World Economic and Financial Surveys

Global Financial Stability Report
Market Developments and Issues

September 2004

International Monetary Fund
Washington DC

Production: IMF Multimedia Services Division
Cover: Phil Torsani
Photo: Padraic Hughes
Figures: Theodore F. Peters, Jr.
Typesetting: Choon Lee

ISBN 1-58906-378-3
ISSN 0258-7440

Price: US$49.00
(US$46.00 to full-time faculty members and
students at universities and colleges)

Please send orders to:
International Monetary Fund, Publication Services
700 19th Street, N.W., Washington, D.C. 20431, U.S.A.
Tel.: (202) 623-7430   Telefax: (202) 623-7201
E-mail: publications@imf.org
Internet:http://www.imf.org

recycled paper

CONTENTS

Boxes

Tables

Figures

The following symbols have been used throughout this volume:

. . . to indicate that data are not available;

— to indicate that the figure is zero or less than half the final digit shown, or that the item does not exist;

– between years or months (for example, 1997–99 or January–June) to indicate the years or months covered, including the beginning and ending years or months;

/ between years (for example, 1998/99) to indicate a fiscal or financial year.

"Billion" means a thousand million; "trillion" means a thousand billion.

"Basis points" refer to hundredths of 1 percentage point (for example, 25 basis points are equivalent to ¼ of 1 percentage point).

"n.a." means not applicable.

Minor discrepancies between constituent figures and totals are due to rounding.

As used in this volume the term "country" does not in all cases refer to a territorial entity that is a state as understood by international law and practice. As used here, the term also covers some territorial entities that are not states but for which statistical data are maintained on a separate and independent basis.

PREFACE

The *Global Financial Stability Report* (GFSR) assesses global financial market developments with the view to identifying potential systemic weaknesses. By calling attention to potential fault lines in the global financial system, the report seeks to play a role in preventing crises, thereby contributing to global financial stability and to sustained economic growth of the IMF's member countries.

The report was prepared by the International Capital Markets Department (ICM), under the direction of the Counsellor and Director, Gerd Häusler. It is managed by an Editorial Committee comprising Hung Q. Tran (Chairman), W. Todd Groome, Jorge Roldos, and David J. Ordoobadi, and benefits from comments and suggestions from Charles R. Blitzer and L. Effie Psalida. Other ICM staff contributing to this issue include Renzo Avesani, Nicolas Blancher, Elie Canetti, Jorge Chan-Lau, Peter Dattels, Toni Gravelle, François Haas, Anna Ilyina, Markus Krygier, William Lee, Chris Morris, Jürgen Odenius, Kazunari Ohashi, Li Lian Ong, Lars Pedersen, Magdalena Polan, Manmohan Singh, Juan Solé, Rupert Thorne, Laura Valderrama, and Yingbin Xiao. Other contributors included Robert Gillingham, Peter Heller, and Dominique Simard of the Fiscal Affairs Department; a staff team of the Monetary and Financial Systems Department that included Robert Corker, Anne-Marie Gulde, S. Kal Wajid, Sean Craig, Gianni De Nicoló, Jan Willem van der Vossen, and Kalin Tintchev; and Kenichiro Kashiwase and Laura Kodres of the Research Department. Martin Edmonds, Ivan Guerra, Silvia Iorgova, Anne Jansen, Oksana Khadarina, Yoon Sook Kim, Ned Rumpeltin, and Peter Tran provided research assistance. Caroline Bagworth, Cynthia Galang, Vera Jasenovec, Elsa Portaro, and Ramanjeet Singh provided expert word processing assistance. Jeff Hayden of the External Relations Department edited the manuscript and coordinated production of the publication.

This particular issue draws, in part, on a series of informal discussions with commercial and investment banks, securities firms, asset management companies, hedge funds, insurance companies, pension funds, stock and futures exchanges, and credit rating agencies in Canada, Colombia, France, Germany, Hong Kong SAR, Italy, Japan, Mexico, the Netherlands, Poland, Singapore, Switzerland, the United Kingdom, and the United States. The report reflects information available up to July 30.

The report has benefited from comments and suggestions from staff in other IMF departments, as well as from Executive Directors following their discussions of the *Global Financial Stability Report* on August 30, 2004. However, the analysis and policy considerations are those of the contributing staff and should not be attributed to the Executive Directors, their national authorities, or the IMF.

CHAPTER I

OVERVIEW

Over the past six months, the global financial system, especially the health of financial intermediaries, has been further strengthened by the broadening economic recovery. The financial system has not looked as resilient as it does in the summer of 2004, in the three years since the bursting of the equity bubble. Financial intermediaries, banks and non-banks alike, have strengthened their balance sheets to a point where they could, if necessary, absorb considerable shocks (see Chapter II, pages 64–73). While it is obviously feasible that one or the other financial institution, such as a hedge fund or even a bank, might succumb to serious mistakes in risk management or to outright fraud, such incidents should be isolated cases with limited, if any, contagion to the system as a whole. Short of a major and devastating geopolitical incident or a terrorist attack undermining, in a significant and lasting way, consumer confidence, and hence financial asset valuations, it is hard to see where systemic threats could come from in the short term. This positive assessment is focused on the financial sector, given its potential to create fast-moving knock-on effects through the wholesale markets. The household sector, in turn, could face certain financial problems going forward, despite its improved balance sheet position. However, from a systemic point of view, the household sector is the ultimate shock absorber.

Consequently, market players are relatively well prepared to deal with the long expected tightening cycle in monetary policy. As discussed in previous issues of the *Global Financial Stability Report* published during 2002, the financial system benefited crucially from two factors during the critical years 2001 and 2002: a strong capital base going into the recession and a preceding paradigm shift in risk management, most clearly among the major internationally active banks. This trend toward risk diversification away from banks, indeed increasingly away from the financial sector as a whole, fundamentally helped the financial system to weather financial shocks. As discussed later in the chapter, this secular trend, while helpful for financial stability, may raise problems in the future. Over the last year or two, the gradually strengthening recovery of the world economy, as well as a steep yield curve, has sharply increased profitability within the financial sector and thus enhanced financial stability. Strong increases in gross revenues as well as a sharp reduction in corporate default rates and in nonperforming loans—both the result of the economic recovery—are providing a strong cushion of comfort for the financial sector (see Chapter II, pages 73–79).

Hence, this *Global Financial Stability Report*, and hopefully the next ones, will focus even more on medium-term structural issues in the financial system. Avoiding complacency, we are looking for fault lines that could ultimately translate into serious financial stresses some time in the future, if and when another downturn in economic activity were to occur.

Over the past two quarters, corporations and financial institutions have generally reported robust earnings. Increases in sales revenues combined with the results of on-going cost-cutting efforts have produced impressive earnings growth in some countries. Consequently, the balance sheets of the corporate and financial sectors have improved further, with many institutions posting high levels of liquid assets. Insurance companies, especially in Europe, have also taken steps to strengthen their risk management capability and strengthened their capital base. By and large, these developments have enhanced the resiliency of international financial institutions.

International financial markets have remained calm so far despite the transition to higher interest rates. During April–May, the unwinding of carry trades in anticipation of Fed tightening raised bond yields and widened emerging market bond spreads. Nevertheless, volatility remained low in major bond and equity markets. Despite reports of increased risk taking reflected in higher value-at-risk levels, many financial intermediaries seem to have been able, so far, to absorb the rise in market interest rates without visible impact on their profitability. This may be attributed to strengthened risk management at many institutions and also to the effective communication strategy by the Fed. This time around, market preparedness for a rate hike stands in sharp contrast to the surprise and volatility that accompanied the Fed's tightening in 1994. By reducing liquidity in the financial system and hence the indiscriminate search for yield that can create financial excesses, the Fed's plan to restore interest rates to a "normal" level could make the economic expansion and benign market situation more sustainable.

After the first hike in the Federal Funds rate in late June, economic data have led market participants to expect inflation to stay under control, allowing the Fed to remove monetary stimulus at a "measured" pace. Consequently, mature and emerging bond markets have recovered part of their earlier losses. Interest rates in forward markets suggest that future modest rate hikes could be absorbed without much negative effect. In particular, the need for potentially unsettling mortgage hedging, which may amplify volatility in long-term rates, is much reduced now, compared to the situation last summer when U.S. bond yields rose abruptly. Basically, due to a record volume of refinancing in 2002 and 2003, most outstanding mortgages in the United States carry a coupon lower than the current long-term mortgage rate. Therefore, further rises in the mortgage rate will not change abruptly the prepayment risk facing mortgage investors, lessening their need to hedge duration risk.[1]

External financing conditions facing emerging market countries have also returned to a healthy and more sustainable level. Even though financing costs have risen from the lows reached earlier this year, they remain much lower than the average for the past five years. After some difficulty in April–May—especially for sub-investment grade borrowers—emerging market borrowers have since gained access to the global capital markets. As about 80 percent of the external bond-issuing program of emerging market countries for 2004 has been completed, some sovereigns are expected to start prefinancing their 2005 needs if market conditions remain favorable.

Risks in the Period Ahead

Overall, when conditions are as benign as they are at the moment, the major risks—especially in the medium term—are on the downside.

The most immediate risk is that market participants may develop a sense of complacency, seeing how smoothly financial markets have adjusted to the initial moves to higher policy rates. This may be reflected in the low volatility observed in major stock and bond markets. Such complacency could lead to a return of indiscriminate risk behavior, due to a strong tendency to "search for yield."

---

[1]U.S. homeowners have increased the portion of variable-rate and interest-only mortgages in new borrowing, thereby taking on more interest rate risk. However, most outstanding mortgages are long-term fixed rate, making the U.S. household sector somewhat interest rate insensitive.

Naturally, if U.S. interest rates were to rise more substantially than currently discounted due to an unexpected acceleration of inflation, the potential impact would be less benign than in the baseline scenario. This would be especially true if the markets were to perceive monetary policy as having fallen behind the curve and needing to catch up. Since the correlation is high between U.S. treasury yields and bond yields in Europe and emerging markets, the spillover effect of such a spike in U.S. yields may be widely felt—whether or not other regions are cyclically ready to absorb higher market interest rates. In the future, and driven by increasingly global asset allocation processes, these linkages will become even stronger as the world moves further toward a common pool of global savings.

Global current account imbalances pose a continued risk, even though it is difficult to forecast how or when the financing of the current account deficits or the adjustment of the imbalances could become disorderly. Data through June show that foreign portfolio flows into the United States remain strong. The sustainability of capital flows to the United States, however, remains a matter of concern. A sharp and disorderly decline of the dollar would, among other things, cause significant losses to many international institutions holding dollar assets or generating dollar income. But in the absence of a compelling alternative to liquid dollar assets within a high-growth area, it is not easy to see why investors would trigger a wholesale shift away from dollar assets without undermining the rationale of their investment decisions.

Overall, global geopolitical risks continue to be elevated and could quickly heighten risk aversion among international investors to the detriment of asset markets—especially those of weak credit quality or limited liquidity. Oil prices, in particular, could spike further, contributing to inflation concerns and potentially hurting financial markets and the economic recovery.

Policy Conclusions for the Short and Medium Term

Now that the Fed and other central banks have successfully managed the first phase of the transition to higher interest rates, the task ahead is to guide market expectations in executing the planned adjustment program. Recent growth and inflation data have brought market participants over to the Fed's vision of a "measured" pace of monetary stimulus removal. The current benign conjunctural situation should be used by the authorities of all countries to address weak spots in their financial systems. In particular, in countries where insufficient profitability has long plagued the banks, a conducive environment should be created to facilitate the consolidation process so as to allow the emergence of a profitable and vibrant banking sector. This would help support the financial system to cope with the next downturn. The benign economic and financial conditions also make the task of policy coordination to reduce global imbalances all the more important and timely. According to the *World Economic Outlook*, these measures encompass policies, including structural policies, to improve the growth performance of Europe and Japan, while achieving fiscal consolidation in the United States over the medium term.

For emerging market countries, the continuation of benign external financing conditions provides an excellent window of opportunity for maintaining strong economic policies and reform efforts to enhance their growth potential and the resiliency of their financial systems. Again, this will enable them to better deal with future shocks.

Beside the conjunctural issues, Chapter II also reviews several structural issues, either mentioned in earlier GFSRs or just emerging, that could have an impact on financial markets. Of particular interest are the sections on the recent developments of hedge funds (page 45) and the growing involvement of financial market participants in energy trading markets (page 58).

Issues for the Long Term: Reforms of the Pension Industry

Chapter III looks at the potential systemic implications of the growth and changes of pension funds within the global financial system. This chapter is the second installment in a series looking at the management of risk in various nonbanking sectors and its impact on financial stability.

Many countries face the challenge of improving the adequacy of pension provisions to cope with rising dependency ratios (i.e., the ratio of retirees to working people). For company-sponsored pension funds, the quick succession from overfunding during the equity market boom years of the late 1990s to underfunding since has given rise to various reform efforts. Among other things, these efforts include improvements to the valuation and disclosure of the assets and liabilities of pension funds.

Another set of measures deals with risk management at pension funds and risk sharing between corporate sponsors and employees. In terms of risk management, the focus among industry members and regulators is shifting from asset portfolio management—frequently benchmarked to the major market indices—to a greater emphasis on asset-liability management, particularly the duration matching of assets to long-term pension liabilities. A growing debate has ensued on the role of governments in providing long-term and inflation-indexed bonds.[2] The focus on asset-liability management has also given rise to a lively debate within the industry concerning the appropriateness of equities or fixed-income instruments in matching pension assets to liabilities. The outcome of such debate could have a considerable effect on

the equity and fixed-income asset classes, as a result of a potential rebalancing of pension assets. In addition, international diversification of pension assets, including to emerging markets, will continue to progress, driven mainly by the uneven demographic developments in different countries, as well as diversification benefits. Given the already dominant size of pension funds in mature markets, even small changes in asset allocations of these funds will have a large impact on relatively illiquid markets, such as emerging markets.

More emphasis on risk management is likely to underpin the shift from defined benefit corporate pension plans to defined contribution plans, or to one of the hybrid plans. This shift has transferred the taking of investment risk from the corporate sponsors to the employees. Potentially, it could give rise to a public policy issue of the role of government if retirees incur losses in their defined contribution plans due to poor investment management or market declines. This issue is becoming quite relevant, since the contribution to retirement income from state pensions is projected to decline in many countries, while individuals' retirement savings are increasingly viewed as insufficient. As mentioned above, the transfer of financial risk outside the financial sector has supported the stability of financial intermediaries. However, once the household sector (and policymakers) fully understand the scope of risk they have incurred and what that could mean for their retirement income, there may be policy implications. The next GFSR will study mutual funds as another important nonbanking financial sector, and the implications that such a trend could have on the financial system more broadly, including new forms of moral hazard ("markets too important to fall" mentioned in the April 2004 GFSR).

Overall, the growing size of pension assets and the focus on asset-liability management

---

[2]In an interesting development, Brazil announced plans to issue new 40-year inflation-index-linked bonds in response to demands from local pension funds.

should strengthen the role of pension funds as stable, long-term institutional investors. This would tend to support financial stability as long as there is an adequate supply of financial assets to meet their demands. However, changes in asset allocation of pension funds would have a large impact on different asset classes and financial markets, especially smaller ones. Understanding these changes in asset allocation, and the subsequent capital flows, thus lies at the heart of multilateral surveillance of financial markets.

Policy Issues for the Pension Sector

Important policy issues are highlighted by the analysis of pension funds and of the changes required to cope with the challenge of an aging workforce. These policy issues are relevant to mature market countries, but could also be applicable to some emerging market countries.

- The aging of the workforce in many countries has intensified the need to promote sufficient and stable retirement savings. First and foremost is the need to better communicate the pension challenges and policy priorities, particularly in countries where the public sector has traditionally provided the bulk of pension benefits. Policymakers should try to establish a broad legal environment (and a tax environment in some cases) conducive to savings growth.
- Within a multi-pillar approach to pension provisions, policymakers should try to work toward a relatively balanced contribution from each pillar. As demographic and cost pressures have increased on Pillar 1 (state pension), the contribution of state plans to pensioners' retirement income is projected to decline in most countries. Therefore, measures to encourage larger contributions from Pillar 2 (occupational pension schemes) and Pillar 3 (individual savings schemes) are increasingly important.
- Measures to strengthen risk management by pension funds. Regulations and tax rules should be designed to foster a closer alignment of pension assets to liability structures. Policymakers should facilitate the development of certain markets and instruments, including long-term, fixed-income and index-linked products. Such securities are necessary to allow pension funds to better match assets and liabilities, as well as to facilitate the supply and pricing of annuity and long-term savings products by market participants, such as insurance companies.
- Risk-based approaches to supervision and to guarantee fund premiums should be enhanced to reflect the riskiness of asset allocations. This would allow for a fairer distribution of the cost of guarantee funds, reduce moral hazard, and encourage risk management.
- As pension funds need to diversify internationally, including to emerging markets, policymakers should aim to remove the frictions that continue to limit international capital mobility. On the other hand, emerging market countries need to strengthen their capacity to absorb such potential capital flows.

Capital Flows Between Emerging and Mature Markets

Conventional wisdom suggests that capital normally flows from mature market countries, enjoying higher capital-labor ratios, to capital-scarce emerging market countries. Indeed this has been the case, except for selected episodes, such as the current period since 2000 when emerging market countries, as a group, have become net exporters of capital (as defined in footnote 1 in Chapter IV, page 121).

As analyzed in Chapter IV, the current episode of net capital outflows follows a series of financial crises in emerging market countries and changes in global imbalances. There are three main themes driving the changes in international capital flows, associated with the net outflow from the emerging market countries.

In the aftermath of crises in the late 1990s and early 2000s, emerging market countries have undergone an adjustment process. Crisis countries had to reduce domestic absorption and increased exports to generate a trade surplus. Many emerging market countries, not just those in crisis, have also reduced their external indebtedness. International banks adjusted their portfolios by reducing exposures to emerging markets. During the adjustment period, countries had to restructure and strengthen their financial and corporate sectors, so as to restore normal financial intermediation and growth.

Second is the unprecedented accumulation of reserves by many central banks, both to maintain a competitive exchange rate and to have insurance against future crises. Various studies point out that a high ratio of reserves relative to external debt, particularly short-term debt, reduces the probability of debt crises. However, the desirable level of reserves varies from country to country, depending on exchange rate policy as well as institutional strengths, including the development of local capital markets, which can facilitate corporate restructuring.

Last but not least is the role of global factors, especially the growing global current account imbalances. Changes in global merger and acquisition activities also affect capital flows. Global risk aversion affects all assets with similar risk characteristics, regardless of their geographical locations. Conversely, abundant global liquidity prompts the search for yield for all emerging markets as an important segment of high-yield assets.

During the period under study, the 2000–01 subperiod was characterized by the adjustment effort, a reduction in private nonresident capital flow into the emerging markets due—among other things—to risk aversion, and a large outflow from emerging market residents. In the subsequent subperiod since 2001, reserves accumulation by central banks

has been impressive, being greater than the rising current account surplus and a rebound in private capital inflows.

Going forward, as emerging market countries recover their economic growth, domestic demand could revive and lead to normal trade developments. Reserves accumulation by many emerging market countries may slow. Beyond a certain level, the opportunity cost and policy complications of acquiring additional reserves may become more evident. Finally, the increase in gross issuance of bonds, equities, and loans by emerging market countries—at an annualized rate of $264 billion year-to-date, compared to $198 billion in 2003—as well as foreign direct investment flows suggest that international investors' appetite for emerging market assets has returned. Indeed, as highlighted in Chapter III, pension funds in mature market countries have a long-term need to diversify a small portion of their assets to emerging market countries. Consequently, the net capital exporting position of emerging market countries could prove to be a temporary development.

To the extent that emerging market countries need to attract stable capital inflows to develop their economies, policy measures can be taken to help change the phenomenon that emerging market countries have become net exporters of capital. Three sets of policy issues correspond to the three factors accounting for the net capital outflow from emerging market countries.

- As emerging markets are becoming more mainstream assets in global portfolios, they have to compete for risk capital vis-à-vis other asset classes in increasingly globalized capital markets. Emerging market countries have to establish a track record of consistently strong economic policies and reforms to enhance their risk-adjusted return prospects to international investors in order to attract stable inflows.
- Policies to self-insure against sudden stops in capital inflows. Implementing a strong economic policy is a necessary condition for

financial stability, but it may not be sufficient in times of global financial turmoil. Accumulating large amounts of reserves can lower the risk of debt crises, but it may become costly, including in terms of posing complications to macroeconomic stability. Implementing financial sector reforms, including the development of local securities markets, can help emerging market countries reduce their reliance on volatile external financing and lower the cost of self-insurance.

• Policies designed to improve the mechanisms for post-crisis balance sheet adjustments. Of particular importance is the need to improve markets for distressed debt to facilitate the transfer of corporate ownership and control, and to produce a better allocation of resources to help revive growth.

CHAPTER II

GLOBAL FINANCIAL MARKET DEVELOPMENTS

Financial markets are adjusting with equanimity to the onset of the interest rate tightening cycle. The well-crafted communications strategy of the U.S. Federal Reserve Board prepared markets fully for the first measured rise in U.S. policy rates in June 2004. The backdrop of resurgent and broad-based economic growth, rising corporate earnings, and stronger corporate balance sheets have helped support equity and corporate bond prices, notwithstanding the prospect of further interest rate increases. Limited inflationary pressure to date has moderated expectations for the pace and degree of tightening in the United States and Europe. Market participants are now focused on the sustainability of the recovery, and its impact on interest rates and asset valuations.

This chapter analyzes key developments in mature and emerging financial markets, focusing on potential sources of risk, especially those arising from changing expectations on the degree and pace of monetary tightening in the United States. It considers developments in the external environment for new issuance by emerging markets and also assesses improvements in the soundness of major emerging market banking systems. It concludes with a review of structural issues in mature markets, focusing on hedge fund activities and the evolution of sectoral balance sheets in Europe, Japan, and the United States.

Overview

Throughout much of 2003, the combination of stimulative monetary policies and strengthening fundamentals contributed to a strong rally in asset prices and a compression of credit spreads on mature and emerging market bonds. In some cases, it appeared that in their quest for yield investors were motivated as much by the push of abundant liquidity as the pull of fundamental valuations. Abundant global liquidity and the steep yield curve for U.S. treasuries had created strong incentives for investors to borrow at low short-term rates to invest in higher-yielding assets. The April 2004 issue of the *Global Financial Stability Report* stressed that the unwinding of these carry trade positions had potential to trigger turbulence in a number of financial markets. It urged investors not to assume that extraordinarily low interest rates would continue indefinitely, and it called on the authorities to be vigilant for excessively leveraged or concentrated positions.

Early this year, as investors adjusted to the prospect of a less accommodative monetary stance, they became more cautious. In the process, some investments that had been encouraged by last year's abundant global liquidity were partly unwound. The resulting adjustments, though pronounced in some emerging and higher-risk markets, resulted in fewer disruptions than had earlier been feared, with all markets so far remaining orderly.

The start of the tightening cycle in the United States was widely anticipated, and investors and intermediaries have had ample opportunity to adjust to a rising interest rate environment. However, some investors may find that the hedges they established are imperfect, and they may have to make adjustments. In addition, considerable uncertainty continues to surround the pace and path of tightening that will be needed to bring interest rates to a cyclically neutral level. Most notably, there is uncertainty about underlying inflationary pressures. Although core inflation remains low, oil and other commodity prices, especially base metals, have risen strongly.

Market expectations of longer-term inflation remain subdued, but the persistence of this view cannot be taken for granted, in particular if the output gap in the main industrialized countries continues to close. The financial authorities in several mature markets have appropriately stressed that they will respond if core inflation rises to levels that threaten price stability. In some cases, the authorities are also concerned about speculative bubbles developing in certain sectors, notably housing.

Emerging markets have weathered the transition in interest rate expectations relatively well. Borrowers had taken advantage of the strong appetite for emerging market assets around the turn of last year to raise the lion's share of their financing needs of the current year. They could afford to be patient when conditions were less favorable in April and May of this year. In the event, appetite returned quickly with some investors, notably life insurers and pension funds, taking advantage of the lower prices of emerging market debt to enter the market, although with a noticeable preference for less risky assets.

Against this backdrop, policymakers can draw some comfort that tightening has commenced with such little disruption. They should also be encouraged that leveraged positions appear to have been reduced, and that financial institutions generally appear well positioned to withstand the move to a higher interest rate environment. At the same time, a number of important risks remain:

- An unanticipated increase in inflation could transform the market's assumptions about the likely pace of tightening and has potential to cause market turbulence. The perception that the U.S. Federal Reserve has fallen "behind the curve" and is chasing, rather than shaping, market expectations for interest rate increases could cause markets to assume interest rates will have to overshoot cyclically neutral levels in order to rein in inflation. Previous episodes have shown that such rapid changes to expecta-

tions can be unsettling. In such a scenario, risk management strategies would be severely tested. Investor assumptions about the ease with which they can exit from carry trades could prove optimistic. Yields and credit spreads could overshoot. For the moment, however, this risk appears remote.

- Extraordinarily low interest rates have encouraged a variety of carry trades and increasing interest in alternative investments. These factors have contributed to an increase in leverage and a proliferation of hedge funds, whose assets under management are estimated to have doubled since 1998 to about $1 trillion. There is a risk of investor herding as particular speculative positions gain wide favor across a number of hedge funds and other leveraged investors. A reversal of such positions could result in a reduction of market liquidity and disproportionate price movements.

- The orderly adjustment of global imbalances remains a challenge. The persistence of these imbalances and the magnitude of the flows involved remain a potential source of vulnerability in currency markets that could spill over to other asset classes.

- Geopolitical concerns remain an imponderable risk factor. In recent months, security concerns have put pressure on oil prices. A further spike in oil prices would dampen economic activity and pressure the external accounts of oil importers. Geopolitical concerns have the potential to heighten risk aversion, leading to widening credit spreads and lower asset prices. Terrorist activity could disrupt the infrastructure supporting financial markets, although a significant amount of work has been undertaken in the major financial centers to assess potential vulnerabilities and put in place procedures and infrastructure in the event of disruptions.

- Rising interest rates in the major financial centers have often resulted in a less hospitable financing environment for emerging markets. History suggests that abundant

Figure 2.1. One-Month Federal Funds Futures Rate
(In percent)

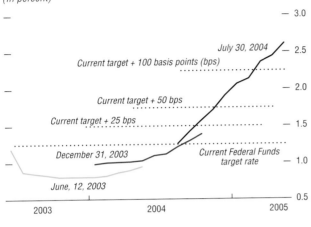

Source: Bloomberg L.P.

Figure 2.2. Strip Curve Interest Rate Expectations
(Three-month LIBOR futures, in percent, as of July 30, 2004)

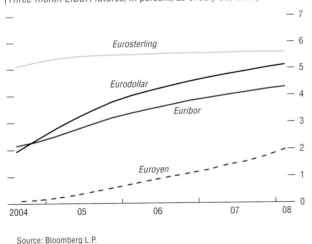

Source: Bloomberg L.P.

global liquidity is a major factor influencing the attractiveness of emerging market assets. Strong growth and the modest financing requirements of some emerging markets will probably mitigate the impact of higher mature market interest rates initially. However, as rates rise, emerging markets may find it increasingly difficult to attract the financing they need. In particular, investors may discriminate between those emerging markets that have made progress on their reform agendas, or are locked into a broader process that is likely to see them converge over time with more mature markets. Increased attention is also being given to debt structures and other balance sheet mismatches as potential sources of risk (Box 2.1, page 13). Although a number of countries have taken steps to improve the structure of their debt by extending maturities and reducing the share of debt indexed to foreign exchange or short-term interest rates, unstable debt structures and mismatched balance sheet positions remain potential sources of instability in a number of key emerging markets.

Developments and Vulnerabilities in Mature Markets

Markets Anticipate Higher Short-Term Interest Rates

Changing policy rate expectations have been the main driver of global financial markets this year. At the start of the year, markets were still anticipating that policy interest rates in the United States would remain, for most of the year, at or close to the exceptionally low levels to which they had been pushed to forestall deflation and stimulate growth.

However, the revised language in the January and March statements of the Federal Open Market Committee (FOMC), combined with strong economic data and signs of stronger employment growth, transformed market expectations for the degree and pace of tightening (Figure 2.1). By the end of July, markets were expecting the federal funds target rate to rise to 2 percent by the end of 2004, following the 25 basis point increase of the federal funds rate to 1.25 percent at the end of June.

In the euro zone, expectations for a possible reduction in interest rates evaporated amid a recent uptick in inflation and as it became increasingly clear that U.S. interest rates were set to rise. Futures markets are now discounting an increase in euro short-term interest rates, although at a slower pace than in the United States (Figure 2.2). Interest rate expectations in Japan remained anchored by the authorities' repeated commitment to the zero interest rate policy and their willingness to supply large amounts of liquidity to the financial system. However, as further evidence of the sustainability of the recovery emerged, and as the yen stopped strengthening even when intervention ceased, markets began to contemplate an exit from the zero interest rate policy. The authorities in Australia, New Zealand, Switzerland, and the United Kingdom had all initiated their tightening cycles before the United States made its first move (Figure 2.3).

Longer-term interest rates rebounded from their lows in mid-March, reflecting expectations of both stronger growth and higher inflation (Figure 2.4). The increase was sharpest in the United States, but was echoed in the euro area and later in Japan. Expectations for long-term inflation—calculated as the yield difference between inflation-indexed and non-inflation-indexed bonds—continued to increase early in the year, although there has been some moderation in recent months, and expected inflation rates remain low by historical standards (Figure 2.5). Until recently, longer-term inflationary expectations were well above actual inflation, but in the United States, actual inflation has now overtaken expectations derived from bond markets. This has yet to happen in Europe, however, as the increase in actual inflation has so far been less

Figure 2.3. Selected Central Bank Policy Rates
(In percent)

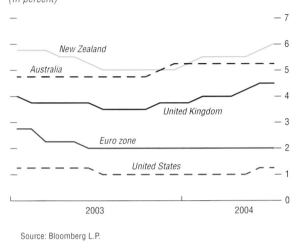

Source: Bloomberg L.P.

Figure 2.4. Ten-Year Government Bond Yields
(In percent)

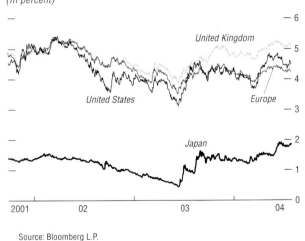

Source: Bloomberg L.P.

Figure 2.5. Long-Term Inflation Expectations
(In percent)

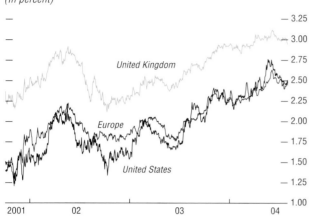

Sources: Bloomberg L.P.; and IMF staff estimates.

Figure 2.6. Implied Volatilities
(In percent)

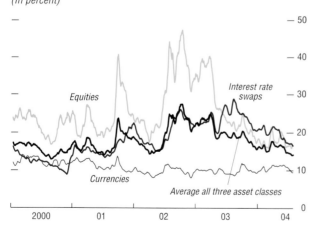

Source: Bloomberg L.P.

marked. In Japan, inflation-indexed bonds are new, and the market for those bonds does not have the depth of those in the United States or Europe. In any case, deflationary expectations have eased in Japan.

As indicated in the April 2004 *Global Financial Stability Report,* low short-term interest rates and the steep yield curve created strong incentives to establish carry trades and other speculative positions. There was a risk that these positions were motivated largely by expectations that short-term interest rates would remain at extraordinarily low levels for an extended period. As interest rate expectations were adjusted in April and May, there is evidence that some of these positions were reduced (Box 2.2, page 15).

Market Volatility Remains Subdued

Nevertheless, options markets were not pricing in major market movements (Figure 2.6). The volatilities implied by the pricing of currency options remained generally low, and those for equity options rose only briefly before falling back to the low levels seen at the end of last year. The volatility priced into options to enter into swaps has also fallen. Low volatility in bond markets reflected in part more continuous and well-diversified hedging activity by holders of mortgage backed securities (MBS). As the pace of prepayments dropped amid rising interest and mortgage rates, and MBS durations increased, only a limited surge in bond option volatility was apparent this year compared to 2003.

A number of factors have contributed to the relatively smooth adjustment of markets to the prospect of higher short-term interest rates. First, the large official purchases of U.S. dollar-denominated bonds, in particular, by Asian central banks, have provided a stabilizing influence in the bond and foreign exchange markets. Second, as already noted, the communications of the U.S. Federal Reserve gave abundant warning to investors and financial institutions to prepare themselves for the start

Box 2.1. Stocks, Flows, and Vulnerability Assessments

While aberrant flows characterize capital account crises, increasing attention is being given to the balance sheet exposures that can engender them. Balance sheet analysis focuses on shocks to stocks of assets and liabilities that can trigger large adjustments in capital account flows. The Asian crisis of 1997–98, in which private sector balance sheet mismatches rather than fiscal imbalances played a key role, gave impetus to research on the risks posed by potentially unstable positions. Such analysis can complement the traditional flow analysis that focuses on the gradual buildup of unsustainable fiscal and current account positions and may be insufficient in fully explaining the dynamics underlying modern day capital account crises.

Balance sheet analysis seeks to identify existing mismatches on the aggregated balance sheet of the corporate, financial, and public sectors. The analysis focuses largely on five sources of vulnerability:

- currency mismatches that may leave a balance sheet vulnerable to a depreciation of the domestic currency;
- maturity mismatches (e.g., long-term, potentially illiquid assets with short-term liabilities) that expose a balance sheet to risks related both to rollover and to interest rates;
- rollover risk if liquid assets do not cover maturing debts;
- interest rate risk, where a sharp increase in interest rates can lead to capital losses to investors and increase the cost to borrowers of rolling over short-term liabilities and cause a rapid increase in debt service; and
- capital structure mismatches if debt-to-equity ratios become too high.

Shocks to interest rates, exchange rates, or market sentiment can bring about a deterioration in the value of a sector's assets compared to its liabilities and lead to a reduction of its net worth. In the extreme case, net worth may turn negative and the sector may become insolvent.

Sectoral analysis is important since the liabilities of one sector are often the assets of another sector and risks can be transferred across balance sheets in severe crisis situations. If a shock causes the corporate sector or the government to be unable to satisfy upcoming liabilities, banking sector assets can be impaired. For example, balance sheet crises that originated in the corporate sector (as in several Asian countries during 1997–98) or the public sector (as in Russia 1998 and recently in Latin America) eventually caused a deterioration in the banking sector. By the same token, if banks restrict credit to prevent further deterioration in banking system assets, risks can feed back into the corporate and government sectors, which may be in need of new financing (as in Turkey in 2001).

The IMF has been using insights based on balance sheet analysis in its surveillance as well as its program work for some time.[1] For example, there has been increased emphasis on adequate levels of official reserves in relation to short-term debt and money aggregates. Balance sheet techniques are also employed in debt sustainability analysis to measure the sensitivity of a country's fiscal and external (private and public) debt to variations in the exchange rate, interest rate, and other variables. Finally, Financial Sector Assessment Programs (FSAP) often include stress testing of the sensitivity of the financial sector's balance sheets to various shocks.

Balance sheet analysis also underpins modern risk management techniques, including credit risk and value-at-risk methodology. The accounting-based approach maps a reduced set of financial accounting variables—such as leverage, liquidity, and profitability—to a risk scale to discriminate between repayment and non-repayment at the corporate level.[2]

A variant of balance sheet analysis called the contingent claims approach (CCA), combines balance sheet information with current financial

---

[1]A recent example is Allen and others (2002).

[2]A prominent accounting-based approach was developed by Altman (1968), who used a linear combination of five accounting and market variables to produce a credit score—the so-called "Z-score." A subsequent seven factor "Zeta model" was later introduced by Altman, Haldeman, and Narayanan (1977) and another variant, the "O-score," was introduced by Ohlson (1980).

Box 2.1 *(concluded)*

market prices to compute probability of default. CCA was developed from modern finance theory and has been widely applied by financial market participants, most notably Moody's KMV, in assessing firm credit risk. CCA can also be applied to aggregated balance sheets to estimate similar risk indicators for the corporate, financial, and public sectors.[3] Extending the contingent claims methodology to a multisector framework allows for examination of the linkages between the corporate, financial, and public sectors, where the potential feedback effects between sectors can be estimated and valued.

CCA uses standard option pricing techniques to derive a measure called the distance to distress. For a firm financed with debt and equity, this measure is defined as the difference between the implied market value of firm assets and the distress barrier based on the book value of debt—or the net worth of the firm—divided by the implied volatility of the market value of assets. The resulting measure yields the number of standard deviations the firm's asset value is from the distress barrier, which can be translated into a default probability. The higher the net worth of the firm, or the lower the volatility of the firm's assets and liabilities, the larger the distance to distress, and the lower the probability of default.

Since market prices represent the collective views and forecasts of many investors, CCA is forward looking unlike analysis based only on a

review of past financial statements. Furthermore, CCA takes into account the volatility of assets when estimating default risk, and this incorporation of nonlinearity is crucial in increasing the predictive power of CCA over standard accounting-based measures. The ability to translate continuously adjusting financial market price information into current estimates of vulnerability is important given the speed with which economic conditions change relative to the time span between releases of consolidated accounting balance sheet information.

Gapen and others found the CCA approach to be useful in identifying vulnerabilities in the corporate sector and in estimating the potential for risk transfer between the corporate, financial, and public sectors. They used the Moody's Macro Financial Risk (MfRisk) model—which is a practical application of the CCA methodology—to assess vulnerabilities retroactively in the corporate sector as well as in a multisector setting for Brazil and Thailand. Their results show the CCA approach holds promise as an early warning indicator of firm credit risk. Naturally, a useful extension of this work is to apply the CCA approach to a wider set of emerging market countries. Here, the analysis does not have to be limited only to assessing corporate sector vulnerabilities but can be usefully applied to estimate the potential for sovereign distress. The CCA approach provides an integrated framework within which policymakers can analyze policy mixes and evaluate which are best suited to countering vulnerabilities.

[3]Examples include Gapen and others (2004); Gray, Merton, and Bodie (2003); and Gray (2002).

of the tightening cycle. As a result, markets had widely anticipated the first interest rate hike in the United States, and the process of price discovery was short as markets swiftly found their new levels. Third, the message that the pace of interest rate increases will be measured is consistent with the market expectations that inflationary pressure is likely to remain subdued. Finally, higher economic growth is supporting the credit quality and

earnings prospects of corporations in the mature markets.

Stronger Corporate Balance Sheets and Earnings Contribute to Stability

Corporate balance sheets have continued to improve, although the strength of the U.S. corporate sector tended to surpass the strength of the corporate sector in Europe.

Box 2.2. Market Repositioning and Deleveraging

While the onset of the latest U.S. monetary tightening cycle was widely anticipated, the financial markets' outlook remained overshadowed by concerns that rising interest rates might spark sudden sales of assets as leverage was unwound. These concerns were reminiscent of 1994, when the rate tightening cycle resulted in elevated financial market volatility and triggered a number of prominent financial failures.

There were at least three reasons to believe that leverage loomed large before interest rate expectations started to rise earlier this year. First, U.S. policy rates were at a 45-year low and leveraged carry trades are a hallmark of low interest rate environments. Second, earnings derived from fixed-income activities of investment banks grew at a rapid pace in recent years. Third, assets under management by the hedge fund industry doubled to an estimated $1 trillion since 1998. Against this backdrop, this box attempts to shed some light on the extent of deleveraging that may have taken place in anticipation of monetary tightening.

Repositioning of U.S. Dealers

Global recoveries spell good and bad news for financial markets. The good news of rising economic returns tends to be accompanied by the bad news of increasing costs of capital. Responding to these forces, investors' portfolio allocations change, thereby setting in motion far-reaching repositioning across financial markets. The nuts and bolts of such a repositioning include the hedging of risks associated with rising interest rates and the attempt to capitalize on potentially higher returns generated by the economic recovery.

Such repositioning appeared to be under way in U.S. fixed-income markets. Security holdings by primary dealers fell by $55 billion from their peak in March 2004 to $68 billion on a net basis at end-June (see the first Figure). This adjustment reflected to a large extent stepped-up hedging activity. Primary dealers built larger short positions in U.S. treasury bonds in order to hedge their interest rate risk on higher-yielding bonds, including corporate and agency

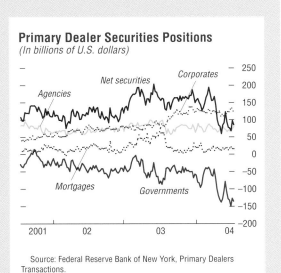

Primary Dealer Securities Positions
(In billions of U.S. dollars)

Source: Federal Reserve Bank of New York, Primary Dealers Transactions.

bonds. In doing so, primary dealers captured the yield spread offered by these bonds over U.S. treasuries, while containing duration risk.

The repositioning appeared to have gone hand in hand with some deleveraging. U.S. primary dealers reduced their secured borrowing by $145 billion to $124 billion since the onset of the repositioning in mid-March to end-June (see the second Figure). Primary dealers, however, represent only one—albeit important and agile—segment of U.S. financial markets. Moreover, commercial banks built up large security portfolios, while risk and leverage can also exist in other less regulated parts of the financial system or through off-balance sheet positions and structured products.

Repositioning in Futures Markets

Leverage and speculation are often intertwined. Many institutional fund managers operate within investment policies that limit or prohibit leverage, while proprietary trading desks at investment banks and hedge funds often have mandates to build leveraged positions. Futures markets provide a useful barometer of overall speculative activity. Trades that take place at the Chicago Mercantile Exchange are distinguished according to their speculative

Box 2.2 *(concluded)*

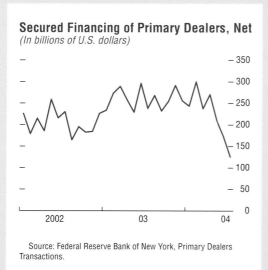

Secured Financing of Primary Dealers, Net
(In billions of U.S. dollars)

Source: Federal Reserve Bank of New York, Primary Dealers Transactions.

Share of Speculative Positions in Futures Markets[1]
(In percent)

	January FOMC Meeting	June 29, 2004	Change
Interest Rates			
3-month eurodollars	6.8	−9.3	−16.0
10-year U.S. treasury notes	−5.8	−16.4	−10.6
Foreign Exchange Rates			
Euro	25.8	12.9	−12.9
Pound sterling	27.9	27.9	0.1
Japanese yen	36.1	8.5	−27.6
Swiss franc	31.0	31.6	0.5
Canadian dollar	20.8	0.4	−20.3
Mexican peso	50.4	−29.9	−80.3
Commodities			
Gold	31.2	17.7	−13.5
Silver	49.5	28.2	−21.3
Platinum	45.6	−7.3	−52.9
Copper	29.9	11.2	−18.6
Cotton	37.6	−38.1	−75.7
Energy			
Crude oil (WTI)	7.7	2.1	−5.6
Natural gas	−10.2	0.3	10.5
Unleaded gasoline	28.9	7.6	−21.3

Source: Commodities Futures Trading Commission; Bloomberg, L.P.; and IMF staff estimates.
[1]Plus (+) sign denotes a net long position, while a negative (−) sign denotes a net short position.

or commercial character. Based on this distinction, the share of speculative positions taken in open futures contracts can be derived for contracts traded on this exchange.

The repositioning and deleveraging observed by primary dealers coincided with a marked reduction of speculative positions in futures markets, although these only capture a small share of overall speculative activity. While high levels of speculative activity prevailed when the Federal Open Markets Committee (FOMC) meeting in January sparked a shift in interest rate expectations, speculative activity eased by mid-year across most major future contracts, especially currency and commodity futures. Speculative activity in interest rate and bond futures, however, heightened, reflecting the shift in interest rate expectations (see the Table). Hedge funds appear to have been particularly sensitive to the first signs of shifting interest rate expectations.

For many firms, sales picked up during the first half of 2004, but they were able to meet the higher demand with existing capacity, or with only limited fresh hiring and investment. As a result, cash flows were strong, and much of the higher revenues fed through to earnings. With interest rates still low, many firms were able to reduce the cost of servicing their debt, and lengthen the maturity of their liabilities. The balance sheets for many companies therefore looked considerably healthier by mid-year than was the case at the start of the year, and this was reflected in a preponderance of ratings agency upgrades. Even some companies that had looked severely strained last year came back from the brink as they have regained access to borrowing. The rate of corporate defaults dropped and credit spreads fell sharply last year as investors positioned themselves in anticipation of the balance sheet strengthening this year. Even as the tightening cycle started, and the cost of financing rose, corporate bond spreads in Europe and the United States have held on to most of last year's gains (Figures 2.7 and 2.8).

The improvements in cash flows and earnings also supported equity prices in mature markets (Figure 2.9). Coming into the year, expectations of impressive earnings growth buoyed equity markets. The technology sector, in particular, was bid up temporarily as it appeared that the long-awaited cycle of reinvestment in technology infrastructure was restarting. Earnings in the first half of 2004 lived up to those high expectations, rising by about 20 percent for the S&P 500 on year-ago levels.

Nevertheless, equity markets have been largely range bound, resulting in modest losses or gains in most major markets during the first seven months of the year. Trading levels were low, and implied volatilities priced into options suggest market participants did not anticipate sharp moves in either direction. Even relatively strong second quarter earnings failed to arrest a general downward drift in major indices. Stronger earnings and lackluster price movements resulted in improved valuations. By mid-2004, forward earnings multiples fell back to levels below their 10-year average in most of the major markets (Figure 2.10). However, the valuation of global technology shares still appeared stretched.

External Imbalances Remain a Potential Source of Volatility

Throughout much of 2003, the level of capital inflows needed to finance the U.S. external current account deficit weighed on the dollar (Figure 2.11). These concerns waned in early 2004 as strong U.S. growth and expectations for higher U.S. interest rates contributed to an appreciation of the dollar. In addition, as investors reduced leverage and unwound carry trades, they reduced long speculative positions in Asian currencies and equity markets and in commodity currencies, and contributed to dollar demand. As a result, currency market

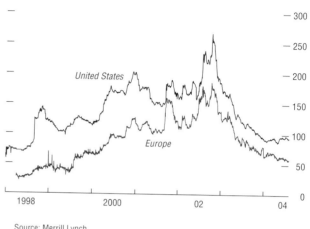

Figure 2.7. High-Grade Corporate Bond Spreads
(In basis points)

Source: Merrill Lynch.

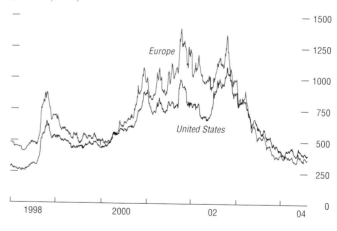

Figure 2.8. High-Yield Corporate Bond Spreads
(In basis points)

Source: Merrill Lynch.

movements were subdued and implied volatility on currency options remained low. Nevertheless, the scale and structure of the financing flows to the United States represent potential sources of instability (Box 2.3, page 35).

Developments and Vulnerabilities in Emerging Markets

The April 2004 GFSR warned of the risk that the transition to higher interest rates in the mature markets and deleveraging could unsettle emerging bond markets. Besides fundamentals and investor attitudes toward risk, the analysis found low policy rates in the major financial centers were a key determinant of the decline in emerging bond market spreads during the rally that began in October 2002 (Figure 2.12).

In the event, shifting interest rate expectations and a temporary heightening of risk aversion triggered an abrupt end to the rally this year that had led spreads to 10-year lows. In a matter of weeks, the results of almost one year of spread compression dissipated, with the spread of the EMBI Global rising to 549 basis points in May 2004. As a result, emerging market bonds experienced a loss in the second quarter this year for the first time since the third quarter of 2002.

Incidentally, the model presented in the April 2004 GFSR, subject to a minor modification, forecast the spread widening that occurred in April and May relatively well (Figure 2.13). In this context, Box 2.4 (page 39) discusses further research on the determinants of emerging bond market spreads.

Changing interest rate expectations—as reflected by the slope of the eurodollar futures strip curve (Figure 2.14)—appear to have contributed to recent spread changes.[1] A

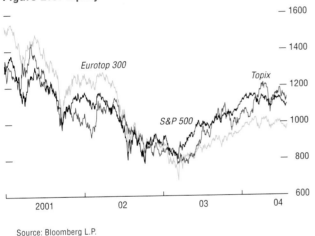

Figure 2.9. Equity Indices

Eurotop 300

Topix

S&P 500

2001   02   03   04

Source: Bloomberg L.P.

[1]The slope of the eurodollar futures strip curve is calculated as the difference in yields (in basis points) between the fifth contract (12–15 months out) and the front contract for immediate delivery (up to 3 months).

brief steepening of the eurodollar futures strip curve at end-January, following a change in language in a statement issued by the FOMC, coincided with an initial widening of emerging market spreads. Subsequently, interest rate expectations started to rise sharply with a further change in language by the FOMC in its statement issued in mid-March. This set the stage for the sell-off in emerging market debt in April and May. Once interest rate expectations stabilized in mid-May, emerging market spreads began to tighten again.

Mounting expectations for higher interest rates affected spreads in part through the unwinding of carry trades. Although data on the extent of these leveraged investments are difficult to come by, investor surveys showed a sizable unwinding of positions by "trading accounts" during April when emerging debt markets suffered substantial declines (losing 5½ percent). These accounts include hedge funds and proprietary trading desks, which are prone to rely on leverage.

In addition to trading accounts, dedicated and crossover investors also reduced their risk during the sell-off by increasing cash levels, moving up in the credit quality spectrum, and reducing the duration of their portfolios. Market commentary and surveys suggest they did so primarily owing to fears over increases in global interest rates, rather than because of concerns about credit fundamentals. In fact, domestic country fundamentals have remained robust and in some cases strengthened for a variety of reasons, including:

- a significant pickup in demand for emerging market exports as the global economy entered a broadly synchronized recovery, notwithstanding a more muted recovery in the euro area;
- higher commodity prices fueled by the global economic recovery and particularly strong demand from China;
- reduced external vulnerabilities stemming from the greater prevalence of floating exchange rates, more dependence on local

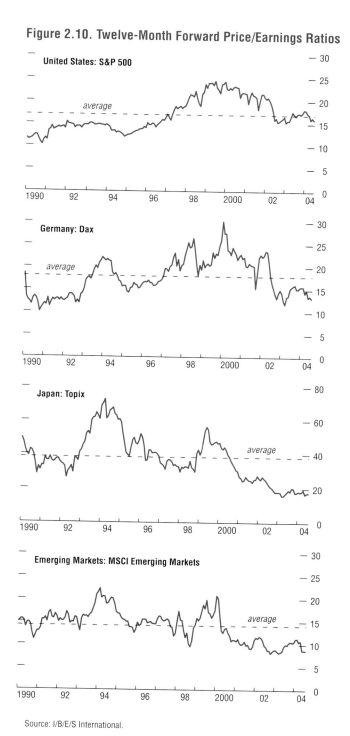

Figure 2.10. Twelve-Month Forward Price/Earnings Ratios

United States: S&P 500

Germany: Dax

Japan: Topix

Emerging Markets: MSCI Emerging Markets

Source: I/B/E/S International.

Figure 2.11. Net Foreign Purchases of U.S. Financial Assets
(In billions of U.S. dollars)

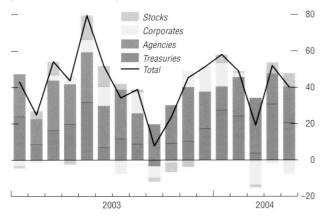

Source: U.S. Department of the Treasury.

Figure 2.12. Emerging Market Debt Spreads
(In basis points)

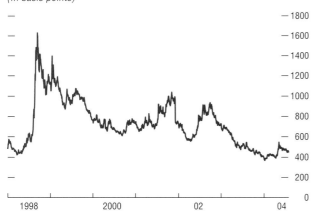

Source: J.P. Morgan Chase & Co.

financing, and higher international reserve levels; and

• active debt management operations by a number of emerging market countries that reduced balance sheet vulnerabilities and/or led to savings on debt-servicing costs. To cite two prominent examples: Brazil has pursued a policy of reducing its dollar-linked liabilities, bringing them down to less than 15 percent of total net public debt from 30 percent at the end of 2002. Mexico implemented an innovative debt swap of global bonds to take advantage of inefficiencies in its global bond yield curve, generate savings, and provide greater liquidity to investors.[2]

The maintenance of overall good country fundamentals has helped the adjustment to higher interest rates remain orderly; there were no severe dislocations for either investors or issuers. However, the brunt of the sell-off was born by higher-yielding credits. Notwithstanding a subsequent recovery, by end-July the Dominican Republic, Brazil, Peru, and Turkey still showed losses year-to-date. (Figure 2.15). The shake up in Russia's banking sector, however, also weighed on bond markets in Russia and the Ukraine.

Nevertheless, sub-investment grade credits outperformed in the rally that followed the sell-off and continued through July this year. The differential between average spreads on B-rated sovereigns compared to BB-rated or investment grade sovereigns began to narrow again following the sell-off in April and May (Figure 2.16).

Looking ahead, the main external risk for the asset class remains the possibility of another round of deleveraging. Expectations for a significantly faster pace of monetary tightening in the United States could lead to further risk aversion and higher spreads on emerging market bonds as speculative posi-

[2]See the April 2004 *Global Financial Stability Report*, Box 2.3 (IMF, 2004a) for case studies of liability management operations by Brazil and Mexico.

tions are reduced. Of less concern is a sharp slowdown in Chinese economic growth, which would most likely affect only selected emerging market countries with resource-intensive exports. Following the renewed spread tightening mid-year, emerging bond market valuations appeared once more stretched. By end-July, emerging bond market spreads relative to U.S. corporate bonds had fallen substantially from their peak in May 2004 (Figure 2.17), although they remained above their lows.

Finally, while the supply and demand balance in primary markets appears largely favorable, excess supply represents a potential concern, in particular due to the still large remaining financing needs in parts of the emerging market corporate sector. There is also a possibility of further Paris Club-related issuance by bilateral creditors, akin to the ARIES deal that liquefied German Paris Club claims on Russia (Box 2.5, page 42). While this transaction allowed Germany to raise deficit financing without issuing debt, a strengthening of public finances would have been more prudent.

Despite these risks, a number of factors are likely to support a favorable external financing environment for emerging markets going forward:

- Financing needs for the remainder of the year are moderate. An estimated 80 percent of planned 2004 issuance for emerging market sovereigns was completed in the first half of the year, despite the temporary lull in issuance by sub-investment grade sovereign borrowers during the second quarter of 2004.

- The credit quality of emerging market sovereigns seems poised to improve. Credit ratings have remained broadly flat since 2002, despite a good deal of progress on fundamentals (Figure 2.18). Thus, there appears to be further scope for upgrades moving forward. Indeed, market participants are anticipating some key upgrades, an expectation buttressed by the results of credit ratings models.

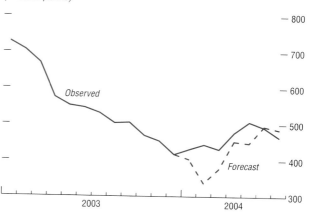

Figure 2.13. Observed and Forecast EMBI+ Spreads
(In basis points)

Sources: J.P. Morgan Chase & Co.; and IMF staff estimates.

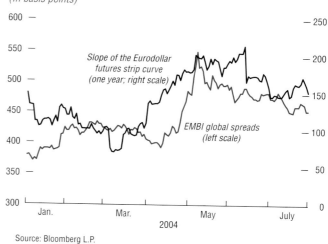

Figure 2.14. EMBI Global Spreads vs. Eurodollar Interest Rate Expectations
(In basis points)

Source: Bloomberg L.P.

Figure 2.15. Emerging Market Debt Returns
(In percent, year-to-date through July 30, 2004)

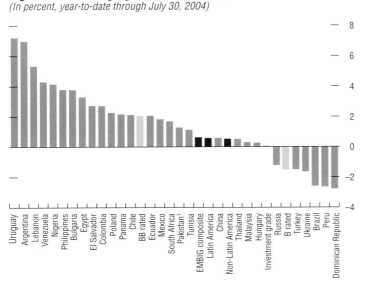

Source: J.P. Morgan Chase & Co.
[1]From inception of the index.

Figure 2.16. Spread Differentials in Emerging Market Debt
(In basis points)

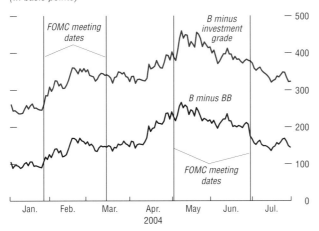

Sources: J.P. Morgan Chase & Co.; and IMF staff estimates.

To the extent that interest rates eventually reach cyclically neutral levels and yield curves flatten, the incentives for leveraged carry trades will diminish. Hence, the importance of domestic fundamentals as the dominant driver of emerging debt markets is likely to reassert itself. This underscores the need to persevere with efforts to reduce balance sheet vulnerabilities, remain vigilant about macro-economic stability, and push forward with growth-enhancing structural reforms.

Shifting Interest Rate Expectations and Local Emerging Markets

The impetus to risk taking provided by low interest rates in the major financial centers was also reflected in local emerging markets. In an environment of abundant global liquidity, foreign flows into local emerging equity and bond markets appear to have been quite strong prior to April of this year. The main beneficiaries of such flows were Asian equity markets and, in the case of local bond markets, countries with the highest yields and deepest markets, including Brazil, Hungary, Indonesia, Mexico, Poland, South Africa, and Turkey.[3] Equity markets experienced a significant reduction in foreign flows in the second quarter of this year, amid changing interest rate expectations in the United States. The effect on flows into local emerging bond markets, however, seemed smaller and largely concentrated on high-yielding markets, particularly Brazil and Turkey. Market feedback suggests that leverage was concentrated in these markets.

Local emerging equity markets sold off with mature markets in April and May in the wake

---

[3]This analysis focuses on countries with liquid local markets and those appearing to provide the highest potential for carry trades. It only covers a subset of the possible ways in which foreigners invest in local markets. Increasingly, foreign investments in local markets are carried out by taking positions in currency or interest rate linked derivatives, the flows of which are more difficult to measure.

of changing interest rate expectations and fears of a slowdown in China. Reflecting the concerns over China, the sell-off was particularly strong in Asia. While portfolio equity inflows to emerging Asia were buoyant in the first quarter of 2004, they slowed significantly in the second quarter. This is evident in the net flows into U.S.-based equity funds investing in Asia (excluding Japan), which reached a record of $1.1 billion in the first quarter but then experienced outflows of $410 million, the highest four-week outflow since July 1997, between April and May this year (IMF, 2004b).

The decline in emerging market equities was highly correlated with the decline in mature equity markets, suggesting that global factors, including shifting interest rate expectations, had ripple effects through mature and emerging markets (Figure 2.19). In fact, equity markets fell across emerging Europe, the Middle East, Africa, Latin America, and Asia.

Unlike emerging equity markets, the sell-off in local bond markets was more differentiated. Spreads of local currency bonds issued by Brazil and Turkey rose sharply in April and May (Table 2.1 and Figures 2.20 and 2.21), while their respective currencies experienced depreciation. Other local markets, however, were not materially affected. This differentiation reflected a combination of factors, including a shift out of the riskier sub-investment grade credits into the less volatile investment grade credits, the varying share of foreign ownership in local markets, and the concentration of leverage in high-yielding credits.

Although offering the third highest yields among select local markets, Hungary's local debt spreads fell during April and May 2004. This reflected its investment grade status and expectations of a continued easing of monetary policy even in the face of rising international interest rates. In South Africa and Poland, local spreads increased marginally in reaction to rising inflation expectations and, in the case of Poland, uncertainty about the

Figure 2.17. Differentials Between Corporate and Emerging Market Spreads
(In basis points)

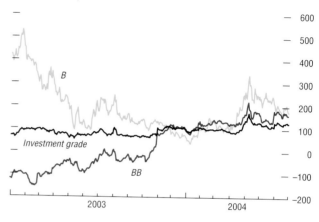

Sources: J.P. Morgan Chase & Co.; Merrill Lynch; and IMF staff estimates.

Figure 2.18. Emerging Market Credit Quality

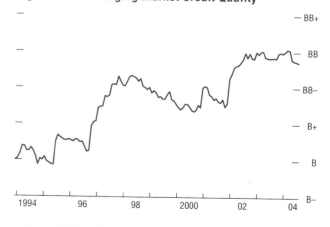

Sources: J.P. Morgan Chase & Co.; Moody's; Standard & Poor's; and IMF staff estimates.

Table 2.1. Selected Local Currency Bond Spreads
(In percentage points, monthly average over U.S. treasuries or German Bunds)

| | Latin America | |
	Brazil 2-yr	Mexico 5-yr
January	13.68	5.38
February	13.78	5.46
March	13.87	5.71
April	14.00	5.35
May	16.26	5.83
June	15.95	6.09
July	14.71	6.24
Change in Spreads—March to May	2.39	0.12

Sources: Bloomberg, L.P.; and IMF staff estimates.

Figure 2.19. Correlations of MSCI World and Emerging Market Indices
(Thirty-day rolling window)

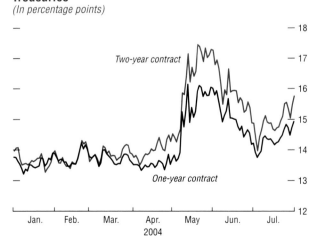

Sources: Morgan Stanley Capital International; and IMF staff estimates.

Figure 2.20. Brazil: Local Market Spreads over U.S. Treasuries
(In percentage points)

Sources: Bloomberg L.P.; and IMF staff estimates.

fiscal outlook. Similarly, spreads of Mexican local instruments rose marginally due to an increased perception of inflation risk and an unexpected tightening of monetary policy by the central bank in April. In Indonesia, spreads fell over the period as monetary policy remained largely accommodative.

Portfolio outflows suggest that high-yielding local currency debt markets appear to have been subject to deleveraging in April and May this year. Nonresident purchases and holdings of local currency debt issued by Brazil increased sharply during the fourth quarter last year and the first quarter this year, before declining in the second quarter (Figure 2.22). Mirroring these developments, nonresident holdings of government debt peaked in April 2004, before declining in May and June (Figure 2.23).

Portfolio flows into Turkey exhibit a similar pattern. Portfolio flows rose sharply toward the end of last year and remained high in the first quarter of 2004 (Figure 2.24). A decline in April proved temporary, however, and inflows resumed in May. Foreign holdings of local currency bonds continued to increase in June and early July (Figure 2.25).

The temporary reduction in foreign holdings of local debt securities issued by Brazil and Turkey suggests that deleveraging in high-yielding local debt markets was limited. Moreover, there is little evidence of substantial

	Emerging Europe, Middle East & Africa			Asia
Turkey 1-yr	Hungary 5-yr	South Africa 10-yr	Poland 5-yr	Indonesia 1-yr
22.20	6.20	5.88	3.34	7.99
22.90	6.43	6.18	3.48	6.99
22.05	5.92	6.52	3.57	6.49
20.99	5.48	6.52	3.79	5.70
27.13	5.72	6.74	4.08	5.73
26.10	5.99	6.77	3.92	5.27
24.97	6.15	6.60	4.07	5.14
5.08	−0.20	0.21	0.51	−0.76

outflows from lower-yielding markets, including Hungary, Indonesia, Poland, and South Africa. Against this background, a renewed unwinding of leverage in mature markets may prove once more unsettling for local debt markets.

Emerging Market Financing

Gross issuance of bonds, equities, and loans by emerging market countries through June 2004 compares favorably with previous years, despite a lull in issuance in April and May as markets adjusted to the prospect of higher U.S. short-term interest rates (Table 2.2 and Figure 2.26). Bond issuance was particularly strong, although sub-investment grade borrowers encountered an unreceptive market in April and May. Equity issuance in the first two quarters of 2004 has also exceeded previous years, despite the lull in April and May. As usual, Asia dominated new equity issuance. Syndicated lending to emerging markets followed a similar pattern, and the level of such lending through June 2004 has been broadly in line with previous years.

On a net basis, emerging market issuance has also been strong, notwithstanding heavy redemptions. In the second quarter of 2004, however, net issuance in Latin America turned sharply negative as some sub-investment grade issuers remained temporarily out of the mar-

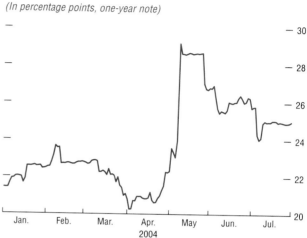

Figure 2.21. Turkey: Local Market Spreads over German Bunds
(In percentage points, one-year note)

Sources: Bloomberg L.P.; and IMF staff estimates.

Figure 2.22. Brazil: Portfolio Investment in Local Currency Debt Instruments
(In millions of U.S. dollars)

Net flows (left scale)

Cumulative (right scale)

Sources: Central Bank of Brazil; and IMF staff estimates.

ket and issuance in loan and equity markets was negligible (Figure 2.27). This was the third successive quarter of negative net issuance for Latin America.

Bond Issuance

After gross bond issuance soared to a record $38.4 billion in the first quarter, issuance dipped sharply in the second quarter only to rebound strongly in late June. Gross bond issuance through June 2004 was well above levels of previous years and has further accelerated in July to start the third quarter at a record pace of some $19 billion (Figure 2.28). Early in the year, strong demand for emerging market assets, low global bond yields, and record low emerging market bond spreads created strong incentives for issuers to accelerate funding plans. Issuers were keen to lock in low financing costs as expectations of a turn in global interest rates became more pronounced. As a result, net bond issuance in the first quarter reached a multi-year high of $13.4 billion, despite record amortization payments. The inclusion of collective action clauses seems now to be widely accepted as industry standard (Box 2.6, page 44).

Primary market access turned decidedly more difficult in late April, causing borrowing costs for many emerging markets to rise rapidly. Several issuers cancelled planned bond issues, and by mid-June, net bond issuance for the quarter had turned negative. Sovereign and corporate issuers in Latin America faced particular difficulties. During the month of May, not a single Latin American bond was launched. By late June, however, bond markets again appeared receptive to new issues from sub-investment grade borrowers as Brazil and Turkey launched bonds that were well received. Turkey came to the market with a $750 million seven-year fixed-rate bond that was heavily oversubscribed. Brazil launched a well-received $750 million five-year floating-rate note (FRN). The FRN capitalized on the growing appetite of investors for protection

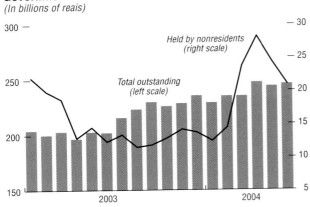

Figure 2.23. Brazil: Nonresident Holdings of Government Debt Instruments

(In billions of reais)

Source: Brazil Ministry of Finance.

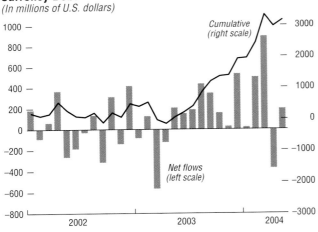

Figure 2.24. Turkey: Portfolio Investment in Local Currency Debt

(In millions of U.S. dollars)

Source: Central Bank of Turkey.

against rising interest rates. Sovereign and corporate issuers in Chile, Mexico, Russia, and Venezuela also issued FRNs.

The bond issues by Brazil and Turkey notwithstanding, issuance in the second quarter was dominated by higher-grade borrowers. In a high-profile transaction, Mexico successfully launched an innovative debt management operation involving the older, off-the-run global bonds for more liquid, on-the-run global bonds. The $3 billion transaction was well received by the markets, as it made the Mexican yield curve more efficient by replacing higher-yielding bonds with instruments that traded more in line with the sovereign yield curve. As suggested earlier, July was a bumper month for primary market issuance, with many sub-investment grade borrowers returning to the market.

In Europe, high-grade issuers successfully capitalized on positive market sentiment toward new EU members. The Czech Republic and Slovak Republic saw solid demand for their respective debut issues in the international bond market, while Poland (in May) and Hungary (in June) returned successfully to the Samurai bond market to issue ¥50 billion ($462 million) each in foreign bonds. The Samurai market saw a burst of activity as Japanese investor appetite for such bonds grew as a yield pickup over domestic yen interest rates. From the issuer's perspective, yield spreads on yen-denominated Samurai bonds were comparatively low due to their limited supply.

Equity Issuance

Driven by robust new issuance in Asia, equity issuance has been on track to top the $41.8 billion in emerging market equity financing raised in 2000 (Figure 2.29). While increased market volatility in April and May triggered a brief pullback in new equity issuance, June saw a solid rebound in equity financing, mainly by Asian issuers. Chinese firms accounted for most of the region's new

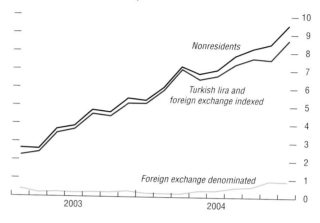

Figure 2.25. Turkey: Nonresident Holdings of Government Debt Instruments
(In quadrillions of Turkish lira)

Sources: Turkey Ministry of Finance; and IMF staff estimates.

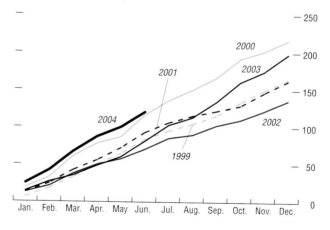

Figure 2.26. Cumulative Gross Annual Issuance of Bonds, Loans, and Equity
(In billions of U.S. dollars)

Source: Capital Data.

Table 2.2. Emerging Market Financing

					2003				2004					Year to Date[1]
	2000	2001	2002	2003	Q1	Q2	Q3	Q4	Q1	Q2	Apr.	May	Jun.	
						(In billions of U.S. dollars)								
Gross issuance by asset	**216.4**	**162.1**	**135.6**	**197.9**	**35.0**	**46.0**	**53.2**	**63.7**	**67.3**	**56.5**	**20.0**	**13.0**	**23.4**	**140.6**
Bonds	80.5	89.0	61.6	97.4	20.1	27.9	24.6	24.7	38.4	26.9	11.3	6.6	9.0	74.0
Equities	41.8	11.2	16.4	28.7	1.2	2.0	7.1	18.4	13.2	10.3	1.6	2.2	6.5	25.2
Loans	94.2	61.9	57.6	71.8	13.7	16.1	21.5	20.6	15.7	19.3	7.1	4.2	8.0	41.5
Gross issuance by region	**216.4**	**162.1**	**135.6**	**197.9**	**35.0**	**46.0**	**53.2**	**63.7**	**67.3**	**56.5**	**20.0**	**13.0**	**23.4**	**140.6**
Asia	85.9	67.5	53.9	86.2	12.9	15.7	25.1	32.5	32.6	26.3	6.4	6.5	13.4	67.0
Latin America	69.1	53.9	33.4	42.8	7.8	12.1	9.1	13.8	12.5	8.3	5.7	0.7	1.9	24.8
Europe, Middle East, Africa	61.4	40.8	48.3	69.0	14.3	18.2	19.1	17.4	22.2	21.9	7.9	5.9	8.1	48.9
Amortization by asset	**114.3**	**148.0**	**129.3**	**124.2**	**22.1**	**34.3**	**29.6**	**38.2**	**38.4**	**33.2**	**12.6**	**7.7**	**12.9**	**n.a.**
Bonds	52.2	60.0	59.8	61.8	10.5	17.5	15.6	18.2	25.0	17.9	6.7	3.3	8.0	n.a.
Equities	0.0	0.0	0.0	0.0	0.0	0.0	0.0	0.0	0.0	0.0	0.0	0.0	0.0	n.a.
Loans	62.1	88.0	69.5	62.4	11.6	16.8	14.0	20.0	13.5	15.3	6.0	4.4	4.9	n.a.
Amortization by region	**114.3**	**148.0**	**129.3**	**124.2**	**22.1**	**34.3**	**29.6**	**38.2**	**38.4**	**33.2**	**12.6**	**7.7**	**12.9**	**n.a.**
Asia	57.1	66.5	56.2	49.4	8.3	12.0	14.5	14.7	16.1	13.2	5.5	3.0	4.8	n.a.
Latin America	32.3	45.9	41.2	40.8	7.6	10.1	8.0	15.1	12.7	13.4	6.2	2.8	4.4	n.a.
Europe, Middle East, Africa	24.9	35.5	31.9	33.9	6.2	12.2	7.1	8.4	9.6	6.6	1.0	1.9	3.7	n.a.
Net issuance by asset	**102.2**	**14.2**	**6.4**	**73.8**	**12.9**	**11.7**	**23.6**	**25.5**	**28.8**	**23.3**	**7.4**	**5.3**	**10.6**	**n.a.**
Bonds	28.3	29.1	1.8	35.6	9.6	10.4	9.0	6.6	13.4	9.0	4.6	3.3	1.0	n.a.
Equities	41.8	11.2	16.4	28.7	1.2	2.0	7.1	18.4	13.2	10.3	1.6	2.2	6.5	n.a.
Loans	32.1	−26.1	−11.8	9.4	2.1	−0.7	7.5	0.5	2.2	4.0	1.2	−0.2	3.1	n.a.
Net issuance by region	**102.2**	**14.2**	**6.4**	**73.8**	**12.9**	**11.7**	**23.6**	**25.5**	**28.8**	**23.3**	**7.4**	**5.3**	**10.6**	**n.a.**
Asia	28.8	0.9	−2.3	36.7	4.7	3.7	10.6	17.8	16.5	13.0	0.9	3.5	8.6	n.a.
Latin America	36.9	7.9	−7.8	1.9	0.2	2.0	1.0	−1.3	−0.3	−5.1	−0.5	−2.1	−2.5	n.a.
Europe, Middle East, Africa	36.5	5.3	16.4	35.1	8.1	6.0	12.0	9.0	12.5	15.3	6.9	3.9	4.4	n.a.
Secondary markets														
Bonds														
EMBI Global (spread in basis points)[2]	735	728	725	403	626	515	486	403	414	482	468	482	490	453
Merrill Lynch High Grade (spread in basis points)	890	795	871	418	757	606	543	418	438	404	388	404	390	393
Merrill Lynch High Yield (spread in basis points)	200	162	184	93	156	120	110	93	94	97	89	97	96	94
U.S. 10 yr. treasury yield (yield in %)	5.12	5.05	3.82	4.25	3.80	3.52	3.94	4.25	4.30	4.33	4.51	4.58	4.48	4.78
						(In percent)								
Equity														
DOW	−6.2	−7.1	−16.8	25.3	−4.2	12.4	3.2	12.7	−0.9	0.8	−1.3	−0.4	2.4	−3.0
NASDAQ	−39.3	−21.1	−31.5	50.0	0.4	21.0	10.1	12.1	−0.5	2.7	−3.7	3.5	3.1	−5.8
MSCI Emerging Market Free	−31.8	−4.9	−8.0	51.6	−6.8	22.2	13.5	17.3	8.9	−10.3	−8.5	−2.3	0.2	−4.4
Asia	−42.5	4.2	−6.2	47.1	−9.3	21.4	14.9	16.3	7.6	−12.2	−6.3	−4.7	−1.6	−9.3
Latin America	−18.4	−4.3	−24.8	67.1	−0.9	22.6	12.4	22.4	6.2	−9.2	−10.9	−1.2	3.2	−0.1
EMEA	−22.3	−20.9	4.7	51.3	−5.3	23.7	11.6	15.8	13.2	−7.4	−11.0	2.0	2.0	2.7

Sources: Bloomberg L.P.; Capital Data; J.P. Morgan Chase & Co.; Morgan Stanley Capital International; and IMF staff estimates.

[1]Gross issuance data (net of U.S. trust facility issuance) are as of July 16, 2004 close-of-business London, and Secondary markets data are as of July 30, 2004 c.o.b. New York.

[2]On April 14, 2000, the EMBI+ was adjusted for the London Club agreement for Russia. This resulted in a one-off (131 basis points) decline in average measured spreads.

share issues during the second quarter, led by China Telecom's $1.7 billion share issue in May and the $1.9 billion initial public offering (IPO) by China's Ping Ang Insurance. The two transactions were the largest share issues in the second quarter, boosting the region's share in global emerging equity financing to some 80 percent. In June, firms in the Emerging

Europe, Middle East, and Africa (EMEA) region also returned to primary equity markets, after having been largely absent for most of the second quarter. In sharp contrast, new equity issuance by Latin American firms remained quite low, following limited issuance in 2003. With only five of the region's corporates having been able to raise funds during the entire first half of the year, Latin America's share in total emerging market equity issues remained stuck at a mere 3 percent.

Syndicated Lending

After a strong first quarter, gross lending to emerging market borrowers slowed in May, but rebounded sharply in late June, in line with activity in primary equity and bond markets (Figure 2.30). On a net basis, lending to emerging markets contracted in May as lenders reduced market exposure in response to the global market sell-off. During the second quarter slowdown, lending to Asian corporates held up well. Loans to firms in the EMEA region declined markedly, however, and lending to Latin American borrowers slowed to a trickle.

Foreign Direct Investment

There are preliminary signs of a modest recovery in foreign direct investment (FDI) flows to emerging markets this year, following declines in 2002 and 2003. FDI flows to Latin America are estimated by the World Bank to have increased significantly in the first quarter of 2004 compared with the first quarter of 2003, led by flows to Chile and Mexico, and to a lesser extent Brazil (Figure 2.31). Asian FDI flows also increased over the same period, and continued to account for the bulk of global FDI flows to emerging economies. Within Asia, flows to China remained dominant. FDI flows to Eastern European countries and Turkey also show signs of increase. On the basis of these initial trends and the prospect of stronger global growth, FDI flows to emerg-

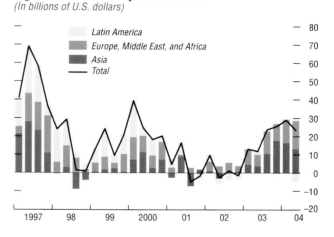

Figure 2.27. Quarterly Net Issuance
(In billions of U.S. dollars)

Sources: Capital Data; and IMF staff estimates.

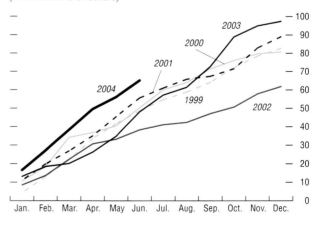

Figure 2.28. Cumulative Gross Annual Issuance of Bonds
(In billions of U.S. dollars)

Source: Capital Data.

Figure 2.29. Cumulative Gross Annual Issuance of Equity
(In billions of U.S. dollars)

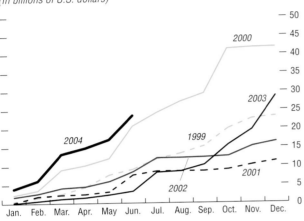

Source: Capital Data.

Figure 2.30. Cumulative Gross Annual Issuance of Loans
(In billions of U.S. dollars)

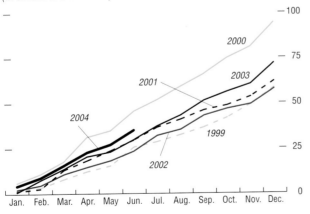

Source: Capital Data.

ing markets are forecast by the World Bank to recover moderately this year. This view is also supported by private sector surveys suggesting increased readiness to undertake cross-border acquisitions and investments.

Banking Sector Developments in Emerging Markets

Since the last GFSR, banking systems in the major emerging markets have continued to recover, with generally improving capital positions, asset quality, and earnings (Table 2.3). In most countries, domestic banks have expanded lending, funded by deposit growth and interbank credits from major international banks. Performance varies across regions, however. In Asia, the financial position of banks has generally strengthened further with the economic recovery, except in a few countries where underlying weaknesses have not been fully addressed. The stabilization of banking systems in Latin America is being sustained, but full normalization is contingent on a supportive global environment and fundamental restructuring to restore solvency of distressed institutions. Banks in emerging markets in Europe continue to perform well, with adequate capital, although rapid credit expansion is a source of risk in a number of countries. In the Middle East and Africa, there has been little change since the last GFSR, but there are encouraging indications of efforts to deal with structural weaknesses in state-owned banks in some countries.

Emerging market banking systems face risks associated with a reversal of the low interest rate environment experienced in recent years. In many countries, low interest rates have allowed a strengthening of banks' balance sheets through capital gains on their interest sensitive assets while the reduction in funding costs probably contributed to a widening of interest rate margins. To the extent that these gains have been distributed and on lent rather than added to capital or reserves, banks would need to adjust to opposite effects on their balance sheets as interest rates rise. Also, profits could be squeezed by a compression of interest margins to the extent that funding costs rise and banks are unable to fully pass this increase on to customers.

Supervisory authorities in emerging markets are also evaluating the implications for their banking systems of the revised Basel Accord (Basel II), which was endorsed by the Basel Committee on Banking Supervision in June 2004 for implementation in 2007. The precise impact of the new accord on banking systems in emerging markets is difficult to gauge. On the one hand, banks from these countries, which are likely to follow the standardized approach, may need to increase capital to allow for greater weighting of riskier credit exposures and to cover operational risk. On the other hand, they could adapt their portfolios to limit the need to provide additional capital. Supervisory authorities may need to ensure their banks have the capacity to meet the additional capital requirements. In addition, they may need to consider the impact of Basel II on the activities of international banks in their banking systems. International banks are more likely to operate under the internal ratings based (IRB) approach and will face higher risk weights on their emerging market exposures.

There are indications of a shift in the pattern of lending activities of major international banks in emerging markets toward interbank and government lending in foreign currency (Table 2.4). The rise in interbank lending is consistent with signs of recovery in many emerging market banking systems. Overall credit extended by these institutions to emerging markets rose on average but the share of foreign currency lending to the non-financial private sector declined noticeably in some regions. However, a significant portion of the increase in interbank lending may have funded part of the increase in lending to this sector by emerging market banks, possibly contributing to their currency and maturity mismatches.

Figure 2.31. Foreign Direct Investment to Emerging Markets
(In billions of U.S. dollars)

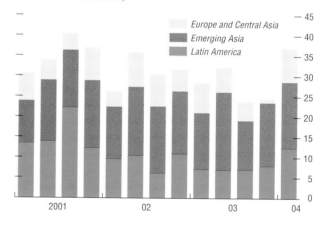

Source: World Bank.

Table 2.3. Emerging Market Countries: Selected Financial Soundness Indicators
(In percent)

	Return on Assets				Nonperforming Loans to Total Loans				Capital to Assets				Moody's Financial Strength Index[1]			
	2000	2001	2002	2003	2000	2001	2002	2003	2000	2001	2002	2003	2001	2002	2003	May 2004
Asia[2]																
Mean	0.3	0.5	0.7	1.0	15.2	14.8	13.3	10.3	6.8	6.8	7.4	7.8	25.9	26.7	27.5	28.4
Median	0.3	0.6	0.8	1.0	16.0	11.4	15.8	10.8	5.7	5.3	6.1	7.5	16.7	18.5	19.4	19.6
Standard deviation	0.9	0.4	0.4	0.4	9.0	9.7	8.8	6.5	3.1	3.2	3.2	3.3	25.4	24.0	23.5	23.1
Latin America																
Mean	0.5	0.4	0.2	1.1	9.5	9.6	10.7	9.6	10.6	10.7	10.3	10.6	27.8	19.7	18.7	19.8
Median	0.9	0.7	1.0	1.4	9.2	9.2	8.6	7.8	10.3	10.0	10.8	10.2	26.9	19.4	15.8	24.2
Standard deviation	1.5	2.2	3.6	2.0	7.1	6.8	9.0	7.7	1.6	2.2	4.2	3.4	12.2	17.0	18.7	19.2
Emerging Europe[3]																
Mean	0.7	0.1	1.5	1.6	12.6	12.3	9.9	8.6	9.8	10.2	10.3	10.4	29.2	28.9	29.8	30.5
Median	0.9	1.0	1.2	1.4	11.1	8.3	8.6	6.0	9.5	9.5	9.8	9.8	29.8	32.1	32.1	33.3
Standard deviation	1.4	3.1	0.9	0.7	9.1	9.1	6.6	7.4	3.5	3.2	3.1	2.6	12.9	13.6	13.3	13.4
Middle East																
Mean	1.2	1.2	1.2	1.2	14.3	14.2	14.6	14.6	8.9	8.7	8.5	8.0	29.8	28.6	28.6	28.6
Median	1.2	0.9	0.7	0.7	13.6	15.6	15.3	14.3	9.2	9.3	8.9	7.3	31.7	29.2	29.2	29.2
Standard deviation	0.6	0.9	0.8	0.9	5.1	3.9	4.8	5.7	2.7	2.8	2.8	2.4	8.9	9.6	9.6	9.6
Sub-Saharan Africa																
Mean	3.7	3.6	2.7	3.4	15.7	13.3	12.2	10.9	9.2	9.4	9.3	9.1	...	...	...	...
Median	3.2	3.3	2.3	3.0	14.6	11.7	8.9	8.0	9.1	9.1	9.4	9.0	...	...	...	...
Standard deviation	3.1	2.7	2.1	2.5	9.2	8.3	9.6	8.5	1.4	1.4	1.3	2.0	...	...	...	...

Sources: National authorities; and IMF staff estimates.
[1]Constructed according to a numerical scale assigned to Moody's weighted average bank ratings by country. "0" indicates the lowest possible average rating and "100" indicates the highest possible average rating.
[2]Excluding Japan.
[3]Includes Central and Eastern Europe, Israel, Malta, and Turkey.

Asia

Banking systems in emerging markets in Asia have continued to strengthen with the economic recovery. Earnings, asset quality, and capital adequacy show a steady improvement on average, helped by better interest margins and operational efficiency. These positive developments are also reflected in higher ratings of banks by private sector rating agencies and stronger relative market valuations of bank stocks, which have trended upwards after a slight correction early in the year (Figure 2.32).

Authorities in a number of countries in the region are moving to address structural issues in their banking systems. In China, the authorities are making efforts to address weaknesses at state-owned banks and two of them have been recapitalized. In addition, they have been required to undertake external audits, tighten provisioning, and maintain

higher capital ratios. Similarly, prospects for commercial banks in India have brightened with the steps taken by the authorities to address key vulnerabilities, including, in particular, the tightening of loan classification requirements. Following market reaction to a proposed securities transactions tax, the authorities have modified the proposal and taken steps to reassure markets.

In Thailand, while distressed assets still constrain banks' balance sheets, profitability of private banks has improved and some banks have been able to raise capital. The Thai Asset Management Company's (TAMC) executive committee has approved resolutions of 90 percent of the assets, but since not all agreements have been signed by debtors and several cases that are currently classified as foreclosure are likely to re-enter the debt negotiation phase, substantial work remains before all of TAMC's nonperforming loans (NPLs) are resolved.

Table 2.4. Exposure of Foreign Banks to Emerging Markets[1]
(In percent)

| | Total Foreign Exposure as a Percent of Domestic Credit | | Foreign Currency Exposure as a percent of Total Exposure to the Country | | Of Which Foreign Currency Exposure to: | | | | | |
| | | | | | Banking sector as a percent of total foreign currency exposure | | Public sector as a percent of total foreign currency exposure | | Nonbanks as a percent of total foreign currency exposure | |
	Dec. 2002	Dec. 2003	Dec. 2002	Dec. 2003	Dec. 2002	Dec. 2003	Dec. 2002	Dec. 2003	Dec. 2002	Dec. 2003
Asia	**18**	**18**	**54**	**55**	**43**	**44**	**9**	**10**	**46**	**44**
China	2	3	89	88	42	43	14	13	41	42
Hong Kong SAR	106	116	33	37	40	43	2	2	57	54
India	13	16	45	54	21	30	20	15	53	51
Indonesia	31	29	84	81	9	9	27	32	64	59
Korea	16	18	70	71	60	61	10	8	28	29
Malaysia	46	49	40	40	15	15	20	26	64	56
Philippines	49	57	77	79	30	33	20	24	49	43
Singapore	186	172	66	64	66	65	1	1	33	34
Thailand	28	27	49	46	19	21	9	12	71	63
Latin America	**82**	**73**	**50**	**50**	**13**	**17**	**15**	**19**	**71**	**64**
Argentina	68	56	71	67	9	19	20	25	71	56
Bolivia	40	21	89	84	42	15	18	2	40	83
Brazil	46	36	51	52	19	23	13	16	67	59
Chile	89	81	48	45	15	23	8	11	77	66
Colombia	61	47	68	60	13	14	24	30	63	56
Dominican Republic	64	63	89	83	33	16	15	30	48	51
Mexico	114	116	31	33	8	13	23	28	69	59
Paraguay	107	120	55	62	15	14	13	13	63	58
Uruguay	45	45	79	75	13	16	20	23	67	61
Venezuela	160	218	71	61	6	3	25	33	69	64
Emerging Europe	**60**	**64**	**65**	**64**	**26**	**29**	**19**	**20**	**55**	**51**
Bulgaria	72	85	72	65	28	19	26	24	46	57
Croatia	116	122	64	64	31	36	20	18	49	45
Czech Republic	122	131	33	27	33	33	4	6	54	54
Hungary	91	97	65	66	32	30	30	34	38	36
Israel	11	13	95	94	28	26	22	26	50	47
Poland	105	108	43	46	19	18	23	29	58	53
Romania	102	109	77	78	15	17	16	25	69	58
Russia	43	45	95	93	27	35	15	12	58	52
Slovak Republic	97	110	38	42	29	33	23	28	47	39
Turkey	35	28	94	94	16	20	24	24	60	56
Ukraine	12	15	79	83	33	29	7	17	60	55
Middle East	**26**	**28**	**77**	**77**	**45**	**43**	**12**	**14**	**43**	**42**
Egypt	13	16	74	76	35	25	35	43	29	32
Jordan	19	18	71	69	26	24	29	33	45	43
Lebanon	15	17	79	80	31	23	6	7	62	70
Morocco	36	32	52	47	18	15	20	28	63	57
Pakistan	22	20	39	37	13	20	12	27	75	53
Saudi Arabia	19	17	100	100	42	40	13	19	45	41
Sub-Saharan Africa	**32**	**26**	**73**	**72**	**26**	**22**	**19**	**26**	**55**	**52**
Kenya	43	44	52	56	6	6	14	17	80	77
South Africa	22	15	82	79	40	35	20	27	39	37
Zimbabwe	24	34	33	37	5	1	47	58	48	41
Total	**30**	**29**	**57**	**58**	**31**	**33**	**13**	**15**	**55**	**51**

Sources: BIS, *Consolidated Banking Statistics*; IMF, *International Financial Statistics*.
[1]These BIS bank data are cross-border consolidated and therefore capture both banks' direct cross-border exposures and exposures incurred through the subsidiaries and branches located in the country (both in foreign and local currency). They include both loan and securities exposures.

Figure 2.32. Emerging Market Countries: Bank Market Valuations
(February 1999 = 100)

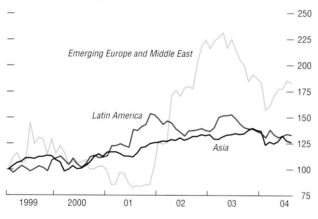

Sources: Datastream; and IMF staff estimates.

Overall, indicators of bank soundness in Malaysia remain solid and systemic risks seem well contained. While the economic recovery there has helped lower the ratio of nonperforming to total loans, provisioning against such loans remains below 50 percent. In Korea, banks have weathered the credit card debt problem without systemic repercussions. In May, the government established a new "bad bank," Hanmaeum Financial, to take over defaulted credit card debts and facilitate their resolution. The banking systems in Hong Kong and Singapore continue to perform well, with improved profitability supported by the ongoing economic recovery.

Bank profitability has improved in Indonesia, helped by reduced funding costs, but financial and governance problems persist in the large state banks. Bank Indonesia has moved to strengthen the banking system in preparation for the removal of the blanket deposit guarantee by intervening in several small banks. However, legislation for a deposit insurance scheme has been stalled due to elections. In the Philippines, scope for remedial action to address potential banking system vulnerabilities is hampered by weaknesses in the regulatory and supervisory framework, including the lack of an effective prompt corrective action framework and legal protection for supervisory intervention.

Latin America

Reflecting the return of stability in the troubled banking systems in the region, banks' earnings, nonperforming loan ratios, and reported capital positions show improvement. Market indicators and ratings, however, suggest that concerns have not abated. Ratings of banks by private rating agencies weakened on average in 2003 before recovering in 2004, and relative market valuations have declined slightly since April 2003. Foreign bank penetration is generally high in Latin America, although there has been a pronounced decline in lending by interna-

Box 2.3. Financing Flows and Global Imbalances

Amid heightening concerns over the sustainability of the financing of the U.S. current account deficit, the U.S. dollar has weakened from its 2002 high. Foreign exchange market intervention coincided in 2003 and early 2004 with pressure on many currencies to appreciate, especially in emerging Asia and Japan. Reminiscent of the late 1980s (see the first Figure at right), surging global foreign exchange reserves boosted official purchases of U.S. treasuries, notwithstanding the notable absence of concerted foreign exchange market interventions that were the hallmark of the 1987 Louvre Accord (see the second Figure below).

In a marked contrast from the late 1980s, concerns over deflation and financial market pressure have been major concerns for policymakers in recent years, most notably in Japan. On signs that a recovery was finally taking hold, global investors started to raise their portfolio weightings in Japan more closer to its weight in benchmark indices. Consequently, foreign purchases of Japanese equities surged in the second half of 2003 and early 2004. Expectations of exchange rate appreciation reportedly resulted in further speculative and leveraged position building, especially in the months following the Septem-

Group of Seven (excluding United States) Reserve Changes
(In percent of U.S. GDP)

Sources: International Monetary Fund, *International Financial Statistics*; and IMF staff estimates.

ber 2003 Group of Seven (G-7) Communiqué (see the third Figure).

Large-scale foreign currency market interventions by Japan in 2003 and early 2004 were undertaken with a view to smooth out undue currency fluctuations. Market participants tended to attribute these interventions also to

U.S. Current Account and Foreign Official Financing

Sources: IMF, *International Financial Statistics*; and U.S. Bureau of Economic Analysis.

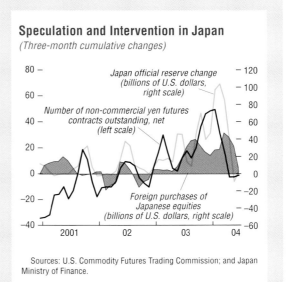

Speculation and Intervention in Japan
(Three-month cumulative changes)

Sources: U.S. Commodity Futures Trading Commission; and Japan Ministry of Finance.

Box 2.3 *(concluded)*

Foreign Ownership of U.S. Securities
(In percent of total market)

Sources: Board of Governors of the Federal Reserve System, *Flow of Funds*; and IMF staff estimates.

the desire to overcome deflation and to minimize the risk that a premature tightening of monetary conditions resulting from currency appreciation could derail the nascent economic recovery. Interventions coincided with a rise in speculative long yen positions registered by the Chicago Mercantile Exchange from September 2003 through mid-February this year. While futures markets capture only a small share of speculative activity, this suggests surging speculative inflows may have contributed to the volatility of the yen.

The Financing of Global Imbalances

• Foreign exchange reserves held by industrial countries and developing countries swelled during the interventions in 1986–88 and 2003–04.[1] The accumulation of reserves, however, was more concentrated during the latter period, with the reserve increase experienced by Japan accounting for most of the increase

[1] The analysis is focused on periods marked by high official financing flows to the United States, namely April 1986 through March 1988 and April 2003 through March 2004; these periods are referred to as 1986–88 and 2003–04.

in industrial country foreign exchange reserves (see the Table).

• The rapid increase of foreign exchange reserves fuelled official purchases of U.S. securities on a large scale during both periods (see the fourth Figure). Nevertheless, official financing flows to the United States rose from 1.2 percent of U.S. GDP in 1986–88 to 2.9 percent of U.S. GDP in 2003–04. This increase outpaced the rise in global foreign exchange reserve holdings in relation to GDP over the past two decades.[2]

• Reflecting the shift from concerted to unilateral interventions, the sources of official financing flows have become significantly more concentrated, with Japan's share in official flows rising particularly strongly.

• Private sector financing flows to the U.S. remained largely stable, averaging nearly 2 percent of GDP during 1987–88 and 2003–04. Nevertheless, foreign direct investment flows have turned negative on a net basis since the first quarter of 2003, as U.S. companies have stepped up their operations abroad. Mirroring these trends, U.S. equity investors have increasingly diversified their portfolios by increasing their foreign equity holdings. FDI and equity outflows on a net basis averaged 1.9 percent of GDP during 2003–04 compared with a 0.8 percent inflow in 1987–88.

Risks to an Orderly Resolution of Global Imbalances

The global imbalances, reflecting the U.S. current account deficit and large surpluses in other parts of the world, pose a continued risk. While the U.S. current account deficit is likely to adjust, the timing and nature of the adjustment are difficult to predict. Even though capital flows to the U.S. have remained buoyant, a slowdown cannot be ruled out, especially in light of the high share of foreign ownership of U.S. assets. Nevertheless, it is not easy to see why investors would engage in a wholesale shift away

[2] Global foreign exchange reserves rose sixfold during 1984–2003, while worldwide nominal GDP grew threefold over the same period.

U.S. Current Account Financing
(Annual rates)

	1986:Q3–1988:Q2	2003:Q2–2004:Q1	1986:Q3–1988:Q2	2003:Q2–2004:Q1
	(In billions of U.S. dollars)		*(In percent of U.S. GDP)*	
Current account balance	−153.3	−537.3	−3.3	−4.8
Official assets, net	57.2	326.8	1.2	2.9
U.S. official reserve assets	5.5	2.0	0.1	0.0
Foreign official reserve assets in the U.S.	51.6	324.8	1.1	2.9
Private assets, net	96.1	210.5	2.1	1.9
Direct investment, net	22.3	−164.8	0.5	−1.5
Inflows	49.4	25.4	1.1	0.2
Outflows	−27.1	−190.2	−0.6	−1.7
Portfolio flows, net	44.7	359.1	1.0	3.2
Inflows	48.8	420.0	1.0	3.8
Outflows	−4.0	−60.9	−0.1	−0.5
Equity flows, net	14.3	−44.7	0.3	−0.4
Inflows	13.3	44.1	0.3	0.4
Outflows	1.1	−88.8	—	−0.8
Bond flows, net	30.4	403.8	0.7	3.6
Inflows	35.5	376.0	0.8	3.4
Treasuries[1]	0.4	163.4	—	1.5
Agencies	n.a	−10.6	n.a	−0.1
Corporates & Others[2]	35.1	223.2	0.6	2.0
Outflows	−5.1	27.9	−0.1	0.2
Other[3]	34.6	16.2	0.6	0.1
Memorandum items:				
Industrial country reserve change	196.9	349.6	4.2	3.1
of which, Japanese official reserves change	55.4	328.2	1.2	2.9
of which, German/ECB official reserves change[4]	47.9	−20.0	1.0	−0.2
Developing country reserves change	70.1	438.1	1.5	3.9
of which, Asia excluding Japan				
U.S. nominal GDP, billions of U.S. dollars	4,671.9	11,166.7		

Sources: Bureau of Economic Analysis; and International Monetary Fund, *International Financial Statistics*.
[1]Reported as "Other private investment in U.S. securities" during 1986:Q3–1988:Q2.
[2]Including Agencies during 1986:Q3–1988:Q2.
[3]Net short term, U.S. official non-reserve assets, and discrepancy.
[4]German reserves 1986:Q3–1988:Q2; ECB reserves 2003:Q2–2004:Q1.

from U.S. dollar assets, in the absence of a compelling alternative to dollar assets in a high growth area, without undermining the rationale of their investment decisions.

- The composition of inflows represents a further risk. Foreign direct investment flows turned negative, and the financing of the U.S. current account deficit increasingly relied on portfolio flows. In addition, there was a shift in the composition of portfolio financing flows from equity to fixed income related flows, which paralleled the growing structural U.S. fiscal deficit.
- The high share of foreign ownership of U.S. assets, in particular U.S. bonds, raises the possibility that a lack of confidence in the U.S. dollar could result in higher yields. These could, in turn, call into question the discounted value of other assets and lead to price declines in other markets.
- The unusually rapid growth of international reserves has facilitated the financing of the U.S. current account deficit. However, a shift in the currency composition, especially by those countries experiencing a continued large buildup or with large holdings of foreign exchange reserves, could undermine the strength of official financing flows to the United States.

tional banks to the nonfinancial private sector and a shift toward interbank and government credit. Local banks' interbank foreign currency exposures may therefore have increased and may need to be more carefully monitored.

The overall regional picture masks continued improvements in the stronger systems and only tentative recovery in the crisis afflicted countries. Financial soundness indicators (FSIs) indicate that the Brazilian banking system is sound and prospects have improved further in light of the ongoing economic recovery. Credit quality and risk management is likely to be enhanced in the future with the recent introduction of the credit rating system by the central bank. FSIs for banks in Mexico have been strengthening steadily. The banking system in Chile remains robust with improved capital adequacy and profitability and stable and low nonperforming loan ratios.

The banking system in Argentina has stabilized but remains fragile. Its prospects hinge critically on increasing profits, given the lack of public sector resources and the unwillingness of shareholders to invest in Argentine banks. Similarly, notwithstanding some progress in restructuring, the banking system in Uruguay remains vulnerable to the need for continued restructuring of the largest bank. Difficulties have also emerged at a smaller cooperative bank. Ongoing political uncertainties in Venezuela have contributed to concerns about the soundness of the banking system, where weaknesses may be masked to some extent by foreign exchange controls and regulatory forbearance.

In the Dominican Republic, conditions in the financial system seemed to have stabilized despite macroeconomic uncertainties. Significant efforts, however, are still needed to increase provisioning and capital. The liquidity drain experienced by banks in Bolivia early this year has stopped, but the system remains vulnerable to liquidity shocks. The authorities are making progress in their efforts to deal with weak banks and facilitate

corporate restructuring. In Ecuador the consolidation of the banking system continues despite persistent structural weaknesses. However, the system remains vulnerable to domestic and external shocks, which would have to be absorbed without the benefit of a lender of last resort.

Emerging Europe

Several indicators point to continued good performance of banking systems in the European emerging markets. The strong earnings shown on average in 2002 were sustained in 2003, and asset quality and capital adequacy strengthened. The favorable developments and prospects are also reflected in continued strong bank ratings and improving relative market valuation of bank stocks, following some retrenchment in the second half of 2003. On the whole, banking systems in the region seem poised to gain further from the economic recovery, although rapid credit growth, especially to the retail sector, poses a risk in some countries. The credit expansion is being intermediated by foreign banks, which have a large presence in many countries in the region. The Bank for International Settlements (BIS) data indicate that their lending in domestic currency has increased substantially, although there has been a shift away from credit to the nonfinancial private sector.

Variation in the situation of banking systems across the region reflects the differing structural issues they face. The restructuring of the banking system in Turkey has progressed and the impending replacement of the blanket guarantee by a limited deposit insurance scheme should provide an important signal and help limit moral hazard. A number of structural issues, however, still remain to be addressed, including privatization of state-owned banks, the sale of nonperforming loans held by the state asset management company, and rationalization of taxation in the banking system.

Box 2.4. Emerging Market Spread Compression: Is It Real or Is It Liquidity?

As the monetary tightening cycle begins and industrial country interest rates rise, calibrating how much of the compression in emerging market spreads was due to improvements in "real" fundamentals and how much was due to excess liquidity could have important ramifications.[1] The impact of an interest rate rise on spreads may be fairly benign if the lower spreads have been primarily the result of improved fundamentals, but a reversal could be quite abrupt if excessive liquidity were to blame, and could be even more pronounced if the excessive liquidity also led to leveraged positions.

To examine this issue, a forecasting model was constructed that takes into account several features of emerging market spreads and how they adjust to domestic fundamentals and interest rates.[2] First, observe that to the extent that rates paid by emerging market borrowers follow industrial country interest rates, a decline in interest rates, all else being equal, implies lower debt burdens for emerging market countries and an improvement in fundamentals as measured by debt service ratios, debt-to-GDP ratios, and the likelihood of default. Thus, in observing an improvement in fundamentals the model should control for the interaction between industrial country interest rates and the domestic fundamentals—improvements in fundamentals need to be *in addition* to the effects of lower interest rates in order to distinguish the effects of liquidity.

Second, many studies use credit ratings as a proxy representing fundamentals as they encapsulate a host of economic variables.[3] While a handy and efficient measure, the measure is "coarse"—there are a fixed number of categories (e.g., AAA, AA+, A, . . . C–, and SD, referring to default) and alterations among them are not associated with a fixed (or linear) response in

spreads. The model below attempts to enrich the informational content of ratings by: (1) using the indications for future up- or downgrades represented by the rating outlook to account for possible future ratings changes; (2) scaling the ratings variable using logarithms to account for their non-linear relation with spreads; and (3) computing predicted values of ratings depending on three types of "fundamentals."[4]

The model proceeds in two steps. First, the ratings with outlooks are regressed on three measures of "fundamentals," which include an overall variable for economic risks, one for political risks, and one for financial risks.[5] A short-term interest rate, as measured by the current level of the U.S. federal funds target rate, is additionally included so that in the second stage any effect of interest rates on spreads will be independent of such effects influencing the fundamentals as proxied by the predicted ratings. Second, the predicted credit rating from the first stage is used in a second stage where the log of spreads at time t is regressed on the following additional variables: time t futures rate for federal funds three months in advance; a dummy variable representing, at time t, an expected rise in the U.S. policy rate three-months ahead; the time t volatility of expected

[1]See Kashiwase and Kodres (forthcoming).
[2]The model represents a reduced-form model for spreads and, as such, does not distinguish between supply and demand factors for debt securities and their influence on spreads.
[3]See, for example, IMF (2004a) and Sy (2002).

[4]Empirically, markets react first and foremost to hints of future ratings changes rather than the actual event when it occurs. Sy (2002) observes that when spreads are "excessively high" a rating downgrade frequently follows, similarly "excessively low" ratings are often followed by upgrades, suggesting market spreads anticipate future ratings changes.
[5]The *International Country Risk Guide* (2003) releases monthly ratings covering three types of risks—political, economic, and financial. The political variable includes various measures of political risk. The economic risk rating includes variables such as annual inflation, budget balance/GDP, and the current account/GDP. The financial variable includes variable such as foreign debt/GDP, foreign debt service/(exports of goods and services), net international liquidity as months of import cover, and a measure of exchange rate stability. The higher the rating, the lower the risk. The rating takes a numerical value between 0 and 100.

Box 2.4 (concluded)

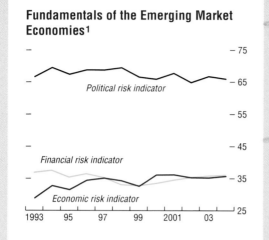

Fundamentals of the Emerging Market Economies[1]

Political risk indicator

Financial risk indicator

Economic risk indicator

Sources: J.P. Morgan Chase & Co.; The PRS Group, Inc., *International Country Risk Guide*; and IMF staff estimates.
[1]The data are a monthly average through May 2004, representing a weighted average of the countries in the EMBI Global Index.

U.S. monetary policy; an interaction term between the volatility and expectations; and time t implied volatility of the stock market (VIX), which serves as a proxy for risk aversion. The interest-rate related variables can be viewed as representing liquidity effects.

The model is run as a panel data set with fixed effects using monthly data from January 1994 through May 2004 for 30 countries within the EMBI Global universe (excluding Argentina). In the first stage regression, all three types of fundamentals are statistically significant, even though the improvement in fundamentals has not been very dramatic for the sample as a whole (see the first Figure). The additional use of the ratings outlook adds several percentage points of explanatory power. In the second stage, the coefficient on the predicted credit ratings variable is the largest and most statistically significant: a one-notch degradation in rating increases spreads by 190 basis points (see the Table). The

Emerging Market Bond Spreads: Fixed-Effect Panel Regression Model

	Unit	Coefficient	Standard Error	*t*-statistics	Impact on the spread (bp.) by one standard deviation increase[1]
Dependent variable: EMBI spreads (bp.)	log				
Explanatory variable:					
(1) Credit ratings predicted[2]	log	0.271	0.009	30.7	190[3]
(2) 3-month ahead Fed Funds futures rate	percent	0.070	0.005	15.4	85
(3) Volatility of 3-month ahead Fed Funds futures minus target rate[4]	log	0.163	0.014	11.8	69
(4) Expectation of rate increase[5]	0 or 1	0.151	0.076	2.0	52
(5) Interaction between the volatility and the expectation	log	0.121	0.031	3.9	99
(6) VIX	level	0.019	0.001	13.3	80
(7) Constant	log	2.452	0.112	22.0	n.a.
R squared:					
Within		0.462			
Between		0.778			
Overall		0.676			
Number of observations:		2,275			

Sources: Bloomberg, J.P. Morgan Chase, The PRS Group, Inc.; *International Country Risk Guide;* and IMF staff estimates.
[1]Given an initial spread of 700 bp, an average across countries over the sample period, the number indicates how much the spread will change in basis points from one standard deviation increase in the variable, ceteris paribus.
[2]An aggregate index of credit ratings and their outlook is regressed in the first stage against economic, financial, and political fundamentals as well as the U.S. policy rate.
[3]Based on a one-notch decline in the long-term sovereign credit rating from BB to BB-.
[4]This volatility measure is based on the 90-day rolling standard deviation of the difference between 3-month ahead Fed Funds futures and target rate.
[5]This dummy variable takes a value of 1 when investors price in more than 50 percent of a 25 basis point increase at the frequency of more than half of the total number of trading days in any given month.

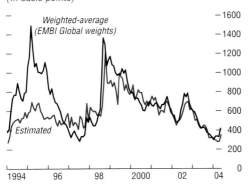

**Emerging Market Bond Spreads
(Excluding Argentina)**
(In basis points)

Weighted-average
(EMBI Global weights)

Estimated

1994   96   98   2000   02   04

Sources: Bloomberg L.P.; J.P. Morgan Chase & Co.; The PRS Group, Inc.; *International Country Risk Guide*; and IMF staff estimates.

coefficient on the anticipated federal funds rate suggests that a fall in the federal funds futures rate results in a fall in spreads and vice versa, as would be predicted by a liquidity effect.[6] But the coefficient is much smaller than that for ratings and is also smaller than the effect of a market "surprise"—the volatility of interest rate expectations. Although the appropriate calibration is not obvious, translated into the effect of a one standard deviation move, both effects as well as the interaction term have sizable impacts on spreads. Thus, if a tightening in the U.S. policy

[6]Other studies have used interest rates (short-term, long-term, and their difference) as an explanatory variable for spreads. The outcomes have not been uniform, with some—Eichengreen and Mody (1998); Kamin and von Kleist (1999); Sløk and Kennedy (2004); and McGuire and Schrijvers (2003)—finding a negative or inconclusive relationship.

rate is not anticipated the effect on spreads of the two coefficients involving the "surprises" is much larger than an anticipated increase.

The model is then used to forecast through June 2005 assuming the following: (1) no change in fundamentals; (2) federal funds futures rates predict future policy interest rates as accurately as they were predicted in 1999 when markets "got it right;" and (3) stock market volatility remains the same as in the first six months of 2004. The second Figure shows the models' predictions and the current EMBI Global index. Looking back, the model predicts relatively well, especially in recent times. Thus, the period leading up to the Asian crisis and most of 2000 suggests spreads were even lower than future federal funds (and other variables) would have predicted. However, like some other models, the model suggests that much of the "overshoot" is gone by 2002, with the elements of the model determining spreads fairly closely even through the reversal in early 2004. Looking forward, the model suggests that if the federal funds rate should rise by 275 basis points by mid-2005 as forecast by futures markets, the EMBI Global spread (excluding Argentina) should rise by another 100 basis points or so. Of course, this conclusion rests on the observation that fundamentals remain the same and the ability of markets to predict future movements in interest rates as accurately as they did in 1999 repeats itself. What is clear from the model is the accuracy of markets' predictions of future interest rates is important and thus the Federal Reserve can play a role in reducing the risk of any disruptions in the emerging bonds market. A clear communication strategy by the Federal Reserve that helps guide market expectations can promote financial stability by keeping the volatility of the expected U.S. monetary policy low, thus contributing a more modest widening in emerging market spreads.

Russia's banking system experienced disruptions in May–July, despite generally strong economic conditions (Box 2.7, page 46). The

authorities were able to contain turbulence and staunch runs on banks, which had only a limited impact on banks in other countries in

Box 2.5. German Issue of Russian Federation Credit-Linked Notes

On July 1, 2004, Germany liquefied €5 billion of its holdings of Russian Paris Club debt (PCD) through the issuance of credit-linked notes (CLNs) by a special purpose vehicle.[1] By issuing new notes to investors linked to Russia's performance on its PCD obligations to Germany, the German authorities generated cash for deficit financing without issuing debt. The issue is the first public transfer of PCD in six years since the securitization by France and Italy of PCD in 1998.

The deal involved some innovative features. In the transaction, Germany agreed to pay ARIES—a special purpose vehicle—the flow of principal and interest it is due on a portion of its PCD. In return, Germany receives an up-front payment from the note issue, effectively monetizing the PCD. There is no change in PCD ownership. Since the PCD has an amortizing schedule giving rise to a different cash flow, the payments the special purpose vehicle receives from Germany have to be swapped into cash flows corresponding to those of the issued bullet bonds. For an event of default to occur, Russia has to be more than 60 days late in payments above a certain size and Germany must decide to publicly announce that Russia has failed to service its PCD. In this event, investors in the CLNs will receive a recovery value of 20 percent in cash.

The CLNs were judged to be inferior in credit quality and recovery value to other Russian sovereign debts. At times of payment difficulties, sovereigns have tended to default on PCD as a first resort. Furthermore, the guaranteed recovery value is below the market's perception of the recovery value on Russian marketable debt. Reflecting these considerations, Moody's rates the CLNs two notches below the sovereign at

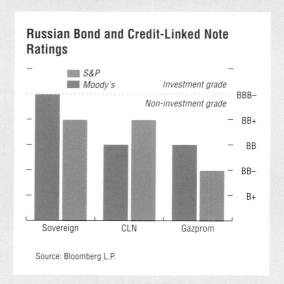

Russian Bond and Credit-Linked Note Ratings

Source: Bloomberg L.P.

"Ba2" (same rating as Gazprom), although Standard & Poor's awards a comparable rating to the sovereign of "BB+" (see the first Figure).[2]

Even though Russia's indebtedness and credit profile are unaffected by the transaction, the issuance of CLNs increased market exposure to Russian sovereign credit risk. Moreover, Germany could issue up additional CLNs. Germany's claims on Russia amount to €14 billion, although not all of these obligations can be transformed into CLNs. The issuance of the CLNs and the potential further additional supply of Russian-linked securities contributed initially to a modest widening of spreads on Russian external debt (see the second Figure). Russian sovereign and corporate markets sold-off when the monetization was announced, but have since recovered, reflecting strong demand for the notes and an easing of concern about the extent of additional supply from such transactions. Nevertheless, further transactions may crowd out borrowing or raise the cost of borrowing for Russian entities, while it would also lower

[1]The issue comprises three tranches. A €2 billion euro-denominated three-year floating rate note was priced at Euribor plus 325 basis points, a €1 billion five-year fixed-rate euro-denominated note was priced to yield 7.76 percent or 420 basis points over euro area government bonds, and a $2.4 billion 10-year fixed rate dollar-denominated note was priced to yield 9.71 percent, or 500 basis points over U.S. treasury bonds.

[2]Standard & Poor's apparently considers only the probability of default on the CLNs and not the expected recovery rate in determining its rating.

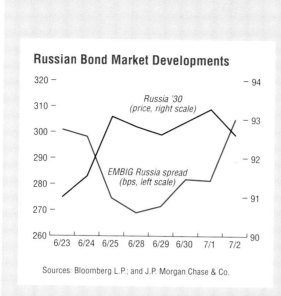

Russian Bond Market Developments

Sources: Bloomberg L.P.; and J.P. Morgan Chase & Co.

debt payments from Russia to Germany in the future.

It is possible that other countries will follow the German example and seek to monetize their PCD. In the case of Russian PCD, additional supply outside of Germany will be somewhat restricted since no other Paris Club creditor has similarly large claims on Russia (see the Table).

Russia's Paris Club Creditors
(In billions of U.S. dollars)

Paris Club debt	48
Of which:	
Germany	20
Italy	5
Japan	4
France	3

Countries with Large Debts to the Paris Club[1]
(In billions of U.S. dollars)

Argentina	3.3
Brazil	9.4
Ecuador	2.5
Peru	8.4
Poland	15.6
Egypt	19.6
Morocco	5.6
Nigeria	23.1
Indonesia	33.6

[1]Approximate Paris Club debt based on debt to official bilateral creditors

There is also potential for similar transactions involving the PCD of other countries. Overall size of the PCD and its concentration in the hands of creditors will determine the likely volume of any transaction.

the region. Passage of interim deposit insurance will help to underpin confidence as the banking system continues to restructure and consolidate. While the authorities' recent measures were successful in calming the situation, more effective bank resolution processes, improved crisis management tools, and a clear and consistent public communications strategy are needed to minimize the impact of individual banks' problems on confidence in the sector as a whole. Elsewhere in the region, rapid credit expansion is the main concern and warrants close monitoring in a number of countries, including the Baltics, Bulgaria, the Czech Republic, Hungary, Romania, Russia, the Slovak Republic, and Ukraine. The associated risks are greater in countries—for example, Ukraine—where a high degree of dollarization, including of loans, exposes banks to direct exchange rate and related credit risk.

Middle East and Africa

Data limitations suggest greater caution in interpreting regional aggregate financial soundness indicators in the Middle East and Africa. Such data tend to be strongly influenced by a few large countries. Against this backdrop, financial soundness indicators (FSIs) point to a marginal weakening in banks' performance in the Middle East, although individual country experiences vary. Favorable economic developments augur well for the banking system in Egypt, where the authorities are also moving to address structural weaknesses in the system, including in

Box 2.6. Collective Action Clauses

Following the first Mexican issue in New York in March 2003, there has been a clear shift toward the use of collective action clauses (CACs) in international sovereign bonds issued under New York law. Since March 2004, sovereign issues containing CACs grew to represent more than 90 percent of total value of new issues, and 40 percent of the value of the outstanding stock of bonds from emerging market countries, largely reflecting the increase in sovereign bonds issued under New York law that included CACs.

After a relatively brief period of uncertainty regarding the degree of standardization between investment grade and non-investment grade countries, it now appears that market practice for bonds issued under New York law has rapidly converged toward a 75 percent voting threshold for majority restructuring provisions. In particular, Brazil lowered the voting threshold in its recent sovereign issues to 75 percent from 85 percent, reflecting the practice followed by a number of non-investment grade countries.

Market acceptance of CACs has continued with no observable impact on pricing even after international liquidity conditions toward emerging market debt gradually tightened in the sec-

ond quarter of 2004. Market reports no longer focus on the inclusion of CACs in bonds issued under New York law, reflecting the acceptance of CACs as market practice.

Since March 2004, seven emerging market countries—Brazil, Israel, Lebanon,[1] Mexico, Peru, the Philippines, and Turkey—again included CACs in their bonds issued under New York law. When reopening a bond issued under New York law in 2002, Jamaica did not include CACs in its New York law bond. Among mature market countries only Italy issued under New York law, and again included CACs in these issues.

There have been several issues that included CACs under English and Japanese law, as it is market practice in those jurisdictions. Cyprus, Croatia, the Czech Republic, Hungary, the Slovak Republic, the Philippines, Ukraine and Thailand, among emerging market countries, and Austria, Greece, New Zealand, and Sweden, among mature market countries, issued under U.K. law. Both Poland and Hungary issued under Japanese law. Jamaica was the only country that issued under German law.

[1]Bonds issued by Lebanon include majority restructuring provisions.

Emerging Market Sovereign Bond Issuance by Jurisdiction[1]

	2002				2003				2004		
	Q1	Q2[2]	Q3	Q4	Q1	Q2	Q3	Q4	Q1	Q2	Q3[3]
With CACs[4]											
Number of issuance	6	5	2	4	9	31	10	5	25	20	5
of which: New York law					1	22	5	4	14	13	1
Volume of issuance	2.6	1.9	0.9	1.4	5.6	18.0	6.4	4.3	18.5	15.4	2.5
of which: New York law					1.0	12.8	3.6	4.0	10.6	9.0	0.8
Without CACs[5]											
Number of issuance	17	12	5	10	14	4	7	7	2	1	2
Volume of issuance	11.6	6.4	3.3	4.4	8.1	2.5	3.5	4.2	1.5	0.9	1.5

Source: Capital Data.
[1]Number of issuance is in number. Volume of issuance is in billions of U.S. dollars.
[2]Includes issues of resturctured bonds by Uruguay.
[3]Data for 2004:Q3 are as of July 30, 2004.
[4]English and Japanese laws, and New York law where relevant.
[5]German and New York laws.

the legal and regulatory areas, nonperforming loans (NPLs) at state-owned banks, and the need to strengthen capital adequacy. In Lebanon, capitalization and profitability have improved and the trend deterioration in the quality of the loan portfolio has ceased. Large exposure to the sovereign and high degree of dollarization remain the main risks. The banking system in Pakistan is performing well and has undergone significant restructuring and privatization. Market and credit risks are the emerging concerns going forward. The banking system in Saudi Arabia remains highly liquid, profitable, and well capitalized, but faces some risk from the potential for a reversal in the rise in oil prices. In Kuwait, the blanket government guarantee of bank deposits was removed in April 2004, which should lessen moral hazard.

Financial soundness indicators (FSIs) for banks in South Africa have improved and the recent robust credit growth has abated. The authorities are also seeking to re-align legislation to be consistent with international best practice. The banking system in Kenya continues to be burdened by a high level of nonperforming loans and weaknesses in supervision, and implementation of reform measures remains slow. Banks in Zimbabwe have shown resilience in the face of adverse macroeconomic developments, but the possibility of systemic difficulties in the near term cannot be ruled out.

Structural Issues in Mature Markets

This section covers six structural issues:
- An update on the insurance industry, following the discussion in Chapter III of the April 2004 GFSR (Box 2.8, page 48).
- The hedge fund industry—developments and practices.
- An introduction to energy trading markets.
- Balance sheets in major mature markets.
- The Basel II Framework.
- Market and credit risk indicators for the mature market banking system.

Hedge Fund Industry: Developments and Practices

Interest in the hedge fund industry by institutional investors has grown significantly in the last five years, resulting in large capital inflows, even as the industry continues to address earlier public and private sector recommendations. The significant growth of hedge funds, driven by institutional investors (e.g., pension funds, foundations, and endowments), has heightened the desire by the official sector to better understand hedge funds and their activities. The hedge fund industry is important to financial stability considerations for several reasons: (1) it is an active and leveraged counterparty to systemically important and regulated financial institutions; (2) broadly speaking, hedge funds can employ leverage much more extensively and diversely than other investment vehicles; and (3) industry assets are growing rapidly, and it is an increasingly important investor base in the international capital markets. As such, people continue to ask if hedge funds may again be a source of systemic vulnerability or market dislocations, similar to the events of 1998 and Long Term Capital Management (LTCM).

The hedge fund industry is composed of a heterogeneous group of pooled investment vehicles—there is no "typical" hedge fund. Nevertheless, hedge funds share several characteristics that distinguish them from traditional asset managers:
- they employ a wider range of financial instruments and investment strategies, including the use of leveraged positions;
- the manager's particular investment strategy is more important to performance than asset class or geographic market selection;
- they may hold large short positions, and often employ active trading strategies; and
- hedge fund managers rely primarily on performance fees for much of their revenue.

In general, the hedge fund structure seeks to ease constraints typically faced by traditional fund managers.

Our study examines how we may achieve a better understanding of hedge funds and

Box 2.7. Russia: Recent Turbulence in the Banking Sector

Despite strong macroeconomic fundamentals, Russia's emerging private banking system endured a period of uncertainty in May–July. The closure of a small bank, Sodbiznessbank, in early May on account of alleged breaches of anti-money laundering laws sparked the turbulence. The subsequent announcement of a default and voluntary liquidation by another small bank and concerns about capital adequacy and money laundering in some other banks added to market nervousness. The events triggered a tightening of interbank credit lines, deposit withdrawals at some banks, and a run-up in interbank interest rates.

To some extent the nervousness in the banking system can be understood as a hard-to-avoid counterpart to the restructuring and consolidation of banks under a desirable reform process. The authorities recognize the tensions entailed by the reform process and during the recent turbulence took steps to reassure depositors. The central bank ensured ample liquidity by halving reserve requirements to 3.5 percent. And, on July 10, the Duma passed emergency legislation extending deposit insurance to all household

deposits under 100,000 rubles (about $3,500) at all banks. The deposit insurance provides a safety net while the process of admitting banks to the system is completed. By mid-July, these measures appeared to have contained the situation and restored confidence, with the banking system regaining deposits and international reserves continuing to increase.

The recent developments also underscored the need for the central bank to have sharper and more independent instruments to resolve problem banks and manage liquidity. This would include more effective bank resolution processes, improved crisis management tools, and a clear and consistent public communications strategy. In this respect, recent passage of deposit insurance for household accounts at all banks and a strengthened bank bankruptcy law aims to make the process of resolving banks more speedy and avoid delays in paying out deposit insurance, which undermine confidence. Russia's central bank should also review its facilities for liquidity management so that more targeted support could be provided to illiquid but solvent banks that face runs in the future.

their market activities, particularly for financial stability considerations. We will not examine issues concerning investor protection, particularly relevant to retail investors, or safeguards against fraud. This study will review and update developments in the hedge fund industry since the previous IMF study in 1998, and consider what progress has been made to satisfy various recommendations and proposals from that time.[4] Our objective is to address the broadly held view that not enough is known about hedge fund activities (i.e., to

"de-mystify" the hedge fund industry). Our operating assumption is that markets work, and that market discipline can be very effective in such areas. However, in conducting our review of progress since the earlier studies, we note that such studies largely concluded that market discipline failed in 1998 with regard to LTCM. Pursuant to our study, we focus on the following issues: (1) counterparty exposure; (2) use of leverage; (3) disclosure and transparency; (4) market discipline; and (5) the impact of hedge funds on smaller and devel-

---

[4]This study is a continuation of an overview of hedge fund activity published in the April 2004 *Global Financial Stability Report* (IMF, 2004a), where we reviewed the industry's growth since 1998 (Eichengreen and Mathieson, 1998). Earlier studies included a broad range of recommendations, seeking to improve counterparty risk management, enhance disclosure and transparency, and strengthen market discipline to improve industry surveillance. See, for example, President's Working Group on Financial Markets (1999), Counterparty Risk Management Policy Group (CRMPG, 1999), and FSF (2000 and 2002).

oping markets. A concluding section discusses the possible future direction of further industry and policy actions.[5] We plan to continue this project, aiming to provide more detail regarding particular hedge fund and counterparty practices, and to cooperate with other official bodies on related work.

Growth of the Industry

The desire by institutional investors to improve risk-adjusted returns has led to significant capital flows into hedge funds. Assets under management among hedge funds were estimated to be over $800 billion at end-2003, and are projected to rise to approximately $1 trillion in 2004, growing on average 15 percent a year since 1999 and accelerating since 2002 (Table 2.5). The number of hedge funds was estimated to be 8,100 at end-2003, compared with approximately 6,000 in 1998. Industry representatives and previous studies have also noted that proprietary trading desks of banks and securities firms have increasingly engaged in trading activities similar to those of hedge funds. While hedge fund assets remain small compared with traditional asset managers, such as mutual funds (approximately $5 trillion in the United States alone), the increasing interest from pension funds and other institutional investors means hedge funds will likely continue to receive significant capital flows into the foreseeable future.[6]

Institutional investors have increased their focus on active asset management. Many large institutional investors have historically pursued passive investment strategies, focused on various broad equity or fixed-income benchmark indices. However, increasingly these investors are looking to integrate investment and risk management practices, and thus seek a blend of "strategies" to meet their invest-

Table 2.5. Hedge Funds: Number of Funds and Assets Under Management[1]

	1999	2000	2001	2002	2003	2004
United States						
Number of funds	4,150	4,250	4,400	4,600	4,875	...
Assets under management[2]	225	280	315	340	420	...
Europe and Japan/Asia						
Number of funds	2,050	2,250	2,600	2,900	3,225	...
Assets under management[2]	225	240	285	310	400	...
Global						
Number of funds	6,200	6,500	7,000	7,500	8,100	8,800
Assets under management[2]	480	520	600	650	820	970

Source: Van Hedge Fund Advisors International.
[1]Historical data and projections for 2004 are estimates by Van Hedge Fund Advisors International.
[2]In billions of U.S. dollars.

ment objectives, while aiming to maintain risks at acceptable levels. A greater emphasis on diversification and asset correlations is reflected in portfolio construction. As such, investors increasingly seek to isolate and enhance returns from active asset management (alpha), and wish to reduce the volatility and returns associated with general market risks (beta). Such investment objectives have encouraged greater hedge fund exposure.

Given the rapid industry growth, market participants question the capacity of some strategies and large funds to generate "alpha." Due to the significant flow of capital and new fund managers into the industry, most market participants anticipate diminishing returns in some hedge fund strategies. From a policy perspective, the concern is that managers will employ more leverage to enhance or maintain historical performance, and some evidence of this exists today. Without adequate transparency, it is often difficult to determine if such activity is taking place or whether it may be destabilizing in some markets. Consequently, many policymakers, regulators, and market participants

[5]Our views on the issues discussed in this section were developed through numerous meetings with fund managers and risk managers from hedge funds, funds of hedge funds, and the main banks and prime brokers in the hedge fund industry, as well as national authorities in several of the major financial centers.
[6]Non-money market mutual fund shares, as reported in U.S. flow of funds accounts (U.S. Board of Governors of the Federal Reserve System, 2004).

Box 2.8. Insurance Industry Update

The April 2004 GFSR discussed the reallocation of risk from banks to the insurance industry, and the factors influencing insurers' willingness and capability to hold and manage risks. It noted that the ability of insurance companies to hedge liabilities and how they invest could be explained by differences in market structure and regulatory frameworks, with accounting standards and credit rating agencies also playing important roles.

The global recovery in equity markets and improvements in credit quality during 2003 and early 2004 have improved insurance company balance sheets, including solvency levels. Insurers have also continued to enhance their risk management techniques, including the adoption of advanced financial risk management techniques from the banking industry. A number of insurers, particularly in Europe, have strengthened their balance sheets by continuing to reduce equity allocations and increase credit exposure.

While risk management practices have improved, insurers continue to face difficulties hedging the complex risks in some legacy and newly developed products. In the 1980s and 1990s, many insurers marketed products (e.g., annuities and universal life policies) with high guaranteed rates of return and other product features with high optionality that were difficult to hedge in the financial markets. Newer products have attempted to shift more of these risks to policyholders. However, weaker demand has prompted insurers to reintroduce some guarantees (e.g., guaranteed minimum income and surrender benefits). These guaranteed benefits are difficult to hedge or properly price, and many reinsurance companies are unwilling to reinsure these products, reflecting in part the difficulty to hedge the exposures.

Regulatory and Reporting Developments

In the United States, the National Association of Insurance Commissioners (NAIC) has proposed measures to streamline the current state-based system of insurance regulation.[1] The framework seeks to promote state adoption of national regulatory standards, including life insurance products, to

ease administrative burdens and make regulation more effective. Some market participants think the NAIC may also consider methods to improve its risk-based capital framework, possibly by introducing different risk weights for different categories of equity holdings.

The U.K. FSA has moved forward in implementing risk-based capital requirements. The FSA released in July 2004, the Prudential Sourcebook (PSB) for insurers, which codifies the changes proposed in CP 195 released in 2003 (see April 2004 GFSR for details of CP 195). As noted in our previous study, the FSA is attempting to link capital requirements for insurance companies more closely to market risk principles, particularly for with-profits products. One investment bank foresaw a likely increase in the use of credit derivatives by insurers to manage credit risks in the investment portfolio.

The European Union's Solvency II project, which seeks to formulate a Basel II-like risk-based capital framework, moved forward with the release in April 2004 of a discussion paper (MARKT/2502/04). Industry representatives indicated that developing appropriate risk models for insurers remained a considerable challenge, including the appropriate role diversification may have in the calculation of risk-based capital requirements. In addition, and as noted in our April report, there is continued concern that national supervisors may not have sufficient resources to evaluate and develop standards for internal risk management models as part of Solvency II.

The International Accounting Standards Board (IASB) recognized that consultation on a completely new international reporting framework for insurance accounting could not be completed in the timetable previously proposed. In particular, it noted that consultation could not be completed on Phase II of its project in time to meet the starting date of 2005 set by the European Union and other jurisdictions. In response to concerns over conceptual and practical issues related to insurance accounting, including the implementation of fair value accounting principles (such as IAS 39), the IASB announced that, before restarting Phase II, it would assemble a small working group of senior insurance professionals to help analyze the issues, starting work in September 2004. In the meantime, it has issued interim guidance on accounting for insurance contracts.

---

[1]For details, see NAIC (2004), which can be found at *http://www.naic.org/docs/naic_framework.pdf.*

have raised the question of how to monitor hedge fund activities, and whether regulation may be required.[7] We attempt to address these questions in the context of the five factors that are the focus of our review.

Counterparty Exposure and Risk Management

Counterparty risk management by banks and prime brokers with regard to hedge funds has improved during the last five years.[8] As in the past, collateral remains a cornerstone of risk management at prime brokers and banks, and their trading and credit activities with hedge funds, particularly equity market activities.[9] In contrast, financing for fixed-income transactions may be more fragmented, with an individual counterparty (often a bank) extending credit with relatively less collateral protection.[10] The collateral coverage relative to the credit extended (i.e., the haircut),

credit terms, and trading margin are now usually set by formal and established credit assessment procedures. Discussions with leading counterparties (banks and brokers) suggest that such assessments generally include many of the following factors: (1) the transparency of the investment strategy; (2) the amount of leverage required by the strategy to be economically viable; (3) the underlying liquidity, concentration, and volatility of investment positions; (4) the amount of liquidity (i.e., cash and equivalents) held by the fund; (5) the size and operational infrastructure of the fund; (6) the degree of "strategy drift" detected in the fund or the fund manager's operating history; and (7) the length and quality of a fund manager's track record.

Established banks and brokers use collateral and other credit terms in an effort to achieve AA or AAA credit quality. Banks and brokers

---

[7]The SEC Commissioners voted on July 14, 2004 to publish for comment a proposed rule that would require the registration of hedge fund advisors under the Investment Advisers Act of 1940. Many of the largest hedge funds are already registered with the SEC (and, for those that are commodity pool operators and commodity trading advisors, with the U.S. Commodity Futures Trading Commission). Requiring the registration of hedge fund advisors would allow the SEC to collect more information about hedge funds, such as the number of funds that an advisor manages, the amount of assets in hedge funds, the number of employees and types of clients, and the identity of persons that control or are affiliated with the advisor. Through this requirement, the SEC staff would have access to all funds with assets in excess of $25 million. However, the threshold amount is one of several issues on which the SEC has requested industry comment until September 15, 2004.

[8]CRMPG (1999) called for the development of liquidation-based estimates of potential credit exposures when assessing credit, and integrated risk management combining market and credit risk, which the FSF also endorsed. Today, credit procedures most often evaluate current and potential exposures, and risk management techniques employed by banks and prime brokers address multiple sources of risks, as well as their correlations. Current exposure is evaluated by marking to market the value of liabilities. Potential exposure uses the calculated value at risk (VaR) for a given period, typically 10 days, and sets loss limits with a confidence interval, typically 95 or 99 percent, of likely losses. This risk management approach contrasts sharply with the silo approach of dividing market, credit, and operational risk commonly practiced in the past.

[9]Prime brokerage traditionally focused on equity trading. For historical reasons, the risk "buckets" into which hedge fund clients are often classified by prime brokers are relatively conservative. Based on a rolling 10-day VaR, margin is set by some brokers to cover potential losses at the 95 percent confidence level for the highest-quality customers, and at the 99 percent level for the lowest-quality counterparty. Margin limits are further adjusted by scrutinizing the portfolio for other sources of risks and characteristics (e.g., liquidity, concentrations, and how positions fit into the broader book at a prime broker).

[10]In contrast to equity transactions, funds engaged in fixed-income trades tend to have more counterparties to trade with, and collateral arrangements may only cover 95 percent of potential losses, as calculated by a rolling 10-day VaR. The principal difficulty is that each leg of a fixed-income transaction is likely to be financed separately. For example, creating a fixed-income position could require a certain amount of collateral from the hedge fund. The fund may then hedge the purchase using a swap arrangement obtained at another bank or broker. The fund could then ask that less collateral be charged on the first transaction because it is now hedged. In addition, the fund could seek further swap or futures trades related to this position, thereby creating different exposures. Most banks and brokers would prefer to finance most or all legs of such transactions; however, hedge funds continue to resist such pressures. Ideally, collateral should reflect the risk profile of the entire trade, not each individual leg. However, in some cases, a more collateralized position on each leg or a particular leg may make the transaction uneconomic.

actively manage counterparty exposure using multiple sources of information, including trading and other relationships, and a variety of risk management tools, including derivatives.[11] Some prime brokers (dealing particularly with equity trades) maintain less than 1 percent uncollateralized exposure to all counterparties (not just hedge funds) on a current and potential exposure basis.[12]

Most prime brokers and banks believe that "hard" requirements for collateral and other credit terms may be inappropriate. Such hard limits may force hedge funds to liquidate positions at the worst time, and possibly exacerbate deteriorating market conditions and weaken the counterparty's position. Consequently, counterparties actively monitor these exposures, requiring more detailed and frequent reporting of portfolio positions, and use qualitative judgments to complement quantitative rules to proactively adjust exposures. In this regard, the larger banks and established brokers seek to combine traditional credit analytics with trading and market experience, and often encourage hedge funds (by offering preferential trading terms) to bring more of their overall business to them in order to gain a fuller picture of their risk profile (albeit with relatively little success to date).

Market participants emphasized that liquidity risk continues to represent a significant challenge. One of the lessons from the failure of LTCM is that liquidity can disappear quickly during periods of market stress, espe-cially when hedge funds and similar activities by proprietary trading desks within banks and securities firms accumulate significant and/or concentrated positions.[13] To manage their liquidity risks, most hedge funds seek to limit concentrations with specific counterparties and instruments, and have explicit (often hard) exit strategies on positions in anticipation of possible market disruptions. Nevertheless, many fund and risk managers, as well as investors, question whether such strategies are realistic for less liquid asset classes or markets dominated by hedge funds and bank trading desks (e.g., distressed securities, and fixed-income or convertible arbitrage strategies). Typically, hedge funds also utilize "lock-up" agreements, often for extended periods (up to two or three years), to manage investor or fund liquidity and capital withdrawals, which is another way that hedge funds manage liquidity risk—thereby transferring or sharing this risk with investors.

Use and Measurement of Leverage

Since 1998, credit providers and hedge funds have developed a better understanding of leverage and, broadly speaking, hedge fund leverage is at relatively moderate levels today. At present, many equity hedge funds report leverage typically less than two times capital, and other styles and strategies are similarly reporting leverage at or below historical norms.[14] Nevertheless, leverage can magnify liquidity, market, and credit risks, as well as returns, and is one of the most important fac-

---

[11]In addition to the steps outlined in footnotes 9 and 10, several brokers recently have attempted to use information from the credit derivatives market to manage collateral requirements—using spread movements on credit default swaps to adjust collateral requirements and exposures.

[12]It should also be noted that Basel II and its market risk approach has also positively influenced the analysis and management of hedge fund exposure by the larger banks and brokers.

[13]The report of the President's Working Group on Financial Markets (1999) observed that risk management weaknesses revealed by the LTCM episode ". . . were also evident, albeit to a lesser extent, in investment and commercial banks' dealings with other highly leveraged counterparties, including other investment and commercial banks." Industry representatives have said that obtaining information about leverage and risk positions among hedge funds alone would provide only a partial picture. Indeed, the FSF broadened its analysis to include proprietary trading desks of regulated banks and securities firms.

[14]By comparison, the report of the President's Working Group on Financial Markets (1999) stated that LTCM leveraged their capital as much as 28 times in 1997 and 1998.

Table 2.6. Leverage Estimates by Hedge Fund Strategy[1]

Fund Strategies[2]	Total Number of Funds	Simple Average Leverage Within Each Strategy	Asset-Weighted Average Leverage Within Each Strategy	Leverage		Volatility of Returns Within Each Strategy[3] (percent)
				Minimum	Maximum	
Fixed income: diversified	21	5.4	8.3	1.0	18.0	6.7
Fixed income: mortgage-backed	30	3.9	4.3	1.0	10.0	10.0
Fixed income: high yield	7	3.0	3.3	1.3	5.2	10.3
Convertible arbitrage	108	2.5	3.0	1.0	7.0	4.9
Equity nonhedge	74	2.2	2.9	1.0	12.0	8.1
Fixed income: arbitrage	74	2.0	2.1	1.0	12.0	7.5
Global macro	54	2.0	2.4	1.0	5.0	11.2
Equity market neutral	36	1.7	1.8	1.0	3.0	6.4
Event-driven multi-strategy	68	1.5	1.4	1.0	10.0	12.4
Merger/risk arbitrage	80	1.4	1.6	1.0	10.0	6.0
Equity hedge	499	1.4	1.4	0.7	20.0	14.5
Distressed securities	89	1.3	1.2	1.0	3.0	4.9
Emerging markets	118	1.3	1.4	1.0	3.0	27.3
Short selling	19	1.2	1.1	1.0	2.0	15.2
Sector composite	103	1.2	1.2	1.0	2.0	17.1
Memorandum item:						
Fund of funds	482	1.2	1.2	1.0	25.0	9.1

Source: Center for International Securities and Derivatives Markets, CIDMHedge database.

[1]Leverage may not be reported consistently across hedge funds. This number can refer to the current reporting period or to some period average, as reported by the hedge fund. In addition, no specific guidance is available as to how the figure is computed. Data for the period December 1997–December 2003, and at December 2003, as appropriate.

[2]See Box 2.9 for strategy definitions.

[3]Volatility is calculated as the standard deviation of the data reported by hedge funds within each strategy.

tors contributing to a hedge fund's overall risk profile. Moreover, hedge fund and risk managers have noted that leverage has shifted to newer and riskier strategies. Many sophisticated investors carefully assess the use and appropriate degree of leverage, which varies from strategy to strategy, and are cautious about investing in highly leveraged strategies. However, increased competition among prime brokers, particularly newer entrants, has made it easier for hedge funds to obtain leverage.[15]

Market participants recognize that leverage must be monitored against acceptable norms for different strategies (Table 2.6 and Box 2.9). As noted above, leverage varies from strategy to strategy, and certain strategies (typically fixed-income and various arbitrage strategies) generally employ more leverage. Despite best practices recommended by hedge fund associations, most hedge funds only report accounting leverage, which is often stated as the market value of gross exposures (the sum of long and short positions) relative to a fund's net asset value.[16] One limitation of this measure is that it does not gauge how underlying market risks are affected by changes in asset prices, which is what an economic measure of leverage would provide. Economic measures of leverage generally begin with a VaR calculation, and may incorporate stress scenarios and some measures of concentration and liquidity of a fund's positions.

Market participants have become concerned about leverage being introduced at the fund of hedge funds (FOFs) and investor levels. Recently, some FOFs have used leverage to compensate for diminishing returns (e.g., due

[15]Recently, 11 of the 36 hedge funds that responded to a Greenwich Associates survey reported an increase in their use of leverage, although not dramatically higher, spurred in part by easier credit terms and more margin credit provided by prime brokers (Greenwich Associates, 2004).

[16]See Managed Funds Association (2003) for a recent compendium of alternative measures of leverage.

Box 2.9. Hedge Fund Strategy Definitions

Relative Value Strategies

1. *Equity Market Neutral*

Seeks to profit by exploiting pricing ineffi-ciencies between related securities, neutralizing exposure to market risk by combining long and short positions.

2. *Convertible Arbitrage*

Involves purchasing a portfolio of convertible securities and hedging a portion of the equity risk by selling short the underlying common stocks.

3. *Fixed Income*

Fixed-Income Composite funds include funds that invest in Fixed-Income Arbitrage, Fixed-Income Diversified, Fixed-Income High-Yield, Fixed-Income Mortgage-Backed.

   3a. *Fixed-Income: Arbitrage.* A market neutral hedging strategy that seeks to profit by exploiting pricing inefficiencies between related fixed-income securities, while neu-tralizing exposure to interest rate risk.

   3b. *Fixed-Income.* These funds invest in non-investment grade debt. Objectives may range from high current income to acqui-sition of undervalued instruments. Empha-sis is placed on assessing credit risk of the issuer. Some of the available high-yield instruments include extendible/reset secu-rities, increasing-rate notes, pay-in-kind securities, step-up coupon securities, split-coupon securities and usable bonds.

   3c. *Fixed-Income: Mortgage-Backed.* These funds invest in mortgage-backed securities. Many funds focus solely on AAA-rated bonds. Instruments include government agency, government-sponsored enterprise, private-label fixed- or adjustable-rate mort-gage pass-through securities, fixed- or adjustable-rate collateralized mortgage obligations (CMOs), real estate mortgage investment conduits (REMICs), and stripped mortgage-backed securities

(SMBSs). Funds may look to capitalize on security-specific mispricings. Hedging of prepayment risk and interest rate risk is common. Leverage may be used, as well as futures, short sales, and options.

Event Driven Strategies

4. *Distressed Securities*

Strategies invest in, and may sell short, the securities of companies where the security's price has been affected by a distressed situation like reorganization, bankruptcy, distressed sales, and other corporate restructuring.

5. *Merger Arbitrage/Risk Arbitrage*

Merger Arbitrage, sometimes called Risk Arbitrage, involves investment in event-driven situations such as leveraged buyouts, mergers, and hostile takeovers.

Other Strategies

6. *Equity Hedge*

The strategy is comprised of long stock posi-tions with short sales of stock or stock index options/futures. The strategy has a long market bias.

7. *Sector Composite*

Sector funds invest in specific sectors. Investments are primarily long energy, financial, healthcare/biotechnology, real estate, and tech-nology sectors.

8. *Emerging Markets*

Involves investing in securities of companies or the sovereign debt of developing or emerging countries. Investments are primarily long.

9. *Global Macro*

Macro strategies involves leveraged invest-ments on anticipated price movements of stock markets, interest rates, foreign exchange, and physical commodities. Macro managers employ a "top-down" global approach.

10. *Short Selling*

Short Selling involves the sale of a security not owned by the seller; a technique used to take advantage of an anticipated price decline.

Source: Center for International Securities and Derivatives Markets (CISDM), Hedge Fund database.

to diversification effects or capacity constraints), and presumably to address potential investor concerns related to their double fee structure.[17] Despite the diversification achieved by FOFs, leverage employed at the FOFs level only serves to amplify the risk of leveraged hedge fund activity. Several established prime brokers indicated that they do not extend credit to FOFs, since they cannot effectively monitor the underlying hedge fund activities, with collateral once removed. Nevertheless, it is understood that FOFs are increasingly employing leverage to enhance returns. Similarly, some retail and institutional investors are being offered leveraged equity interests in hedge funds and FOFs, as well as a variety of structured products, including principal protected or capital guarantee products.[18] In short, these multiple layers of leverage increase the risk profile of these institutions and investors.

Disclosure and Transparency

In general, disclosure has not changed significantly, and has become more varied since the recommendations of the President's Working Group on Financial Markets (1999). The goal of disclosing more information for investors and counterparties to better assess the risk profiles of hedge fund portfolios, while not revealing proprietary information, generally remains elusive.[19] Disclosure standards vary considerably depending on the target audience, such as investors, counterparties, or regulators, and to some degree improvements to disclosure practices have been cyclical, depending on the need for fund managers to accommodate investor and counterparty requests.[20] Historically, large institutional investors were able to request and receive a high level of transparency. However, more recently, in large part because investor demand is so strong, many hedge funds do not wish to accept added administrative or reporting burdens. Although there was broad support for prior recommendations to improve disclosure practices by hedge funds, follow-through has been less enthusiastic. For example, in a recent update regarding the recommendations of the Multidisciplinary Working Group on Enhanced Disclosure concerning the disclosure of financial risks, the Joint Forum noted: ". . . the Working Group was unsuccessful in obtaining the cooperation of a sufficient number of hedge funds to provide a meaningful basis for further review."[21]

Banks, prime brokers, and administrators have access to more information and receive greater transparency than most investors. The vast majority of industry participants agree that in general hedge fund counterparties have much better transparency today, including data with reasonably granular detail (e.g.,

---

[17]FOFs charge investors administrative and performance fees (often 1 percent of total assets under management and a 10 percent performance fee), in addition to passing along the fees of the underlying hedge funds (e.g., generally 1 to 2 percent of assets, and 20 percent (or more) for performance).

[18]Interestingly, several hedge funds and FOF managers we met believed the recent poor performance of convertible arbitrage strategies was exacerbated in part due to FOFs withdrawing capital from this non-core strategy to satisfy liquidity requirements related to principal or capital protected products. It should also be noted that a few insurance companies have begun to market these structured credit products to FOFs in competition with traditional bank providers.

[19]As part of our study, we reviewed a variety of reports for investors and counterparties. We found that a typical hedge fund's monthly or quarterly report provides a summary update on performance, exposure represented by the top 5 or 10 positions, attribution of returns, aggregated exposures by sector and/or geographic area, concentrations of these sectoral breakdowns, and, for some, an assortment of risk management metrics, including volatility and VaR. Those funds providing monthly or quarterly risk management data represent a growing minority—and are considered best practice by larger hedge funds.

[20]The availability of hedge fund products to retail investors in Western Europe (e.g., France, Germany, and Italy), Hong Kong, and Singapore has raised regulatory attention concerning disclosure standards for retail investors.

[21]See Joint Forum (2004), page 3.

many credit institutions measure particular exposures across the entire institution, broken down by asset class or sometimes by fund strategy). As such, some market participants believe industry-wide or strategy aggregation of certain risk parameters is feasible. However, many hedge funds avoid allowing any counterparty to obtain full transparency to its trading and investment strategies, based largely on a desire to protect proprietary information and avoid front-running by trading desks within these institutions. Therefore, while better information and transparency appear available, a degree of coordination would be required to compile a reasonable risk profile of particular strategies or market activities.

Market Discipline

Earlier studies identified market discipline as the principal means by which risk-taking is controlled in a market-based economy.[22] A key requirement for effective market discipline is the availability of relevant information. The improvements in risk management and counterparty practices discussed earlier must be complemented with greater transparency for market discipline to be effective. Moreover, such studies also recognized that as the demand for hedge funds grew, the desire to diversify across many hedge funds would bolster the role of FOFs and weaken the incentive or ability of investors to perform sufficient due diligence, placing more of the responsibility on FOF managers.[23]

Industry participants expressed skepticism about the ability of investors and other market forces to exert material discipline on hedge funds. Most simply, market participants believe the strong demand from investors for hedge fund capacity and increasing competition among regulated counterparties may undermine these sources of market discipline. Many market participants noted that the current strong demand to place capital with hedge funds by institutional investors (including FOFs) may limit their ability to gain greater transparency or to monitor hedge fund activities in a comprehensive manner.[24]

Banks and prime brokers also have been viewed as sources of market discipline. Many of these institutions actively monitor hedge fund activity and receive much better transparency than in the 1990s. However, this effort is, by its nature, focused on the hedge funds they service and is intended to manage their own exposures, which the largest banks and brokers seem to do well. Nevertheless, the picture obtained from the improved bilateral transparency and monitoring is unlikely to fully address financial stability issues (e.g., it does not evaluate broader aggregate market, credit, and liquidity risks, as well as concentrations, amplified by the use of leverage, across particular strategies or asset classes, or the potential for disruptive market dynamics). Moreover, with significant competition among banks and brokers for hedge fund business, there is potential for this form of discipline to disappoint. Therefore, at least at present, it would seem inappropriate to rely on market discipline as the primary source of surveillance and monitoring of hedge fund activities, particularly regarding potential systemic risks.

---

[22]The President's Working Group on Financial Markets (1999) and FSF (2000) are two prominent examples. Indeed, the President's Working Group on Financial Markets (1999) concluded that it was the breakdown of market discipline that led to an unusually large buildup of leveraged positions in LTCM's portfolio, and high risk exposures for its investors and counterparties (p. viii).

[23]See FSF (2000) for further discussion.

[24]FOFs often require monthly reporting by hedge funds so as to update their own valuations and reports to their investors. However, a more thorough review of a hedge fund for strategic shifts and changes in risk profile generally occurs once or twice a year for newer hedge fund investments, and may only be triggered by specific events or poor performance for older investments.

Hedge Fund Impact on Smaller and Developing Markets

Market participants, including hedge fund managers, agree that hedge fund activity can produce adverse market volatility in smaller and less liquid markets. There is broad agreement in the market that hedge funds, like other large investors, may be disruptive in smaller and developing markets. However, there is little empirical evidence that hedge funds have been a primary source of disruption during periods of emerging market turbulence, such as the Mexican or Asian currency crises of 1994 and 1998.[25]

Market participants emphasized that hedge fund impact on market volatility should not be solely assessed according to national or regional markets. While hedge fund managers agreed that active trading in relatively smaller markets may be disruptive, many managers also emphasized that the diversity of investors in a given market (or asset class or strategy) is a more significant determinant of market dynamics. For example, convertible arbitrage and many fixed-income strategies are dominated by hedge funds (often estimated to represent 80–90 percent of market activity), which are likely to behave in a broadly similar fashion in response to market developments. As such, these markets are likely to experience significantly greater volatility than a market populated by a more diverse investor group (e.g., insurance companies, mutual funds, and pension funds). In recent years, traditional emerging markets have benefited from a more dedicated and diverse investor base. As smaller markets develop and become more liquid, and thereby more attractive to hedge funds, efforts to further diversify and broaden the investor base should enhance financial stability in those markets. Most hedge fund man-agers cited particular asset classes and strategies (as above), not national or regional markets, as those markets most likely to suffer from significant hedge fund concentration. For policymakers, this implies that financial market surveillance could benefit from an operational metric to gauge the diversity of players in a particular market, in addition to those for depth and liquidity.

Preliminary Conclusions

The demand by institutional investors to place capital with hedge funds continues to grow, and is likely to continue for some time. This trend is fueled by investors' desire to enhance returns from active asset management, and to seek greater portfolio diversification. Institutional investors should be encouraged to press for more information from hedge funds and FOFs (e.g., as a product of fiduciary duties to their underlying investors), to ensure that they understand the factors contributing to investment returns and portfolio risks.

Since 1998, banks and prime brokers have improved their management of hedge fund exposures, as well as their credit and risk management practices. Best practices have emerged and are more broadly adopted. Consistent with Basel II implementation, we find the established brokers and larger banks (and hedge funds) are using sophisticated credit and market metrics to measure and monitor counterparty exposures, including hedge fund exposure. However, it is doubtful whether regulated counterparties have sufficient transparency to allow them to fully assess risks across all of a large hedge fund's activities (particularly potential systemic risks) or across a particular trading strategy (e.g., fixed-income or convertible arbitrage).

[25]See Eichengreen and Mathieson (1998) and Chapter IV of IMF (2004a) for further details. Eichengreen and Mathieson (1998) noted that while hedge funds sometimes take sizable positions, so do banks and other institutional investors. Moreover, hedge funds are concerned about the liquidity and other risks of their positions, not just returns, and are therefore less inclined to take large positions in small, relatively illiquid markets. Fung, Hsieh, and Tsatsaronis (2000) also present similar empirical evidence on the role of hedge funds during the Asian crisis.

Despite the relatively moderate use of leverage by hedge funds today, there is the potential for leverage to rise. In an attempt to maintain performance, funds may pursue more risky strategies, supported by more leveraged positions. Moreover, with new entrants and strong competition among brokers, credit is more readily available to hedge funds today. In addition, FOFs have begun to employ leverage to enhance returns. This layering of leverage may significantly increase the potential for amplifying volatility and market disruptions.

Disclosure and transparency are core issues, and without better transparency it is doubtful market discipline can be relied upon to effectively monitor hedge fund activity. Improving disclosure and transparency on a broader basis would support the effectiveness of market discipline.[26] Banks and brokers generally receive much better transparency today from their hedge fund counterparties, which helps to manage bilateral exposures, but not necessarily systemic risk. The largest hedge funds utilize multiple counterparties, and remain uncomfortable with broad transparency. In part, this may be justified, as many counterparties are also competitors through their proprietary trading desks. Likewise, there is a large variance in investor disclosure, and given the current strong demand for hedge fund investments we question investors' ability to impose market discipline. In short, the hedge fund industry has not embraced earlier recommendations to develop improved standards for disclosure and reporting. Consequently, many in the official sector have questioned whether hedge fund regulation, or monitoring of their activities through regulated financial institutions, may be needed to provide adequate financial surveillance.

The primary goal of most official bodies is to better understand hedge fund operations and their potential impact on systemic risk, not necessarily to regulate these funds. Gaining a greater knowledge of hedge fund activities seems a logical ambition, particularly since hedge funds represent a significant counterparty to systemically important financial institutions. As such, it seems appropriate to monitor their market activities. Similarly, we believe it would be in the best interest of the hedge fund industry to more broadly and proactively encourage increased transparency, particularly as it grows and matures. In those cases where wholesale regulation of even institutional hedge fund activity is advocated, we question such an approach at this time, and whether the appropriate resources will be applied.

Despite the challenges, we believe hedge fund activities and potential systemic risks can be monitored in the main financial centers.[27] A monitoring exercise could occur in two ways. First, as the hedge fund industry becomes more mature, with many managers institutionalizing their investment management businesses, we found managers of some of the largest hedge funds willing to provide risk information to national authorities on a voluntary basis. If many of the hedge funds with $2 billion or more in assets under management provided such information (covering approximately 70 hedge fund groups, representing approximately 40 percent of industry assets, and located primarily in New York and London), a substantial picture of the risk profile of hedge fund activity (by strategy and other criteria) would be available to better monitor systemic risks. Second, and independently, while perhaps challenging to implement, we believe the major prime brokers and banks may be able to provide supervisors with sufficient disaggregated information to allow officials to obtain a more complete assessment of particular risk profiles, potentially at the level

---

[26]The FSF, in the 2000 Report of the Working Group on Highly Leveraged Institutions, noted that *"A number of conditions are necessary for market discipline to operate effectively . . . [including] information on counterparties' liabilities and risks."*
[27]The FSF (2000) noted that *"National monetary authorities, supervisors and regulators should consider proactive market surveillance as a means to help provide useful early warning signals about speculative activity in financial markets."*

of particular hedge fund strategies and financial instruments. Supervisors have always focused on various industry exposures and market risks that they believed required special review. As such, the supervisory structure already exists to monitor hedge fund exposure and activity. Of course, hedge funds operate across national and legal jurisdictions, so a reasonable level of cross-border cooperation would be required among financial supervisors. It is not clear that sufficient cooperation and coordination exists today. In either case, agreement about a common matrix of information, which would include qualitative observations and assessments as well as quantitative data, to properly aggregate and analyze available information would be a significant step forward.[28] Given the improvement in risk management techniques by the largest hedge funds and their regulated bank and broker counterparties, we believe the opportunity exists to improve our understanding of hedge fund activities and potential systemic risks.

Some argue that to regulate or to monitor hedge funds would create moral hazard. The regulation or monitoring of hedge fund activities may be perceived as providing an implicit safeguard for investors, and regulated banks and brokers, possibly leading to more risk taking. Some authorities also worry that monitoring may be more problematic than regulation, particularly concerning how a regulator should act upon information or data obtained. We understand these concerns; however, we do not believe they differ in this context from the general supervisory process, or outweigh the benefits of better understanding hedge fund activities. Moreover, reacting to concerns through regulated entities may also prove the most effective means to influence hedge fund behavior and practices, including immediate risk positions and longer-term transparency issues.

Looking forward, as the hedge fund industry continues to grow and mature, we observe several themes likely to emerge in relation to our work. In particular, given the current and expected capital flows from traditional institutional investors into hedge funds, the largest banks and brokers are increasingly organizing themselves to attract this capital and participate in the "institutionalization" of the hedge fund industry. It is estimated that many of the largest banks and brokers will each manage $20 billion to $30 billion of hedge fund capital within five years. As such, the regulation or monitoring of such activities would become subsumed within existing supervisory mechanisms of the parent institutions. Moreover, some of these institutions also anticipate stronger retail demand for hedge fund products, which may contribute to the U.S. SEC's recent initiative. Among the larger and more established hedge funds, we observe a similar institutionalization of activities, and they broadly anticipate a period in which lower returns produce a shakeout in the industry. While we share much of this view of future industry developments, we remain focused on the potentially sloppy and volatile transition process, and related financial stability issues.

We support efforts to develop a broader understanding of hedge fund activities, which we believe will enhance financial stability. Hedge funds are an established investor group in international capital markets, and a constructive influence on efficient market behavior. Nevertheless, they are a leveraged and active counterparty to systemically important financial institutions, and efforts by authorities to better monitor and influence their activities, including through regulated financial institutions, should be encouraged. Hedge funds, like other institutional investors,

[28]We recognize that it may be challenging to design and maintain such a common matrix. However, we remain hopeful that authorities can cooperate and agree on a set of at least basic common and useful information. Furthermore, we believe, from a financial stability perspective, that much can be gained from a more comprehensive view and understanding of regulated institutions' exposures to hedge funds and those entities engaged in related activities.

can contribute to or may adversely impact financial stability. As such, we still do not know what we do not know about hedge funds, and efforts to improve our surveillance and understanding of their market activities should be supported.

An Introduction to Energy Trading Markets

Energy trading markets have become more important to financial stability in recent years as trading volume and the diversity of instruments and participants have grown rapidly. They have become more interconnected with other financial markets as investment banks, hedge funds, and other institutional investors have become more involved. We discuss below the main features of these highly volatile markets.

The growth in the financial energy trading markets has been tremendous over recent years, with energy-related contracts now being the second most heavily traded category of futures contracts on organized exchanges, after more traditional financial products. The structure of the energy market has also changed, as trading in electricity contracts, mainly over-the-counter (OTC), has grown significantly, particularly with the recent deregulation of electricity generation and transmission in the United States and Europe. Moreover, the range of participants actively trading energy-related financial instruments has expanded over the last three to four years. In addition to the traditional actors, such as oil and gas producers, utilities, refiners, and other industrial consumers, the market now also includes global investment banks as well as hedge funds. While the higher activity by investment banks and hedge funds likely increases the liquidity, depth, and efficiency of the energy markets, it also implies an

increase in exposure to energy market risks. Consequently, there is an increased need for authorities to understand the dynamics of these energy markets, as they are more likely to impact the performance and stability of global financial intermediaries. In what follows, we review the types of instruments traded and of activities undertaken by traditional and newer market participants.

Deregulation is the main catalyst for much of the development of financial energy trading activity, which is largely centered on exchange-traded and OTC derivative contracts.[29] Deregulation of domestic petroleum products and natural gas occurred in the 1970s and 1980s, and in the 1990s for wholesale electricity. Prior to that time, stable and regulated prices were the norm, and producers and consumers of these commodities faced little price risk. With deregulation, traditional energy firms faced greater spot price volatility, and energy derivatives became a natural outgrowth of this process, as firms sought to manage (hedge) the new or increased price risk.

Growth and Characteristics of Energy Markets

Energy prices tend to vary more than the prices of many other commodities and financial instruments, such as stocks and bonds. Table 2.7 compares the daily price volatility of oil, natural gas, and electricity to the euro-dollar exchange rate, S&P 500, and U.S. bond indices, as well as a few other commodities. Financial instruments tend to demonstrate the lowest volatility, while electricity has by far the highest level of volatility. The higher volatility of wholesale electricity and natural gas is in part related to the impact on these prices of nonfinancial market events, like weather. Demand can increase quickly in response to weather, and it is impossible or very costly to

---

[29]This section focuses on financial energy trading rather than physical trading. These are forward dated (derivative) contracts, whereas physical or spot trading is on a more "traditional" customer-to-supplier basis. However, on some organized exchanges, particularly in Europe, financial energy contracts tend to be traded in parallel with "spot" or physical markets.

Table 2.7. Price Volatility for Energy and Other Financial and Nonfinancial Instruments
(In percent)

Product	Volatility	Period
Energy		
Electricity (peak-load)[1]	403.3	1995–2003
Natural gas[2]	78.0	1992–2001
WTI crude oil	42.1	1990–2003
Financial		
S&P 500	14.3	1970–2003
U.S. Bond[3]	7.7	1980–2003
U.S. dollar/euro	10.2	1980–2003
Other commodities[2]		
Copper	32.3	1989–August 2001
Gold	12.0	1989–2001
Cattle	13.3	1989–August 2001
Corn	37.7	1994–2001

Sources: Bloomberg L.P.; Datastream; U.S. Department of Energy (2002); and IMF staff estimates.

[1]Electricity volatility is based on peak-load prices for the Pennsylvania-New Jersey-Maryland region.

[2]Natural gas and other commodities volatility measures are from Table 3 of U.S. Department of Energy (2002).

[3]U.S. bond volatility is based on 7- to 10-year bond index prices.

increase production in the short run for these commodities. Second, and related, neither electricity nor natural gas can be easily transferred or delivered to meet short-term demand spikes, and local storage capacity is either limited (gas) or nonexistent (electricity).

After deregulation, energy trading began in petroleum products, followed by gas and then electricity. The New York Mercantile Exchange (NYMEX) and the International Petroleum Exchange (IPE) have become the dominant organized exchanges for oil and gas trading, with on average 9 million and 2.7 million futures and options contracts traded per month in 2003 on the NYMEX and IPE,

respectively.[30] The growth in energy derivatives trading has been substantial, as exchange-traded options and futures have grown on the NYMEX from a monthly average of 3 million contracts in 1989 to its current level (see Figure 2.33). The exchanges are also expanding their energy contract offerings. In April of 2003, NYMEX introduced a futures contract on electricity and the IPE is planning to do so in 2004.[31]

Although these figures pale in comparison to the turnover of interest rate, currency, and equity index futures and options trading—with an average North American monthly turnover of 109 million contracts—energy is nonetheless the second most active category of futures and options trading. Moreover, open interest in non-bullion commodities rose from $445 billion in 2000 to $608 billion in 2003, with oil and gas accounting for roughly 70 percent of global non-bullion commodity market growth.[32]

Because exchange-traded futures and options specify delivery at a particular location, traders desiring delivery or price protection at other locations must contend with locational differentials, a specific form of basis risk. This is particularly important for natural gas and (even more so) for electricity, where location arbitrage does not work well, since transportation is limited by pipeline (gas) or grid (electricity) infrastructures.[33] Consequently, energy market participants look to the OTC market, especially specialized energy traders within this market, for hedging instruments (Box 2.10, page 61). The greater flexibility of OTC con-

[30]The underlying monetary value of this trading activity is significant. For example, the IPE traded a record 2.07 million Brent futures contracts in April 2004, which represents 2.07 billion barrels of crude oil and an underlying value of approximately $73 billion. In June of 2004, roughly 3.3 million oil futures contracts traded on the NYMEX. This translates to an underlying value of approximately $129 billion.

[31]NYMEX also lists several other electricity futures and options contracts on ClearPort, its electronic trading system. The IPE is slated to introduce a new electricity futures contract in 2004.

[32]Figures taken from Davey (2004).

[33]That is, gas and electricity customers and producers are constrained, as they cannot buy/sell supplies transported via means other than through pipeline and grid systems that have a limited number of delivery points (gas) or regionally organized distribution systems (electricity). As a result, price differences can persist between more or less independent, localized markets. Roughly speaking, gas is less localized than electricity, with oil being the least localized market.

Figure 2.33. Total Number of Energy Options and Futures Contracts¹
(Average monthly volume; in millions)

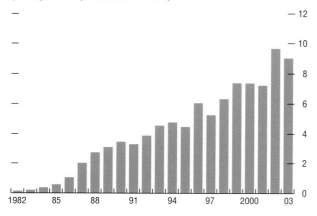

Source: New York Mercantile Exchange (NYMEX).
¹The total volume of options and futures contracts traded on NYMEX.

tracts allows users to negotiate contract terms that more closely reflect their hedging needs. However, the increased contract flexibility comes at a cost of greater counterparty risk exposure and lower liquidity.

Traditionally, in most financial OTC derivative markets, such as interest rate swap contracts, large investment banks dominate, as these intermediaries are best able to hedge the risk from the derivatives contracts. However, it was only with the advent of the internet and the entrance in 2000 of energy traders (also known as merchant energy traders, distributors, or marketers), such as Enron or Duke Energy, that OTC energy trading really grew and began to encompass the broader energy complex. Enron in particular established an internet based trading platform (EnronOnline), in which all trades with Enron as a counterparty were executed. As a result, at that time, the energy derivative affiliates of the investment banks were less dominant in the gas and electricity OTC markets than the energy trading firms.

The energy traders specialized in providing OTC hedging instruments to traditional energy producers and consumers who needed protection from, for example, locational basis risk. The trading firms, who were in general affiliates of traditional energy firms, leveraged their physical assets (mainly wholesale unregulated power generation plants) to become essentially OTC dealers (market-makers) in electricity and, to a lesser extent, in oil and gas.[34] Many of these energy trading firms have fallen from prominence since 2002 and the Enron debacle. As energy dealers, these firms relied upon strong credit ratings and funding liquidity. As such, their trading operations were particularly sensitive to negative credit

[34]These firms were structured substantially differently from typical integrated utilities, in that their assets consisted to a large extent of stand-alone (unregulated) electricity power plants in various locations, primarily selling electricity to (regional) wholesale markets.

Box 2.10. Sample of Popular Energy Contracts

The following are some popular energy contracts. The descriptions are largely based on U.S. Department of Energy (2002).

Forwards

These are similar to futures contracts traded on the energy commodity exchanges, except that they offer a greater variety of future delivery dates and locations than is available with exchange-traded contracts. Natural gas and electricity are more likely to be traded in the forward market than oil, for which forward hedging needs tend to be met via exchange-traded futures contracts.

Basis Swaps

There are a variety of basis contracts that allow participants to hedge locational, product, or even temporal differences between, typically, exchange-traded energy futures and options contracts, and the circumstances of the contract buyer or seller. For example, an OTC trader could agree to pay a local industrial gas consumer the difference between the Henry hub gas price, which is the delivery point for the NYMEX natural gas futures contract, and the gas price at its local gas delivery hub, in exchange for a fixed regular payment. Some other basis spreads of note in energy trading are Brent-WTI spreads (Brent crude oil versus West Texas Intermediate crude oil), gasoline-heating oil spreads, and crack and spark spreads, discussed below.

Crack Spreads

Typically, the profits of industrial users of oil, refiners, and petrochemical firms are significantly affected by the spread or difference in price between crude oil and the refined products they produce. Because industrial users of crude oil can predict their costs other than that of crude oil itself, the spread is their major price uncertainty. Crack spread contracts are in essence bundled forward positions in both crude oil and one or several refined products, such as heating oil and gasoline. For example, an oil refiner seeking to lock in future profits would purchase (sell) crack spread contracts that implicitly bundle a long position in oil forward contracts with a short position in heating oil or gasoline forward contracts.

Spark Spreads

This contract has similar underpinnings as the crack spread contract, except it is producers of electricity that are typically trying to hedge their profit risk. The contracts are in essence a combination of forward contracts and are formulated as a long (short) position in wholesale electricity forward contracts and short (long) forward position in the electricity generators fuel input (typically natural gas, which is used in gas-turbine generators).

Crack/Spark Spread Options

These are options on the crack/spark spread that specify threshold spread levels over (under) which these options are in (out of) the money. This is useful for some industrial users, who are comfortable with price movements within certain limits. These options are somewhat unusual in that they protect the holder from the growth or shrinkage in the difference between prices rather than, as is typical, the movement of one underlying price (such as call options on the S&P 500).

Swing Options

These contracts provide flexibility as to quantity delivered—a swing feature or swing option. A typical swing contract may have the following form. Producer A agrees to sell to gas pipeline company B 100 gas units per day at a fixed price for a one-month period. B has the right the day before to alter the amount it purchases by 10 gas units from the previous day's level (the swing). However, B's purchases cannot be less than 50 gas units nor greater than 150 gas units. In addition, B must purchase 3,000 gas units over the month. The decisions rest entirely with company B. In this case, B will tend to choose the amount and the sequencing of purchases that maximize the value of this contract.

Box 2.11. European Energy Trading

As in the United States, Europe has also undergone a recent phase of energy deregulation that has led to the further development of energy trading markets. An interesting feature of European energy trading, which differs from the United States, is the development of organized electricity exchanges, the first created by the Norwegian and Swedish electricity stakeholders. The Nordic region was the first to experience electricity deregulation, leading to the creation in 1993 of the Nord Pool, a wholesale electricity exchange. Nord Pool is made up of three separate market operations: a physical-delivery market, a financial contracts market, and the clearing organization that deals with Nord Pool's financial contracts and external OTC bilateral wholesale Nordic electricity contracts. Total trading volume, including OTC clearing, was €55 billion in 2003, consisting of 9 percent in spot, 34 percent in financial, and 57 percent in OTC contracts. Another wholesale

electricity exchange, the European Energy Exchange (EEX), was established in Germany. In July, 2004, the EEX announced that monthly open interest reached €3.75 billion, which translates roughly to a total yearly figure of €45 billion. This figure is more than double the open interest observed over the same period on the EEX in 2003.

Of course, as is the case in the United States, the dominate share of trading activity (particularly for natural gas and electricity) occurs in OTC energy markets. Moreover, the evolution of European energy markets has taken on a similar pattern to that of the United States, in that it was specialized energy trading firms that initially dominated these markets. This was followed by a marked decline in market liquidity with the departure of these firms in 2002, and a renewed growth as new players, including investment banks, have recently expanded their trading business in European energy trading products.

events. Following Enron's collapse, many of these firms were forced to cease operations or be retrenched from the energy trading business, and OTC energy trading activity declined in both the United States and Europe (Box 2.11). However, the decline in activity was short-lived, as much of the market activity has shifted to internet-based OTC trading systems, interdealer brokers, and investment banks, which have recently expanded their OTC energy trading businesses.

New Participants

Although internet-based electronic trading platforms were established when the energy merchants were active, it was not until the collapse of Enron (and the withdrawal of energy traders from the market) that trading activity really grew on these trading systems. In the United States, the largest of these firms are TradeSpark, which posts U.S.-based gas and electricity contracts, and the Intercontinental Exchange (ICE), which posts U.S. and

European oil, gas, and electricity contracts. Trading on these systems has grown since being established in 2000, with between $2.5 billion and $4 billion per day (notional amounts) in mainly energy trading on the ICE in 2004. A fast-growing business line for the ICE is their clearing services for bilateral OTC trades, driven largely by the credit concerns that emerged post-Enron regarding the energy trading firms. Clearing reduces the credit risk inherent in bilateral OTC trading and reduces the amount of collateral required to back trading commitments. NYMEX has also introduced a popular clearing service for OTC energy trades.

The advent of cleared OTC trading also increases the number and diversity of potential counterparties for traditional energy trading. For example, the new OTC clearing services make it easier for investment banks to trade OTC oil derivative contracts with a utility. These clearing systems have facilitated the expansion of investment banks' energy trading activities. Moreover, it also makes it easier for traditional energy market participants to trade with institutional investors, such as hedge funds.

Over the last two to three years, just as energy trading firms dropped out of the energy trading markets, investment banks have expanded not only their dealer activities, but have also invested in physical energy assets. These assets are mainly power generation plants and long-term power supply contracts largely purchased from the fallen energy trading firms. Goldman Sachs has been particularly active in this area, purchasing over $2.5 billion of mostly power plant assets in 2003.[35] Most of these acquisitions were viewed as "distressed" equity purchases, which the investment banks expect to gain in value as power prices rise. Morgan Stanley also owns three wholesale unregulated electricity plants.[36] Many of these purchases help the investment banks expand their dealer activities in the electricity trading markets, as these plants enable them to physically deliver on contracts rather than requiring them to seek out sometimes costly offsetting hedges.

Investment banks have also expanded (or reconstituted) their activities in the energy trading business in response to increased demand from nonfinancial corporations and institutional investors, including hedge funds, both to hedge against the rise in energy prices and to speculate (see Figure 2.34). Anecdotal evidence indicates that hedge funds were particularly active in the oil markets during the latter part of 2003 and early 2004, mainly taking long positions in derivative contracts, with the view that demand increases were of a more fundamental or structural nature, and therefore likely to persist. Other institutional

[35]Goldman Sachs purchased 26 power plants from Cogentrix Energy in October 2003.

[36]Morgan Stanley is an electricity power marketer in the United States and owns equity interests in three unregulated wholesale generators, from which Morgan Stanley (solely or acting with a joint venture partner) is the exclusive purchaser of electric power.

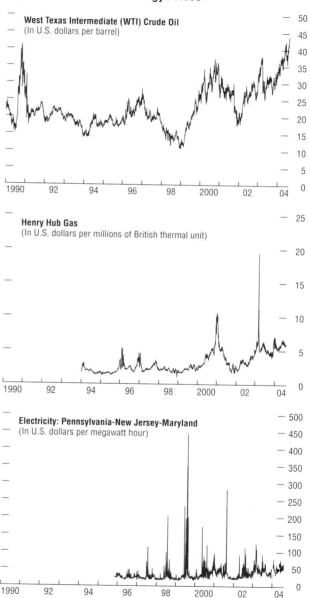

Figure 2.34. Selected Energy Prices

West Texas Intermediate (WTI) Crude Oil
(In U.S. dollars per barrel)

Henry Hub Gas
(In U.S. dollars per millions of British thermal unit)

Electricity: Pennsylvania-New Jersey-Maryland
(In U.S. dollars per megawatt hour)

Source: Bloomberg L.P.

investors, such as pension funds, have also begun to invest in commodities, including energy, as low recent equity and bond market returns have led them to seek a wider range of asset classes, particularly those less correlated with their traditional portfolio allocations (see Chapter III for more on this subject).

The increased participation of traditional finance institutions, such as investment banks, hedge funds, and other institutional investors, in the energy markets implies that they now have greater exposure to energy risks, including the counterparty risk from transactions with traditional energy producers and consumers. This may also imply an increased need for policymakers to understand the dynamics of these energy markets, as they may impact the performance and stability of these financial intermediaries, as well as in a broader economic sense. Moreover, we tend to share the view of some analysts that many of these energy markets are undergoing significant structural changes, with the largest energy consuming and producing nations experiencing different, fundamental issues (including energy dependence, potential capacity constraints, national security, and environmental), as well as increasing demand from fast-growing emerging markets such as China and southeast Asia. For all of the above reasons, we will increase our efforts in monitoring energy trading and broader energy market developments.

Sectoral Balance Sheets

Household Sector

Household balance sheets improved during the first quarter of 2004, as rising equity prices and low interest rates proved supportive. Household debt, particularly mortgage debt, however, remained on a rising trend in the United States and in Europe, notably in the United Kingdom.

A lower flexibility of household balance sheets in the euro area and Japan, compared to the United States and the United Kingdom, may be a factor behind the differences in debt-to-GDP ratios and savings ratios. In the United Kingdom and in the United States, a variety of financial products (e.g., mortgage equity withdrawal and home equity loans, mortgage refinancing, and reverse mortgages) allow households to more easily borrow against the value of their home. While the ability to obtain liquidity from housing assets may help sustain economic activity and, to some extent, help balance sheet restructuring, it may also increase the sensitivity of balance sheets to economic shocks, and precipitate or amplify downward trends.

With the rebound in equity markets, sustained increases in house prices, and further strong income growth, *household balance sheets in the United States* have continued to improve. In particular, the net worth of U.S. households posted its sixth consecutive quarterly increase in the first quarter of 2004 (see Figure 2.35). It rose by 14 percent over the first quarter of 2003, with much of the gain driven by a rise in home and equity prices.

Household debt accumulation has continued to decelerate. Relative to the previous quarter, the amount of consumer credit that U.S. households owed declined in the first quarter of 2004, while mortgage debt continued to grow at an 11 percent annualized rate, down from the 14 percent pace before the end of the mortgage refinancing boom in August 2003. Moreover, household leverage registered its first decline since 1999, as household asset growth outpaced that of debt.

Although household debt accumulation has decelerated, its growth continues to outpace GDP (see Figure 2.36). Many commentators have expressed concerns that, given these high debt levels, rising interest rates could lead to debt service problems for households. However, low interest rates have supported households' ability to service this debt and, as the recovery continues, the recent stronger income growth (up 6.1 percent from a year earlier in the first quarter of 2004 versus 4.7

percent in 2003) should further alleviate the debt service burden. To a significant extent, the growth in household debt over the past few years has reflected sustained mortgage refinancing activity, which hit new records as interest rates declined (until most recently). This refinancing activity has allowed many households to lock in low long-term mortgage rates, not only lowering their interest costs but also partially shielding them from the effects of future interest rate increases. This latter factor makes U.S. household finances overall relatively insensitive to interest rate rises.

A related concern is the possibility that much slower growth, or even declines, in U.S. house prices might remove one of the underpinnings of households' improved net worth. Empirical work in the September 2004 *World Economic Outlook* estimates that expected interest rate rises over the last three quarters of 2004 would slow the growth of nominal house prices, but there is no compelling evidence that a drop in real house prices is in the offing.

In the *euro area*, bank lending to households grew at a 6.9 percent annual pace in May 2004 (from 6.4 percent at end-2003). Household debt/GDP, while significantly lower in the euro zone than in the United States and the United Kingdom, has increased, to reach 48 percent in early 2004 (Figure 2.37). Continuing low interest rates accelerated mortgage borrowing in the recent period, with the annual growth of bank lending for house purchases reaching 8.8 percent in May 2004, from 8.0 percent at end-2003. Consumer credit rebounded further, reaching an annual growth rate of 4.4 percent in the second quarter of 2004, albeit well below the 8 percent level that prevailed until late 2000.

In the *United Kingdom*, borrowing by households has continued to increase sharply in recent months, fueling a continued rise in house prices. As a result, the debt-to-GDP ratio of U.K. households rose to 95 percent in the first quarter of 2004, up from 75 percent at end-2000. Growth in unsecured borrowing

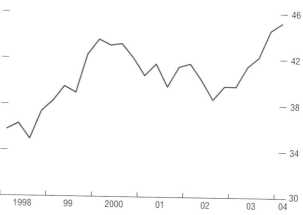

Figure 2.35. United States: Household Net Worth
(In trillions of U.S. dollars)

Source: Board of Governors of the Federal Reserve System, *Flow of Funds.*

Figure 2.36. United States: Household Debt as a Percentage of GDP
(In percent)

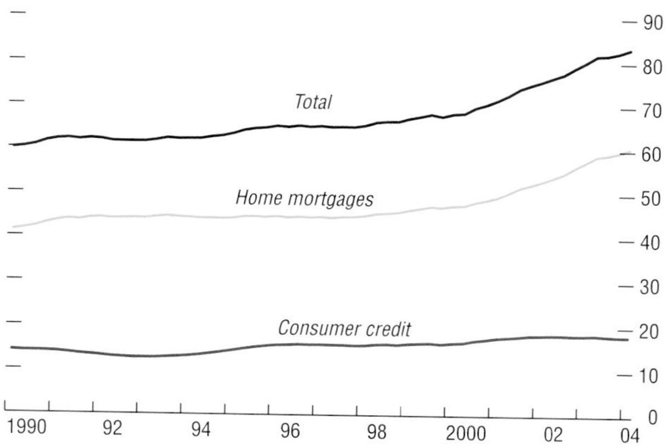

Total

Home mortgages

Consumer credit

Source: Board of Governors of the Federal Reserve System, *Flow of Funds.*

Figure 2.37. Euro Area and United Kingdom: Ratio of Household Debt to GDP
(In percent)

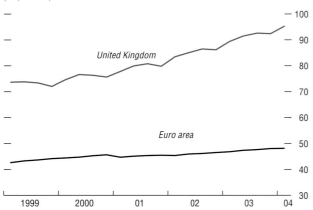

Sources: European Central Bank, *Monthly Bulletin*; and U.K. Office for National Statistics.

Figure 2.38. Japan: Household Net Worth
(In trillions of yen)

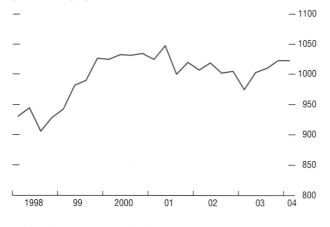

Source: Bank of Japan, *Flow of Funds*.

remained above a 12 percent annual rate in the first quarter of 2004, while secured borrowing was running at a 15 percent annual rate over the same period, the highest in more than a decade. Successive rises in official interest rates have thus far had little effect on overall household credit growth. According to the Nationwide Building Society index, in July 2004, house prices were rising 20.3 percent annually. However, in the most recent months, some indicators of housing activity point to a slowdown. As households increasingly turn to mortgages that are fixed-rate in the first years rather than the more standard variable-rate mortgages, the effective mortgage rate has remained low, below 5 percent at end-March 2004, muting the impact of higher short-term interest rates on households' debt service burden. U.K. monetary authorities recently warned that, although the risk of a market fall in real house prices was small, stress testing by banks for low-probability but high-impact scenarios for household balance sheets was important and, in the longer term, lower inflation meant that high levels of household debt and debt servicing would be eroded less quickly.[37]

The *Japanese household sector*'s net worth continued to improve, albeit marginally, through the six months to the end of March 2004 (Figure 2.38). As in the previous period, the increase derived primarily from valuation gains in equity holdings. Households realized capital gains through the sale of equity (which still increased from 7.4 percent to 8.2 percent of their total assets) and diversified by investing in newly created retail-targeted government bonds (with total issue size of 6.5 trillion yen), securities investment trusts, and foreign currency deposits (asset classes that, in total, represent less than 4 percent of total assets). The slower growth of investment in traditional demand deposits in recent years also demonstrates greater diversification.

[37]See Bank of England (2004).

Corporate Sector

Further improvement in nonfinancial corporate balance sheets, whether measured by leverage, financing gap or asset quality, was noticeable in early 2004. Progress appears uneven, however, from one country—or region—to another. In the United States and to a lesser extent in Japan, strong cash flow has allowed nonfinancial corporations to increase capital expenditures. In Europe, particularly the euro zone, the ongoing buildup of liquidity positions has not yet translated into increased investment.

U.S. nonfinancial corporate balance sheets continued to strengthen since the last GFSR. In aggregate, these firms registered record profits, reflecting the rebound in economic activity. As a result, their leverage—measured by the debt to net worth ratio—continued to decline, reaching 49 percent at end-March 2004, its lowest point since the fourth quarter of 1989 (Figure 2.39).

Driven by strong profits, and cash flows that rose by 24 percent from a year earlier (see Figure 2.40), corporate debt growth was subdued during the period. The sharp rise in profits and cash flows reflected the rapid growth in sales and improved profit margins. Moreover, manufacturing activity continues to rebound and many analysts predict that it will get stronger still over the second half of 2004.

Capital expenditure continued to accelerate, growing by 14 percent over the same period in 2003, having remained at depressed levels through the second half of 2003. As such, the strong rebound in expenditures is likely a reflection, not only of increased economic activity, but also of an unwinding of pent-up capital investment demand in the corporate sector, making use of their currently strong cash position.

Despite the increase in capital expenditures, the financing gap—the difference between capital expenditures and cash flows—remained in negative territory in the first quarter of 2004 (for the fourth consecutive quarter), indicating that corporations con-

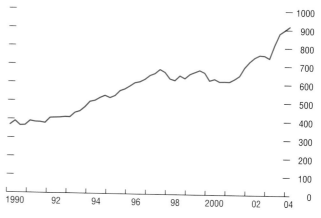

Figure 2.39. United States: Debt to Net Worth Ratio of Nonfinancial Corporations
(In percent)

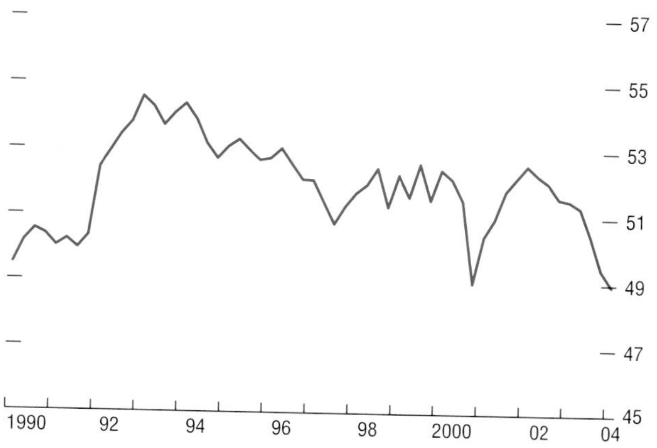

Source: Board of Governors of the Federal Reserve System, *Flow of Funds*.

Figure 2.40. United States: Cash Flow of Nonfinancial Corporate Business
(In billions of U.S. dollars)

Source: Board of Governors of the Federal Reserve System, *Flow of Funds*.

Figure 2.41. United States: Financing Gap of Nonfinancial Corporations
(In billions of U.S. dollars)

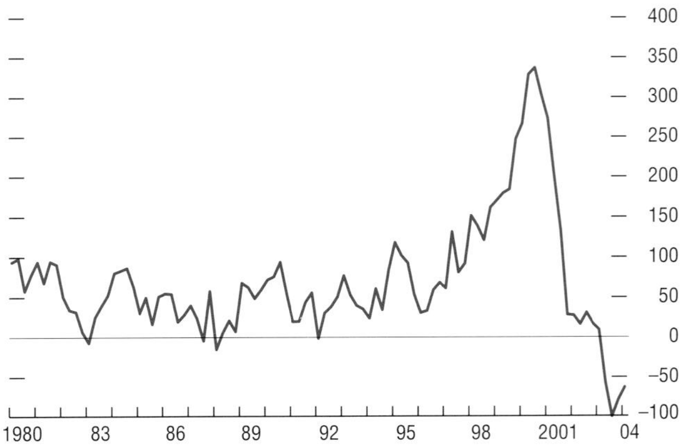

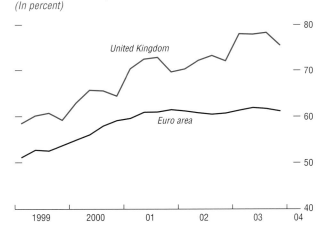

Source: Board of Governors of the Federal Reserve System, *Flow of Funds.*

Figure 2.42. Euro Area and United Kingdom: Ratio of Nonfinancial Corporate Debt to GDP
(In percent)

Sources: European Central Bank, *Monthly Bulletin;* and U.K. Office for National Statistics.

tinue to enjoy high liquidity (see Figure 2.41). This excess liquidity is also an important contributory factor to the decline in leverage mentioned above.

In the euro area and in the United Kingdom, corporates continued to deleverage during the period. The debt-to-GDP ratio of nonfinancial corporations slightly decreased in the second half of 2003, reaching 75 percent in the United Kingdom and 61 percent in the euro area (Figure 2.42). But these ratios are still high by historical standards, and highlight the potential fragility of the corporate sector to higher interest rates (most notably in the United Kingdom) and/or disappointing economic activity (especially in the euro area). At the same time, nonfinancial corporations do not appear to be facing liquidity constraints and, in the euro area, at end-March 2004, deposits with banks by nonfinancial corporations were growing at a 9 percent annual rate. In the euro area, balance sheet restructuring has continued and slowing bank borrowing and securities issuance reflect cautious business investment by nonfinancial corporations as economic activity remains slow to pick up. Overall, the profitability of nonfinancial corporations continued to improve, with weakness mostly concentrated among small and medium-sized enterprises.

Reflecting the improvement of the corporate sector, the default rate of European speculative-grade issuers has dropped close to multi-year lows, to a mere 1.1 percent in the last six months, from 2.4 percent in 2003 and 13.9 percent in 2002. Despite the improving economy, fears have been expressed that tighter liquidity conditions ahead will lead to a sharp rise in the default rate for speculative-grade issuers that have, up to now, taken advantage of the low interest rate environment. During the first six months of 2004, more than 40 percent of corporate bond issuers in Europe were rated speculative grade.

Japanese corporations appear to have regained balance-sheet strength comparable to the early 1980s pre-bubble period, though many still need to further improve profitability. The levels of both corporate capital and cash flow have recovered to historical peaks following a long but steady restructuring process. The capital/asset ratio of Japanese corporates has further improved in recent months, both on a book and a market value basis, primarily reflecting the continued accumulation of retained earnings (Figure 2.43). In fact, the mark-to-market capital/asset ratio of nonfinancial corporates is now restored to the 1990 peak, when capital values were significantly inflated. While their debt-to-GDP ratio remains roughly 25 percent above the 1984–85 pre-bubble level, their cash flow/GDP ratio has exceeded this level through a steady improvement since 1994, reflecting corporate restructuring efforts (Figure 2.44). The impact of any interest rate increase will likely be able to be absorbed within their improved profits.

Asset quality has also improved. Japanese corporations have reduced their holdings of inefficient and risky assets not directly related to their core businesses. The weight of receivables, inventory, and traded securities has declined by nearly a half to 26 percent of total assets, compared to the pre-bubble period. On the other hand, the proportion of assets that reflects ongoing corporate restructuring (intangible fixed assets, investment and other assets, and investment securities) has doubled to 29 percent of total assets. These assets include deferred tax credits from the sale of subperforming assets, goodwill from mergers and acquisitions, and equities invested in subsidiaries created by company splits. It should be noted, however, that these intangible assets could be seen to inflate asset values, albeit to a limited extent.

Banking Sector

A milestone in the regulation of internationally active banks was reached in June 2004 with the Basel Committee on Banking Supervision's issuance of the Revised Capital Framework (Basel II). Potential implications

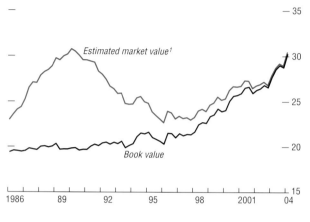

Figure 2.43. Japan: Capital to Asset Ratio of Corporate Sector
(In percent)

Sources: Ministry of Finance, *Financial Statements Statistics on Corporations by Industry;* and IMF staff estimates.
[1]For capital and assets, equity and real estate are marked to the market.

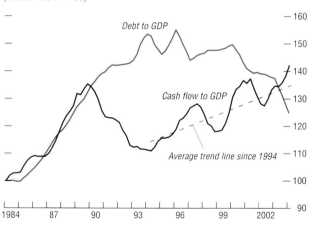

Figure 2.44. Japan: Corporate Debt and Cash Flow Relative to GDP
(March 1984 = 100)

Sources: Ministry of Finance, *Financial Statements Statistics on Corporations by Industry;* and IMF staff estimates.

Box 2.12. The Revised Basel Capital Framework for Banks (Basel II)

On June 26, 2004, the Basel Committee on Banking Supervision (BCBS) issued the Revised Capital Framework (Basel II), which may have a profound effect on the way banks and their supervisors measure and manage banking risks.[1] The Framework contains a mix of options of increasing sophistication and complexity. Most BCBS member countries are expected to implement the simpler of the new approaches (i.e., the standardized and foundation internal ratings based approaches for credit risk, and the basic approach to operational risk), from end-2006.[2] More advanced methodologies are to be implemented a year later, by end 2007, and two years of parallel capital calculation (comparison of old and new standards) will be applied until end 2009.

The revised Framework seeks to upgrade capital regulation, enhance risk measures, and explicitly address the issue of operational risk. Banks may choose from several approaches, tied to different levels of risk management. Basel II also incorporates guidance on the supervisory review process of bank risk management, and seeks to promote greater market discipline through enhanced disclosure requirements. Responding to extensive international consultations on earlier drafts, the published Framework incorporates many changes, such as a simplified standardized approach for less developed banking systems and, provided certain conditions are met, lower risk weights on retail lending, lending to small and medium-sized enterprises (SMEs), and residential mortgages.

The development of the Basel II Framework was both prompted by and has itself encouraged significant improvements in the risk management practices of internationally active banks, and the Framework enhances the ability of supervisors to exercise better, more risk-oriented supervision. The BCBS will continue to refine the Framework, in particular after the first trial years, including the development of a more robust definition of capital, and address unresolved issues, such as the treatment of concentration risk and trading book issues.

Some observers believe that Basel II will foster significant changes in the strategy and market behavior of many banks. Most simply, banks may scale back business lines that could attract higher capital charges. These include securitization, non-OECD lending, equity holdings (particularly large cross-shareholdings), and nonbanking activities such as insurance and asset management. On the other hand, business lines such as retail and SME lending may generate lower capital charges, and could attract additional bank lending. The new capital Framework is also expected to facilitate the trading of credit derivatives, as part of broader credit risk management, where banks make up a significant proportion of trading activities.

Market participants broadly welcomed the Framework, but point to major implementation challenges, including the development of effective systems for cooperation between home and host supervisors.[3] Internationally active banks may be asked to compute capital requirements according to both home and host country criteria. This would add to the regulatory burden. At the same time, supervisors in host jurisdictions need to understand and be able to execute their supervisory responsibilities, regarding the capital adequacy of foreign banks and broader supervision within their jurisdiction.

Concerns have also been expressed that capital flows to developing and potentially lower-rated

[1]The Basel II framework comprises three pillars: Pillar 1 revises the 1988 Accord's guidelines by aligning the minimum capital requirements more closely to each bank's actual risk of economic loss. Pillar 2 recognizes the need for effective supervisory review of banks' internal assessments of their overall risks, and Pillar 3 looks to increase the effectiveness of market discipline by enhancing the degree of transparency in banks' public reporting.

[2]The BCBS member countries are Belgium, Canada, France, Germany, Italy, Japan, Luxembourg, Netherlands, Spain, Sweden, Switzerland, United Kingdom, and the United States.

[3]See press releases from the Institute of International Finance (2004) and the International Swaps and Derivatives Association (2004).

countries could be affected, as capital requirements for lending to such countries and domestic corporates may increase. However, many market observers believe the larger and more sophisticated banks have already incorporated such country and credit risks into their lending activities, independent of the new capital requirements. Competitive concerns have also been raised, as domestic banks in developing countries fear that foreign banks could gain advantage from lower group-wide capital requirements.

Finally, premature implementation of the Framework could weaken rather than strengthen banking systems. Countries may face major implementation challenges: insufficient market infrastructure (rating agencies, export

credit agencies, credit registers), insufficient human resources both at banks and at supervisory agencies, and insufficient data and technology required even for the simpler approaches. Countries should, therefore, first seek to strengthen their supervisory systems through improved compliance with the Core Principles of Effective Banking Supervision before attempting to implement Basel II.

The Basel Committee, as well as the IMF and World Bank, have reiterated in different fora that non-BCBS countries considering implementation of Basel II should do so at their own speed, and according to their own priorities, and neither the Bank nor the IMF is pushing countries to adopt Basel II.

for banks of the new framework are discussed in Box 2.12.

Meanwhile, in the most recent period, bank balance sheets in the United States, Japan, and Europe have continued to strengthen to varying degrees. Supportive financial markets during the first quarter of the year, improvements in asset quality, the ongoing dynamism of household loan demand, and continued cost-cutting and restructuring policies have sustained this process. Significant contrasts remain, however, between and within countries and regions.

U.S. banks continue to be well capitalized, displaying record profit levels. Improved returns largely reflect the pickup in capital market activities that began in 2003 as well as the sustained, albeit moderating, mortgage demand from households. As a result, commercial banks recorded a 9 percent increase in net income in the first quarter of 2004 over the same period in 2003. Loan growth, outside the household sector, continued to be lackluster, with demand for commercial and industrial loans declining further through the first quarter of 2004. Together with the low rate of delinquencies on loans, this illustrated

the strong financial and cash flow position of the corporate sector.

Loan portfolios at U.S. commercial banks displayed improved credit quality as nonperforming loans declined to 1.08 percent of total loans in the first quarter of 2004 from 1.28 percent in the third quarter of 2003. Moreover, delinquency rates in all major loan categories declined further, with the sharpest declines being in commercial and industrial loans, reflecting the improved health of U.S. corporate balance sheets.

Japanese bank balance sheets have continued to improve during the year to end-March 2004, as the economic recovery and the equity market surge continued. Nonperforming loans in the banking system have been reduced by 25 percent during the same period, reflecting improved corporate profitability and further progress in restructuring delinquent borrowers. Within this overall figure, regional banks showed a 13 percent reduction in nonperforming loans. Major banks remain on course to meet the government's target of halving their aggregate nonperforming loan ratio to approximately 4 percent by April 2005. The process of unwinding cross-shareholdings is also in progress. Japanese banks, excluding trust banks, sold 12 percent of their stockholdings during the year to end-March 2004.

With the solvency crisis broadly viewed as behind them, major banks are increasingly focusing on efforts to improve profitability, and most look to retail banking, including small and medium-sized enterprise (SME) and mortgage loans, for attractive opportunities. This trend may likely prompt further consolidation among Japanese financial institutions, and recent mergers and the formation of alliances represent attempts to broaden retail franchises. Some industry observers point out that major banks have already started to penetrate regional bank markets and compete for SME borrowers. The recent introduction of the government scheme for injecting public capital into weakly capitalized banks should also promote consolidation among regional banks, as well as between regional and major banks, as the scheme is designed to provide a strong incentive for weaker regional banks to merge with healthier peers. The stock market has generally welcomed these developments, and bank shares have been rising generally.

European banks' earnings improved in the first quarter of 2004, continuing the trend of last year. Trading and capital market revenues, particularly from fixed income, contributed to the rise in bank income, especially for banks with substantial investment banking activities. Cost discipline has also been a continuing theme among European banks. In 2003, the average cost-to-income ratio among the major European banking groups declined by almost 4 percentage points, to 67 percent. Further reductions are expected in 2004, albeit at a diminishing pace. Meanwhile, the pickup in global activity and the stabilization of asset quality allowed provisioning to be scaled down by most banking groups.

Lending by large U.K. banks to the commercial property sector continued to grow sharply, at a 15.5 percent annual rate in the first quarter of 2004. Concerns have been expressed over an excessive concentration of risk by U.K. banks in this sector, in light of rising interest rates, as close to 50 percent of all property loans in the commercial property market will mature (and thus need to be refinanced) within the next five years. In this context, the proposed development of Property Investment Funds, modeled on U.S. real estate investment trusts (REITs), is welcome, as it should increase the liquidity and the depth of the market.

Overall, return on equity ratios (RoEs) illustrate the improving situation of European banks, but also highlight significant differences from country to country, with U.K., Spanish, Benelux, and Swiss banks exhibiting the highest RoEs, while those of large German banks declined in 2002 and 2003 (Figure 2.45). While profitability of the large German banks has broadly improved in the first half of 2004, revenue generation is likely to remain an issue in the highly competitive and fragmented German commercial banking sector. The need to increase profitability and reorganize business lines will increasingly be the focus of the Landesbanks, as their funding costs are expected to rise after state guarantees are lifted in July 2005.

Banks' issuance on the European covered bond market has grown only slowly in recent months. For the first quarter of 2004, primary market activity is estimated to have been around €70 billion, down €12 billion from the same period last year. The decreasing supply of German Pfandbriefe, particularly by the public sector, accounts for most of the decline in issuance. German Pfandbrief jumbo issues were estimated to represent 69 percent of outstanding jumbo issues at end-March 2004, down from 77 percent in late 2003. With tight spreads between covered bonds and government securities, investor appetite for covered bonds may have diminished. However, the range of issuers in the euro covered bond market continues to expand, with additional U.K. issuers entering the market and the arrival of Eastern European issuers. (FHB bank recently launched the first Hungarian euro-denominated covered bond issue—a five-year, €500 million issue.) Meanwhile, the securitization market continues to develop (see Box 2.13).

Market and Credit Risk Indicators for the Mature Market Banking System

The last year has been a period of relatively low equity price volatility and tight credit spreads for financial institutions (as well as for the wider market). This reflects a generally benign current outlook for global financial markets, with reduced concern about financial stability. Nevertheless, past experience suggests that periods of very low levels of volatility (particularly prolonged periods) can be brought to an abrupt end, and a sudden increase in volatility can be a particular concern for financial stability (see Chapter III, of the September 2003 GFSR for a further discussion). We discuss below some newly developed measures of aggregate market conditions, which may also provide insight on current conditions.

There are several reasons to develop aggregate risk indicators for the mature market financial sector (i.e., banks and large complex financial institutions, or LCFIs). First, we wish to focus on measures that indicate the market's perception of the overall risk profile of the financial sector and certain subsectors. Second, we can develop a historical perspective from which to better understand the current environment, such as the current low market volatility of the equity values of financial institutions. Finally, by looking at the distinct behavior of different groups of financial institutions, we may gain a better understanding of these dynamics from a policy perspective.

We have constructed market indicators for banks and securities firms, and we intend to extend the analysis to insurance companies in future issues of the GFSR. Our approach is to

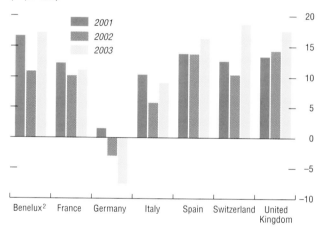

Figure 2.45. Selected Countries: Banks' Return on Equity[1]
(In percent)

2001
2002
2003

Benelux[2]   France   Germany   Italy   Spain   Switzerland   United Kingdom

Source: ©2003 Bureau van Dijk Electronic Publishing-Bankscope.
[1]Return on average equity of five largest commercial banks.
[2]Composed of Belgium, Luxembourg, and the Netherlands.

Box 2.13. Recent Developments in Securitization Markets in Europe and Japan

The euro-denominated securitization market remains dominated by Residential Mortgage-Backed Securities, which accounted for 56 percent of total issuance volume (€62 billion) during the first quarter of 2004. Italian, Spanish, and U.K. assets remain the primary source of ABS and MBS issuance, representing 14 percent, 17 percent, and 41 percent of the underlying assets.

In Germany, the infrastructure of the True Sale Initiative was formally established in April 2004, and the securitization platform is now able to start issuing securities. However, as German bank balance sheets have begun to improve, the immediate benefit and enthusiasm that could have been expected from the securitization of assets such as loans to small and medium-sized enterprises may have declined somewhat. At the same time, interest from nonbank financial service providers to securitize receivables appears to be growing.

In Japan, major banks are enhancing securitization and credit transfer techniques, with a view to improving credit portfolio management. In addition to sales of large corporate loans, major banks have steadily increased their use of credit derivatives. Last year, some major banks started the securitization of SME loan portfolios. Japanese banks also launched a domestic syndicated loan market. The Bank of Japan is actively promoting the development of these markets by accepting these instruments as collateral. However, these markets remain relatively small and illiquid. Many market analysts believe that loan valuation techniques are one of the key impediments to the development of these markets. Japanese banks are accustomed to evaluating loans based on underlying collateral value, while securitization requires loan valuation based on expected cash flows. Collateral-based valuations tend to overestimate the values of lower credit quality borrowers, especially in the case of distressed debt sales (see Box 4.3 in Chapter IV).

consider the financial sector as a portfolio of different institutions, and examine how the market perceives the risk of these portfolios in the context of two indicators: a Market Risk Index (MRI), based on the Value at Risk (VaR; see Box 2.14 for a definition) of the equity values, and a Credit Risk Index (CRI) as an indicator of default risk, based on Credit Default Swap (CDS) spreads.[38,39]

These two indicators can be viewed as two different perspectives from which to analyze the same phenomenon. They are connected at the theoretical level: asset volatility (and therefore equity volatility) is an important determinant of default risk embodied in credit spreads.[40] We should therefore expect these two measures to be highly correlated. At the same time the two indicators are complementary, since the MRI represents sector-wide risk, while the CRI has been designed to capture the credit risk profile of the individual institutions.

We examine a group of the largest internationally active banks and securities firms in mature market economies. In addition to a full portfolio of these institutions, we also look at subportfolios, distinguished by the main activities performed by the firms (e.g., investment banking versus commercial banking) and their geographic location. By focusing on these subportfolios, we can highlight the market perception of vulnerabilities to different types of market events.

[38]Some of the largest internationally active financial institutions release quarterly VaR figures, which attempt to measure levels of risk. Such measures are very useful to understand the evolution over time of the risk profile of a single institution but, at this stage, they are very difficult to use on a comparative basis, given the differing types and degree of financial activities at the different institutions.

[39]A complementary approach to define a credit risk indicator in terms of distance to default, derived from balance sheet and market data, has been recently developed by De Nicoló, Hayward, and Bhatia (2004). For an application to emerging market banks, see Chan-Lau, Jobert, and Kong (2004).

[40]Merton (1974).

The subgroups under review are, by type of institution:

    i) LCFIs,[41] and

    ii) commercial banks;[42]

and by geographic region:

    iii) Canada and the United States,

    iv) Europe, and

    v) Japan/Asia and Australia.

For the MRI, we collected, on a daily basis, the equity price for each institution since June 2000.[43] In our portfolio, each price has been weighted by the firm's relative market capitalization.

The CRI is constructed along similar lines. We collected the spreads for five-year (the most liquid contract) CDSs on senior debt. We weighted each spread in the CRI index in the same way as for the MRI. The time series for the CDS spreads are much shorter than for the equity prices, and due to limited data availability, we are restricted, for the time being, to the CDS prices of LCFIs only.

Market Risk Index

During the period under review the impact of several major events can be examined by the MRI:

- the equity market decline in the spring of 2001;
- the events of September 11, 2001;
- the period of extreme volatility during 2002 caused by credit events, particularly in the United States and Latin America, and general fears of a global recession; and
- the sharp, but temporary, rise in interest rates during the summer of 2003.

Box 2.14. Definition of Value at Risk

Value at Risk (VaR) is the maximum potential loss that can be incurred on a given financial position over a determined time period, and at a certain level of probability. This measure was originally developed for monitoring and managing the market risk of asset portfolios, and is widely used as the basis for financial institutions' internal risk management models. Here we use it as a monitoring tool, which provides us with a market-based measure of the combined risks of a group of institutions with correlated risk sensitivities.

Box 2.15. Volatility Estimation

The graphs show at each point in time the maximum potential loss for our portfolio over a 10-day period at the 95 percent confidence level (i.e., the standard time horizon and confidence level for VaR analysis). The correlation matrix and the volatilities used in the VaR computations are, at each point in time, daily estimates over a 75-day rolling period. They are obtained using an exponential smoothing technique, which gives more weight to the most recent observations.

Following these events, financial markets have enjoyed a recovery phase, broadly characterized by low volatility (Box 2.15 describes how the volatility estimates were made).

---

[41]The definition of LCFIs is the same as applied by the Bank of England in the *Financial Stability Review*, December 2003, and comprises: ABN Amro, Bank of America, Barclays, BNP Paribas, Citigroup, Credit Suisse, Deutsche Bank, Goldman Sachs, HSBC Holdings, JP Morgan Chase, Lehman Brothers, Merrill Lynch, Morgan Stanley, Société Generale, and UBS.

[42]The Commercial Banks selected for our portfolio are: Bank One, Wachovia, HBOS, Royal Bank of Scotland, Royal Bank of Canada, Bank of Nova Scotia, Toronto Dominion, CIBC, Mizuho Financial, Mitsubishi Tokyo Financial, UFJ Holdings, Sumitomo Mitsui Financial, Fortis Group, KBC Bancassurance Holding, Credit Agricole, Commerzbank, HVB Group, Banca Intesa, Unicredito, Sanpaolo IMI, ING Groep, Banco Bilbao Vizcaya Argentaria, Santander Hispano Group, Skandinaviska Enskilda Banken, Svenska Handelsbanken, Nordea, National Australia Bank, Australia and New Zealand Banking Group, Westpac Banking Corporation, Development Bank of Singapore, and Bank of East Asia.

[43]The starting date was based on availability of data.

Figure 2.46. Large Complex Financial Institutions (LCFIs) and Commercial Banks: Market Risk Indicator (MRI)
(In percent of aggregate market capitalization)

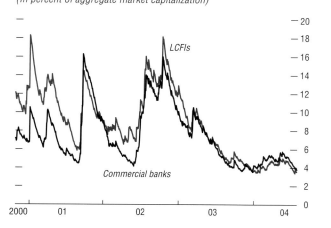

Sources: Bloomberg L.P.; and IMF staff estimates.

Figure 2.47. Entire Portfolio: Market Risk Indicator (MRI) and Diversification[1]

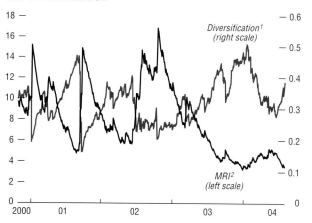

Sources: Bloomberg L.P.; and IMF staff estimates.
[1]As a proportion of undiversified value at risk.
[2]In percent of aggregate market capitalization.

The VaR for the entire portfolio of financial institutions, as well as those shown for the LCFIs and commercial banks subportfolios, have three clear peaks corresponding to the first three events listed above (Figure 2.46). From October 2002 onward, with the exception of a smaller spike at the start of the war in Iraq, the VaRs have steadily declined. The effect of the interest rate volatility in summer 2003 is very minor, suggesting that the market believed that financial institutions were generally well hedged against relatively sharp interest rate moves.

The pattern of the VaR measures for the LCFIs and commercial banks shows great similarities, but there are some differences, partly reflecting the nature of their individual businesses. For example, the investment banking operations of the LCFIs made them more sensitive to the equity market decline in early 2001, but commercial banks were more impacted by the events of September 11. Although the interest rate spike of 2003 was in aggregate modest, there was particularly high sensitivity for a very small group of European commercial banks.

Correlations

From a financial stability perspective, the degree of correlation within the financial sector is important. A high degree of correlation may imply an amplification of systemic volatility, particularly if it persists, and such correlation may pose severe problems in the event of an adverse shock.

We can analyze the effects of correlation by comparing two different VaR measures. We use the VaR computed thus far (i.e., by taking account of correlations), and the VaR calculated as the simple sum of the individual VaRs of each institution, the undiversified VaR, which will always be higher than the first measure. By taking the difference between these two VaR measures, we capture the diversification effect embedded in the portfolio. When this difference is small, it means that the equity prices are highly correlated, and therefore shocks or short-term increases in volatility are more likely to impact (with amplifying effects) the financial sector and the market as a whole.

During periods of relative stability, the diversification effect (i.e., the difference between the two VaR measures) is usually quite high, and on average it is around 30–35 percent. This may be because with a lower level of broad market volatility, market participants are discriminating and valuing different strategies, credit strength, and relevant national or regional economic conditions of the different institutions. However, this measure is subject to wide variations. During periods of increased volatility, the diversification effect is strongly reduced (Figure 2.47). Interestingly, since the beginning of 2004, the diversification effect has been decreasing quite steadily from rather high levels, indicating at present an increasing level of correlation during this relatively prolonged period of low market volatility.

Figure 2.48 also shows that there is almost always less diversification effect among LCFIs than among commercial banks, perhaps reflecting greater national or regional variations between commercial bank activities than those of LCFIs. This may reflect the global nature of many of the LCFIs' operations and risk profiles, with a wide variety of business activities, while more traditional commercial banks continue to operate national or regional banking businesses. At the same time, the degree of correlation between commercial banks tends to rise sharply (approaching that of LCFIs) when a significant shock occurs, such as September 11 and the credit events of 2002. This may reflect the market's immediate reaction to such events as it perceived a common impact across the entire financial sector, or it may reflect the withdrawal of wholesale and broad market liquidity.

The Geographic Dimension

The various market events had different impacts on our geographic subgroups. U.S.

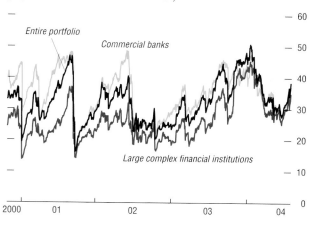

Figure 2.48. Difference Between Undiversified and Diversified Value at Risk
(In percent of undiversified value at risk)

Sources: Bloomberg L.P.; and IMF staff estimates.

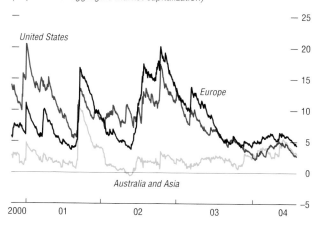

Figure 2.49. Selected Countries: Value at Risk Sensitivity
(In percent of aggregate market capitalization)

Sources: Bloomberg L.P.; and IMF staff estimates.

Figure 2.50. Large Complex Financial Institutions: Market Risk Indicator (MRI) and Credit Risk Indicator (CRI)

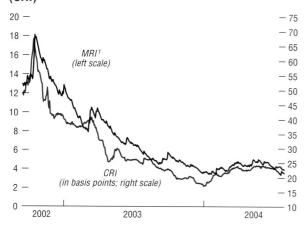

Sources: Bloomberg L.P.; and IMF staff estimates.
[1]In percent of aggregate market capitalization.

banks were more affected by the stock market fall of 2001 and the credit events of 2002, while the impact of September 11 was less significant, despite the location of the actual events (Figure 2.49). Within that group, the 2002 credit events had a stronger impact on institutions for which the commercial banking component of their activities was larger.

Within the portfolio, European firms had a lower sensitivity to the spring 2001 equity market fall; however, they were more sensitive than the U.S. firms to the 2002 credit events. Most affected were the Spanish banks, having high Latin American exposure, and U.K. banks. By contrast, the Scandinavian banks demonstrate the lowest level of volatility throughout the period of analysis. The pattern may reflect the differing degrees of international versus domestic exposure, with those banks operating on a more local basis experiencing less volatility.

The VaR of the Japanese, other Asian, and Australian banks is generally lower than for other regions throughout the sample period. The regional VaR level is similar to that of U.S. banks after September 11, but much lower for the 2001 stock market fall and the 2002 events. This is also reflected in the VaR measures for LCFIs and commercial banks (see Figure 2.46). Within the LCFI group, institutions with significant Asian operations show the lowest sensitivity to the 2002 credit events, suggesting that these events had a geographically differentiated impact. Meanwhile, part of the increase in the VaR in recent months is due to increased volatility among the Japanese banks, perhaps because of their China exposure and also the market response to regulatory actions relating to one bank's nonperforming loan portfolio.

Credit Risk Index

Movements in the CRI are generally consistent with those of the LCFIs' MRI (Figure 2.50), showing a strong reduction in perceived credit risk since 2002.[44] However, from the beginning of 2004, there has been a somewhat gradual increase in credit spreads, more than represented by (MRI) equity market volatility. The increase in credit spreads predates the observed (slight) increase in MRI at the beginning of 2004, perhaps suggesting (as market participants often believe) that credit spreads may be a better indicator of changes in market sentiment.

Conclusions

In conclusion, at present the market is characterized by a relatively low level of volatility, or perceived risk. This also can be seen in the broader S&P 500 index and other measures (see earlier in this Chapter 2). Nonetheless, our analysis also indicates that there is an increasing level of correlation between financial institutions' market prices. This may suggest that, if the current prolonged period of relatively low volatility in financial markets is disrupted, for any reason, by a significant rise in volatility, the relatively higher correlations among a large group of financial institutions may act to amplify that volatility and prove disruptive to broader market conditions. All else being equal, given higher correlations, a market shock could produce such amplified volatility.

We plan to continue to monitor and develop these indicators for the March 2005 GFSR, including the coverage of a wider range of financial institutions (such as insurance companies).

References

Allen, Mark, Christoph Rosenberg, Christian Keller, Brad Setser, and Nouriel Roubini, 2002, "A Balance Sheet Approach to Financial Crisis," IMF Working Paper No. 02/210 (Washington: International Monetary Fund).

Altman, Edward I., 1968, "Financial Ratios, Discriminant Analysis and the Prediction of Corporate Bankruptcy," *Journal of Finance*, Vol. 23 (September), pp. 589–609.

———, Robert G. Haldeman, and P. Narayanan, 1977, "A New Model to Identify Bankruptcy Risk of Corporations," *Journal of Banking and Finance*, Vol. 1 (June), pp. 29–54.

Bank of England, 2004, *Financial Stability Review* (London, June).

Chan-Lau, Jorge, Arnaud Jobert, and Janet Kong, 2004, "An Option-Based Approach to Bank Vulnerabilities in Emerging Markets," IMF Working Paper No. 04/33 (Washington: International Monetary Fund).

Counterparty Risk Management Policy Group (CRMPG), 1999, "Improving Counterparty Risk Management Practices" (June).

Davey, Emma, 2004, "The Bull Run," Energy and Commodities, a supplement to *FOW* (January).

De Nicoló, Giovanni, Peter Hayward, and Ashok Bhatia, 2004, "U.S. Large Complex Banking Groups: Business Strategies, Risks, and Surveillance Issues," in *United States: Selected Issues*, Country Report No. 04/228 (Washington: International Monetary Fund), pp. 72–86.

Duffie, Darrell, and Kenneth J. Singleton, 2003, *Credit Risk: Pricing, Measurement, and Management* (Princeton, NJ: Princeton University Press).

Eichengreen, Barry, and Ashoka Mody, 1998, "What Explains Changing Spreads on Emerging Market Debt: Fundamentals or Market Sentiment?" NBER Working Paper No. 6408 (Cambridge, Mass.: National Bureau of Economic Research).

Eichengreen, Barry, and Don Mathieson, 1998, *Hedge Funds and Financial Market Dynamics*, IMF Occasional Paper No. 166 (Washington: International Monetary Fund).

Financial Stability Forum (FSF), 2000, "Report of the Working Group on Highly Leveraged Institutions" (April).

———, 2002, "The FSF Recommendations and Concerns Raised by Highly Leveraged Institutions (HLIs): An Assessment" (March).

Fung, William, David A. Hsieh, and Konstantinos Tsatsaronis, 2000, "Do Hedge Funds Disrupt

[44]From the CRI, for a Loss Given Default level, one could also obtain a distance to default for the portfolio as implied by the market (see Duffie and Singleton, 2003, which can be compared with the one in De Nicoló, Hayward, and Bhatia, 2004).

Emerging Markets?" (Basel: Bank for International Settlements).

Gapen, Michael T., Dale F. Gray, Cheng Hoon Lim, and Yingbin Xiao, 2004, "The Contingent Claims Approach to Corporate Vulnerability Analysis: Estimating Default Risk and Economy-Wide Risk Transfer," IMF Working Paper No. 04/121 (Washington: International Monetary Fund).

Gray, Dale F., 2002, "Macro Finance: The Bigger Picture," *Risk* (June).

———, Robert C. Merton, and Zvi Bodie, 2003, "A New Framework for Analyzing and Managing Macrofinancial Risks of an Economy," MfRisk Working Paper No. 1–03. Available via the Internet at *http://www.moodys-mfrisk.com.*

Greenwich Associates, 2004, "For Hedge Fund Investors, New Notes of Caution," (Greenwich, CT).

IMF, 2004a, *Global Financial Stability Report,* World Economic and Financial Surveys (Washington: International Monetary Fund, April).

———, 2004b, "Private Capital Flows to Emerging Asia: Stylized Facts and Issues," background paper for the high-level seminar "Managing Short-Term Capital Inflows" sponsored by the IMF and the Bank of Thailand (Bangkok, July 9).

Institute of International Finance, 2004, "IIF Welcomes Basel II Framework. Implementation Poses Key Challenges," Press Release (Washington, June 27).

International Country Risk Guide, 2003, "Brief Guide to the Ratings System" (East Syracuse, NY: The PRS Group).

International Swaps and Derivatives Association, 2004, "ISDA Commends Basel Committee on New Capital Accord," News Release (June 28).

Joint Forum, 2004, *Financial Disclosure in the Banking, Insurance and Securities Sectors: Issues and Analysis,* Basel Committee on Banking Supervision (Basel: Bank for International Settlements, May).

Kamin, Steven B., and Karsten von Kleist, 1999, "The Evolution and Determinants of Emerging Market Credit Spreads in the 1990s," BIS Working Paper No. 68 (Basel: Bank for International Settlements).

Kashiwase, Kenichiro, and Laura Kodres, forthcoming, "Emerging Market Spread Compression: Is It Real or Is It Liquidity," IMF Working Paper (Washington: International Monetary Fund).

Managed Funds Association, 2003, *Sound Practices for Hedge Fund Managers* (Washington).

McGuire, Patrick, and Martijn Schrijvers, 2003, "Common Factors in Emerging Market Spreads," *BIS Quarterly Review* (Basel: Bank of International Settlements, December).

Merton, Robert C., 1974, "On the Pricing of Corporate Debt: The Risk Structure of Interest Rates," *Journal of Finance,* Vol. 29, pp. 449–470.

National Association of Insurance Commissioners (NAIC), 2004, "Modernizing the Insurance Regulatory Framework for a National System of State-Based Regulation." Available via the Internet: *http://www.naic.org/docs/naic_framework.pdf.*

Ohlson, James, 1980, "Financial Ratios and the Probabilistic Prediction of Bankruptcy," *Journal of Accounting Research,* Vol. 19, pp. 109–131.

President's Working Group on Financial Markets, 1999, "Hedge Funds, Leverage, and the Lessons of Long-Term Capital Management" (Washington, April).

Sløk, Torsten, and Mike Kennedy, 2004, "Factors Driving Risk Premia," OECD Economic Department Working Paper No. 385 (Paris: Organisation for Economic Co-operation and Development).

Sy, Amadou, 2002, "Emerging Market Bond Spreads and Sovereign Credit Ratings: Reconciling Market Views with Economic Fundamentals," *Emerging Market Review,* Vol. 3, Issue 4, pp. 380–408.

U. S. Board of Governors of the Federal Reserve System, 2004, *Flow of Funds* (Washington, June).

U. S. Department of Energy, 2002, "*Derivatives and Risk Management in the Petroleum, Natural Gas, and Electricity Industries,*" Energy Information Administration (Washington, October).

RISK MANAGEMENT AND THE PENSION FUND INDUSTRY

As financial markets develop, a variety of nonbank institutions, such as insurers, pension funds, mutual funds, and hedge funds, have been increasing their exposure to market and credit risks. This chapter is the second in a series on the financial stability implications of this reallocation and transfer of risk, following the chapter, "Risk Transfer and the Insurance Industry," in the April 2004 GFSR. This chapter focuses on pension funds, as significant institutional investors.

Pension funds have an impact on the stability of financial markets in several ways, most significantly through their investment behavior. The global size and projected growth of the pension fund sector mean that this investor class can move markets in its own right. Any sizable reallocation of assets, say between fixed income and equities, could have a bearing on financial market stability. Such strategies are not only driven by fundamental business models but also by cyclical factors and risk management considerations, as well as by official policies in areas such as taxation, regulation, and financial accounting. The changing needs of aging pension fund members also have a longer-run impact. As such, an analysis of the pension funds' impact on financial stability will have to cover all of the above elements.

This chapter looks at the longer-term challenges pension funds face as populations age, and the key issues to address in order to enhance their risk management practices and their role as long-term investors. The chapter focuses primarily on Japan, the Netherlands,

Switzerland, the United Kingdom, and the United States, where funded pension plans are most developed. The size of pension savings in these countries, their projected growth (whether managed by the state, corporations, or individuals), and the more recent development of funded pension schemes in other countries, such as France, Germany, and Italy, highlight the fast-growing importance of pension funds for international capital markets and to financial stability.

How pension funds manage risk has a very important bearing on the distribution of financial and other risks among the different sectors of the economy. As employers and governments have become more aware of the funding challenges pension funds face from aging populations, and more conscious of the investment risks involved in funded pension plans, they have sought to manage that risk in a variety of ways. Reductions in state pension benefits in most countries, and movements from defined benefit (DB) to defined contribution (DC) pension plans by many businesses, have increasingly transferred retirement risk (including investment, market, longevity risks, etc.) to the household sector.[1]

National pension systems are typically represented by a "multi-pillar" structure, with the sources of retirement income derived from a mixture of government, employment, and individual savings. A variety of definitions of the pillars are used in academic literature, generally dependent on the purpose of each study. In this chapter, we identify and discuss three pillars, based primarily on the source of

[1]Defined benefit schemes are those in which the employer commits to provide specific benefits related to an individual's wages and length of employment, while under defined contribution plans the commitment is to make specific contributions to a pension fund, with the benefits dependent on the level of contributions to the scheme and the investment return. For definitions of other pension terminology see the glossary.

savings (i.e., government, employment, or individual): *Pillar 1*—the state, often a combination of a universal entitlement and an earnings-related component; *Pillar 2*—occupational pension funds, increasingly funded, organized at the workplace (e.g., DB and DC, and newer hybrid schemes); and *Pillar 3*—private savings plans and products for individuals, often tax-advantaged. These are the definitions commonly used by industry participants and analysts, and are particularly suitable for our focus on risk transfer.[2]

This chapter primarily focuses on Pillar 2, as collective funds organized through the workplace. Our focus reflects the role of Pillar 2 funds as a major institutional investor class. The design of Pillar 1 programs will not be discussed, as this is primarily a fiscal issue, although it should be noted that in some advanced economies, such as Japan, France, and Canada (and certain developing economies), some public sector schemes are (at least partially) funded.[3] This chapter will only briefly discuss Pillar 3 and efforts by some governments to encourage long-term retirement savings generally, as we plan to discuss the fund management industry and household sector in more detail in the March 2005 GFSR. Indeed, the economic characteristics of DC plans, including their allocation of risk, are very similar to Pillar 3, and this chapter focuses more on the management of DB plans and the forces moving funds from DB to DC, rather than on the management of DC plans themselves.

Pillar 2 funds can enhance financial stability by acting as a stable, long-term investor base; however, increasingly a variety of factors are influencing their structure, investment behavior, and management of risks. These factors, and how we arrived at a point many call "a

pensions crisis," are discussed in the chapter. Similar to our previous work, we have highlighted influencing factors, such as market characteristics, regulatory and tax policies, and accounting principles. Finally, we look at different investment strategies and risk management approaches, and how these may help pension funds take a long-term perspective, and thereby support financial stability objectives.

Why Pension Funds Are Important for Financial Stability

An Aging Workforce

The importance of pension savings has increased dramatically in recent years, particularly as populations mature. Historically, low proportions of pensioners in the overall population and the relatively larger workforce from the "baby boom" generation kept the burden of pension outlays somewhat modest. DB schemes seemed a manageable and even attractive (due to benefit deferral) proposition to many companies. But as populations age, the relative size of pension liabilities and investment risk grows. The growth in liabilities has been greater than expected, as increases in longevity have consistently exceeded earlier actuarial forecasts. Questions of managing and maintaining funding levels have become more urgent, and some pension providers will find it increasingly difficult to meet their payment obligations according to their existing benefit structures. For policymakers, the relative burdens and merits of each of the three pillars are increasingly a prominent topic of political and social debate.

Advanced economies are confronted with a variety of retirement challenges associated

---

[2]Another definition used in pension studies, particularly for emerging markets, was first developed in World Bank (1994). It describes Pillar 1 as "non-contributory state pension," Pillar 2 as "mandatory contributory," and Pillar 3 as "voluntary contributory." This definition has been most useful for considering questions of social safety nets, redistribution of income, and related issues.

[3]Many emerging market economies also wholly or partially fund public sector pension schemes. Emerging market pension issues will be discussed in future GFSRs.

Table 3.1. Life Expectancy at Birth: Estimates and Projections
(In years)

	1955	1980	2000	2020	2050
United States	68.9	73.3	76.2	78.7	81.6
Japan	63.9	75.5	80.5	84.3	88.1
Selected European countries[1]	67.6	73.3	77.7	80.5	83.2

Sources: United Nations, *World Population Prospects: The 2002 Revision;* and IMF staff estimates.

[1]Weighted average for France, Germany, Italy, the Netherlands, Switzerland, and the United Kingdom; weights are based on the countries' total population data for 2000.

with population aging, reflecting in part two long-term trends:[4]

- *Increasing longevity.* In recent decades, life expectancy at birth has consistently increased in all advanced economies, from an average of about 68 years in the postwar period to 78 years today (Table 3.1 and Figure 3.1), and is projected to reach 80 years or more by 2020. Importantly for pension costs, life expectancy after age 65 is also rising steadily, from 18 years currently, to a projected 20 years or more in 2020 in the United States and some selected European countries, and rising steeply in Japan (Figure 3.2).

- *Low and declining fertility rates.* In advanced economies between the early 1950s and the late 1990s, fertility rates have dropped from about 2.8 to 1.7 children per woman, and are below the replacement rate in most advanced economies, except the United States.

While population aging is a global phenomenon, it is happening rapidly in some countries. The aging trend is particularly visible in Italy, Japan, and Switzerland, where the

---

[4]We have explicitly excluded the health and medical issues from the scope of this study, in order to focus on funded pensions. However, health and medical costs are rising rapidly in all the mature markets, and to the extent that such private schemes are funded at all, the funding levels are significantly lower than pensions. (For example, for companies in the Standard & Poor's 500 at the end of 2003, the average funding levels were approximately 87 percent for pension liabilities and 15 percent for medical and health care plans.)

Figure 3.1. Life Expectancy at Birth
(In years)

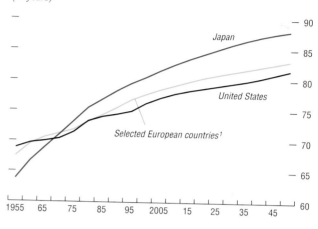

Sources: United Nations, *World Population Prospects: The 2002 Revision;* and IMF staff estimates.

[1]Weighted average for France, Germany, Italy, the Netherlands, Switzerland, and the United Kingdom; weights are based on the countries' total population data for 2000.

Figure 3.2. Remaining Life Expectancy at Age 65
(In years)

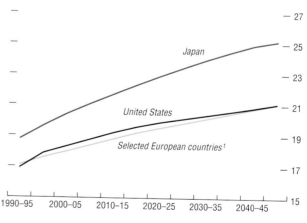

Sources: United Nations, *World Population Prospects: The 2002 Revision;* and IMF staff estimates.

[1]Weighted average life expectancy at age 65 for France, Germany, Italy, the Netherlands, Switzerland, and the United Kingdom; weights are based on the countries' total population data for 2000.

Figure 3.3. Median Age of Population, by Country[1]
(Medium fertility variant)

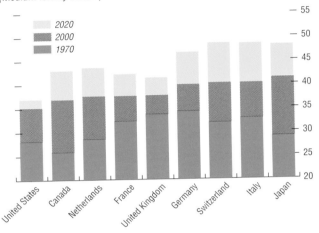

Source: United Nations, *World Population Prospects: The 2002 Revision.*
[1]Countries are shown in increasing order of the median age of population in 2000. The United Nations' medium fertility variant assumes that fertility levels converge to 1.85 births per woman in all countries.

Figure 3.4. Dependency Ratio for Selected Countries[1]
(In percent)

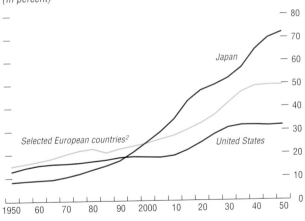

Sources: United Nations, *World Population Prospects: The 2002 Revision;* and IMF staff estimates.
[1]Population aged 65 and over as a percentage of population aged 15 to 64.
[2]Weighted average dependency ratio for France, Germany, Italy, the Netherlands, Switzerland, and the United Kingdom; weights are based on the countries' total population data for 2000.

median age is already above 40 years today, and projected to approach 50 years by 2020 (Figure 3.3). Moreover, national differences in median age are projected to widen in the coming years.

A direct implication is the continued increase in the dependency ratio—the ratio of pensioners to working age population. The dependency ratio is currently about 20 percent in Europe, Japan, and North America, and is projected to increase rapidly once the "baby boom" cohort begins to reach retirement age around 2010. By 2030, this ratio may reach 30 percent in North America, 45 percent in Europe, and 55 percent (and rising rapidly) in Japan (Figure 3.4). The demand for retirement income relative to contributions from working income will be proportionately greater, and this pressure will be felt by private companies (particularly in older or declining industries) as well as by public/state programs.

Policymakers have started to address these challenges and to rethink their pension systems. Thus far, pension reforms frequently have been aimed at reducing the generosity of existing systems in various ways: reducing benefits, increasing contributions (e.g., taxes to pay for state pensions), redefining risk sharing between sponsors and beneficiaries, and increasing the retirement age. Given the scale of the problem, it is likely that actions on several of these fronts will be needed.[5] Increased funding of pension obligations, by both the public and private stctors, and greater retirement savings by individuals (Pillar 3), are increasingly part of the solution.

Pension Funds Are Significant Investors in Global Financial Markets

Funded pension plans' size and importance to financial markets vary sharply between different countries. The countries we have studied can be broadly classified into two groups:

---

[5]See, for example, Turner (2003) and Moody's Investors Service (2004).

those where pension assets represent more than 60 percent of GDP, including the Netherlands, Switzerland, the United Kingdom, and the United States; and those where pension assets represent less than 20 percent of GDP, including France, Germany, Italy, and Japan (Table 3.2).[6]

In a number of countries, pension funds are the largest class of institutional investor. Pension funds represent about 50 percent or more of institutionally held assets in the Netherlands and Switzerland; over 33 percent in the United Kingdom and the United States; and about 20 percent in Japan. The proportion remains negligible in countries where private pension savings are not well developed or are chiefly managed by insurance companies, for instance in France and Germany (Table 3.3).

The investment behavior of pension funds can have a significant effect on markets, as they hold a large and growing proportion of overall financial assets. As of the end of 2001, pension funds in the United Kingdom and the United States held domestic equities equal to 18 and 22 percent, respectively, of total domestic equity market capitalization (Table 3.4). Meanwhile they held domestic bonds (both credit and government securities) equivalent to 11 and 9 percent, respectively, of total domestic bond market capitalization. In the Netherlands, pension funds' total equity allocation (both domestic and foreign) equals 36 percent of the country's domestic equity market capitalization, and Swiss pension funds' total bond allocation (domestic and foreign) equals 59 percent of the domestic bond market capitalization, leading pension

funds from both countries to invest substantial proportions abroad. In contrast, pension funds' relative holdings in Germany, Italy, and Japan are much smaller.[7] But with these and other countries moving toward increased funding of pension liabilities, the global pension fund industry and its impact on financial markets can be expected to grow.

Changes in Pension Funds' Asset Allocations Could Impact Financial Markets

There is an ongoing debate on the merits of pension funds holding bonds versus equities, raising the question of whether bond and equity markets could be impacted by major portfolio reallocations. Equity allocations are currently as high as 50–70 percent in many pension funds in Japan, the Netherlands, the United Kingdom, and the United States (Figure 3.5). Fund managers, pension consultants, and market analysts increasingly believe that regulatory and accounting changes (under consideration or recently adopted) could trigger a significant reallocation of pension assets from equities into bonds, as sponsor companies seek to reduce funding risk and accounting volatility (see the section, "Asset Allocation and Risk Management," later in this chapter). An immediate or short-term reallocation from equities could have a significant impact on financial markets and asset prices in the short term. However, such a shift would seem unlikely given the reluctance of many pension fund managers to move from equities to bonds (or pursue more closely matched risk management strategies) while they remain significantly underfunded.[8] The

[6]The Japanese figures exclude assets held by the Pillar 1 Government Pension Investment Fund (GPIF). Although this public pension scheme is a pay-as-you-go system, it has accumulated a surplus from contributions worth ¥150 trillion, invested in government bonds, equities, and foreign securities.

[7]In Japan, in addition to occupational pension funds, the GPIF's equity holdings amount to 3 percent of domestic stock market capitalization.

[8]In the appendices to CIEBA (2004), a Morgan Stanley research report estimates that an abrupt reallocation could lead to a temporary 10 to 15 percent reduction in U.S. equity prices and a 75–150 basis point flattening of the U.S. government bond yield curve, while a Goldman Sachs paper estimates only a 1 percent reduction in equity prices and a 10 basis point reduction in long-term yields.

Table 3.2. Asset Allocation of Autonomous Pension Funds[1]
(In percent of total financial assets of pension funds, unless otherwise noted)

	1992	1995	1998	2001
Germany				
Cash and deposits	1.5	1.8	1.8	2.0
Bonds	49.5	54.9	55.8	57.4
Equities	0.2	0.0	0.0	0.1
Loans	48.1	43.0	42.2	40.5
Other	0.8	0.2	0.2	0.1
Memorandum items:				
Financial assets (in billions of U.S. dollars)	56.6	65.3	69.3	60.5
Financial assets (in percent of GDP)	2.9	2.7	3.1	3.3
Italy				
Cash and deposits	32.4	38.5	45.4	36.0
Bonds	42.2	33.3	36.1	40.5
Equities	0.1	2.2	0.9	6.8
Loans	0.0	0.0	0.0	0.0
Other	25.3	26.1	17.7	16.7
Memorandum items:				
Financial assets (in billions of U.S. dollars)	38.3	39.0	38.7	47.3
Financial assets (in percent of GDP)	3.1	3.5	3.1	4.4
Japan[2]				
Cash and deposits and other	2.2	1.9	2.5	2.7
Bonds	28.9	27.1	30.7	31.5
Equities	19.4	25.3	46.9	52.3
Loans	8.9	5.5	2.2	1.5
Insurance	40.3	39.9	17.7	12.1
Memorandum items:				
Financial assets (in billions of U.S. dollars)	416	634	619	611
Financial assets (in percent of GDP)	10.7	13.1	13.9	16.0
Netherlands				
Cash and deposits	1.9	2.1	1.5	1.5
Bonds	22.8	27.4	33.5	34.7
Equities	17.8	27.2	40.1	49.5
Loans	48.3	35.7	19.1	8.8
Other	9.2	7.6	5.8	5.4
Memorandum items:				
Financial assets (in billions of U.S. dollars)	244.8	352.1	444.2	397.5
Financial assets (in percent of GDP)	76.0	84.8	107.5	105.1
Switzerland[3]				
Cash and deposits	10.0	11.3	10.7	8.5
Bonds	40.5	36.9	35.5	35.9
Equities	13.1	25.5	31.9	39.0
Loans	34.8	23.4	19.3	13.8
Other	1.6	2.9	2.6	2.9
Memorandum items:				
Financial assets (in billions of U.S. dollars)	145.0	217.5	269.2	280.8
Financial assets (in percent of GDP)	59.6	80.0	97.5	113.5
United Kingdom				
Cash and deposits	3.6	4.0	4.4	3.3
Bonds	9.9	13.4	15.8	14.5
Equities	74.8	70.8	66.8	63.5
Loans	0.1	0.0	0.0	0.0
Other	11.6	11.7	13.0	18.8
Memorandum items:				
Financial assets (in billions of U.S. dollars)	552.4	759.7	1,136.5	954.0
Financial assets (in percent of GDP)	52.7	68.2	79.3	66.4

Table 3.2 *(concluded)*

	1992	1995	1998	2001
United States				
Cash and deposits	4.5	3.7	3.7	3.7
Bonds	31.1	26.9	21.1	23.1
Equities	46.5	54.3	62.5	59.8
Loans	2.8	1.8	1.6	1.8
Other	15.0	13.2	11.0	11.5
Memorandum items:				
Financial assets (in billions of U.S. dollars)	3,011.6	4,226.7	6,231.9	6,351.3
Financial assets (in percent of GDP)	50.0	57.1	71.0	63.0

Sources: OECD Institutional Investors Yearbook; Japanese Pension Fund Association; and Bank of Japan, *Flow of Funds.*
[1]Occupational and personal pension funds, legally separated from the plan/fund sponsor taking the form of either a special purpose legal entity (a pension entity) or a separate account managed by financial institutions on behalf of the plan/fund members.
[2]Asset allocation shares are those of Employee Pension Funds only. Memorandum items include all pension fund assets.
[3]For 1995 and 2001, data refer to 1996 and 2000, respectively.

impact of a more gradual reallocation is more difficult to assess, especially as broader changes in the risk management practices of pension funds can be expected in the coming years.

Pension fund demand could have a particularly pronounced impact on certain asset classes. Pension funds are increasingly focusing on asset-liability management (ALM) (i.e., ensuring that liabilities are sufficiently covered by suitable assets) and in particular the relative duration of assets and liabilities. Many market participants highlight the relatively short supply for this purpose of long-term bonds (i.e., 20 to 30 years or longer), and particularly inflation-indexed bonds (see Table 3.5). At present, even a relatively modest reallocation of pension assets into these long-term securities would overwhelm the market, as liquidity constraints could lead to significant short-term price volatility. Over time, however, the supply of long-term and inflation-indexed bonds may increase, possibly with government leadership, and we would expect pension funds to be a significant investor.

The potential for greater international diversification by pension funds could also have a strong impact on international capital flows. In particular, as populations age in the mature markets and their need for retirement savings grows, this creates potential demand to make additional investments in countries

Table 3.3. Financial Assets of Institutional Investors, 2001[1]
(In percent of total financial assets, unless noted otherwise)

	Total Financial Assets[2]	Investment Companies[3]	Pension Funds	Insurance Companies	Other
France	131.8	47.7	...	52.3	0.0
Germany	81.0	44.9	4.1	51	0.0
Italy	94.0	35.6	4.7	23.7	35.9
Japan	94.7	10.0	19.5	63.7	6.8
Netherlands[4]	190.9	11.9	55.0	32.3	0.8
Switzerland[5]	232.7	13.8	48.8	37.4	0.0
United Kingdom	190.9	14.4	34.8	50.8	0.0
United States	191.0	34.3	33.0	21.2	11.5

Source: OECD Institutional Investors Yearbook.
[1]Institutional investors are insurance companies, investment companies, and pension funds.
[2]In percent of GDP.
[3]Open-end and closed-end investment companies.
[4]For 2001, excluding nonlife insurance.
[5]For 2001, including total assets of pension funds.

Table 3.4. Pension Fund Holdings Compared with the Size of Domestic Market, 2001
(In percent)

	Equities[1]		Bonds[2]	
	Domestic	International	Domestic	International
Japan	7.4	. . .	3.2	. . .
Netherlands	6.5	29.4	15.2	23.3
Switzerland[3]	6.9	5.8	38.1	21.1
United Kingdom	18.1	9.8	11.2	3.4
United States	22.4	5.1	8.7	0.2

Sources: OECD Institutional Investors Yearbook; BIS; Bank of Japan, *Flow of Funds*; World Federation of Exchanges; Datastream; UBS Global Asset Management; and IMF staff estimates.

[1]Holdings of equities as a percentage of total domestic market capitalization.

[2]Holdings of securities over one year in maturity as a percentage of total public and private domestic debt securities outstanding.

[3]Data refer to 2000.

Figure 3.5. Asset Allocation of Autonomous Pension Funds, 2001[1]
(In percent of financial assets of pension funds)

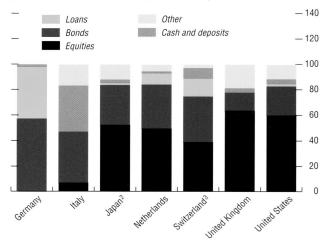

Sources: OECD Institutional Investors Yearbook; Japanese Pension Fund Association; and Bank of Japan, *Flow of Funds*.

[1]Occupational and personal pension funds, legally separated from the plan/fund sponsor taking the form of either a special purpose legal entity (a pension entity) or a separate account managed by financial institutions on behalf of the plan/fund members.

[2]For Japan, "other" refers to insurance sector; and "cash and deposits" refer to cash, deposits, and other. Allocations are those of Employee Pension Funds (EPFs) only.

[3]For Switzerland, data refer to 2000.

with younger labor forces (in particular, emerging markets), and raises questions about the ability of those markets to absorb substantially greater flows.

The Funding Challenge

The debate over the design and asset allocation of pension funds has taken on more urgency as the industry has swung from overfunded to underfunded status in recent years. These factors have focused attention on the investment and other risks associated with traditional DB plans. This has led to a closer consideration of the merits of different asset classes in matching pension liabilities and accelerated the industry's consideration of DC and hybrid pension plan alternatives to traditional DB schemes.

How Pension Funds Became Underfunded

Several factors have led pension funds to become underfunded in recent years.[9] This section focuses on the rising level of DB plan promises, especially relative to contributions, and on the impact of falling equity markets and interest rates.

[9]See, for instance, IMF (2003).

Table 3.5. Selected Countries: Total Outstanding Long-Term Bonds
(In billions of U.S. dollars)

	United States		United Kingdom		France		Italy		Japan	
	2000	2003	2000	2003	2000	2003	2000	2003	2000	2003
Corporate and government long-term bonds[1]	1,143	1,257	144	202	74	128	81	223	250	368
Inflation-indexed government bonds[2]	115	166	99	139	12	59	1	11	. . .	. . .
Memorandum item:										
Total pension fund assets (at end-2001)	6,351		954		. . .		47		711	

Sources: U.S. Department of the Treasury; U.K. Debt Management Office; Agence France Trésor; Italy, Ministry of Economics and Finance; Japan, Ministry of Finance; Merrill Lynch; and OECD, *Institutional Investors Yearbook 2003*.
[1]Total amount of 10-year and above maturities. For the United Kingdom, France, and Italy, government bonds only.
[2]For France and Italy, also includes bonds indexed on euro area inflation.

Pension funds in North America and parts of Europe historically have held significant amounts of equities in their portfolios. This reflected a belief in the greater long-run returns expected from equities compared with bonds. In the United States, this also partly reflected the interpretation of the "prudent person" rule introduced as part of the Employee Retirement Income Security Act (ERISA) in 1974, which in part requires "diversifying investments . . . so as to minimize the risk of large losses, unless under the circumstances it is clearly not prudent to do so," which led many pension funds to more systematically diversify across asset classes.[10]

During the 1990s, as equity prices rose, the funding ratio of many DB plans rose well above 100 percent. While accounting and actuarial smoothing of market valuations reduced the immediate impact of equity prices on funding ratios, the steady rise in equity prices fed through over time (Figures 3.6 and 3.7). In some cases, the "overfunding" was further exaggerated by the use of above-market or relatively fixed discount rates for funding ratio calculations, even as market rates for bonds fell throughout most of the 1990s.[11]

Moreover, projections of future returns, based largely on recent performance, further boosted calculated funding ratios by extrapolating forward these current strong equity market returns.

Sponsor companies often acted to "realize" these gains, thereby weakening the capacity of pension funds to absorb future shocks. In particular:

- Many sponsor companies reacted to their pension fund's overfunding (both real and exaggerated) by reducing or eliminating contributions. Sponsor companies were able to reduce their annual contributions (or, in some cases, tax regulation penalized further contributions) and in many cases take "contribution holidays" of a decade or more. In other cases (such as in Switzerland or in the U.S. public sector), contributions by employees were reduced as well.

- Companies with surplus pension funding also frequently increased the size and scope of benefits, including through indexation. The costs of these benefit increases did not directly affect companies' reported profits. But in practice they introduced permanent increases in liabilities and greater risk to the

---

[10]Asset allocations became more similar in the U.S. pension fund industry after the adoption of ERISA, as the "prudent person" rule contributed significantly to a convergence in asset allocation between different pension funds. In 1970, the equity allocation of state and local government pension funds was 23 percent, whereas that of private trusteed pension funds was 54 percent. By 2000, the allocations were much more similar, at 58 percent and 48 percent, respectively.

[11]In Japan, the Netherlands, and Switzerland, fixed discount rates for liabilities were used, while U.K. discount rates allowed a large element of actuarial discretion and were typically set well above market rates (although a market-related element was increasingly used from the mid-1990s onwards).

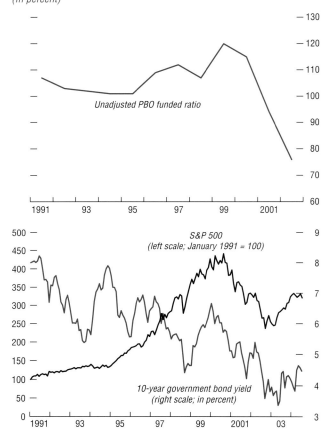

Figure 3.6. United States: Ratio of Assets to Projected Benefit Obligations (PBOs) for the Fortune 500
(In percent)

Unadjusted PBO funded ratio

S&P 500
(left scale; January 1991 = 100)

10-year government bond yield
(right scale; in percent)

Sources: Hewitt Associates; and Bloomberg L.P.

financial strength of pension funds, with the costs and risks further magnified by increases in longevity beyond earlier actuarial projections. In some cases, generous early retirement packages were used to increase turnover in the workforce and to phase out DB plans and introduce new DC-style plans for younger employees.

Japan also experienced overfunding, but with a different timing. Overfunding developed in the late 1980s during the asset market bubble. However, poor returns in the 1990s on both equity and fixed-income markets, together with returns of 5.5 percent required on Pillar 1 pension contributions managed by employers, led to 66 percent of private pension funds becoming underfunded by 1996.[12] Overfunding briefly occurred again following the abolition of investment limits in 1996, which allowed an increase in equity holdings. (Under previous limits, pension funds were required to invest more than 50 percent of their assets in bonds, and less than 30 percent each in equity and foreign securities.) Japanese pension funds raised their allocation in equities to above 50 percent by 2000, and at that time 82 percent of Japanese funds were overfunded (Figure 3.8).[13]

Between 2000 and 2002, pension funds worldwide became significantly underfunded. The equity market fall of 2000–02 sharply cut the funding ratios of pension funds that, in many cases, held equity allocations of 50 percent or more (see Table 3.2). Moreover, market interest rates, which increasingly were being used in some jurisdictions (such as Japan and the United Kingdom) as the basis

[12]In Japan, employers providing Pillar 2 pensions in the form of Employee Pension Funds (EPFs) are also required to administer (as agents) the government's Employee Pension Insurance (EPI) for their employees, withholding contributions from employees' salaries and managing the funds to provide a fixed return. In return, the EPFs are allowed to be overfunded, with the profit or loss from investing EPI returns absorbed into the overall EPF funding position.
[13]See Watson Wyatt (2003).

for discounting liabilities, fell significantly, thereby increasing the present value of liabilities and creating the "perfect storm" for pension funds.[14] In the United Kingdom, the shift from contribution holidays to large annual contributions was made all the more extreme by the fact that Minimum Funding Requirement (MFR) thresholds began to dictate funding policy at many firms. (The MFR funding calculation uses more market-related discount rates—i.e., at that time, lower rates—and hence larger valuations of liabilities, than previously controlling actuarial funding calculations.) Even the assets held in the form of fixed-rate bonds failed to grow in value as fast as liabilities, largely because the average duration of such assets was typically much shorter than the duration of liabilities. By the end of 2002, over 90 percent of pension funds in Japan, the United Kingdom, and the United States were underfunded, and the rise in interest rates and equity prices since has led to only a partial recovery (Figure 3.9).

The impact of falling equity markets and bond yields on asset and liability valuations was significant. Figure 3.10 shows one estimate of the effect of valuation changes on pension funds in different countries and regions. It illustrates the impact of market changes on a hypothetical pension funding ratio, assuming that the fund started with a funding ratio of 100 percent at the beginning of 2000, and that it had a typical asset allocation and liability structure for that country or region.

Although the fall in equity values has been most often credited as causing the underfunded position of many pension funds, the fall in bond yields (and the greater use of market-related discount rates for liabilities) has been at least as important. Given the typically long duration of pension fund liabilities, changes in yields (and thus discount rates) have a major impact on the calculated value of liabilities. In the United States, for

[14]See Hewitt Investment Group (2001) and Custis (2001).

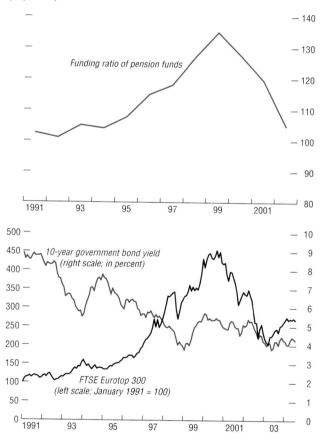

Figure 3.7. Netherlands: Funding Ratio of Pension Funds
(In percent)

Sources: Netherlands Pension and Insurance Supervisory Authority; Van Ewijk, and van de Ven (2003); and Bloomberg L.P.

Figure 3.8. Japan: Employee Pension Funds[1]
(Number of funds)

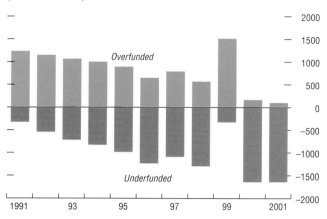

Source: Pension Fund Association.
[1]Fiscal years; before 1996, data shown on book value basis; for 1996 and after, data shown on fair market basis.

Figure 3.9. United States: Distribution of Corporate Defined Benefit Pension Plans by Funding Ratio, 2003[1]
(Number of pension plans)

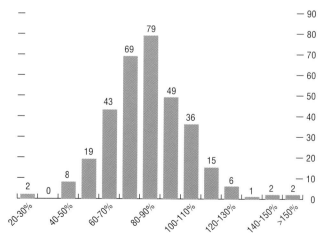

Source: Wilshire, *2004 Corporate Funding Survey on Pensions.*
[1]Survey of 331 companies in S&P 500 Index.

instance, it has been said as a rule of thumb that each 10 basis point change in the discount rate leads to a 1 percent change in projected benefit obligations (PBOs) (Standard & Poor's, 2004a). Meanwhile, a recent actuarial estimate suggested that the aggregate underfunding of the 200 largest U.K. DB schemes would be eliminated by either a 30 percent rise in equity prices or a 1 percentage point rise in bond yields (Aon Consulting, 2004). This demonstrates the significant, and often underappreciated, influence market-related discount rates can have on funding ratios.

Companies have only limited scope in the short term to address their underfunding by reducing benefits or increasing contributions. Companies have had little room to reduce recently increased benefits—in fact, they were sometimes legally constrained from scaling back benefits (for instance, in the United Kingdom indexation up to a cap of 5 percent became a regulatory requirement in 1997). Weaker corporate profitability in 2001–02, and the ongoing decline in the financial strength of older industries, also restricted the ability of some sponsor companies to raise contributions.

The deterioration in funding levels, and the questions raised in some cases about the corporate sponsor's ability to meet future obligations, brought urgency to the debate about pension fund structures and strategies. The viability of DB schemes has been questioned, as well as the appropriate risk sharing between employer and employee (Pillars 2 and 3), public and private sector responsibilities, and related social and tax policy issues. The rapid deterioration of funding ratios accelerated the shift to DC schemes, and led to the development of new approaches to pension and retirement programs.

The Move from DB to DC and Hybrid Plans

Even before the deterioration in market conditions and funding levels, there was a growing belief that many DB schemes, as traditionally constructed, may need to be redesigned. DB schemes had become less flexible, in large part through greater benefits and increasing longevity. In addition, the DB structure may be less suitable as employees become more mobile—in fact, newer industries (often less unionized) and their generally younger workforces favor DC pension schemes, as more mobile employees are attracted by the portability of pension benefits. The move to more market-based accounting principles has also increased the perceived volatility of DB plan balance sheets.

In the United States, the use of DC plans has been growing for 30 years. The introduction of ERISA in 1974, the creation of the Pension Benefit Guaranty Corporation (PBGC), which imposed insurance premiums on DB funds, the strengthening of funding requirements, and, for some firms, a desire to reduce contribution levels supported the growth of DC plans (Figure 3.11). Over time, many DB plans have closed to new employees and/or frozen benefits at existing accrued levels, and shifted all employees to new plans. By 1985, over 35 percent of assets under management (AUM) by U.S. private pension funds were in DC plans. Since then, DC plans (e.g., 401(k) plans) have continued to increase in popularity in the United States, reaching close to 55 percent of AUM by 2000, and growing further since then.

In the United Kingdom, the trend was initially slower, but the recent introduction of FRS 17 and a fair value accounting framework (to be fully implemented by January 2005) has accelerated the move away from DB schemes. In 2000, 80 percent of active participants in private sector pension funds still belonged to DB plans, but more recent information suggests that 60 percent of DB schemes (weighted by the number of employees) are now closed to new members (Jackson, Perraudin, and Trivedi, forthcoming). Many U.K. firms are also taking the

Figure 3.10. Estimated Valuation Effects on Projected Benefit Obligation (PBO) Funded Ratios¹
(In percent)

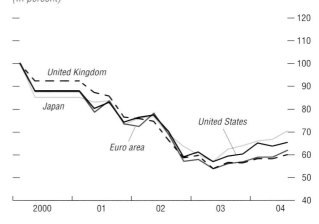

Source: Towers Perrin.
¹The series show the effect of asset and liability valuation changes on a hypothetical pension fund in each country or region with a typical asset allocation and liability structure, and with a funding ratio of 100 percent at the beginning of 2000, without allowing for contributions to the fund during the period.

Figure 3.11. United States: Assets Under Management of Private Pension Schemes
(In billions of U.S. dollars)

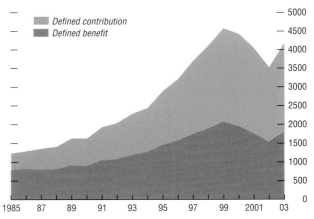

Source: Board of Governors of the Federal Reserve System, *Flow of Funds*.

opportunity to cut contribution levels as they move to DC.

In Japan, DC schemes have not grown very quickly, despite reforms in 2001 to allow DC plans to complement or replace traditional DB pension funds. Tax Qualified Pension Plans, as they exist today, will be progressively phased out by 2012, and replaced by new externally managed DB and/or DC schemes.[15] Companies with EPFs (see footnote 12) are given an option whether to transform themselves into the new DB or DC schemes. The increasing mobility of employees, and the introduction of a more transparent accounting framework in 2000, which revealed funding gaps on sponsor companies' balance sheets, prompted these reforms. The recent scaling back of Pillar 1 (cutting the benefit level by, on average, 10 percent of final salary) has also encouraged the development of DC plans.[16] However, the growth of DC plans also has been impaired by the limitation of tax deductions for employers (¥432,000 per year, per employee), and the fact that employees are not allowed to contribute to the new corporate DC schemes.

To date, the move from DB to DC schemes has not altered asset allocations a great deal. In the United States, individuals participating in DC plans have tended to allocate the majority of their funds to equity investments, which is not substantially different from DB plans (60 percent of AUM in DC plans have been invested in equity on average since 1990, compared with 53 percent for DB plans). But the shift to DC is important to financial markets, including, among other reasons, because of its transfer of risk from sponsor companies to households. It remains to be seen whether the current asset allocation pattern will continue, particularly as aging populations approach retirement age.

Despite these statistics, many consultants argue that households often remain too risk averse. Financial consultants advise individuals to hold relatively large allocations of higher risk instruments, such as equities, in pension savings when they are young, and to gradually switch to assets with more stable values, such as bonds, as they approach retirement. Consultants in a number of countries repeatedly stated that, while it may be tax efficient to hold bonds within pension savings, households generally hold too little investment risk overall. This is especially so for younger savers, particularly when looked at in the context of their overall savings (including other non-pension savings). However, in recent years a variety of "life cycle" savings products have been developed, which address asset allocation and adjustment issues related to aging.[17] (A broader discussion of household sector savings will be discussed in the March 2005 GFSR.)

The reconsideration of DB plans has also led to the development of "hybrid" pension plans (see Box 3.1). Many sponsor companies have sought to share market and longevity risk, and to adjust benefits depending on business conditions, while still guaranteeing a minimum benefit to employees. Such hybrid plans incorporate elements of both DB (as the sponsor makes contributions and bears at least some investment or guaranteed return risk) and DC plans (as benefits are often expressed in terms of an account balance and often result in a lump sum payment at retirement).

---

[15]Tax Qualified Pension Plans are the second largest form of pension plan in Japan, after EPFs, and are so called because they meet Corporate Tax Law conditions for tax exemptions on contributions.

[16]See IMF (2004b).

[17]In the United States, "life cycle mutual funds" were first developed in the 1990s. In order to match the presumed and recommended changing risk tolerance of individuals during their life, such funds provide greater risk taking in the early years, before automatically and gradually adjusting the asset allocation to a more conservative approach (e.g., reducing equity and increasing fixed-income investments) as the individual approaches retirement.

Table 3.6. Sources of Retirement or Replacement Income
(In percent of total income)

	Germany	France	Italy	Netherlands	Switzerland	United Kingdom	United States	Japan
Public sources[1]	85	79	74	50	42	61	41	34
Private/all other sources[2]	15	21	26	50	58	39	59	66
Memorandum item:								
Overall replacement rate (percent)[3]	82	79	80	78	81	69	67	75

Sources: Adapted from Börsch-Supan (2004); Employee Benefit Research Institute; Pensions Policy Institute; Japanese Ministry of Public Management, Home Affairs, Posts and Telecommunications, Survey of Household Economy; and IMF staff estimates.

[1]Pillar 1 includes France's AGIRC/ARRCO, the U.K.'s State Second Pension Scheme (S2P), and Japan's EPI.

[2]All private sources of retirement income, including occupational pension income as well as income from financial assets (including income from the reinvestment of lump sums paid by Pillar 2 schemes), use of bank deposits (particularly important in Japan), and earnings from work (in the United States, earnings from work are estimated to represent close to 20 percent of retirement income).

[3]Pension income, just after retirement, as a percentage of total income just before retirement, for an average two-person household; excludes sources of income other than pensions.

The use of hybrid schemes is growing in the United States, Europe, and Japan. In the United States in 2000, 21 percent of PBGC-covered plan members belonged to hybrid plans. We anticipate further growth of such plans, but legal uncertainties and technical difficulties linked to conversion from traditional DB schemes in some cases may slow their development in the near term. Many European companies are also developing hybrid Pillar 2 schemes, which give employers some flexibility over the provision of inflation protection and longevity risks (see below). In Japan, due to the greater inflexibility in DC plans (as legislated), many companies have adopted "cash balance" plans as part of their amendment of DB schemes following the 2001 reforms.

Dutch regulatory proposals have also moved their system closer to a hybrid model, and the United Kingdom has reduced the degree of required indexation. The planned regulatory reforms (including the development of a risk-based capital system, described below) encourage the traditionally indexed DB Dutch pension system to make pension indexation explicitly conditional on market conditions. Meanwhile, the United Kingdom has decided

to halve the cap on required inflation indexation to 2½ percent.

New National Approaches to Pension Schemes

European countries that have been developing Pillar 2 and 3 systems in recent years benefited from the experience of countries with more established funded pension schemes. They have been conscious of the financial constraints arising from an aging population, and new designs have generally followed a DC or hybrid plan approach.

Currently, the relative importance and contribution of Pillars 1, 2, and 3 differ significantly from country to country (see Table 3.6). In countries such as the Netherlands, Switzerland, the United Kingdom, and the United States, the public pension system operates in part as a safety net, designed to provide a basic pension income, while Pillars 2 and 3 provide a much more significant contribution to retirement or replacement income than in other countries.[18] In contrast, in most continental European countries the state has traditionally been the main source of retirement benefits (generally pay-as-you-go, or PAYG), and Pillars 2 and 3 are typically

[18]See, for example, Queisser and Vittas (2000).

Box 3.1. Hybrid Pension Plans

Hybrid pension plans, in essence, have some features of defined benefit (DB) plans, but often with a greater sharing of risks by beneficiaries. Similar to traditional DB plans, the employer/trustee invests the plan assets and typically bears some of the investment risk. However, hybrid plans also operate in many ways like defined contribution (DC) plans, in that the employee typically has an individual account and can receive the account balance either in annuity form or as a lump sum at separation, thereby assuming more longevity risk. The portability and relatively earlier accrual of benefits typically provided by hybrid plans are often very attractive to today's more mobile workforce. At the same time, hybrid plans provide to employees some of the advantages of DB plans in terms of guarantees and assurance. Indeed, the terminology is not always well-defined and some "hybrid" schemes in effect provide defined benefits.

Hybrid plans take a variety of forms across countries, for example:

- In Japan, the United Kingdom, and the United States, "cash balance plans" (CBPs) are the most common form of hybrid pension plan. CBPs in those countries are plans in

which a fraction of an employee's salary is deposited in a notional account (or "cash balance"). Notional accounts are used for record-keeping purposes only, as the funds are not invested for each individual separately, but for the plan as a whole. The benefits are usually based on an average rather than final salary, and may or may not contain a variable element related to market returns (in Japan they reflect asset returns with minimum guarantees), and accrue more evenly over an employee's career than under traditional DB schemes. In the United States, CBPs are legally classified as DB plans, and as such are insured by the PBGC.

- In Germany, the growth of hybrid plans reflects (in part) the impact of regulations on capital guarantees imposed on pension funds. New vehicles introduced under the Riester reform, including the Pensionsfonds, are required to guarantee a minimum benefit equivalent to principal protection. Similarly, since 2002, other vehicles, including the Pensionskasse and Direktversicherung, also need to provide such guarantees in order to benefit from state subsidies and tax deductions.

underdeveloped. In Germany, for instance, while many employers have for years provided Pillar 2 (traditionally DB) schemes, the benefit represents a modest share of aggregate pension income.[19] In France, the earnings-related mandatory AGIRC/ARRCO system,[20] even if managed and funded by contributions from both employees and employers, is in essence an additional layer of Pillar 1 (some-

times referred as "Pillar 1A"). In Italy, the *Trattamento di Fine Rapporto* system, under which employers pay a lump sum when an employee leaves the company, has long been the closest proxy to a Pillar 2 scheme, but has represented only a small part of retirement income. While the framework for new DC schemes was established in 1993 in Italy, DC plans have gained momentum only since

---

[19]Pillar 2 pension benefits are estimated to represent approximately 5 percent of retirees' overall income. At end-March 2003, 43 percent of private sector employees (46 percent in western Germany and 27 percent in eastern Germany) were members of occupational pension schemes. Pension fund membership has been greater in the manufacturing sector than the service sector, and much greater in large companies than small and medium-sized corporations. Indeed, pension fund membership tends to be relatively greater in large companies than smaller companies in many advanced economies.

[20]*Association Générale des Institutions de Retraites des Cadres* (AGIRC) and *Association des Régimes de Retraites Complémentaires* (ARRCO).

1999, and by 2003 15 percent of the eligible population had enrolled in DC plans.

In many countries, the newer designs generally are intended to develop multi-pillar funded schemes, to supplement Pillar 1 as the traditional primary source of retirement income. These reforms include major changes (often reductions) in Pillar 1 programs, expanded funded corporate schemes (generally DC or hybrid), and the development of individual retirement savings vehicles.[21]

Germany, for example, is moving toward funded hybrid pension schemes.[22] The existing Pillar 2 schemes are primarily DB plans. Among them, *Direktzusage* (or "book reserve"—historically the most popular DB scheme with large German corporates) has not been funded by segregated assets, but the pension fund liabilities are included directly in the company balance sheet, backed by the operating assets of the sponsor company and considered "internally funded." The range of occupational pension schemes has been expanded in 2001 with the creation of *Pensionsfonds*, which can be set up as either DB or DC schemes. Furthermore, "hybrid" schemes (in Pillar 2 and in Pillar 3) are growing in Germany, many of which provide principal protection and minimum guaranteed returns on accrued contributions in order to qualify for favorable tax treatment. Employees typically are required to take an annuity on retirement.

Italy and France, through *Fondi Pensione* and *Plan d'Epargne Retraite Collectifs (PERCO)*, have established pure DC schemes for all private sector employees (and public sector employees in Italy).[23] In both countries, these DC schemes are required to offer participants a menu of investment options with different risk-return profiles. As in Germany, the tax regime in Italy encourages the payment of benefits at retirement through annuities, rather than as a lump sum.

Key Influences on Pension Funds' Financial Management

In addition to the challenge of aging populations, a number of other factors influence the management of pension funds. National financial market characteristics, regulations and tax policy, pension guarantee schemes, and accounting standards have a significant effect on asset allocation and risk management strategies.

Financial Market Characteristics

As discussed in the April 2004 GFSR study on the life insurance industry, national market characteristics play a significant role in influencing institutional investment styles and preferences. Pension funds, like other institutional investors, show a high degree of home bias in their investment strategies. As such, national markets may supply or limit the investment alternatives desired by pension funds to meet their specific investment needs.

However, pension fund investment behavior can be quite different from other institutional investors in the same country or region, suggesting that regulatory and other factors are also influential. In markets with relatively developed funded DB plans, equities form a large part of pension funds' aggregate investments. In some countries, this contrasts sharply with the life insurance industry. For example, in the United States, pension funds are much more heavily invested in equities than insurers, despite the large domestic availability of corporate bonds and other credit

[21]See, for example, Allianz Dresdner Asset Management (2003).

[22]Changes in German pension schemes are taking place in the context of the "Riester Reform" (2000–02).

[23]Loi Fillon (2003) in France and the Berlusconi measures of 2003–04 in Italy. The recent Italian measures followed the 1992–93 d'Amato reforms and the Dini-Prodi reforms of 1995–97 that introduced one of the most radical pension reforms across industrial countries, switching from a PAYG DB scheme to a DC system.

instruments. Similarly, in European countries pension funds have not followed insurers, which have increased corporate credit investments following recent pressure on solvency margins and improvements in risk management techniques. This suggests that the lack of risk-based incentives, implemented perhaps through funding requirements or pension insurance premiums, or the relative sophistication and adoption of risk management techniques may be at least as important a determinant of investment strategies as the characteristics of local or regional capital markets.

An important issue for pension funds is the availability of long-term and index-linked bonds. As routinely stressed by pension fund managers, financial products such as annuities and long-dated and index-linked debt instruments may better match pension liabilities with an average duration often beyond 20 years, as well as addressing the needs of individuals for Pillar 3 savings products. The market for long-term bonds is deepest in the United States (although, even there, the size of the market for maturities beyond 10 years is relatively modest). A number of countries—for instance, France, the United Kingdom, and the United States—have small but growing markets for index-linked bonds (see Table 3.5). The United States has recently widened its maturity range of issues to include a 20-year Treasury Inflation Protected Security (TIPS) bond, and Germany and Switzerland have also announced their intentions to issue their first inflation-linked bonds in 2005. But in all mature markets such long-term instruments remain small compared with the size of pension fund portfolios.

As a result, pension funds have sought other ways to increase or match duration, and

some have turned to equities for long-term hedges. Given supply constraints on long-term or index-linked bonds, some pension funds have relied on equities or other instruments to provide more duration or inflation hedges. This explains the relative significance of equity holdings or real estate in many pension fund portfolios. In addition, derivative instruments (such as swaps) have attracted some pension fund managers seeking to increase asset duration or obtain some form of inflation protection.

Certain policy actions may be needed to stimulate further issuance of long-term and index-linked bonds and to support these markets. The availability and development of such instruments should be supported by national governments, including through government issuance and clear and consistent tax policy regarding long-term bonds. This should enhance pension funds' ability to act as long-term providers of capital and support financial stability. Corporate issuers desiring long-dated funding exist in most mature markets, such as capital-intensive industries, utilities, financial services (banks and insurers), and housing. In some areas (e.g., Europe), the development of securitization and structured credit markets may also provide such instruments. Insurance companies will undoubtedly have an important role to play in the expansion of annuity markets; however, even here, insurers need long-term market instruments to efficiently hedge and price annuity risk.[24] One particular factor that may inhibit the supply of annuities by insurers may be the difficulty of managing longevity risk of the extreme elderly as average life expectancy continues to rise (often by more than earlier projections). Backstop government funding of this "tail risk" could be an option to consider

---

[24]Annuities may provide payments either for the lifetime of the beneficiary or for a fixed term. In the United Kingdom, DC pension funds are required to provide 75 percent of pensions via lifetime annuities, and increasingly fewer insurers are willing to sell such products. In the United States, by contrast, most annuities are fixed-term, thus presenting fewer hedging challenges. For a broader discussion of the challenges in developing such markets, see Jackson, Perraudin, and Trivedi (forthcoming).

Box 3.2. Individuals' Life-Cycle Savings and Global Capital Markets

Aging is expected to have far-reaching implications for the global distribution of growth, labor, and capital. While aging is a global trend, there are large differences in its speed across countries and regions. These differences, combined with the reforms of numerous national pension systems, may have a significant impact on the overall supply of capital, the performance of capital markets, and international capital flows.

Life Cycle and Supply of Capital

According to the traditional life-cycle theory of consumption and savings, national savings rates are expected to decrease in an aging economy. To make up for lower income during retirement, individuals would save an increasing fraction of their income during their working life and dissave during retirement. This would result in a hump-shaped savings profile over a person's life (see the Figure).

Recent reforms toward multi-pillar pension systems are likely to validate this theory. For instance, in European countries with predominantly public PAYG systems (e.g., France, Germany, and Italy), no old age dissavings has been observed (indeed, intergenerational transfer of savings to younger relatives is taking place), whereas in the Netherlands and the United States, where a large share of retirement income is provided through private pension schemes, the hump-shaped life-cycle savings profile is evident. This suggests that reforms toward more balanced multi-pillar pension systems may induce both increased savings for retirement among European workers and a decline in savings rates at or near retirement.

The Potential Benefits of International Diversification

Investing pension assets internationally may be good not only for risk diversification but also to realize better returns. With the growth of funded pension plans and the removal in some cases of investment restrictions, increased attention has been paid to the international investment of retirement savings. Overlapping generations models applied to advanced

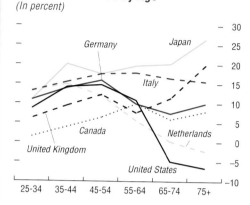

Estimated Personal Savings Rates for Selected Countries by Age[1]
(In percent)

Sources: Schieber (2003); and Börsch-Supan (2004).
[1]Ages are of the household head/reference person; and savings rate in each age group is for all households in their respective samples.

economies show that substantially higher aggregate savings rates can be expected in an open economy than in a closed economy. In a closed industrialized economy, an increase in national savings leads to a larger capital stock and to a decrease in the rate of return on capital, which acts to crowd out additional savings. In an open industrialized economy, more savings are generated as the rate of return does not change significantly. Indeed, research indicates that not only a country or region's absolute age structure (and thus capital supply) but relative differences in age structure across countries or regions are an important determinant of capital flows.[1]

However, the degree to which relative aging may determine capital flows will also depend on the international mobility of capital. In this regard, existing frictions, such as taxation or foreign investment limitations, together with investors "home bias," may limit the benefits of international diversification.

[1]See for example Higgins (1998), Reisen (2000), and Lührmann (2002).

if it avoids a greater Pillar 1 cost arising from a shortage of supply of annuities.

International diversification can help overcome national or regional market constraints and support macroeconomic savings patterns. National savings rates are likely to decline in aging societies, due to life-cycle effects. This may encourage greater investment of pension assets into the economies of younger, economically faster-growing countries or markets. Indeed, there is evidence that such international diversification not only provides benefits from risk diversification, but may also provide higher returns on capital (Box 3.2). This highlights the importance of pursuing regulatory efforts to eliminate domestic investment restrictions and promote improvements in risk management at pension funds.[25]

Taxation and Regulation

Regulatory and tax constraints on investment behavior and national funding rules significantly influence pension fund strategies. Among the rules set by a variety of bodies, tax rules tend to have the greatest influence on annual funding decisions by pension sponsors and on individuals with regard to retirement savings.

Taxation

In many cases, tax rules on pension contributions effectively set upper and lower bounds for funding decisions. This is the case in the United States, where contributions that would increase the funding level beyond a 100 percent funding ratio are not tax deductible, and even attract an additional 10 percent excise tax. At the same time, tax policies and penalties also aim to prevent large funding deficiencies, such as through the imposition of a tax of 100 percent of the deficiency in case of failure to correct it.

Taxation and other rules can create disincentives or prohibitions to annual contributions or the withdrawal of surplus assets, thereby further discouraging precautionary overfunding. In the United States, excess assets cannot be withdrawn by companies from pension schemes unless the scheme is terminated, and then up to a 50 percent duty plus standard corporation tax would need to be paid. Meanwhile, as noted above, the loss of annual deductibility and a 10 percent excise tax on contributions to overfunded schemes were driving factors behind the contribution holidays in the 1990s, and increase the potential risk of schemes becoming underfunded in the event of adverse market or other developments. Allowing more deductible (or at least not penalized) contributions, up to some reasonable overfunding limit (e.g., two or three years of "normal" contribution rates) would give sponsors and pension managers a greater ability to prudently plan for cyclical downturns.

Tax rules for savings products play a strong role in determining how individuals save (Box 3.3). Tax rules are generally designed to give preferential treatment to retirement savings, and as an incentive for individuals to start saving early. Indeed, if private savings are insufficient to ensure adequate old-age income in the long run, the cost of providing a safety net will ultimately fall on the government (via Pillar 1). As such, the fiscal cost of tax incentives for retirement savings may be viewed as preventative of potentially much larger costs that may be incurred later to support persons with inadequate pension savings.

However, it remains unclear whether tax incentives help raise overall pension savings, or merely shift existing savings. In particular, complex taxation regimes favoring certain types of pension plans may simply reallocate savings with little or no increase in the overall savings level. Empirical evidence is mixed, but

---

[25]See, for example, Schieber (2003) and Deutsche Bank Research (2003).

Box 3.3. The Tax Treatment of Pension Plans: a Comparison for Selected Industrial Countries

The tax treatment of pension plans in most OECD countries is broadly as follows (see the Table):

- *Contributions* by employees into approved pension schemes are deductible from the employees' taxable gross income (i.e., they are made before tax), and contributions by employers are deductible from the employer's earnings. In general, the total deductible contributions are limited to a maximum percentage of the employee's income.
- *Income* earned by approved pension funds from their investments is exempt from tax.
- *Pension income* received by individuals is normally subject to tax on the same basis as wages, and early distributions or distributions less than a minimum required level are both generally subject to additional taxes.

Tax systems usually treat qualified pension plans preferentially, with the net fiscal cost of these incentives varying widely in the countries shown in the Table. The fiscal cost is measured as the difference, over the length of the investment, between the amount of taxes collected when (a) the money is saved in a pension plan and (b) if it were invested in a benchmark non-retirement saving vehicle. Estimates for 2000 range from 1.7 percent of GDP in the United Kingdom and 1.5 percent in Switzerland, to 1.0 percent in the United States and the Netherlands, and 0.2 percent in Japan. However, the revenue forgone from tax incentives for private pensions remains a small fraction of the governments' spending on public pensions. In Germany, spending on public pensions was about 100 times larger than the forgone revenue from pension savings in 1997 (0.1 percent of GDP), while it was eight times in Japan, seven times in the Netherlands, six times in the United States, and three times in the United Kingdom.

However, poorly designed tax systems may result in simply substituting one form of savings for another, with little or no additional pension savings, and larger deadweight losses. Complex taxation regimes can generate distortions in favor of one type of pension plan versus another, or in favor of pension plans relative to other saving vehicles. There have been moves to simplify tax regimes and, in some countries, grant a single tax treatment for all types of occupational pension schemes. In France,

Tax Treatment of Pension Plans

Countries	Contributions	Fund Income	Pension Benefits	
			Annuities	Lump sum
France	T/PE[1]	E	T/PE	T/PE
Germany	T/PE	E	T	T/PE[2]
Italy	T/PE[3]	E	T/PE[4]	T/PE[5]
Japan	E	E	T/PE	T/PE
Netherlands	E	E	T	T
Switzerland	E	E	T	T
United Kingdom	T/PE	E	T	T/PE[6]
United States	T/E[7]	E	T/E[8]	T/E[8]

Source: OECD (2004b).

Legend: T = taxed; E = exempt or deductible; PE = partially exempt or deductible.

[1]Deductible up to 19 percent for up to 8 times the annual social security ceiling (€44,360 in 2003).

[2]Tax-free allowance of 40 percent of pension payments granted up to €3,072 at age 63 or higher.

[3]Tax exempt up to 2 percent of gross employee earnings.

[4]Taxed only for 87.5 percent of their gross amount.

[5]Taxable base limited to the part over the employee's contribution to the fund.

[6]Tax-free lump sum of up to 25 percent of fund value.

[7]Exemption up to $12,000 for 401(k) plans (employees) and up to 3 percent of employee compensation (employers matching dollar for dollar contributions). Contributions to Roth IRA are not tax deductible.

[8]Income from Roth IRA is tax exempt.

pension reforms have set up a new legal framework for all private retirement savings (Pillars 2 and 3), consisting of an annual global tax deduction. The same global approach, encompassing Pillars 2 and 3, has been introduced in Germany, but the complexity of tax incentives and savings subsidies is inhibiting the take-up of retirement savings products.

While an important goal of tax incentives targeting occupational pension funds and other retirement saving is to raise the level of national savings, empirical evidence in this regard is mixed. In general, studies have found a minimal impact of occupational pension plans on national savings. However, many methodological issues affect the reliability of the results. A recent survey (OECD, 2004b) finds that about 60 to 75 percent of savings in tax-favored pension vehicles simply displaces other savings. Some studies also indicate participation rates in pension schemes are affected by taxes. A U.S. study (Reagan and Turner, 2000) found that a 1 percentage point increase in marginal tax rates leads to a 0.4 percentage point increase in the proportion of full-time employees participating in a pension plan.

a recent survey (OECD, 2004b) finds that about 60 to 75 percent of savings in tax-favored vehicles represent a reallocation from other savings (see Box 3.3).[26] Even such a reallocation of savings, however, may be beneficial in encouraging retirement planning if it represents a shift from short-term to longer-term and more stable savings.

Regulation

Supervision of pension funds traditionally has been conducted by bodies primarily concerned with labor and benefits, rather than financial markets. Thus, to date much of pension fund regulation has focused on the protection of pensioner and employee rights, and ensuring that pension fund assets are segregated for the benefit of employees, rather than reviewing the risks and long-term dynamic process of assessing whether the obligations will be met. Nevertheless, pension regulators often set minimum funding requirements and, in some cases, restrict certain investments or asset holdings, and thus influence investment behavior.

The choice of the discount rate for minimum funding requirements heavily influences pension fund asset allocation strategies.[27] Pension fund managers wishing to limit the volatility of their regulatory funding ratio may hold a larger allocation of assets with a high correlation to the discount rate used for liabilities. Corporate bond yields are increasingly used by regulators as the discount rate for liabilities, and this should increase pension funds' demand for credit instruments. In the United Kingdom, discount rates based on inflation-linked yields stimulated growing demand for such products. In the late 1990s, a shift to government yields, at a time of shrinking government debt supply, led to very low (and at times quite volatile) yields on

these instruments. The more recent move to AA corporate bond yields provides a wider range of potential issuers for investment and hedging purposes, and removed the regulatorily driven pressure on government yields.

In the United States, the discount rate for funding calculations has been temporarily amended to a corporate bond rate, in an effort to provide short-term relief to underfunded plans. For two years, the discount rate used to determine DB scheme liabilities and sponsor companies' required contributions (as well as their PBGC premiums) will be a four-year weighted average of long-term high-grade corporate bond yields, replacing the 30-year U.S. treasury bond yield. In addition, certain industries (for example, steel and airlines) benefit from specific financial support—for instance, only 20 percent of annual contributions that would be otherwise required to address underfunded situations are to be contributed each year, thus spreading out the required increased payments— (Federal Deposit Insurance Corporation, 2004).

Regulations also influence asset allocation through "prudent person" rules and formal limits on certain investments. In many countries, regulators explicitly restrict the range of investment options by imposing quantitative investment limits, usually by asset class (Yermo, 2003). Although some countries continue to place upper limits, for instance, on investments in foreign securities, regulatory constraints on pension fund allocations rarely act as a major constraint on investments today.[28] The "prudent person" rules generally establish a principle of "diligence that a prudent person acting in a like capacity would use" (Galer, 2002). Fear of liability under those rules can lead fund managers to invest in portfolios that are substantially similar to their peers, and

---

[26]OECD (2004b).

[27]See, for example, Blake (2001).

[28]In the past (as described earlier), Japanese restrictions on allocations both to equities and to foreign securities acted as a strong constraint on pension fund allocation strategies, but these were abolished in 1997.

therefore can constrain pension funds from developing innovative or new approaches, and quite possibly from developing more modern risk management approaches. It can also induce herd behavior, and thereby introduce more volatility to capital markets.

Historically, many industry observers described pension fund regulation as unsophisticated in dealing with solvency and risk management, but there are signs of change. The regulatory factors mentioned above do not deal explicitly with the risk of investment portfolios. They often focus, in a more limited way, on the current level of funding, and are based on a variety of qualitative assumptions about future performance, and not on the risks inherent in the pension fund's asset-liability mix. However, some regulators are beginning to take a more sophisticated approach to evaluating the risk profile of pensions. In the Netherlands, a combined regulator has been established for insurers and pension funds, the *Pensioen & Verzekeringskamer* (PVK), and its merger with the banking regulator is expected to be formally completed in January 2005. PVK is importing many of the risk principles and measures applied to financial institutions into its pension supervision (Box 3.4). In addition, pension guarantee funds, like the PBGC or the Pension Protection Fund (PPF) being developed in the United Kingdom, are considering taking account of portfolio risks in the premiums they establish for individual pension plans. The developments essentially act to introduce risk-based capital or funding requirements to the pension system.

Initial steps have been proposed to establish international minimum standards for pension regulation. The OECD (2004a) recently issued *Core Principles of Occupational Pension Regulation*. While rather general in scope, they have proposed principles relating to, among other things, full funding of pension schemes and the enhancement of portability. We encourage further progress to apply and develop principles such as these.

Pension Guarantee Funds

The social objective of encouraging and protecting private pension savings has also led to the creation of pension guarantee or insurance funds. Guarantee funds are intended to diversify the risk of pension fund failures among the general population of pension plans, and should eliminate or (at least) reduce the potential cost to the government, if it were to act as the ultimate safety net for pensions. Guarantee funds are likely to increase in importance, as more countries look to increase the role of private pensions. The United States (PBGC), Germany *(Pensions Sicherungs Verein)*, and Switzerland (the Guarantee Fund) have long-standing insurance funds, and the United Kingdom is looking to establish such a fund (PPF).

However, this insurance protection may create other risks, depending on how guarantee funds are designed or operate. Most importantly, guarantee funds may generate moral hazard, to the extent they lead weaker sponsors to increase investment risk in the pension fund in the hope of reducing or limiting contributions. In the United States, for example, PBGC "risk-based" premiums relate only to the degree of underfunding and do not take into account the asset mix or liability structure. In addition, if a guarantee fund's own investment portfolio tends to have a similar asset mix as that of the covered pension funds, then the guarantee fund may be experiencing difficulties when claims from distressed pension funds are greatest. This may be exacerbated if pension funds tend to become underfunded when sponsor companies face more difficult business conditions (i.e., cyclical).[29]

[29]These challenges are illustrated by the PBGC, whose deficit reached a trough of over $11 billion at the end of its 2003 financial year, after having a surplus of $10 billion in 2000.

Box 3.4. Proposed Risk-Based Capital System for Pension Funds in the Netherlands

A proposed redesign of pension fund supervision in the Netherlands aims to ensure that pension funds remain fully funded at almost all times. Strict rules are being proposed for the rebuilding of funding levels in pre-specified timescales, either by increasing funding or reducing the indexation of benefits. Pursuant to the proposal, three parallel funding tests would be applied:

- *a minimum test*, requiring pension funds to maintain a minimum 105 percent funding ratio, even if their assets and liabilities are perfectly matched;
- *a continuity test*, requiring pension funds with conditional indexation clauses to have a long-term plan to meet their conditional goals during the next 15 years; and
- *a solvency test*, reflecting the composition of the fund's assets.

The solvency test, in particular, would introduce an innovative risk-based capital framework for pension funds. The risk parameters would be set so as to guarantee at a 97.5 percent confidence level that the funding ratio will stay above 105 percent over one year (taking account of expected contributions and expenses during the year). In other words, the funding ratio for funds meeting this requirement would only be expected to fall below 105 percent once every 40 years.[1] If the funding ratio fell below the risk-based floor, the fund would be granted a period of 15 years to address this gap (either through increased contributions or reduced investment risk). This risk component is meant to provide, like Basel II, a standard risk measure set by the supervisor, or alternatively allow funds (where appropriate) to use their own risk models and capital calculations.[2]

For the standard calculation, assets would be marked-to-market, and liabilities measured with a "market" yield curve. The discount rate would be set according to the duration of liabilities, and may reflect a government yield curve. The volatility parameters for assets would be based on a long-term historical run of data, reflecting the long-run orientation of pension funds. Liability measures also are expected to assume further increases in longevity (e.g., a two-year lengthening of average life spans).

Companies would also be required to state whether they have a "conditional" or "unconditional" inflation-indexation policy for pensions. If the policy is unconditional, the 105 percent regulatory floor would need to be against inflation-linked liabilities. However, if the policy is conditional, liabilities need only be measured in nominal terms. Since most pension funds seem to have opted for this conditional form, benefit commitments would generally be assured in nominal terms, and indexation would be contingent on investment performance or a company's willingness (but not legal commitment) to increase contributions. This requirement is viewed as a means to communicate the risk and protections provided to pension beneficiaries.

Overall, the proposed rules will give pension funds multiple hedging goals. Such a regulatory framework will lead pension funds to view asset-liability management (ALM) as an exercise in hedging both nominal liabilities (to meet their supervisory funding floor) and, possibly, real liabilities (to meet a conditional indexation goal, if retained). Which of these aims is more important will depend on their funding position. Weaker pension funds may begin hedging with bonds and abandon an indexation goal, while stronger funds, operating above their risk-based capital floor, may continue to target higher real returns, using greater amounts of equities and index-linked bonds, where available. However, many funds are expected to pursue a mixed approach, holding nominal bonds to meet their 105 percent liability floor, and investing the surplus in riskier assets in order to possibly achieve indexation goals. While Dutch pension funds currently tend to hold diversified portfolios (with a typical portfolio consisting of 50 percent equities, 40 percent bonds and loans, and 10 percent real estate and other investments), some funds have already reduced their equity allocations and sought to increase the duration of fixed-income assets to meet the proposed supervisory framework. However, to date such portfolio changes have not been widespread.

[1]Although the exact parameters have yet to be established, the supervisor estimates that a fund invested 50/50 in bonds and equities, and with a typical bond duration profile of five years, could be expected to have a minimum risk-based capital requirement of 130 percent of projected liabilities.

[2]The supervisor expects about 10 to 20 of the largest pension funds to apply internal models, and others to use the standard measures.

We support the inclusion of more risk-based elements in the design of guarantee funds. Risk-based premiums are being considered in the United Kingdom that may (at a minimum) take account of the investment or market risk in pension fund portfolios. More generally, risk-based premiums could be based on various criteria, including funding levels (based on accumulated benefit obligations, or ABOs, which seem particularly appropriate for an insurance fund), asset composition, liability structure (e.g., average maturity or duration), and degree of asset/liability matching of the pension fund.

Finally, whether and how guarantee funds or regulators should take account of the sponsor company's financial strength remains an open question. In principle, the cash flow and balance sheet strength of the sponsor company should play a role in determining the pension fund's ability to meet its liabilities. However, in practice, the great diversity of companies across a wide range of industries would make the evaluation of their financial strength an even more difficult task for supervisors than they currently face for single industries, such as banking or insurance. Moreover, the deterioration of a pension plan's funding level and/or an increase in its holding of "risky" assets may reflect its own ability (or not) to support the pension fund, and therefore these criteria may satisfy the supervisory need to set objective risk-based premiums.

Accounting

Accounting is frequently cited as the most important factor affecting pension fund management, and the shift from DB to DC or hybrid schemes.[30] Pension obligations can introduce volatility in the sponsor company's financial statements, depending on how they are measured and recorded. Indeed, industry observers frequently assess that a move to market-based, fair value accounting principles would significantly increase the shift away from DB pension plans and may encourage greater short-term trading and investment styles.

Current Practices

In most jurisdictions, the impact of short-term pension gains and losses on the financial accounts of sponsor companies are smoothed over several periods. Historically, a variety of smoothing practices have been applied to various components of a pension sponsor's financial statements, including investment returns (actual against expected), and actuarial gains and losses (i.e., changes in liability values). The current international accounting standard (IAS 19) and national accounting standards in most of continental Europe, Japan, and the United States incorporate various smoothing mechanisms (see Box 3.5).

Another important accounting principle is the choice of the discount rate used to measure pension liabilities.[31] This rate has a significant influence on the measurement of the obligation, as a higher rate reduces the present value of pension obligations. Indeed, some analysts have suggested that the rate selected or movements in rates have a greater influence on pension fund balance sheets than asset performance, given the typically long average duration of liabilities. Some jurisdictions have allowed the same discount rate to be used for liabilities as for expected returns on assets, thus further smoothing the impact of market movements (such as the projected yield on equities). However, in accordance with IAS 19, many jurisdictions now require a rate approximating a high-quality (AA or equivalent) corporate bond yield. In other countries, like Germany, the discount

---

[30]See, for example, CIEBA (2004).

[31]The discount rate used in the financial accounts is not always the same as the discount rate used for regulatory purposes.

Box 3.5. Comparison of U.S. FAS 87, U.K. FRS 17, and Proposed IAS Standards

Approaches to pension accounting differ significantly across countries. The differences largely relate to the degree to which the accounting permits smoothing in consideration of uncertainties associated with pension-related costs and obligations, the subjective and complex process of estimating the obligations, and the long-term nature of the obligation. This box compares three pension accounting regimes, namely, U.S. FAS 87, U.K. FRS 17 (to be fully implemented in January 2005), and proposed IAS requirements (IAS 19, effective January 2005).

How Pension Assets and Obligations Are Measured and Presented in Corporate Balance Sheets

Under all three regimes, the sponsor company recognizes pension obligations net of pension assets. However, in measuring pension assets and liabilities, the U.S. regime (FAS 87) allows more smoothing than FRS 17. Both IAS 19 and FAS 87 permit amortization of unrecognized gains or losses over the remaining working life of active employees, but also permit more rapid, and even immediate, recognition. Under IAS 19 and FRS 17, pension assets are measured by market values. Under FAS 87, pension assets are measured at either market value or a calculated value that recognizes changes in fair value over not more than five years (referred to as "market-related value"). Under all three regimes, liabilities are measured by the projected benefit obligation (PBO). PBO measures obligations on the assumption that the plan remains a going concern, and so is meant to capture the impact of future wage increases and unvested benefits, actuarial assumptions, and discount rates determined as of the current measurement date. Pension liabilities, under FAS 87, are measured based on the PBO with a requirement to recognize an additional minimum liability if the accumulated benefit obligation (ABO), which represents essentially a liquidation value, exceeds the fair value of plan assets; both the ABO and PBO amounts are disclosed in the notes to the financial statements.

If there is a net surplus in the pension fund, the sponsor company may record all or part of it as an asset. While FAS 87 sets no explicit limit on the amount that may be recognized, IAS 19 and U.K. FRS 17 limit it to the amount that would be recoverable by the sponsor through a refund or a reduction of future contributions.

Regarding the discount rate to be applied to pension liabilities, IAS 19 prescribes yields of high-quality corporate bonds; U.S. FAS 87 gives a choice of either high-quality corporate bonds or insurance annuity rates; and U.K. FRS 17 recommends AA or equivalent corporate bond yields.

Smoothing Principles in the Profit and Loss Account

In general, when evaluating pension fund investment results, sponsors may take a long-term view by smoothing short-term performance volatility. For this purpose, IAS 19 and U.S. FAS 87 reflect expected returns rather than actual returns on pension assets. The difference between actual and expected returns is subject to amortization in future periods, or at times may be entirely deferred if it does not exceed a minimum threshold. The rate of expected return reflects each company's view about the future performance of its pension portfolio.

Under IAS 19 and U.S. FAS 87, smoothing also exists in actuarial gains and losses (i.e., projected liabilities), which are also amortized and reflected in earnings over future periods. If the difference between actual and expected returns, together with other actuarial gains or losses, is within a range of 10 percent of the higher of plan assets or liabilities (the "corridor"), the amount is not required to be amortized. Under IAS 19 and FAS 87, plan sponsors may elect a systematic method of amortization that must be applied consistently (see the Table).

The United Kingdom's FRS 17 also uses expected returns; however, the differences between expected and actual returns, as well as actuarial gains and losses, are recognized in the period in which they are incurred in a separate *Statement of Total Recognized Gains and Losses* (STRGL). Use of the separate account, instead

Important Differences in the Three Accounting Standards

	IAS 19	U.S. FAS 87	U.K. FRS 17
Measurement of pension obligations	Projected Benefit Obligations (PBO).	PBO. Accumulated Benefit Obligations (ABO) (minimum recognition): PBO and ABO are reported in the notes to the financial statements.	PBO.
Measurement of pension plan assets	Fair market value: no smoothing allowed.	Market-related value: companies are permitted to use fair market value or a calculated value that smoothes up to five years for purposes of determining the asset value for use in the return on assets and 10 percent corridor computation. The value of assets disclosed in the notes is the fair market value.	Fair market value: no smoothing allowed.
Smoothing of gains or losses in earnings statements	Unamortized past service costs are amortized over the remaining service period. Actuarial gains or losses within a "corridor" may be ignored (the higher of 10 percent of the present value of the obligation or 10 percent of the market value of assets). Actual gains or losses over a "corridor" may be amortized over the remaining working life of active employees (immediate recognition is permitted).	Unamortized past service costs are amortized over the remaining service period. Actuarial gains or losses within a "corridor" may be ignored (the higher of 10 percent of the present value of the obligation or 10 percent of the market-related value assets). Actual gains or losses over a "corridor" may be amortized. The minimum required amortization is based on the remaining working life of active employees.	Unamortized past service costs are amortized over the period in which the benefits vest. The difference between actuarial gains, losses, and adjustments is recognized in the period incurred in a separate note in the financial statement (STRGL), i.e., not smoothed.
How future investment returns are calculated	Long-term estimates of expected returns.	Long-term estimates of expected returns.	Long-term estimates of expected returns. However, the difference between expected and actual returns is recorded in STRGL.

Sources: Standard & Poor's (2003); and Financial Accounting Standards Board.

of direct reporting in the profit-and-loss statement, is an attempt to avoid introducing excessive volatility into headline income figures. Recently, the IASB has issued a proposal on the possible introduction of a separate account to allow companies to report the annual cost (with or without smoothing). It should be noted that IASB and U.S. FAS 87 also allow immediate recognition of the difference between actual and expected returns at the company's option.

rate is fixed by the authorities and only rarely adjusted.

Recent Trends

The trend among standard setters is toward limiting the scope for pension fund smoothing, by introducing more market sensitive or fair value principles. The United Kingdom is moving toward a fair value approach with the introduction (to be completed in 2005) of a new accounting rule (FRS 17). Under this rule, although the "headline" profit and loss account continues to show the actuarial version of pension gains and losses, the unsmoothed mark-to-market version of the gains and losses are shown in a separate *Statement of Total Recognized Gains and Losses* (Box 3.5). The International Accounting Standards Board (IASB) has also introduced changes in its pension accounting standards that will permit reporting according to fair value principles in a form similar to the United Kingdom—EU countries agreed to adopt IAS 19 in January 2005.

In many jurisdictions, steps are also being taken to ensure greater disclosure of a pension fund's financial condition. Pension liabilities are increasingly reflected like other debt obligations of the sponsor company. Japan began recording pension liabilities as debt obligations of the sponsor in 2000—previously Japanese companies were required only to recognize annual contributions as an expense in the profit and loss account. This move has forced many small and medium-sized enterprises to terminate their pension plans due to the sudden reporting of large funding gaps in their balance sheets.

Potential Impact

The use of fair value accounting principles would address the arbitrariness that characterizes traditional pension fund accounting practices. It is widely recognized that the various smoothing mechanisms used in the accounting for pension plans introduce an arbitrary and inconsistent application of current accounting standards, which some argue substantially limits the usefulness of financial reports. In particular, the use of subjective assumptions, which frequently vary between companies, may hamper comparative analysis, and the financial risks borne by the sponsor companies may be underestimated (Shilling, 2003).

However, it is also argued that by generating greater volatility in sponsor companies'

balance sheets, fair value accounting principles may misrepresent (i.e., over- and under-state) a pension fund's financial condition and accelerate the shift away from DB plans. Recent experience in the United Kingdom indicates that fair value principles may accelerate moves to DC and hybrid plans, which allow companies to reduce their risk concerning pension obligations and transfer investment and market volatility to employees/beneficiaries. Similar effects can be seen in Japan and the United States. Greater sensitivity to market price volatility may also in the future encourage fund managers to focus on short-term asset management strategies, or alternatively to seek to immunize themselves from short-term accounting volatility by reallocating their portfolios from equities to bonds.

Rating Agencies

Rating agencies now explicitly recognize the underfunded amount of pension plans as debt of the sponsor company. The rating agencies treat the difference between the PBO and the fair value of plan assets like any other long-term debt obligation of the sponsor company,[32] and use various adjustors to unwind some of the smoothing introduced by current pension accounting practices.[33] This shift in ratings analysis has resulted in several ratings downgrades at least partly based on pension issues, particularly in continental Europe. Such actions often affect companies in older industries, with an aging workforce and/or a perceived weaker cash-flow strength or financial flexibility. Increased attention to the rating impact of pension funding levels seems also a factor in the shift from DB plans to DC and hybrid schemes.

Recently, some rating agencies have started to make explicit statements regarding pension investment strategies, giving greater support

---

[32]By accepting a portion of their compensation on a deferred basis, employees essentially become creditors of the sponsor company.
[33]See, for example, Moody's Investors Service (2003).

to fixed-income pension assets. Fixed-income assets are seen as providing greater security to beneficiaries—at the expense of higher returns. Most simply, based on this view, the more closely a pension's projected obligations are matched with a portfolio of high-quality fixed-income securities, the greater its ability to meet its liabilities as they fall due. While this analysis seems sound, the ability to achieve such asset/liability matching is difficult, and the availability of market securities may be lacking.

Asset Allocation and Risk Management

The ultimate purpose of pension schemes is to meet their committed future pension liabilities. The fund manager's duty is to manage the fund for the benefit of the plan members in order to meet those liabilities, rather than to earn an excess return. Given the liabilities' generally long-term structure, this implies a long-term focus to investment. A number of risks need to be managed as part of the ALM process, including the duration of both assets and liabilities, inflation, longevity, and the ability of the sponsor company to meet future contribution needs. Challenges and constraints also arise, such as those concerning the availability of appropriate financial instruments, the impact of pension fund performance on the sponsor company's accounts, and the general desire to keep the level of contributions down.

Asset Allocation

There is no consensus among pension and investment experts on the appropriate asset allocation for DB or hybrid pension funds. Although there are many different approaches to investment management for pensions, asset allocation approaches generally fall into one of three different styles.

Primarily Equity-Based

Many in the pension fund industry favor a portfolio consisting primarily of equities, largely because they believe that in the long run the extra return from equities will outweigh the short-term volatility. In their view, although equity returns can be volatile in the short run, equities are much more likely over the long-term average life of pension liabilities to outperform bonds, and thereby reduce contributions or allow for increased benefits. Accordingly, they also generally oppose "fair value" accounting methods, arguing that it does not reflect the long-term nature of pensions or pension investment.

Many advocates of this position also view equities as a better inflation hedge than nominal bonds, and that, given the lack of supply of long-dated bonds, equities are a more practical way to match the duration of pension liabilities. Equities are seen by some as a good inflation hedge because their value reflects future expected profits, and hence may be seen as likely to rise with future wage and price growth in the long term. Some also argue that equities have a much longer duration than bonds, because their dividends represent a stream of cash flows with no final maturity or because their price movements can be quite large in response to interest rate movements.[34] This would imply that they could be useful as a hedge for long-term liabilities. On the other hand, other market analysts find the correlation between equities and bonds is often weak, or too variable over time, to be relied upon as a duration hedge. The equity market fall in 2000–02, which effectively implied negative duration of equities for that period, was the largest two-year fall in major markets since the Great Depression, leading some to reduce their equity allocations. Nevertheless, supporters of an equity-based strategy argue that the high returns of the 1990s outweigh the two years of losses.

[34]For instance, Standard & Poor's (2004b) have estimated a current duration of 15 years for the U.S. equity market.

Primarily Bond-Based

A recent body of opinion favors a portfolio based wholly or primarily on fixed-income securities. The argument is that, as a pension fund's liabilities form a future stream of payment obligations that closely resemble a portfolio of bond payments, a bond portfolio can best provide the certainty that the pension fund will meet its liabilities as they fall due. At the same time, sponsor companies should not seek or accept additional business, leverage, or investment risks through their pension fund. Shareholders, it is argued, do not desire this additional market exposure. If shareholders seek a diversified portfolio of this type, they can more efficiently build one themselves.

Many companies indicated that they would consider moving to a much larger bond allocation if their funding ratio rebounded to 100 percent or more. The most publicized example of this strategy has been the U.K. retail firm Boots, which moved to a 100 percent bond allocation in 2001. However, the company has more recently announced that it intends to invest up to 15 percent in other assets, to better match very long-dated liabilities, which extend beyond 35 years, and for which it is not possible to purchase equivalent-duration bonds. A few other employers (in various countries) have also moved to a more bond-based investment strategy. However, many companies are reluctant to make significant short-term contributions or switch to currently highly priced fixed-income instruments given their current weak funding levels.

A "Balanced" Portfolio, with Bonds, Equities, and Other Assets

Some pension funds, and their consultants, argue that a diversified investment portfolio composed of a variety of asset classes offers the best way to balance risk and return. Pension fund managers supporting a balanced portfolio approach often also favor certain "alternative investments" (such as private equity, real estate, commodities, and more recently hedge funds) in addition to bonds

and equities (Greenwich Associates, 2003). Fund managers may employ the balanced approach to seek to enhance return through active management of a variety of asset classes, while diversifying risk and perhaps matching near-term cash flows. Such an investment policy has also been attractive to funds (for instance in Switzerland or, historically, the Netherlands) that measured their liabilities with a relatively fixed discount rate and therefore had a fixed asset return target, or managed the assets against benchmark indices rather than against liabilities. The relatively small domestic markets in the Netherlands and Switzerland have also led funds in these jurisdictions to diversify internationally.

A vigorous debate is currently taking place in the pension fund industry on the merits of these different approaches. The debate on these different strategies is also closely related to discussions regarding broader risk management, and accounting and regulatory issues. To illustrate some of the arguments regarding the relative merits of bonds and equities, two U.K. market analysts whom we met during the preparation of this study agreed to provide short pieces on their differing analyses. These are presented in Boxes 3.6 and 3.7.

Policymakers need not take a view on optimal asset allocation, but should ensure that decisions are guided by appropriate risk management practices. Given the long-term nature of pension provision, some asset and liability risks certainly are being taken. These risks need to be understood and assessed by fund managers, and appropriate safety margins encouraged through risk management strategies (e.g., a prudent level of overfunding). Policymakers can encourage this through regulation and tax policy.

Risk Management

There is great variation in the sophistication of pension fund management. Some of the largest funds commit considerable staff and other resources to internal trading capacity,

Box 3.6. Defined Benefit (DB) Pensions and Corporate Finance Theory

Shareholders Are the End Risk Bearers

Default scenarios aside, shareholders in a corporation bear the asset versus liability risk within its pension plan (with gains or losses in assets reflected in adjustments to the contribution rate). Shareholders should therefore be broadly indifferent to the following three options: holding equities (say) within the DB pension plan of the company they invest in; holding equities of other firms directly on the balance sheet of the corporation; or holding these equities in the shareholders' personal portfolios. This analysis is similar in principle to the Modigliani and Miller (1958) indifference proposition. Furthermore, as with the Modigliani and Miller proposition, despite the apparent indifference at first sight, factors such as tax and frictional costs are the key to understanding optimal structures in practice.

Arguments in Favor of Matching

Among the reasons why a shareholder should prefer the assets and liabilities of a pension plan to be closely matched are:
• The company reduces the likelihood that financial losses in the pension plan disrupt the core business activity.
• The actions of management are more easily monitored and the scope for internal cash windfalls being lost or misallocated is reduced.
• Internal and third party management costs and fees are minimized.
The cost of defined benefit obligations cannot be reduced by investing in equities except in so far as the value of the benefits to plan members are reduced, by increasing default risk. Overall,

Note: This box was prepared by Jon Exley of Mercer Investment Consulting.

shareholders can only gain by this if they can avoid the policy rebounding in the form of higher wage costs, adverse publicity, or government responses (e.g., restrictions on corporate activity).

Defined Benefit Liabilities Can Be Matched by Using Nominal or Inflation-Linked Bonds (or Swaps)

Debate over the close matching of DB liabilities often focuses unnecessarily on the link with future salaries. However, few would disagree that the accumulated benefit obligation (ABO) can be very closely matched with bonds without taking a view on future salaries, and, in fact, there are strong arguments in favor of viewing the ABO as the economic liability, on the grounds that increases in the liability due to future salary increases accrue only when the increases are awarded (see, for example, Exley, Mehta, and Smith, 1997). Valuing and hedging of the ABO with bonds thus forms the basis of a practical risk management approach.

Even if we consider projected benefit obligations (PBOs), in many plans the proportion of liabilities linked to future salary increases (and the duration of the linkage, which does not usually extend beyond retirement) may in practice be quite small. Furthermore, to the extent that liabilities are regarded as linked to future wages, the empirical evidence for a link between equities and salary growth is weak (see Smith, 1998), as is the economic justification. (Even if a link existed between aggregate corporate earnings and wages, this does not necessarily imply a link between earnings per share and wages per employee.) More practically, no proposed links have met the acid test of a workable hedging algorithm. Although less accurate than the ABO hedge, inflation-linked bonds also provide the best hedge for the salary-related element of a PBO liability.

risk analysis, and/or the management of external fund managers. In other cases, medium-sized (and some larger) funds have only a handful of employees to evaluate benefit obligations and determine asset allocation, and often have delegated much of the detailed work to consultants and external managers.

Box 3.7. Economics and Pension Fund Asset Allocation

The issue of asset allocation and pension funds has broad economic significance and raises important questions of long-run economic and financial relationships. In particular, it raises the question of whether a defined benefit (DB) pension scheme that is open and operated on an ongoing basis ought to be 100 percent invested in bonds, as some practitioners have proposed, or whether equities should play a substantial role, as is the case in most pension fund portfolios.

Salaries, profits, and dividends are all relatively stable components of GDP. As such, the established view has been that equities ought to be a good hedge against salary-linked liabilities (e.g., Black, 1989, in the United States and Blake, 2001, in the United Kingdom). Advocates of bond investments question this. Some have even suggested that the negative correlation of the two series shown in the first Figure means that claims on profits, such as equities, were not a good match for salaries (Exley, Mehta, and Smith, 1997). However, if the data are displayed in nominal terms over time (as in the second Figure), the relationship becomes clearer. To understand whether investment in equities should form a standard part of a pension fund's portfolio, the correct approach is to consider whether changes in the value of future salaries are correlated with changes in the value of future profits. Using rolling 25-year windows, Giles (2004) demonstrated that the correlation between changes in the present values of future profits and salaries was in excess of 80 percent. That is, holding a profit-linked security, like equities, would have been a highly effective hedge for salary-linked liabilities over the period.

Further arguments put forward in support of the proposition that funds should be 100 percent invested in bonds are also difficult to sustain:

• Pension funds should hedge expected projected benefit obligations (PBOs), and not merely the contractually certain accumulated

Note: This box was prepared by Tim Giles of Charles River Associates.

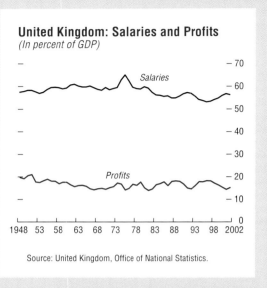

United Kingdom: Salaries and Profits
(In percent of GDP)

Source: United Kingdom, Office of National Statistics.

benefit obligations (ABOs). In general, firms hedge because future prices are *not* contractually certain. Companies and pension funds that are operated as going concerns are concerned with *expected* liabilities, not just those that are contractually certain. This has fundamental significance when it comes to asset allocation.

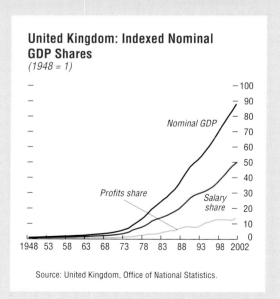

United Kingdom: Indexed Nominal GDP Shares
(1948 = 1)

Source: United Kingdom, Office of National Statistics.

- Unless salaries are completely diversifiable or deterministic, an economic valuation would not rely on a bond rate. An economically important variable, such as salary levels, will be highly correlated with systematic risk. The appropriate discount rate is likely to be close to the firm's overall discount rate or, if that is unknown, the weighted average return on all asset classes rather than a bond rate.
- It is futile to promote the superiority of an asset allocation policy if it is based on securities that are not available in sufficient quantity. When considering the matching of future salary obligations, 100 percent bond proponents suggest that pension funds should invest in index-linked bonds—in spite of the lack of supply. They simply make the assumption that governments or even corporations will alleviate the scarcity of index-linked bonds by issuing more. However, there is no obvious fundamental incentive for either to do so.

Accordingly, it is possible that the market for index-linked liabilities could expand in the face of increased demand from pension funds but, in all likelihood, this would be at an equilibrium price that reflects an excess of demand over supply.

The Capital Asset Pricing Model (CAPM) and its extensions tell us that the notional "average investor" should hold a portfolio equivalent in its risk/return characteristics to the "market" of all assets. Pension funds do have peculiar characteristics, particularly DB schemes. Therefore, asset allocations may deviate from the market portfolio. It has not yet been demonstrated, however, that the difference between the average risk-reward trade-off, and that of pension fund members or sponsors, is sufficiently stark to justify a 100 percent bond portfolio. In fact, the available evidence supports the widely held view that equities are an important component of the portfolios of open DB pension funds.

Consultants have a significant influence over pension fund management. Many pension funds rely upon and commission their risk analysis to be done by external consultants. In addition, the corporate governance structure of pension funds, with the overall direction set by trustees or a benefits committee, which may have limited expertise on investment matters, leads to considerable reliance on consultants for expert advice. Nevertheless, consultants often seem reluctant to propose substantial changes in ALM strategies or portfolio composition, particularly if it would strongly deviate from their previous advice or with consensus industry practices. Therefore, historically pension fund strategies have been quite stable, but the reliance on consensus presents some risk of herding within the industry, and may retard the development of newer risk management practices.

Financial and risk management practices within pension funds still focus much more

on the asset than the liability side of the balance sheet. This is a distinct difference from insurance companies, which traditionally placed much greater focus on liability risk rather than asset risk, as described in the April 2004 GFSR. With pension funds, this partly reflects the fact that assets are more easily adjustable (particularly in the short term) than pension liabilities. The stronger emphasis on assets also reflects the greater difficulty in recalculating liabilities than assets, with full actuarial recalculations typically only performed once every three years and partial updates (reviewing assumptions such as inflation, discount rates, and prospective investment returns) only once a year. As such, there is a tendency for funds to regard the value of liabilities as fixed between actuarial revaluations, and this has created much less focus on liability risk.

Therefore, many pension funds measure asset performance against broad market indices rather than against the underlying liabilities. But the focus on such indices may distract managers' attention from the real goal (i.e., to ensure funds are managed to meet liabilities as they fall due), and may further increase the risk of herding. Moreover, in some jurisdictions, this passive investment style also led pension fund managers to pursue very short-term investment strategies, including chasing yesterday's attractive markets and returns.

Greater focus on ALM and risk management practices needs to be encouraged. There has been increased use of ALM by some pension funds, driven partly by the "perfect storm" of recent years, but also by greater sensitivity to market values and movements through new accounting standards and market-related discount rates for liabilities. Some of the more sophisticated pension funds have begun to use risk management techniques from other areas of finance, instead of a focus primarily on actuarial methods. Even if liabilities are recalculated infrequently, these funds now may employ stochastic approaches such as Monte Carlo simulations to study a variety of different scenarios and their impact on both the asset and liability side of the pension balance sheet. But there is much still to be done to encourage and employ ALM techniques more broadly in the pension industry.

Several types of risks must be addressed in the pension ALM process. Pension fund liabilities can vary through structural changes in the workforce, the longevity of pensioners, future salary increases for workers, and the indexation of payments to prices or wages. Structural changes in the workforce are hard to hedge through the asset portfolio. However, annuities can hedge longevity risk, and salary and inflation-protected pension benefits may be in large part hedged by index-linked bonds.

Index-linked securities may be very useful for risk management but, as noted, the supply of such instruments and their role in pension portfolios have been limited to date. Their limited use in portfolios partly reflects the limited indexation of pension obligations in some countries, and funding methodologies that do not fully reflect changes in inflation expectations. Of course, the current low real yields available on index-linked securities (especially since most of the supply is of government debt) may also limit demand. But changes in accounting and regulatory principles could increase demand, and this could in turn stimulate increased supply from a wider range of issuers, including corporates.

A modest allocation to alternative investments may also play a useful role in pension fund portfolios. Currently, many pension funds have alternative investment allocations of around 10 to 15 percent, primarily in private equity and real estate. Hedge funds are also being increasingly considered, although (despite some media reports) aggregate amounts invested, or reasonably expected to be invested in the immediate future, remain modest, and few pension funds have made allocations to hedge funds above 5 to 10 percent of their investment portfolio.[35]

Increased international investment brings challenges as well as benefits for risk management. As described earlier, international investments may provide both diversification and higher returns. However, they will also require a greater focus on currency risks and credit risks to a wider range of countries, borrowers, and instruments, as well as broader progress on addressing obstacles to international capital mobility.

Pension funds should be free to choose their desired asset mix, within the bounds of prudent and (ideally) risk-based funding principles. A degree of overfunding can provide a prudent cushion against the risk of market

---

[35]See, for example, Astérias (2002).

movements. Merely aiming to achieve a funding ratio of 100 percent makes a pension fund's future level of contributions or benefits more sensitive to investment and market risk. Pension funds can increase the likelihood that their assets will be able to meet their liabilities by aiming to achieve a prudent measure of overfunding—the amount of which can be thought of as the "capitalization" of the fund—taking into account the level of risk arising from the asset mix and the financial strength of the sponsor company.

Within this analysis, the financial strength of the sponsor company is an important (and often overlooked) factor when considering ALM or risk management of pension funds. The strength of the sponsor is important in assessing the ability of a pension fund to meet its PBOs as a going concern (while the strength of the pension fund as a stand-alone entity may be more important to assess the ability to meet ABOs in the event of a plan closure). Financially strong companies in growing industries may have more flexibility to take investment risk and manage short-term funding shortfalls. On the other hand, older-industry firms with a higher proportion of retirees to active workers, and with large pension obligations in relation to the size of the overall company or with less dependable cash flows, will have less flexibility to increase contributions as needed. Therefore, we believe the appropriate funding level, or the risk profile of a pension fund's portfolio, should not be considered in isolation from the financial strength and flexibility of the sponsor company.

In sum, policymakers should seek to ensure that a pension fund's obligations can be met by its funding and investment strategy, consistent with its risk management practices. During our study, we frequently observed the stronger or "wealthier" sponsor companies moving to remove risk from their pension fund and more often seeking to match or overfund projected liabilities, while weaker firms continued to pursue riskier investment strategies in the hope of "growing out" of

underfunded positions. In this respect, the existing regulatory incentives and structure for pension funds are producing very different behavior when compared to life insurers, many of whom reallocated from equities to bonds in response to weakened solvency positions. Although this may in part also reflect the longer time horizon and liability structure of pension funds, it suggests that risk-based approaches to funding and related regulations may be useful to encourage greater risk management practices by pension funds.

Conclusions and Policy Recommendations

The growth of funded pensions and the growing emphasis on risk management should strengthen the role of pension funds as stable, long-term institutional investors. Overall, this development should enhance global financial stability.

Pension funds and their weakened financial position have received significant attention in recent years. No doubt, this can be attributed in large part to the 2000–02 equity market decline and falling interest rates. However, the deeper causes of this deterioration have been building for many years. Nevertheless, pension funds have a very significant role to play in mature market societies, particularly as providers of retirement income and as investors of long-term savings. At present, a number of factors challenge the very existence of traditional pension structures in many advanced economies, and the following discussion and recommendations are intended to highlight how pension funds may continue to be a home for long-term savings, and thus an important contributor to social and financial stability goals. The recent partial recovery in funding ratios (arising from improved market conditions, particularly rising market interest rates) provides a window of opportunity for policymakers to introduce measures to encourage better risk management practices, and to reduce the risk of another cycle of over- and underfunding.

Promoting Sufficient Retirement Savings

As a first priority, policymakers need to more effectively communicate the pension and savings agenda. In virtually every jurisdiction, public and private sector officials we met highlighted the need to better communicate the pension challenges and policy priorities. While this seems universally the case, it is perhaps particularly true in countries where the bulk of pension benefits have been traditionally provided by the state. Indeed, in part due to insufficient communication, some recent pension reforms aimed at the household sector (Pillar 3) have received little support or enthusiasm. The long-term need for greater savings is not going to dissipate, and for current pension reform efforts to succeed a broad-based understanding and support by the general public is necessary.

Policymakers should provide effective incentives for the development of long-term savings. This does not require legislation or regulation that provides detailed product design, but rather the development of a tax and legal environment that is relatively simple, stable, and facilitates retirement savings growth. The private sector is best equipped to design and provide a wide variety of savings products, and the public sector should focus on building the necessary framework and incentives. If the incentives are properly established and communicated, we believe attractive products will emerge.

In designing a multi-pillar approach to pension provision, policymakers may be best served by targeting a relatively balanced contribution from each pillar. With demographic and cost pressures increasing on Pillar 1, the contribution of state plans is projected much lower in most advanced economies. Increasingly, many state pension programs see their goal as providing a much lower or even minimum level of replacement income. Therefore, efforts to facilitate larger contributions from Pillars 2 and 3 are a practical necessity. As such, the role of retirement savings through occupational pension schemes (Pillar 2) and/or individual savings schemes (Pillar 3) will need

to grow significantly, as individuals seek to supplement state benefits. However, due primarily to differing national preferences for risk sharing between sectors, these pension and savings programs will likely be designed very differently.

As part of pension reform efforts, the workplace (Pillar 2) would seem to be the most efficient location to organize and accumulate retirement savings. Through occupational pension schemes, employers can most effectively organize the funding of employees' retirement savings. Moreover, employees seem more prepared to contribute wages at source to long-term, work-related, pension schemes, whereas efforts to attract funds in various Pillar 3 schemes in many mature market countries have experienced less success. In addition, by bundling employee savings and creating a menu of financial products, employers are well positioned to negotiate lower investment costs and obtain professional advice to the benefit of employees and beneficiaries.

Traditional DB schemes and principles should not be uniformly discarded, and we believe the development of hybrid plans should be encouraged. Rather than being a flawed concept, many traditional DB plans and benefits were mispriced and lacked adequate funding strategies and risk management practices, as revealed by the recent market slump. Nevertheless, at least some of the risks related to pensions may be better managed at the institutional than the individual level, and various hybrid plans that aim to guarantee a minimum level of benefit and corporate pension contribution, while sharing some (not all) of the investment and longevity risks with employees, may strike the right balance. A particular concern of many sponsors and industry analysts is longevity risk, and special consideration for the extreme elderly may support the broader market availability of annuities and related insurance products. At the same time, Pillar 2 schemes must be suitable for a more mobile workforce, including portability, proportionate benefits and vesting schedules.

Promoting Strengthened Risk Management Practices

Policymakers should consider ways to facilitate the development of certain markets, including more long-term (20 years and longer) fixed-income and index-linked products. Such securities and markets are necessary to allow pension funds to better match assets and liabilities, as well as to facilitate the supply and pricing of annuity and long-term savings products by traditional market participants, such as insurance companies. We believe public sector leadership in this area (including issuance) will be followed by greater private sector issuance. In several jurisdictions, the number of institutions providing annuity products continues to decline, and pricing is increasingly unattractive or unavailable due to the limited supply of market instruments to hedge such risk.

Financial stability can be enhanced by regulatory policies that are more closely aligned with the purpose and liability structure of pension funds, while encouraging the development of better risk management systems. Regulators should encourage funded plans to develop investment portfolios (including international investments) appropriate to the pension's liability structure. Such measures would encourage fund managers to focus more on risk management, rather than benchmarking performance against various indices, and should also reduce the risk of herd behavior. This may imply quite different allocations between equities, bonds, and other assets by different pension funds and, possibly, more fixed-income investments by pension funds with a rapidly aging workforce or closed to new participants.

Tax and related regulations should be designed to reduce or remove barriers to prudent, continuous funding policies. One of the key reasons for the contribution holidays in the late 1990s was the loss of preferential tax treatment (i.e., deductions) or even tax penalties applied to further contributions once pension funds became somewhat overfunded. The inability to continuously fund and to build a funding cushion left many funds exposed to a market down-

turn, and created the need for relatively large contributions to meet minimum funding standards. Tax rules that would allow a certain level of annual contributions, including as tax deductible payments, even during overfunded periods, and which do not penalize firms for building up a prudent funding cushion (e.g., two or three years of normal contributions), would help to encourage long-term, stable pension strategies. Moreover, based on OECD statistics, such policies should not represent a material drain on tax revenue. Of course, a balance has to be reached to prevent pension funds from becoming tax shelters, and thresholds for continued tax deductibility could perhaps be coordinated with risk-based concepts of adequate funding levels set by supervisors.

Risk-based approaches to supervision and to guarantee fund premiums should be enhanced. Guarantee fund "risk-based" premiums need to take account of the pension fund asset-liability mix, and not only the level of current funding. This should provide a fairer distribution of guarantee funds' cost, reduce moral hazard risk, and encourage better risk management practices. The Dutch proposal for risk-based standards is an interesting and innovative approach, applying supervisory expertise from other financial sectors. It would seem useful to also consider the financial strength of the sponsor in setting risk-based capital or premiums; however, we recognize the practical difficulties, and we encourage the adoption of risk-based approaches whether or not that factor is included.

Policymakers and standard setters should ensure that financial accounts provide an accurate reflection of the financial condition of companies, including their pension plans, and we continue to encourage enhanced disclosure standards rather than an emphasis on single-point accounting measures. Our recommended approach here is similar to that expressed in the April 2004 GFSR for insurance companies. A factor frequently cited by pension fund managers for the move away from DB plans is the trend to fair value accounting principles in many mature market jurisdictions. While this view may understate the demographic and cost pressures also at work against DB plans, it is not clear that the volatility associated with fair value accounting measures accurately reflects a pension fund's true risk profile or properly focuses the management of pension risks. We believe a broader disclosure of the asset and liability structure (including the maturity profile of pension obligations, and market and interest rate sensitivities) of funded pension plans, and a discussion of risk management practices and funding or capital cushions, would provide investors and beneficiaries with appropriate information. Indeed, while we support the approach of rating agencies to treat the unfunded portion of pension obligations like other forms of corporate debt, the agencies acknowledge that such accounting volatility creates its own ratings pressure and possibly more immediate funding constraints. Sophisticated investors are certainly aware of pension issues, and relevant disclosure should ensure broader market understanding of pension risks.

An important contribution to pension reform and the growth of long-term savings may include the promotion of international diversification of pension assets. In time, a shift of capital from advanced economies to younger and faster-growing economies may provide substantial benefits in terms of higher returns and diversification and, ultimately, in helping advanced economies deal with the macroeconomic implications of aging. This reinforces the need of policymakers to address the numerous frictions that continue to limit international capital mobility, and the need to strengthen the capacity of developing countries to absorb such potential capital flows.

From a financial stability perspective, pension funds represent a truly long-term institutional investor base. However, following the 2000–02 market downturn and low interest rate environment, which many analysts have called a "perfect storm" for pensions, we observe a sig-

nificant effort by sponsors to lower the risk profile of their pension funds and to shift a variety of risks to pension beneficiaries (i.e., the household sector). It seems increasingly clear that households and individuals can be expected to have a greater responsibility for securing their retirement, deciding how much to save, where and how to invest, and to increasingly bear other risks related to their pensions and retirement. This risk transfer raises the question of how well equipped households are to bear such risks, as well as the appropriate sharing of risks between the household and other sectors. These questions will be addressed further in the March 2005 *Global Financial Stability Report* chapter on the fund management industry and the household sector in general.

References

Allianz Dresdner Asset Management, 2003, "European Pensions: Reform Trends and Growth Opportunities" (Munich).

Aon Consulting, 2004, "Pension Crisis Overstated Says Leading Pensions Consultancy," press release (London, June 22).

Astérias Ltd., 2002, *U.K. Pension Fund Survey— August 2002* (London, October).

Black, Fischer, 1989, "Should You Use Stocks to Hedge Your Pension Liability?" *Financial Analysts Journal,* Vol. 22 (January/February), pp. 10–12.

Blake, David, 2001, "U.K. Pension Fund Management: How Is Asset Allocation Influenced by the Valuation of Liabilities?" Discussion Paper PI-0104 (London: The Pension Institute, University of London).

Börsch-Supan, Axel, 2004, "Mind the Gap: The Effectiveness of Incentives to Boost Retirement Saving in Europe," Discussion Paper No. 52–04 (Mannheim Research Institute for the Economics of Aging, June).

Committee on Investment of Employee Benefit Assets (CIEBA), 2004, "The U.S. Pension Crisis—Evaluation and Analysis of Emerging Defined Benefit Pension Issues" (Bethesda, MD: Association for Financial Professionals, March).

Custis, Thomas, 2001, "Defined Benefit Pension Plans Face the 'Perfect Storm'" (Seattle: Milliman USA, December 19).

Deutsche Bank Research, 2003, "Aging, the German Rate of Return and Global Capital Markets," *Current Issues: Demography Special* (Frankfurt: December 4).

Exley, C. Jon, Shyam J. B. Mehta, and Andrew D. Smith, 1997, "The Financial Theory of Defined Benefit Pension Schemes," Group for Economic and Market Value Based Studies, pp. 72–81. Available via the Internet at *http://www.gemstudy.com/ DefinedBenefitPensionsDownloads/Financial_Theory_ of_Defined_Benefit_Pension_Schemes.pdf.*

Federal Deposit Insurance Corporation, 2004, "Could a Bull Market Be a Panacea for Defined Benefit Pension Plans?" (Washington: FDIC).

Galer, Russell, 2002, "Prudent Person Rule Standard for the Investment of Pension Fund Assets" (Paris: Organisation for Economic Co-operation and Development, November).

Giles, Tim, 2004, "The 100% Bonds Proposition: Does the Underlying Analysis Stand Up?" (London: Charles River Associates, April). Available via the Internet at *http://www.crai.co.uk/ pubs/pub_3653.pdf.*

Greenwich Associates, 2003, "As Funding Gaps Resist Rally, U.S. Investment Plans Shop for Smarter Strategies" (Greenwich, CT, February 9).

Hewitt Investment Group, 2001, "The Perfect Storm: How Pension Funds Should Navigate Through Troubled Waters" (Lincolnshire, IL: October).

Higgins, Matthew, 1998, "Demography, National Savings, and International Capital Flows," *International Economic Review*, Vol. 39 (May), pp. 343–69.

International Monetary Fund, 2003, "Underfunding of Corporate Pension Plans: Macroeconomic and Policy Implications," in *United States: Selected Issues,* Country Report No. 03/245 (Washington: IMF). Available via the Internet at *http://www.imf.org/ external/pubs/cat/longres.cfm?sk=16785.0.*

———, 2004a, *Global Financial Stability Report,* World Economic and Financial Surveys (Washington: IMF, April).

———, 2004b, "Pension Reform Issues in Japan," in *Japan: Selected Issues,* Country Report No. 04/247 (Washington: IMF). Available via the Internet at *http://www.imf.org/external/pubs/cat/ longres.cfm?sk=17621.0.*

Jackson, Patricia, William Perraudin, and Kamakshya Trivedi, forthcoming, *Defined Benefit Pensions, Hedging and UK Companies* (London: Bank of England).

Lührmann, Melanie, 2002, "The Role of Demographic Change in Explaining International Capital Flows," MEA-Discussion Paper (Universität Mannheim).

Modigliani, Franco, and Merton H. Miller, 1958, "The Cost of Capital, Corporation Finance, and the Theory of Investment," *American Economic Review*, Vol. 48 (June), pp. 261–97.

Moody's Investors Service, 2003, "Analytical Observations Related to U.S. Pension Obligations" (January).

———, 2004, "The Effects of Aging on Public Sector Pensions and Healthcare Systems: A Rating Agency Perspective" (May).

Organisation for Economic Co-operation and Development, 2004a, "Recommendation on Core Principles of Occupational Pension Regulation" (Paris: OECD)

——— 2004b, "Tax Favoured Retirement Savings Plans: A Review of Budgetary Implications and Policy Issues," Working Paper No. 1 on Macroeconomic and Structural Policy Analysis, Economics Department, Economic Policy Committee (Paris: OECD).

Queisser, Monika, and Dimitri Vittas, 2000, "The Swiss Multi-Pillar Pension System: Triumph of Common Sense?" Policy Research Working Paper No. 2416 (Washington: World Bank).

Reagan, Patricia, and John Turner, 2000, "Did the Decline in Marginal Tax Rates During the 1980s Reduce Pension Coverage?" in *Employee Benefits and Labor Markets in Canada and the United States,* ed. by William T. Alpert and Stephen A. Woodbury (Kalamazoo, MI: W.E. Upjohn Institute).

Reisen, Helmut, 2000, *Pensions, Savings and Capital Flows: From Ageing to Emerging Markets* (Cheltenham, U.K.: Edward Elgar).

Schieber, Sylvester J., 2003, "Global Aging: Opportunity or Threat for the U.S. Economy?" testimony before the U.S. Senate Special Committee on Aging (Washington, February 27).

Shilling, A. Gary, 2003, "Pension Profits Become Corporate Costs," *Business Economics* (October).

Smith, Andrew D., 1998, "Salary Related Cash Flows: Market Based Valuation," Group for Economic and Market Value Based Studies. Available via the Internet at *http://www.gemstudy.com/ DefinedBenefitPensionsDownloads/Salary_Related_ Cash_Flows_Market_Based_Valuation.pdf.*

Standard & Poor's, 2003, "Navigating the International Pension Accounting Maze" (May 16).

———, 2004a, "Update on Postretirement Benefits Obligations" (April 29).

———, 2004b, "Using Equity Duration in Pension Fund Allocation" (January 27).

Turner, Adair, 2003, "Demographics, Economics and Social Choice," transcript of lecture at London School of Economics (November 6).

Van Ewijk, Casper, and Martijn van de Ven, 2003, "Pension Funds at Risk," CBP Report 2003/1 (The Hague: Central Plaanbureau, April).

Watson Wyatt, 2003, "Pensions in Crisis," *Insider*, Vol. 13, No. 9 (September).

World Bank, 1994, *Averting the Old Age Crisis: Policies to Protect the Old and Promote Growth*, World Bank Policy Research Reports (New York: Oxford University Press).

Yermo, Juan, 2003, "Survey of Investment Regulation of Pension Funds" (Paris: Organisation for Economic Co-operation and Development, November).

EMERGING MARKETS AS NET CAPITAL EXPORTERS

Emerging markets have become net capital exporters since 2000.[1] This development, which was highlighted in the September 2003 GFSR, has raised questions and concerns among market analysts and policymakers. Conventional wisdom suggests that capital should flow from capital-abundant mature markets to capital-scarce emerging markets. However, this general presumption does not hold for an individual country when it needs to adjust its international investment position as a result of a financial crisis, or when risk-adjusted returns shift global asset allocation away from emerging market assets. Moreover, when different types of risks and capital market imperfections are incorporated into the analysis, it is not unlikely that a particular emerging market country could become a net capital exporter—at least for a short period of time.

Macroeconomic policies are central to post-crisis adjustment in emerging markets, as well as to ongoing global current account imbalances.[2] While recognizing the importance of macroeconomic policies, and the difficulties in disentangling savings-investment gaps from financing issues, this chapter focuses mainly on capital account, or financial and balance sheet issues in the major emerging markets, as well as their interaction with global markets.[3] After an examination of the main stylized facts on capital flows over the last decade, the chapter argues that there are three key themes behind the perceived anomaly of emerging markets as net capital exporters: the overlapping adjustments to a sequence of crises in major emerging markets; the accumulation of reserves and a greater reliance on local financial markets; and the asset allocation implications of mature markets risk-adjusted returns and macroeconomic imbalances.

An examination of the stylized facts on capital flows suggests that the period in which emerging markets became net capital exporters (2000–04) can be divided into two subperiods, and that private (residents and nonresidents) and official sectors play different roles in each subperiod. In the first subperiod, 2000–01, there is a substantial reduction in nonresident inflows to emerging markets—the end of the sharp decline in flows that started in 1997—combined with an also relatively large outflow from emerging market residents. In the second subperiod, 2002–04, a rebound in private sector inflows is dominated by a considerable accumulation of net international reserves (NIR) by the official sector.

Most systemically important emerging markets were engulfed in a sequence of crises that involved large reversals in capital inflows, as well as deep and protracted balance sheet adjustments. The confluence of some of these adjustments, and a few new crises around the turn of the century, marked the trough of the pronounced cycle in capital flows to emerging markets of the 1990s. For this confluence of crises and adjustments to be quantitatively important, the restoration and strengthening of balance sheets had to be sufficiently long and profound. The chapter shows that this was indeed the case in some crisis countries, and argues for focusing on both sides of the

---

[1]For the purpose of this chapter, a country is a net capital exporter when its balance in the current (capital and financial) account is positive (negative), assuming all errors and omissions belong in the capital account.

[2]See, for instance, Ghosh and others (2002) on the role of IMF policies in capital account crises, and IMF (2003b) on global imbalances.

[3]Lane and Milesi-Ferretti (2003 and 2004) and Gourinchas and Rey (2004) argue that fluctuations in external accounts are better understood by focusing on financial markets rather than goods markets.

balance sheet adjustment, which reinforce each other in terms of their impact on emerging markets investment position. In particular, the chapter shows an important accumulation of net foreign assets by emerging market residents that coincided with the reduction in external liabilities. The depth and length of the external deleveraging process is also studied, and implications for bank and bond markets are discussed.

In the more recent subperiod 2002–04, an unprecedented accumulation of net international reserves (NIR) and increased borrowing from local securities markets to reduce reliance on external financing were the main factors that made emerging markets net capital exporters. In many cases the large accumulation of reserves has stemmed from attempts to prevent nominal exchange rate appreciation in the face of increasing capital inflows. However, while there has been much controversy about the adequacy of reserve levels and some empirical studies suggest that NIR levels are excessive (in particular, in Asia), precautionary or "self-insurance" arguments could be used to justify higher levels of international reserves relative to the level suggested in those studies. The chapter also argues that the desirable level of reserves depends on the degree of risk aversion of the monetary authorities, as well as on the development of local financial markets, which could provide an alternative mechanism to self-insure against sudden reversals in capital flows.

Finally, in an increasingly globalized capital market, flows to emerging markets cannot be dissociated from global factors stemming from developments in the mature markets. Despite the string of crises, emerging markets have become an established asset class in global portfolios, and the global asset allocation

process of international investors involves a comparison of risk-adjusted returns across asset classes as well as across countries. In this context, events such as the bursting of the global equity bubble, the increasing role of China in global production and trade, and the persistence of global imbalances have a direct bearing on the supply of funds available for emerging markets and, hence, on whether they become net capital importers or exporters. The chapter shows that risk-adjusted returns favored allocations toward U.S. assets between 1996 and the early 2000s—facilitating the financing of increasingly large U.S. current account deficits—while emerging market securities became more attractive in 2003–04.

After an analysis of the stylized facts on capital flows, and of the key themes behind the emergence of emerging markets as net capital exporters, the chapter concludes with a discussion of a corresponding set of policy implications.

Stylized Facts

Emerging markets *as a whole* have become *net exporters* of capital since 2000. Prior to 2000, emerging markets were, in aggregate, *net importers* of capital, with financing largely driven by private sector inflows since the late 1980s.[4] This section focuses on key trends in capital flows to and from emerging markets, with particular emphasis on the differential behavior of residents and nonresidents. The differential behavior of private (resident and nonresident) and official sectors is manifest in two markedly different subperiods during which emerging markets became net capital exporters: 2000–01 and 2002–04. In the first subperiod, the nonresident private sector

[4]The main trends in net capital flows to emerging markets were reported in the September 2003 GFSR. Some differences across both chapters are due to different sets of countries included in the Emerging Markets group. In this chapter, the IMF's *World Economic Outlook* (WEO) data and definitions are used for most of the analysis, but the country classification is somewhat broader here; it also includes Bosnia and Herzegovina, Brunei, Cyprus, Eritrea, Israel, Serbia and Montenegro, and Timor-Leste.

flows completed the decline from emerging markets, with inflows reaching the trough in 2001, while resident outflows were at or above trend levels. In the second subperiod, the private sector (resident and nonresident) saw more normal levels of flows (moderate outflows and inflows, respectively), while the official sector became the key driver of emerging market outflows through an unprecedented level of NIR accumulation (see Figure 4.1).

Resident and Nonresident Private Sector Flows

Nonresident private capital inflows rose sharply through much of the 1990s, peaking in 1997, before slowing significantly following the onset of several emerging market crises (see Figure 4.1). This trend was largely driven by foreign direct investment (FDI), which has been the dominant source of private external financing for emerging markets. Indeed, FDI in emerging markets remained relatively stable through the crisis and recovery years, before slowing somewhat in 2002 and 2003. In contrast, net debt flows to emerging markets fell markedly following the Asian crisis, driven mostly by a retrenchment in bank lending. Meanwhile, external bond financing has been more resilient as retrenchments by lenders have been more sporadic during the same period. Interestingly, the spike in debt inflows in 1997 is similar to that in 1981, in the lead-up to the 1980s debt crisis. The difference is in the steep decline in the late 1990s, which was also followed by a much sharper rebound in 2003–04.

At the same time that emerging markets experienced a surge in private sector (nonresident) inflows in 1994–97, there was a somewhat smaller increase in private (resident) outflows (see Figure 4.2).[5] This pattern is common across regions, albeit less pro-

[5]This simultaneous surge in inflows and outflows is consistent with a sharp rise in gross foreign asset and liability positions for emerging markets (see Lane and Milesi-Ferretti, 2004).

Figure 4.1. Capital Flows to Emerging Markets

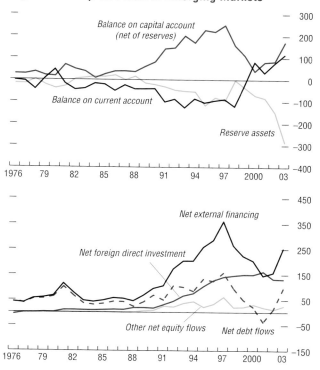

Source: IMF staff estimates based on data from the *World Economic Outlook*.

Figure 4.2. Private and Official Outflows/Inflows of Residents and Nonresidents in Emerging Markets
(In billions of U.S. dollars)

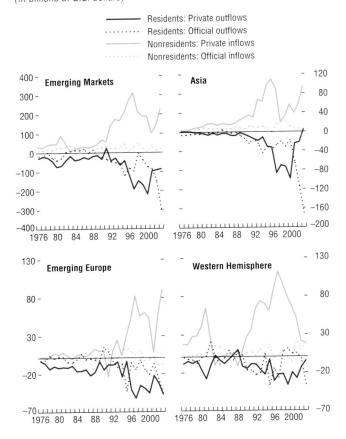

——— Residents: Private outflows
········· Residents: Official outflows
——— Nonresidents: Private inflows
········· Nonresidents: Official inflows

Source: IMF staff calculations based on data from the *World Economic Outlook*.
 Note: Private resident outflows are defined as current account balance minus change in reserves minus external financing. Official nonresident inflows are defined as equity securities constituting foreign official assets plus net credit and loans from the IMF plus other official debt flows. Private nonresident inflows are defined as net foreign direct investment (excluding debt-creating liabilities) plus equity securities constituting foreign private assets plus net external borrowing from commercial banks plus net external borrowing from other private sources. Capital transfers are excluded from the calculation of nonresident inflows.

nounced in Latin America.[6] Indeed, the increase in resident outflows predates the reversal in nonresident inflows for all regions, and reinforces the latter between 1997 and 2000. These outflows are represented by recorded private investments offshore, as well as unrecorded capital flight (recorded as errors and omissions in a country's balance of payments), and reached almost $250 billion in 2000.[7] Portfolio investment in overseas markets made up an important component of outflows during this period. Moreover, despite the sharp slowing in total resident outflows since 2001, portfolio outflows have continued to increase, reaching $77 billion in 2003 from $16 billion in 1997. Meanwhile, direct investments abroad by residents of emerging markets increased from $19 billion in 1997 to $38 billion in 2003.

Regional Trends

There are, however, important regional differences observed during these two subperiods. In Asia, the pickup in nonresident private inflows started already in 1999, even as the resident private outflows increased before slowing markedly in 2001. Importantly, net FDI inflows into the region have remained relatively stable despite the crisis, with China being the most preferred destination of FDI among emerging markets, even

---

[6]However, Latin American countries were the largest recipients of capital inflows in the late 1970s and early 1980s, and they also experienced a large outflow from residents during the period of large inflows from non-residents that preceded the 1980s debt crisis.

[7]A common definition of "capital flight" is that of funds fleeing across national borders in search of a safe haven (Brown, 1992). Dornbusch (1990) provides a distinction between two types of capital flight. The first is motivated by the fear of discrete losses as a result of expected major changes in the exchange rate, political risk, financial repression, and tax considerations. The second is "low-level capital flight," which is the steady outflow motivated by tax considerations or the inability to diversify a portfolio. See also Gunter (2004) for a discussion on different definitions and views of the capital flight issue.

Table 4.1. Emerging Markets: Balance of Payments Errors and Omissions
(In billions of U.S. dollars)

	1997	1998	1999	2000	2001	2002	2003
Emerging markets	−71.4	−41.0	−48.7	−46.6	−31.6	−4.3	10.2
Africa	−1.8	−1.3	−1.5	−0.5	0.4	−0.2	0.8
Asia	−44.7	−22.9	−23.4	−24.9	−8.7	4.5	7.0
Emerging Europe	−10.1	−13.2	−7.1	−12.4	−9.0	−10.3	−3.9
Middle East	−7.5	2.1	−9.6	−6.0	−7.8	7.6	5.9
Western Hemisphere	−7.4	−5.8	−7.2	−2.8	−6.5	−5.9	0.3

Source: IMF staff estimates based on the *World Economic Outlook*.

replacing the United States as the single largest recipient in 2003. In 2001, NIR accumulation in the region began its exponential growth, following a gradual increase after 1997. Overall, the net result is that short-term official outflows (in the form of NIR) from this region far exceed net private sector imports of capital.

While emerging Asia has been a large net capital exporter for the past six years, emerging Europe has been exporting capital since 2000 and Latin America only (and marginally) in 2003. In emerging Europe, nonresident private inflows slowed sharply in the first subperiod (2000–01), followed by an equally sharp rebound in subsequent years to a historic high in 2003. This rebound was driven by debt and FDI inflows on the back of EU membership expectations, as well as post-crisis recoveries in Russia and Turkey.[8] As in other episodes of sharp rebounds in capital inflows, resident private outflows have also increased in 2003, reaching almost 1997 levels. Meanwhile, nonresident private inflows to Latin America have slowed sharply since 1997, while resident private outflows have also moderated since then. The region's share of FDI, which surpassed that of Asia during the 1997 to 1998 period, slowed significantly since 2002 and has yet to pick up. The region continued to be a net capital importer until 2002, and aggregate NIR declined between 1999 and 2002, as the Argentina and Brazil crises unfolded. Both

regions also experienced a marked increase in NIR in 2003, albeit smaller than Asia. In other regions, capital flows to Africa have followed similar trends to emerging markets as a whole, while flows in the Middle East have been somewhat more idiosyncratic (see Box 4.1).

The return to emerging markets of unrecorded resident capital outflows over the past year has been remarkable and has mitigated recorded outflows. Capital flight initially surged to $71 billion in 1997 and continued at high levels until 2000, but subsequently moderated and finally reversed to post a positive $10 billion in 2003. The pattern of errors and omissions is quite volatile and is largely driven by the trends in Asia, which represented almost two-thirds of the total during the Asian financial crisis period, and then became positive in 2002 and 2003 (Table 4.1). Much of this repatriation of residents' funds is said to be driven by the anticipation of an appreciation in the Chinese yuan. In Eastern Europe, errors and omissions outflows have been more volatile, and have largely coincided with the Russia and Turkey crises, although these outflows also slowed significantly in 2003. In Latin America, errors and omissions in the second half of the 1990s were at their highest levels since the second half of the 1980s, corresponding to the series of crises in the region.

An examination of the official sector indicates a dichotomy in the trend of official capi-

---

[8]Accession countries have remained net capital importers since 1995.

Box 4.1. Capital Flows to Africa and the Middle East

The trends in capital flows to Africa and the Middle East have been distinctly different (see the Figure). In Africa, net outflows in the official sector (nonresident inflows minus resident outflows) have tended to be less than private sector net inflows (nonresident inflows minus resident outflows), making the region a net importer of capital until 1996–97 and then again in 2000–01. Meanwhile, the Middle East has been a net exporter of capital through both the official and private channels.

Capital inflows to both Africa and the Middle East have exhibited different patterns through the 1990s. In Africa, nonresident private inflows—largely in the form of FDI—have become increasingly important for the region, surging sharply through the 1990s before moderating in recent years, in accordance with trends in other emerging markets. These flows have been *concentrated in the oil sector*, with the major oil-exporting countries receiving about half of the FDI flows into the region in 2003. Meanwhile, the sharp surge in portfolio equity flows into Africa—predominantly to South Africa—in the mid-1990s was followed by an equally sharp decline in the second half of the decade. The nascent recovery in 2002 and 2003 has been driven by the strong economic performance in South Africa. Meanwhile, debt flows into Africa—which had been the dominant means of financing in the 1980s—had become less important in the 1990s and have actually declined in recent years. In contrast, nonresident private flows to the Middle East have been somewhat flat since the late 1990s, as FDI flows to the region were among the lowest in emerging markets. Portfolio flows to the region have been unremarkable, while debt inflows have remained the most important source of financing for the most part of the 1990s. Debt flows to this region recovered slightly in 2003, following some retrenchment in the late 1990s and early 2000s.

Similarly, private outflows between the two regions have behaved differently. In Africa, resident private outflows increased through 1997, before slowing to almost negligible amounts in

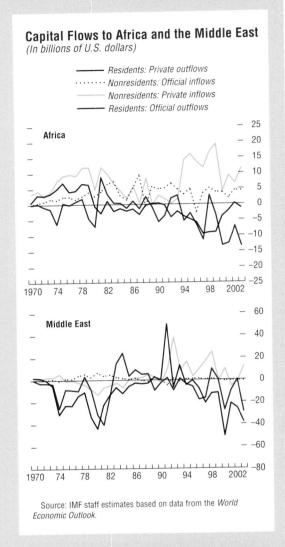

Capital Flows to Africa and the Middle East
(In billions of U.S. dollars)

——— Residents: Private outflows
·········· Nonresidents: Official inflows
——— Nonresidents: Private inflows
——— Residents: Official outflows

Africa

Middle East

Source: IMF staff estimates based on data from the *World Economic Outlook*.

2003. Interestingly, errors and omissions in the region's balance of payments had become slightly positive in the past year, following some capital flight in the 1990s. In the Middle East, *recorded* resident private outflows increased between 1995 and 2000, peaking at $50 billion in 2000. It has since moderated, with the errors and omissions data also indicating some repatriation of *unrecorded* capital back to the region.

Official flows to Africa have been more important than for the Middle East. Official flows to

Africa in the second half of the 1990s were dominated by the IMF's and World Bank's Heavily Indebted Poor Countries (HIPC) Initiative, which led to the decline in debt stocks and debt service. As a result of this initiative, poverty-reducing expenditures were made possible and donor assistance increased. In 2002, gross official flows to 27 HIPC countries rose by 50 percent to almost $12 billion, from $8 billion in 1997. In contrast, nonresident official inflows into the Middle East have been almost negligible since the late 1980s.

tal flows relative to the private sector. While nonresident private capital inflows to emerging markets have been large through the 1990s, official sector flows have been significantly lower, except for minor spikes during periods of crises. In recent years, outflows of medium- to longer-term official sector capital from some regions have been largely offset by inflows of official sector capital to Latin America, from the IMF and other official sources. In contrast, Asia's official sector—led by the crisis-affected countries—is recording outflows in medium-to-longer term official capital, partly attributable to repayments of IMF loans. That said, short-term official capital—built up through favorable post-crisis adjustments in the current account and renewed private capital inflows—has been the main source of capital exports from emerging markets in the last two years.

Trends by Markets

Uncovering trends and turning points in international banking and securities markets is somewhat more difficult, owing to structural changes in the financial services industry as well as data limitations. It is generally acknowledged, however, that bank retrenchment was an important driver of the net exports phenomenon in the first subperiod (2000–01), but that banking flows appear to have returned to more normal levels in the second subperiod (especially in 2003–04; see Box 4.2). A more informative perspective can be obtained from changes in outstanding loans and bonds—rather than from flow figures.

In sharp contrast to the retrenchment in cross-border lending to emerging markets during 1997–2002, lending through the local subsidiaries of foreign banks increased quite rapidly in all regions (Table 4.2). While international bank lending to emerging markets—including both cross-border lending and lending by locally based foreign banks—continued to grow in 1997–2002, domestic bank lending remained stable over the same period. International bank lending to Asia fell after the financial crisis, while lending to Eastern Europe and Latin America actually increased—more than compensating for the slowdown in domestic bank lending.

In contrast to developments in banking markets, domestic bonds outstanding increased at a faster pace than external bonds in 1997–2002, while total bonds outstanding also slowed down relative to the pre-crisis period (1994–96, Table 4.3). The growth of external bonds slowed down to 4 percent (from 12 percent) in Latin America, and to 5 percent (from 33 percent) in Asia in the post-crisis period. In contrast, the growth of external bonds accelerated to 8 percent (from 5 percent) in Eastern Europe. Overall, the data suggest that the bond market has been more resilient for emerging market borrowers than bank lending, during the crisis years and after.

The stock market capitalization of emerging markets as a whole has risen by 25 percent

Table 4.2. Bank Lending in Emerging Markets

	Total Lending, 1996 (Billions of U.S. dollars)	Average Annual Growth, 1993–96[1] (Percent)	Total Lending, 2002 (Billions of U.S. dollars)	Average Annual Growth, 1997–2002 (Percent)
East Asia				
Domestic banks	769.5	18.1	876.1	2.4
Local subsidiaries of foreign banks[2]	29.8	15.4	84.9	21.2
Cross-border[3]	282.2	29.0	130.3	−11.6
Latin America				
Domestic banks	563.7	17.3	484.8	−2.7
Local subsidiaries of foreign banks	58.5	28.6	241.7	31.2
Cross-border	199.9	6.2	166.1	−2.8
Eastern Europe				
Domestic banks	242.5	9.4	252.8	0.8
Local subsidiaries of foreign banks	9.6	80.5	96.3	48.5
Cross-border	74.7	1.6	70.4	−0.6
All Emerging Markets				
Domestic banks	1,575.7	12.7	1,613.7	0.4
Local subsidiaries of foreign banks	97.8	24.4	422.8	29.4
Cross-border	556.7	14.5	366.9	−6.5

Sources: Bank for International Settlements (BIS); and IMF staff estimates.
[1]For domestic banks, the average annual growth rates for East Asia and Latin America are from 1990–96 and from 1991–96 for Eastern Europe and all Emerging Markets.
[2]"Local subsidiaries of foreign banks" includes local currency claims on local residents.
[3]"Cross-border" lending refers to external loans and deposits of BIS reporting banks vis-à-vis individual countries.

Table 4.3. Debt Securities in Emerging Market Countries

	Amount Outstanding, 1996 (Billions of U.S. dollars)	Average Annual Growth, 1994–96 (Percent)	Amount Outstanding, 2002 (Billions of U.S. dollars)	Average Annual Growth, 1997–2002 (Percent)
Asia[1]				
Domestic debt securities	558	16	1,170	14
Debt securities issued abroad	83	33	116	5
Total	641	19	1,285	13
Latin America[2]				
Domestic debt securities	385	70	401	2
Debt securities issued abroad	190	12	245	4
Total	575	51	646	3
Eastern Europe[3]				
Domestic debt securities	53	13	129	22
Debt securities issued abroad	15	5	18	8
Total	68	11	147	20
All Emerging Markets				
Domestic debt securities	996	28	1,699	10
Debt securities issued abroad	288	16	379	4
Total	**1,284**	**25**	**2,078**	**9**

Source: Bank for International Settlements (BIS).
[1]China, India, Korea, Malaysia, Philippines, and Thailand.
[2]Argentina, Brazil, Chile, and Mexico.
[3]Czech Republic, Hungary, and Poland.

between 1996 and 2003, notwithstanding the crises experienced in several regions.

However, given the weak trend in net portfo-lio equity flows into each region, this suggests that much of the improvement in market capi-talization is likely attributable to local investor activity.[9] In turn, international equity issuance collapsed with the string of emerging market crises, as well as the bursting of the global equity bubble in 2000, contributing to reduced capital inflows to emerging markets. That year, China's international initial public offerings (IPOs) dominated emerging market equity issuances, with almost one-third of total emerging market international IPOs. The subsequent recovery in equity issues in the second subperiod was notable for the large international IPOs in China in 2003, totaling almost one-fifth of all emerging market issuances (see Figure 4.3). This follows a drop to 19 percent of all international equity issuance by emerging markets in 2001 and to 13 percent in 2002. By comparison, FDI into China has continued to increase, even as FDI to other developing countries has fallen since 2001.

In sum, emerging markets became net capital exporters in 2000–04 as a result of a sharp decline in inflows and an increase in residents' outflows in 1997–2001, and because of an unprecedented increase in net international reserves in 2002–04. In the next sections, the chapter argues that both of these facts can be interpreted as a result of post-crisis behavior by the private and official sectors, as well as by determinants of investors' global asset allocation decisions.

The Post-Crisis Balance Sheet Adjustment Process

The general presumption that capital flows from mature to emerging market countries does not hold when a country needs to adjust its international investment position as a result of a financial crisis. The emerging market crises of the late 1990s and of early 2000 were dubbed capital account crises because

Figure 4.3. International Equity Issuance and FDI in China vs. All Other Emerging Market Countries
(In billions of U.S. dollars)

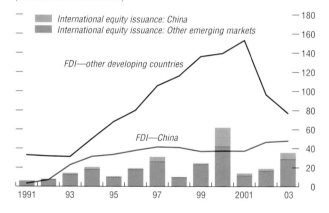

Sources: IMF, *World Economic Outlook*; and Dealogic.

---

[9]With the exception of Korea, which publishes data on the proportion of foreign holdings in local equities, there is little information available for the other emerging markets.

Box 4.2. Data Sources and the Trends in Bank Lending Flows to Emerging Markets

A comparison of the data sourced from the IMF, the World Bank, or the Institute for International Finance (IIF) on *bank lending flows*—specifically, the category "bank loans and other debt (net)"—suggests that the scope of these flows is relevant in determining the pattern and volatility of net flows to emerging markets.[1] This category of data is said to explain more than 80 percent of the differences in observed total inflows over the 1990s, depending on the data source. In the IMF data, bank lending includes items such as loans, trade credits, currency and deposits, and kindred assets and liabilities of banks and other financial institutions. Similarly, the IIF data also include transactions in debt securities, the financing portion of merger and acquisition (M&A) activity, and nongovernment trade finance, albeit by nonresident commercial banks only.

In addition to the composition of that category, IMF lending flows are reported on a net basis—that is, they are net of repayments and repatriations—while the IIF and World Bank do not record deposits of residents in other countries in calculating the flows for "bank loans and other debt (net)." This is in addition to the different sets of countries included in each data series, which manifest some differences in the data.[2]

[1]See Dobson and Hufbauer (2001) for a detailed discussion for the differences in capital flow data across the different sources.
[2]Korea is included only in the IIF set of emerging market countries.

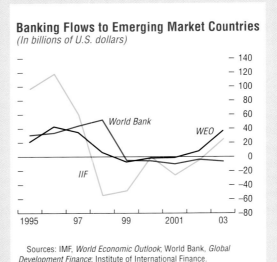

Banking Flows to Emerging Market Countries
(In billions of U.S. dollars)

Sources: IMF, *World Economic Outlook*; World Bank, *Global Development Finance*; Institute of International Finance.

Thus, it is not surprising that the different sources of data show different trends in bank lending flows.

The resulting differences in the data are shown in the Figure. The IMF figures are less volatile than the IIF numbers, presumably due to the net nature of loans and repayments. They show that banks have resumed net lending to emerging markets since 2002, while the World Bank data suggest that net retrenchments are still occurring. This is probably due to the World Bank's exclusion of short-term loans, which picked up substantially in 2003.

they were triggered by sudden reversals of capital inflows and were propagated by financial factors. In this context, this section argues that post-crisis balance sheet adjustments explain, to a large extent, why emerging markets became net capital exporters in 2000–01.

The section characterizes the pattern of adjustment for the main crisis and non-crisis countries following two avenues. First, the aggregate behavior of crisis and non-crisis countries is analyzed, with the second group acting as a benchmark that captures aggregate trends in international capital markets. Second, the section analyzes the pattern of balance sheet adjustments followed by the major crisis countries. In particular, the depth, length, and composition of the external deleveraging process and other balance sheet adjustments are studied, in connection with the size of the original financial shock and the behavior of different segments of the debt markets.

Table 4.4. Capital Flows in Crisis and Non-Crisis Countries
(In billions of U.S. dollars)

	1996	1997	1998	1999	2000	2001	2002	2003
All Emerging Markets								
Nonresidents: private inflows	271.2	310.4	211.4	189.0	188.1	100.2	140.1	225.1
Nonresidents: official inflows	3.7	24.5	44.3	22.8	4.7	32.7	9.9	18.3
Total nonresident flows	**274.9**	**334.9**	**255.7**	**211.8**	**192.8**	**132.9**	**150.0**	**243.4**
(In percent of GDP)	*4.6*	*5.4*	*4.3*	*3.6*	*3.1*	*2.1*	*2.3*	*3.4*
Residents: private outflows	−118.4	−191.3	−148.6	−169.4	−217.6	−97.7	−91.7	−86.1
Residents: official outflows	−82.2	−96.3	−2.8	−37.2	−74.2	−85.2	−148.8	−295.1
Total resident flows	**−200.5**	**−287.6**	**−151.5**	**−206.6**	**−291.9**	**−182.9**	**−240.5**	**−381.1**
(In percent of GDP)	*−3.4*	*−4.6*	*−2.5*	*−3.6*	*−4.6*	*−2.9*	*−3.7*	*−5.3*
Total net flows	**74.4**	**47.3**	**104.2**	**5.2**	**−99.1**	**−49.9**	**−90.5**	**−137.7**
(In percent of GDP)	*1.3*	*0.8*	*1.7*	*0.1*	*−1.6*	*−0.8*	*−1.4*	*−1.9*
Crisis Countries[1]								
Nonresidents: private inflows	139.0	114.9	58.3	50.0	53.7	−26.4	21.1	37.7
Nonresidents: official inflows	−0.3	14.0	17.9	0.8	−5.2	20.0	−7.3	−1.9
Total nonresident flows	**138.8**	**128.9**	**76.2**	**50.8**	**48.6**	**−6.3**	**13.7**	**35.8**
(In percent of GDP)	*6.3*	*5.7*	*4.0*	*3.1*	*2.7*	*−0.4*	*0.9*	*2.0*
Residents: private outflows	−67.0	−73.8	−55.1	−56.8	−72.4	−34.5	−51.7	−46.8
Residents: official outflows	−18.2	9.7	−2.4	−15.6	−10.1	10.4	−19.7	−61.0
Total resident flows	**−85.2**	**−64.1**	**−57.5**	**−72.4**	**−82.5**	**−24.1**	**−71.4**	**−107.8**
(In percent of GDP)	*−3.9*	*−2.9*	*−3.0*	*−4.5*	*−4.6*	*−1.5*	*−4.6*	*−5.9*
Total net flows	**53.6**	**64.8**	**18.7**	**−21.6**	**−33.9**	**−30.4**	**−57.6**	**−72.0**
(In percent of GDP)	*2.4*	*2.9*	*1.0*	*−1.3*	*−1.9*	*−1.8*	*−3.7*	*−3.9*
Non-Crisis Countries								
Nonresidents: private inflows	132.2	195.5	153.0	139.0	134.4	126.6	119.0	187.4
Nonresidents: official inflows	4.0	10.5	26.4	22.0	9.8	12.7	17.3	20.2
Total nonresident flows	**136.2**	**206.0**	**179.5**	**161.0**	**144.2**	**139.3**	**136.3**	**207.6**
(In percent of GDP)	*3.7*	*5.2*	*4.4*	*3.8*	*3.2*	*3.0*	*2.8*	*3.8*
Residents: private outflows	−51.3	−117.6	−93.5	−112.7	−145.2	−63.2	−40.0	−39.3
Residents: official outflows	−64.0	−105.9	−0.4	−21.5	−64.1	−95.6	−129.1	−234.1
Total resident flows	**−115.3**	**−223.5**	**−93.9**	**−134.2**	**−209.4**	**−158.8**	**−169.1**	**−273.4**
(In percent of GDP)	*−3.1*	*−5.6*	*−2.3*	*−3.2*	*−4.6*	*−3.4*	*−3.5*	*−5.1*
Total net flows	**20.9**	**−17.5**	**85.5**	**26.8**	**−65.2**	**−19.5**	**−32.8**	**−65.8**
(In percent of GDP)	*0.6*	*−0.4*	*2.1*	*0.6*	*−1.4*	*−0.4*	*−0.7*	*−1.2*

Source: IMF staff estimates based on the *World Economic Outlook*.
[1]Crisis countries include Argentina, Brazil, Indonesia, Malaysia, Philippines, Russia, Thailand, and Turkey.

The Confluence of Overlapping Adjustments

The string of capital account crises in the late 1990s and early 2000s led to strong adjustments in the external position of the affected countries and, to a lesser extent, of the non-crisis countries as well. Although countries that did not experience crises were also net capital exporters during the period under study, crises countries are the driving force behind emerging markets' status as net capital exporters in 2000–04 (see Table 4.4). Despite their smaller size, crisis countries had an average outflow of $48.5 billion during 2000–04, compared to an average outflow of $45.8 billion for the non-crisis countries.[10] Moreover, crisis countries' net outflows are larger in

[10]Crisis countries are Argentina, Brazil, Indonesia, Malaysia, the Philippines, Russia, Thailand, and Turkey. Their aggregate GDP for 2003 was $1.8 trillion, compared to $5.4 trillion in the rest of the emerging market universe in our sample.

Figure 4.4. Capital Flow Trends for Crisis and Non-Crisis Countries
(In billions of U.S. dollars)

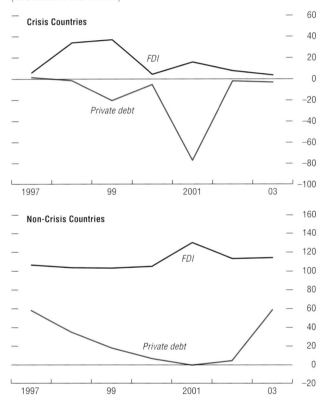

Source: IMF staff calculations based on *World Economic Outlook* data.

absolute size in all the years—except for 2000.[11] The fact that non-crisis countries also became net capital exporters, even if to a lesser extent than crisis countries, suggests that the former group also became more cautious in its borrowing behavior and that global factors also had an impact during this subperiod. The outflows from both crisis and non-crisis countries were driven by post-crisis balance sheet adjustments that involved both a reduction in external liabilities—external deleveraging—and an increase in foreign assets.

A notable feature of private flows to emerging markets is the sizable reduction in overall inflows by nonresidents from 1997 to 2001, which was driven mostly by the countries that experienced financial crises during that period (Table 4.4). Nonresident private inflows to all emerging markets declined by $210 billion from their peak in 1997 to their trough in 2001; the corresponding decline in crisis countries is $140 billion, exactly two-thirds of the total amount. Also, private inflows to non-crisis countries are much more stable and resilient than those to crisis countries, and they never become negative.

The behavior of residents' outflows—that is, their accumulation of net foreign assets—is more difficult to gauge, in part because of data limitations. Resident private outflows were above average during most of the period in crisis countries, in particular in 2000. However, these outflows were also above average in 2000 for non-crisis countries. The trends for the non-crisis group, in particular for this component of outflows as well as for official outflows, is dominated by outflows from China.[12] Also, it is likely that attractive risk-adjusted returns in the mature markets have pulled capital away

---

[11]Private outflows in non-crisis countries are unusually large in 2000; should they have been at average levels, crisis countries would have also dominated the overall result in 2000.

[12]See Gunter (2004) for a thorough discussion of capital flight from China in 1984–2001.

from emerging markets at the peak of the global equity market bubble.

Before turning to the deleveraging process, it is important to note the differential trends in FDI versus debt flows. Whereas FDI flows to non-crisis countries remained resilient throughout 1997–2001, showing an overall tenuous upward trend, FDI in crisis-countries exhibited significant volatility (see Figure 4.4). As noted in the Capital Markets Consultative Group Report, or CMCG (2003, pages 5–6), crisis episodes heighten perceptions of regulatory, taxation, and expropriation risks, thus undermining FDI flows. Moreover, the relatively long time horizon of FDI serves as an automatic stabilizer in response to short-term developments. Indeed, the fact that FDI flows and private debt flows to crisis countries appear to have been moving in opposite directions during 1997–2001 meant that FDI inflows were in part mitigating the impact of debt outflows set off in crisis periods.[13]

The pattern exhibited by bond flows also differed markedly between crisis and non-crisis emerging markets during 1997–2003. Cumulative net bond issuance by crisis countries declined slightly since early 2000, while issuance by non-crisis countries continued to rise steadily (Figure 4.5). The fact that growth in net issuance by non-crisis sovereigns continued unabated throughout the entire sample period suggests that an increase in global risk aversion encouraged investors to become more selective and to move up the credit spectrum, instead of pulling out from all high-risk assets. Sovereign bond issuance was also more resilient than corporate bond issuance.

In contrast with FDI and bond flows, the swings in bank lending appear to have been more synchronized between crisis and non-crisis countries. As noted in the stylized facts section, cross-border lending fell in all regions

---

[13]Froot and Stein (1991) note that sharp depreciations make domestic assets very attractive in post-crisis depreciation episodes, which could be manifested in a negative correlation between FDI and debt flows.

Figure 4.5. Cumulative Net External Debt Issuance: Crisis vs. Non-Crisis Countries
(In billions of U.S. dollars)

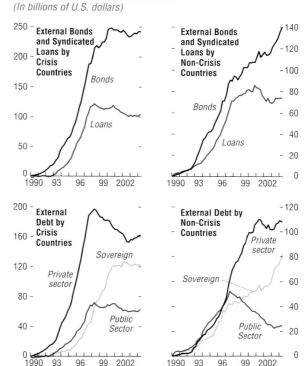

Sources: Dealogic; and IMF staff estimates.

during 1997–2002. As discussed in IMF (2003c), the retrenchment in commercial bank lending was associated with weak balance sheets and earnings, greater risk awareness, consolidation, and an ongoing shift in business strategies.[14] Moreover, the cumulative net issuance of syndicated loans by all emerging markets countries was virtually flat during 1998–2003, with a brief recovery in late 2000 led by the technology, media, and telecommunications (TMT) sector (Figure 4.5). The fact that there was almost no new net syndicated loan issuance from crisis countries throughout the entire sample period suggests that the Asian crisis may have triggered a structural shift in the syndicated loans market for emerging markets, with both global factors and crises in Brazil and Argentina contributing as well.[15]

The Depth and Length of Post-Crisis External Deleveraging

The process of external deleveraging—the post-crisis reduction of external liabilities—is thus a key determinant of the fact that emerging markets became net capital exporters in 2000–01. The process started in 1997 in some Asian countries and is still ongoing in some of them. It was reinforced by other crises in major emerging markets thereafter. The fact that there was a confluence of adjustment processes from different crises is related to the issue of how long and profound the adjust-

ments had to be. Thus, the determinants of the depth and length of this deleveraging are analyzed in this section.

The post-crisis deleveraging process depends on a number factors, including individual countries' *financial market conditions*, the extent of *official support* received from international financial institutions (IFIs), and local *economic fundamentals and policies*.[16] The focus here is mostly on financial conditions, which are particularly relevant because they were among the main causes and propagation mechanisms of the crises. Indeed, the hallmark of recent emerging market crises has been a sudden stop or reversal of capital inflows, generally associated with "twin" banking and balance of payments crises.[17] The sudden stop triggers a sharp fall in asset prices (including the exchange rate) and a collapse in economic activity. The persistence of the effects of the initial shock depends on the specific financial market initially hit by the sudden stop. In principle, an associated banking crisis may give rise to a more protracted adjustment given the inherent procyclicality of bank credit. This procyclicality is, in turn, driven by the fall in asset prices that reduces the value of collateral and forces a further (endogenous) reduction in foreign liabilities.[18]

The size of the initial sudden stop and the persistence in the decline in GDP, associated with the fall in asset prices, are illustrated in Figure 4.6 for a sample of crisis countries. The mechanism described above is particularly evi-

---

[14]Ferrucci and others (2004) show that factors specific to creditor countries ("push" factors) and those specific to debtor countries ("pull" factors) are equally important in explaining bank flows to emerging markets.

[15] During 1994–97, emerging Asia was the largest recipient of syndicated loan flows in the emerging markets universe. Also, a large share of syndicated loan issuance by emerging market entities was from the TMT sector and also driven by M&A activity. See IMF (2001).

[16]The focus here is on the financial aspects of the adjustment. Reference to macroeconomic conditions and/or IMF programs is made only when it may be directly relevant to financial market developments and conditions. For a thorough discussion of macroeconomic policies and IMF programs in capital account crises, see Ghosh and others (2002).

[17]See Calvo (1998) and Kaminsky and Reinhart (1999).

[18]Kiyotaki and Moore (1997) show how the existence of collateral constraints amplifies the impact of an exogenous shock through declines in the value of collateral pledged by borrowers in order to access imperfect credit markets. Christiano, Gust, and Roldos (2002) extend their analysis to a small open economy and quantify the effects on external deleveraging in a prototypical Asian crisis country.

dent for the Asian countries—with the exception of the Philippines. A rather large capital outflow, amounting to 20–25 percent of quarterly GDP in Indonesia and Thailand and 15 percent of GDP in Korea, was followed by a more protracted decline in quarterly GDP.[19] Moreover, the decline in stock prices accompanied further capital outflows, as corporates were forced to deleverage by even larger amounts over time. Stock market indices rebounded in late 1999–early 2000, as a result of spillovers of the global TMT bubble, while real estate price indices suffered a larger and much more persistent decline. The pattern of adjustment was somewhat different in the other crisis countries. In Russia and Turkey, sizable initial outflows had a lesser impact on GDP and asset prices, owing to a reduced role of banks in the financial intermediation process. In Brazil, smaller outflows and a resilient banking system resulted in a smaller contraction in GDP and asset prices.

The length of the deleveraging process can be measured as the peak-to-trough in the total external debt stock of a particular country.[20] Based on the length of deleveraging in the financial market, the sample of crisis countries can be broken down into two groups: *"long-adjustment"* countries (over two years), including Indonesia, Korea, Malaysia, Philippines, Russia, and Thailand; and *"short-adjustment"* countries (less than two years), including Brazil and Turkey (see Table 4.5).[21]

[19]The persistence of the negative effect of the financial crisis on GDP is best described by the time it took for quarterly GDP to recover to its pre-crisis level: 15 quarters in Thailand, 20 in Indonesia, and only 6 quarters in Korea.

[20]Note that the "peak" may not always coincide with the currency devaluation or debt default that follows the pullout of external capital. Instead it may either precede or lag the latter by a few months. Also, for the Philippines, which did not experience a pronounced decline in total external debt stock (unlike other Asian emerging markets), the peak-to-trough in Table 4.5 refers to the stock of foreign bank loans.

[21]Malaysia's external debt was much lower than other "long adjustment" countries, when measured relative to GDP (see Ghosh and others, 2002).

Figure 4.6. Selected Emerging Market Crisis Countries: Sudden Stops, Asset Prices, and GDP

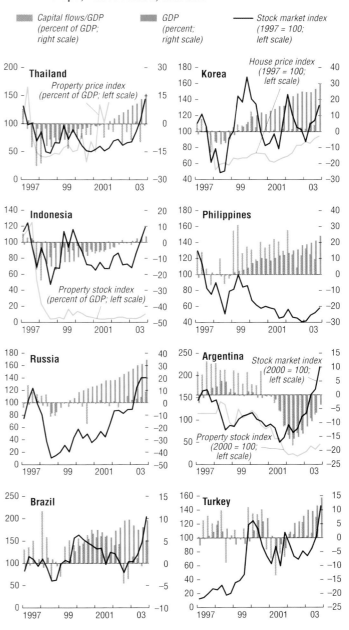

Sources: IMF, *International Financial Statistics*; Bloomberg L.P.; CEIC database; and Standard & Poor's, Emerging Markets Database.

Table 4.5. The Post-Crisis External Debt Adjustment in Selected Emerging Markets
(In billions of U.S. dollars, unless otherwise noted)

Country	External Debt Financing	External Debt Structure at the Peak (Percent)	Peak	Trough	Change	Percent Change	Length of Decline in Private Financing (Number of years)
Crisis Countries/Long Adjustment							
Thailand (1997:Q2–2003:Q2)	Private financing	*92*	107	26	−81	−76	**5+**
	Official financing	*8*	9	16	7	71	
	Total		116	42	−75	−64	
Indonesia (1997:Q4–2003:Q2)	Private financing	*63*	69	29	−39	−57	**5+**
	Official financing	*37*	40	59	19	46	
	Total		109	88	−21	−19	
Korea (1997:Q2–2001:Q4)	Private financing	*97*	149	93	−56	−38	**4.5**
	Official financing	*3*	5	16	11	214	
	Total		154	108	−46	−30	
Russia (1998:Q3–2002:Q3)	Private financing	*63*	71	45	−26	−36	**4.0**
	Official financing	*37*	42	16	−26	−61	
	Total		113	61	−52	−46	
Malaysia (1997:Q3–2000:Q3)	Private financing	*92*	42	29	−12	−30	**3.0**
	Official financing	*8*	4	4	0.4	12	
	Total		45	33	−11.9	−26	
Philippines (1997:Q4–2000:Q3)	Private financing	*59*	25	28	3	14	**2.75**
	Official financing	*41*	17	21	4	22	
	Total		42	50	7	17	
Crisis Countries/Short Adjustment							
Argentina (2001:Q2–2003:Q2)	Private financing	*84*	133	117	−16	−12	**2+**
	Official financing	*16*	26	33	6	24	
	Total		159	149	−10	−6	
Brazil (1998:Q2–1999:Q3)	Private financing	*91*	180	137	−43	−24	**1.25**
	Official financing	*9*	19	28	10	52	
	Total		199	166	−33	−17	
Turkey (2000:Q4–2001:Q4)	Private financing	*84*	65	54	−12	−18	**1.0**
	Official financing	*16*	12	23	11	91	
	Total		77	77	−1	−1	

Source: Joint BIS-IMF-OECD-WB external debt database.
Notes:
"Peak" refers to the peak in the stock of foreign debt (bank loans and debt securities issued abroad. and "trough" refers to the inflection point. The exact dates for each country are presented in the parentheses. For Argentina, Thailand, and Indonesia, the 'trough' is the end of the sample period.
Bank loans data are from the BIS location banking statistics, which are based on the country of residence of reporting banks.
Debt securities issued abroad include Brady bonds.
These figures may sometimes differ from those obtained from local sources due to differences in methodology. Trade credits are not included.

The length of the adjustment period is positively correlated with the depth of the decline of external debt, and both the depth and length of the adjustment are related in turn to the size of the initial shock, the financial market most affected by the crisis, and the level of development of alternative financial markets. Countries that suffered a large sudden stop (i.e., more than 10 percent of GDP) and had a major banking crisis experienced a deleveraging process that lasted from three (Malaysia) to five years (Indonesia and Thailand). Countries displaying a large share of securitized external debt recovered relatively faster than those issuing primarily bank debt. Finally, countries where domestic bond markets were relatively underdeveloped (Thailand, Indonesia, and Russia) and hence could not serve as an alternative source of funding for local banks and corporates exhibited longer periods of adjustment.

In particular, the length—and efficiency—of the deleveraging process depends on the speed of the banking sector cleanup process

Box 4.3. Distressed Debt Markets: Recent Experiences in Mature and Emerging Markets

Well-functioning distressed debt markets are an essential ingredient for an efficient corporate sector deleveraging process, and they can reduce the depth and length of such a process following a crisis. While many analysts stress the legal and cultural aspects of corporate restructuring, there are capital market features that are critical to the efficiency of the process. In particular, a secondary market for trading (and pricing) of nonperforming loans, the existence of a debtor-in-possession (DIP) facility under bankruptcy proceedings, and a market for exit finance are essential to an efficient restructuring. The investor base of these markets has grown, especially in the United States after the Savings and Loan crisis in the 1980s, and comprises two types of investors—speculators who buy debt only for trading purposes and corporate turn-around/private equity specialists who invest in "fixable" companies to restructure the balance sheet.

Distressed debt investors realize the lengthy periods of time that they may be locked into situations with significant market-to-market risk and their investments require a special kind of risk capital that is not benchmarked to any index. These investors typically invest in issues that trade significantly below par, roughly in the 20 to 40 cent range. Distressed funds have provided sizable capital to mature markets; in fact, the U.S. distressed debt market, including defaulted debt, is estimated at $100 billion to $150 billion, or about a quarter of the U.S. high-yield market of roughly $600 billion.

Although mature markets (especially the United States) have attracted risk capital since 1980, only during the early 1990s, in the aftermath of the Brady plan, did emerging markets begin to attract distressed debt investors. This box illustrates how risk capital continues to facilitate corporate restructuring in the mature markets and discusses the increasing role of distressed debt investors in emerging markets during post-crisis periods, including balance sheet adjustments in corporate and financial sectors.

Mature Markets

United States and Europe

The legal framework for corporate restructurings is instrumental in the structure and evolution of a distressed debt market and varies significantly on either side of the Atlantic. Some analysts agree that the U.S. distressed debt market under the umbrella of Chapter 11 legislation has allowed for a superior and faster restructuring than in other jurisdictions. In addition, the sizable risk-capital available in this market allows for unparalleled and innovative capital market structures. Debtors filing for bankruptcy in the United States, in contrast to Europe, continue to have access to credit via the DIP facility under bankruptcy (or, Chapter 11) proceedings. The DIP facility offers a number of legal inducements, including, in exceptional cases, super-priority status to the new lenders, giving them a first call over collateral assets. However, other analysts suggest that the easy access to new funding and suspension of some obligations during bankruptcy often encourages distressed corporates to file for Chapter 11. In Europe, banks remain the primary source for corporate funding and laws have been designed to protect the banking system. European policymakers view that companies in U.S. bankruptcy proceedings often continue to incur losses at the expense of the creditors and are forced into liquidation anyway; in fact, about 30 percent of all companies that have reorganized under U.S. Chapter 11 go into liquidation, merge in distress, or file for bankruptcy, again, within five years (LoPucki and Kalin, 2000).

Both frameworks have their pros and cons, as they are designed to protect different sets of creditors. However, with the globalization of capital markets and the development of new asset classes (subordinate debt and asset-backed securities), analysts estimate that legal frameworks and market structures will begin to converge.

Japan

The market for corporate restructuring (i.e., "turn-around" business) is presently in its

Box 4.3 *(concluded)*

infancy and remains illiquid, especially for a mature market. Market participants suggest banks view their claims (in particular nonperforming loans) as perpetual debt and book them in line with optimistic valuations of the underlying collateral, often as high as 60 cents to 80 cents on the dollar. Distressed debt investors presently view their investments as equity stakes that are valued in terms of cash flows; their bids for nonperforming loans usually range from about 20 cents to 35 cents on the dollar. The asymmetry in the two valuation methods is likely to result in fewer nonperforming loans to be cleared by the market, especially with collateral prices increasing on the back of an economic recovery in Japan (Ohashi and Singh, 2004). However, recent transactions, including Shinsei's turnaround and successful initial public offering by a distressed debt investor, continues to buoy the incipient distressed debt market.

Emerging Markets

Although in the mid- to late 1980s, intermarket dealers and major international banks traded in defaulted sovereign loans, high-net-worth individuals from emerging market countries were some of the first investors that had an appetite for distressed debt. Major international banks that still had commercial operations in Latin America were limited by regulations to trade in external debt that made it difficult to unwind their exposure. In addition, the accounting regulations were conducive to allowing banks to provision at their discretion.[1] The concentration of a country's debt with a few large banks—and not distressed debt investors—provided support to the debt prices in early to mid-1980s (Fernandez and Ozler, 1991). Only

toward the late 1980s, high-net-worth individuals started repatriating their funds buying distressed assets, which in turn triggered a steady recovery in these assets. The balance between banks, the original holders, and traders had shifted over time. Subsequently the larger banks, who initially held Brady bond positions in minimum lots of $250 million, sold their holdings to institutional investors and the retail sector in smaller denominations.

The post Brady plan era was the first time that distressed assets attracted sizable risk capital. Distressed debt investors were instrumental in facilitating and concluding the Brady agreements (Collyns and El Erian, 1993). Distressed debt investors have continued to provide a "floor" to emerging market debt prices by investing at sub-par prices. The increasing role of distressed debt traders continues to gain importance, as was evident from the recent distressed episodes, including Ukraine (2000), Moldova (2002), Brazil (2002), Uruguay (2003) and in the Asian (1999–present) and Argentine corporate workouts (2002–present).

Unlike the 1980s, the Asian crisis sparked an intrinsic desire for risk capital that provided a floor to distressed asset prices. In a region where foreign investors historically were prevented from holding a majority interest, the crisis altered the cultural inhibitions toward them. However, corporate restructuring required immediate reform—a novelty that was initially opposed by the local entrepreneurs. By 1999, just two years after the crisis, the regional nonperforming loans attracted distressed debt investors. With the bursting of the TMT bubble and the equity slowdown in 2001, buy-side firms also showed interest in distressed assets in the region and were soon joined by the regional banks that had recapitalized and were investing in nonperforming loans along with hedge funds. About six years after the crisis, at the end of 2003, about a trillion dollars of distressed loans had been removed from the banking sector (Ernst and Young, 2004).

Recent experience from Asia suggests that although asset management corporations

---

[1]The guidelines for the Federal Accounting Standards Board (FASB) allowed that restructured debt, under certain conditions, could be carried on the books at the original face value even though it traded at submarket interest rates—an important regulatory niche exploited by many banks when undertaking debt-conversion and/or the Brady bonds with submarket interest rates.

(AMCs) have removed a substantial amount of distressed corporate assets from the banking system, there is insufficient evidence to suggest if these restructured loans are resolved. Market participants and analysts suggest that "resolution—in its purest form—is realized only when the nonperforming loans is in some way converted to cash" (e.g., Fung and others, 2004). Only the Korean and Japanese AMCs (Korean Asset Management Company and Reconstruction and Collection Corporation, respectively) and, to some extent, Malaysia's Danaharta, have resorted to sizable recovery in the form of cash.

Market participants acknowledge that a sound legal infrastructure along with governmental support for efficient market resolution and realistic asset pricing were fundamental factors that attracted cash from distressed investors. Recent experience with Argentine corporate and quasi-sovereign workouts (e.g., City of Buenos Aires) also suggests that swift restructurings with corporate creditors, in cash or equity, is possible even if the sovereign is stalled in protracted negotiations. Investors with risk capital, if not crowded out by the official sector, will likely cushion balance sheet adjustments due to interest rate or commodity price shocks in the near future.

and the existence of a relatively well-functioning distressed debt market. Market participants have noted that the asset management corporations (AMCs) set up in the aftermath of the Asian crisis were efficient in carving out nonperforming loans from the banking system, but that they were slow in disposing of the assets. Although distressed debt markets are a relatively new development even in mature markets, analysts have noted that Korea has made substantial progress in this area and this has contributed to a smoother and more efficient adjustment process (see Box 4.3). Illiquid asset markets in other crisis countries have allowed the pre-crisis owners of small and mid-size Asian corporates to deleverage by buying back their debts at extremely low prices, while retaining corporate control. Market participants have also noted that the persistence of weak corporate governance, combined with insufficient structural reforms to improve investment returns, contributes to the persistence of savings-investment gaps and the fact that local entrepreneurs prefer to export their capital rather than invest it locally.

Finally, the external deleveraging process was accompanied by a simultaneous increase in domestic currency–denominated debt,

resulting in marked changes in the liability structure of both crisis and non-crisis countries. The shift from foreign to local financing was driven by several factors: first, the need to reduce balance sheet mismatches; and, second, by supportive expansionary monetary policies in many mature and emerging market countries that have kept interest rates at historic lows over the past five years. Examples of the interaction of these balance sheet and macroeconomic factors are provided in the next section.

Balance Sheet Adjustments and Macroeconomic Stability

The external deleveraging process was an important component of the balance sheet adjustment in crisis countries. However, as noted above, the private sector also increased the accumulation of net foreign assets as part of such adjustment—and, perhaps, even before the crises. Adjustments in both sides of the balance sheet underlie the process that led emerging markets to become net capital exporters. However, the achievement of macroeconomic stability has also contributed to a more resilient balance sheet picture in these countries.

Box 4.4. Distance to Distress as a Measure of Balance Sheet Vulnerability

The distance to distress is a default risk indicator, based on the contingent claims analysis, that captures corporate balance sheet vulnerabilities. This indicator essentially combines asset value, leverage, and business risk into one single measure of default risk. In the case of a firm financed with both debt and equity, this measure is equal to the implied market value of the firm's assets minus the distress barrier, scaled by the implied asset volatility. The result produces the number of standard deviations (in terms of asset values) that the firm is from distress, which can also be used to derive a default probability. In other words, the higher the asset value, the lower the leverage and the asset volatility, the larger the distance to distress (i.e., the farther away the firm is from distress and the less likely the firm is to default).

The distance to distress is a useful measure of balance sheet vulnerability, not just for firm-level analysis, but also for sectoral analysis (see Gray, Merton, and Bodie, 2003). This is shown in the Figure derived from an example on the utility sector in Brazil (see Gapen and others, 2004). The market value of assets in that sector follows a stochastic path, and when there is a negative shock to the sector, its asset value may fall relative to its distress barrier. Therefore, the distance to distress shrinks, indicating the sector is moving closer to default. This became rather clear when the Brazilian utility sector was exposed to the financial turbulence of the summer of 2002.

The utility industry in Brazil operates primarily in the local market, with revenues collected in local currency and some liabilities denominated in foreign currency. It raised large amounts of funds during 1998–99 in dollar loans largely related to privatization efforts. The subsequent devaluations in the currency in 1999 and 2002 along with the rationing of power in 2001 resulted in balance sheet weaknesses. Prior to the financial market volatility, the difference between the asset value and the distress barrier in the sector reached $18 billion and the asset volatility was at 22 percent, which yielded a distance to distress of about 2 standard deviations in March 2002. The subsequent mapping of this

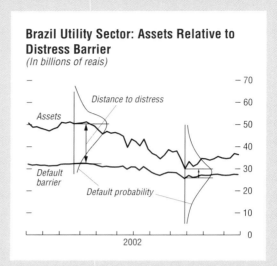

Brazil Utility Sector: Assets Relative to Distress Barrier
(In billions of reais)

distance to distress into probability of default indicated that the aggregated industry had a one-year-ahead probability of default equal to 5 percent.

The turbulence in Brazilian financial markets during the summer of 2002 took its toll on the balance sheet of the sector, which has recovered thereafter. As illustrated in the Figure, the distance to distress in the sector narrowed steadily and hit its trough in September 2002. At that time, the difference between the asset value and the distress barrier declined by $15 billion because of the slump in the market value of the assets, while the implied asset volatility surged to 40 percent as a result of the currency depreciation. Therefore, the distance to distress for the sector dropped to a bottom level of 0.2, which was equivalent to a one-year-ahead probability of default of around 30 percent for the sector as a whole. Following the successful political transition, the utility sector has recovered—together with the rest of the Brazilian corporate sector (see Figure 4.7 in text).

Hence, the distance to distress has proven to be a powerful measure to gauge corporate balance sheet vulnerability. The analysis has also shown to be rather useful in predicting bank ratings downgrades (Chan-Lau, Jobert, and Kong, 2004).

An efficient way to summarize the impact of balance sheet adjustments and improved macroeconomic stability on the financial strength of different sectors of the economy is through the use of the "distance to distress" measure. Distance to distress is a measure of assets minus liabilities, divided by the volatility of assets. While the value and volatility of assets are obtained from market values, the measure of liabilities is the book value of short-term debt plus one-half of long-term debt (see Box 4.4). Hence, an increase in the distance to distress signals a combination of an increase in assets, and a decrease in liabilities (or in the share of short-term debt), as well as a reduction in the volatility of the value of assets—including exchange rates.

A comparison of the distance to distress indicator during and after crises for a sample of crisis countries illustrates the degree of balance sheet (and macro) adjustment achieved by these countries (see Figure 4.7). The cases of Thailand and Korea show that the government and the corporate sectors have improved their balance sheets substantially, while banking sectors have lagged behind in relative terms. In contrast, Brazil and Russia show major improvements in the government and banking sectors, but the corporate sector lags behind in relative terms. In all cases, a higher value of assets relative to liabilities is boosted by a decline in the volatility of assets—attributed mostly to a decline in exchange rate volatility.

Accumulation of Reserves and Reliance on Local Markets

The severity of crises and associated adjustments, combined with the fact that almost all systemically important emerging markets suffered some sort of crisis during the last decade, has increased policymakers' risk aversion, and led many countries (both crisis and non-crisis) to self-insure against future capital account crises. These efforts to self-insure are one of the factors behind the large net inter-

Figure 4.7. Distance to Distress in Selected Emerging Market Crisis Countries

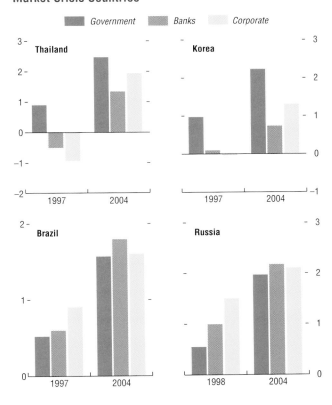

Source: Moody's/MfRisk estimates.

national reserves accumulation during 2002–04, and explain, to some extent, why emerging markets continue to be net capital exporters even after relatively sizable adjustments in the private sector.

The increase in reserves is undoubtedly a result of efforts to prevent exchange rate appreciation and pursue export-led growth policies, especially during the resumption of private nonresident inflows in 2003–04. However, some analysts have argued that self-insurance vis-à-vis financial crises continues to be a relevant consideration in many policymakers' objective function, especially in the absence of adequate market instruments for such purpose. Indeed, both motivations can be viewed as complementary: the exchange rate is managed to stimulate exports and discourage imports, thereby allowing for the accumulation of net foreign assets (and a reduction in external vulnerabilities). However, too much reserve accumulation could also be destabilizing, as it may lead to excess liquidity and quasi-fiscal deficits—as a result of costly sterilization efforts—as well as encourage poor lending decisions. This section follows up the analysis in IMF (2003b), which stresses macroeconomic aspects of net international reserves accumulation—including efforts to maintain competitiveness and its implications for inflation and macroeconomic stability—and assesses the plausibility of the self-insurance argument in relation to other self-insurance mechanisms—in particular the development of local financial markets.

Central banks usually attempt to restore reserves to pre-crisis levels, but in the current adjustment period they have gone beyond such levels. For some countries, including Indonesia, Malaysia, and Korea, pre-crisis reserve levels were restored in less than two years. Reserve levels have exceeded not only their pre-crisis levels, but also several "rule-of-

thumb" ratios used to measure their adequacy—such as the one that states that net international reserves should cover one year of external debt amortization (Table 4.6). These developments are even more significant given the adoption of more flexible exchange rate regimes in many of these countries.

Reserve levels are subject to considerable debate even now, when most empirical studies suggest current levels may be excessive. An optimal level of reserves should trade off the opportunity costs of holding reserves versus the macroeconomic costs incurred in the absence of reserves. Recent empirical studies suggest that starting in 2002 countries accumulated reserves well beyond the levels justified by economic fundamentals.[22] These studies have found that international reserves are correlated with indicators of economic size, capital account vulnerability (financial openness and the ratio of broad money to GDP), and current account vulnerability (ratio of imports to GDP and export volatility). Current account vulnerabilities appear to be more important in explaining reserve levels than capital account vulnerabilities, and opportunity costs do not appear to be important determinants of reserve levels. It is unclear, however, whether capital account vulnerabilities—or more precisely the benefits of insuring against them—are adequately captured in the specified regressions.

Opportunity and sterilization costs are relatively low and they have not deterred countries from building up substantial reserve levels. Emerging market countries' borrowing costs exceed the yields earned on mature market government securities, the assets most commonly held as reserves by central banks.[23] Since bond spreads are positive, countries accumulating reserves are paying an opportunity cost, as they could alternatively use the reserves to repay external debt rather than

---

[22]See Edison (2003) and references therein for further details.
[23]See McCauley and Fung (2003) for recent trends in reserves management and composition.

Table 4.6. Reserves and Related Ratios for Selected Countries as of End-2003

	Reserves (Billions of U.S. dollars)			Reserves/GDP (In percent)	Spreads* Reserves/GDP[2]	Reserves/ Short-Term Debt	Reserves/Bank Deposits[3] (In percent)
	1996	2003	Most recent[1]				
Asia							
China	107.0	408.2	463.1	28.9	0.17	14.2	n.a.
India	20.2	98.9	115.4	17.2	n.a.	6.4	31.1
Indonesia	18.3	36.2	34.9	17.4	n.a.	1.5	34.4
Korea	34.0	155.3	166.5	25.7	0.19	3.4	34.7
Malaysia	27.0	44.5	53.6	43.2	0.43	5.4	46.2
Philippines	10.0	13.5	13.4	17.0	0.70	1.6	34.5
Thailand	38.7	42.1	44.2	29.5	0.20	2.1	32.0
Eastern Europe							
Czech Republic	12.4	26.8	26.4	31.3	n.a.	4.7	42.3
Hungary	9.7	12.7	13.1	15.4	0.04	1.3	35.0
Poland	17.8	32.6	35.3	15.6	0.12	1.7	40.8
Russia	11.3	73.2	81.8	16.9	0.43	3.1	77.4
Turkey	16.4	34.0	33.4	14.2	0.44	1.8	60.4
Latin America							
Argentina	18.1	14.2	16.2	10.9	5.98	1.2	47.5
Brazil	58.3	49.1	50.4	9.9	0.45	1.8	34.9
Chile	15.0	15.8	16.1	22.0	0.20	1.5	53.5
Colombia	9.8	10.8	11.2	13.9	0.59	3.8	56.8
Mexico	19.4	59.0	60.3	9.4	0.19	2.2	39.3
Venezuela, Rep. Bol.	11.8	16.0	18.9	18.9	1.11	5.1	103.4

Sources: IMF staff estimates based on *International Financial Statistics;* Bank for International Settlements; and J.P. Morgan.
[1]As of May 2004 for all countries, except for Indonesia (as of June 2004).
[2]EMBI Global spreads as of December 31, 2003.
[3]Bank deposits include demand, time, savings, and foreign currency deposits.

invest in lower interest rate securities.[24] Illustrative calculations of this opportunity cost in Table 4.6 suggest that it seldom exceeds 0.5 percent of GDP. However, since NIR increases are often sterilized, the relevant marginal cost may be the domestic interest rate paid in such operations. This is likely to increase the opportunity costs of reserve holdings.[25] For instance, in Brazil the spread between the three-month domestic interest rate and the three-month U.S. treasury bill was 14½ percent or the equivalent to a cost of 1.4 percent of GDP for sterilizing an increase of reserves equal to 10 percent of GDP in the absence of an exchange rate depreciation. Central banks normally do not mark to market their NIR holdings, but the opportunity

cost should also include potential losses due to exchange rate and interest rate fluctuations. As most NIR are held in U.S. dollar assets, these are likely to be large in the event of a U.S. dollar depreciation.

These results suggest that the precautionary (or self-insurance) and other motives for holding reserves may outweigh the financial costs of accumulating reserves. Reserves play an important role as a first line of defense against sudden stops in capital inflows (Tweedie, 2000). Moreover, when a financial crisis actually strikes, costs are substantial; holding net international reserves helps to deflect these costs. To the balance sheet adjustment costs discussed in the previous section, sharp declines in economic activity, increased unem-

[24]This argument would have to be qualified by the fact that net international reserves are usually of lower duration than external debt, and that a liquidity premium has to be paid for the liquidity service that they provide.
[25]However, in some cases, such as China currently, yields on U.S. securities exceed the interest rate paid on bills sold by the People's Bank of China.

ployment, and the inability of banks and financial markets to function effectively, among other things, would have to be added. Some analysts estimate that the net cost to Asian governments of the banking crises of 1997–98 ranged from 23 percent of GDP in Korea to 52 percent in Indonesia (Hoelscher and Quintyn, 2003). Others estimate the cost of the crises as the output loss relative to potential GDP (IMF, 2000). In this case, the maximum cost for a typical emerging market with a slow recovery from crisis would be 18.9 percent of GDP. It is likely, however, that central banks would want to be ready to have the necessary cash flow to finance—in a noninflationary way—the transfers needed to prevent the output costs. If this is the case, the stock of reserves needed to self-insure vis-à-vis a crisis would be closer to the first estimates. Other authors have suggested that since most balance-of-payment crises are associated with banking crises, reserves should cover a nontrivial fraction of bank deposits (in particular, if they are dollarized): in most emerging markets, NIR cover more than one-third of bank deposits, a relatively safe coverage.[26,27]

Smoothing capital flow volatility and preventing associated balance-of-payment and banking crises appear to be important determinants of a desirable level of reserves, especially when monetary authorities' preferences are characterized by "loss aversion." If a crisis increases the volatility of shocks and/or the authorities' loss aversion, it will greatly increase the demand for international reserves.[28] Using a framework that incorporates these features, Aizenman and Marion (2003) are able to rationalize, to a large extent, the recent accumulation of NIR in Asian countries.[29] They show that, in the aftermath of crisis, countries that face higher perceived sovereign risks and costs of higher fiscal liabilities—including for preserving financial stability—opt to increase their demand for reserves. The authors also show that higher discount rates, political instability, or corruption could explain why other countries decide to hold smaller precautionary NIR balances.

In this vein, large holdings of international reserves have an important role in reducing the likelihood of a financial crises. Macroeconometric models of currency crisis, such as the IMF's two core early warning system models, have shown that higher ratios of NIR to short-term debt, which ensure that countries can meet external cash flow needs and avoid rollover problems, reduce the probability that a country experiences a *currency* crisis.[30] Similarly, Chan-Lau (2004) shows that a higher level of reserves reduces the probability of a *debt* crisis.[31] In particular, the crisis probability is affected not only by the level of reserves but also by their volatility since for the same level of reserves, higher volatility makes liquidity problems more likely. More important, Figure 4.8 shows that further reductions in default probabilities require

---

[26]Blejer and Schumacher (1998) suggest that the role of central banks as guarantors of financial stability, and their commitment to prevent systemic banking crises, should be explicitly taken into account in the assessment of the vulnerability of central bank balance sheets.

[27]Bank runs in Uruguay affected around 50 percent of deposits, but this was due to the (regional) offshore center nature of the banking system and the close connection to Argentina.

[28]Loss aversion refers to the tendency of agents to be more sensitive to negative shocks that reduce their consumption than to positive ones. The optimal level of reserves is hence larger than the level needed to smooth short-term, high-frequency fluctuations in exchange rates. On the latter, see BIS (2004) and Hviding, Nowak, and Ricci (2004).

[29]However, a large enough degree of loss aversion could rationalize *any* level of reserves. It is questionable whether such high levels of risk aversion would be realistic.

[30]See IMF (2002).

[31]In normal times, high levels of NIR also lower borrowing costs by lowering perceptions of sovereign risk, as shown by Kamin and von Kleist (1999), Eichengreen and Mody (1998), and Ferrucci (2003).

more than proportional increases in reserves, and that the ratios increase with the volatility of NIR to short-term debt ratios.[32]

Adequate reserve ratios would be lower if market-based insurance mechanisms were more widely available (see Box 4.5 for a description of market-based insurance mechanisms). A recent study by Lee (2004) suggests that optimal reserve ratios could be lower than traditional estimates if countries could insure themselves against crises using put options. Under this assumption, the optimal reserve to GDP ratio is bounded and between 20–40 percent. These figures are roughly consistent with those observed in industrial countries, as well as in most emerging markets (Table 4.6). Furthermore, if contingent credit lines or other market-based insurance mechanisms are available, optimal reserve ratios can be further reduced.[33]

Developed local securities markets could also reduce the adequate level of international reserves. Countries with underdeveloped local securities markets need higher levels of reserves for at least two reasons. First, underdeveloped local securities markets result in inefficient intermediation of local savings and many times fail to provide a meaningful alternative source of funding to external debt. Second, corporates facing highly imperfect local markets tend to underestimate the insurance value of domestic currency debt against an exchange rate depreciation and, as a result, issue excessive foreign currency debt

---

[32]The relationship between reserves to short-term ratios and default probabilities was estimated using a structural model of default risk. The model assumes that reserves to short-term ratios are constant but subject to random shocks. The volatility of the random shocks for each country analyzed was obtained by calibrating the model using average credit default swap prices for the first half of 2004. See Chan-Lau (2004) for details.

[33]Official insurance mechanisms are discussed elsewhere. In particular, the role of the IMF's recently expired Contingent Credit Lines as a precautionary line of defense vis-à-vis capital account crises and alternative official mechanisms for crisis prevention are discussed in IMF (2004a).

Figure 4.8. Reserves to Short-Term Debt Ratios and Sovereign Default Probabilities

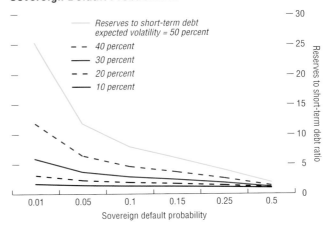

Source: Chan-Lau (2004).

Box 4.5. Market-Based Insurance Mechanisms

In principle, insuring partially or fully against drastic declines or sudden reversals of capital flows can be achieved through market-based mechanisms. These mechanisms include the use of contingent credit facilities and other alternative insurance initiatives.[1]

Contingent Credit Facilities

Private provision of contingent credit facilities could potentially help sovereign borrowers to cope successfully with short-lived liquidity problems (Feldstein, 2003). For instance, in December 1996 the Central Bank of Argentina established a $6.7 billion contingent credit line with a number of private banks. The contract allowed the central bank to sell Argentina public bonds for dollars subject to a bond repurchase. The contract duration was two years with an "evergreen" clause allowing an extension of the credit line for another three months every three months. Banks, however, could walk out of the contract if Argentina defaulted on its international bonds (Gonzalez-Eiras, 2002).

Privately provided contingent credit facilities have some drawbacks. For instance, there are opportunity costs similar to those incurred by holding reserves because countries need to post collateral with the lending banks. Credit made available to large countries with substantial external financing needs may not be enough to cushion them adequately against a sudden stop in capital flows. Hence, privately provided contingent credit facilities may suit small countries' needs better. Also, banks extending contingent credit lines may well choose to cut other financing to offset the contingent credit exposure (Kletzer and Moody, 2000). Finally, markets may interpret the use of the credit facility as a bad signal and require a premium, thereby driving up the country's borrowing costs, including those associated with the roll of the contingent credit facility.

Alternative Insurance Initiatives

Buiter and Sibert (1999) have proposed that foreign currency debt should have attached a universal debt rollover with a penalty (UDROP) provision.

This provision entitles the borrower to extend the maturity of performing debt for a period of three to six months at a penalty rate negotiated between debtor and creditor. The UDROP provision allows debtors to increase the maturity of their foreign currency debt and could help them cope with liquidity crises. Because the maturity is extended only for a short period of time, the UDROP would protect only countries facing liquidity crises rather than solvency crises. As with contingent credit lines, there are concerns that there could be a creditor run if the country triggers the UDROP provision.

An international insurance corporation could also insure investors against sovereign debt defaults (Soros, 1998). The insurance cost would be paid in advance by borrowing countries at the time they issue bonds or arrange loans, with borrowing limits set up by institutions like the IMF. To prevent moral hazard, mechanisms to ensure that uninsured debt is not bailed out in case of default would need to be established. In practice, establishing an international insurance corporation faces many obstacles since determining the insurance fee and maximum borrowing amounts are not trivial issues. Also, there is no guarantee that countries would not be bailed out for strategic or political reasons (Rogoff, 1999).

Structuring parallel loan agreements among countries with imperfectly correlated business cycles and growth trends has been proposed by Shiller (2003). These loan agreements would allow countries to insure themselves against underperforming economic growth vis-à-vis the other countries participating in the agreement. Caballero (2003) proposes that emerging market countries issue bonds with payoffs contingent on economic and financial variables correlated with a country's economic activity but not easily manipulated by a country's authorities. Private sector participation in insuring against economic slowdowns using these instruments may be possible if structures such as collateralized debt obligations (CDOs) are used. As pointed out by Mendoza (2004), though, implementing these initiatives requires international cooperation, which may be better coordinated by international financial institutions, such as the IMF.

[1]See Espinosa-Vega and Vera-Martín (2004) for an analysis of market-based mechanisms.

(Caballero and Krishnamurthy, 2003). Under such circumstances, it may be necessary for the authorities to provide some degree of insurance by holding a higher level of NIR.

A careful assessment of self-insurance policy options suggests that emerging markets with different levels of local market development may have to resort to different policy mixes. In a recent study, Solé (2004) develops a framework to analyze the question of whether and how central banks should insure their economies against the risk of default caused by large exchange rate depreciations. In particular, the author compares the welfare implications of three policies.[34] Under a laissez-faire policy, the decision to hedge foreign exchange risk is costly and is left to private firms. If firms decide not to hedge, their creditors perceive them as riskier and charge higher interest rates, which, in turn, reduce the level of economic activity and social welfare (this is represented by a solid line in Figure 4.9). Under a policy of intervention in foreign exchange forward markets, the government bears the cost of hedging activities—measured on the horizontal axis—and charges higher taxes (with the level of welfare falling more smoothly, as in the dotted line). Finally, a policy of stocking reserves involves the use of current tax revenues to acquire foreign currency, and since this is independent of the cost of hedging, it is represented by the flat line in Figure 4.9.

If local securities and derivatives markets are highly underdeveloped, self-insurance has to be done by accumulating international reserves. This is represented by region III in Figure 4.9. As local markets develop and hedging costs decline, the authorities intervene in the forward market to finance a future

Figure 4.9. Welfare Effects of Self-Insurance Policy

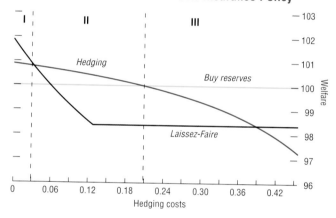

Source: Solé (2004).

---

[34]The policies studied are (1) buying and holding foreign reserves as a buffer stock; (2) intervention in the foreign exchange forward market to acquire contracts that deliver foreign currency at a future date; and (3) a laissez-faire policy in which no bailout takes place.

Figure 4.10. Global Imbalances
(In billions of U.S. dollars)

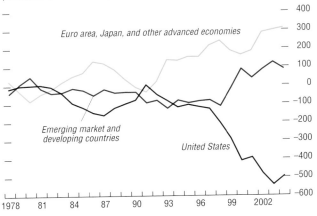

Source: IMF, *World Economic Outlook.*
Note: Summary of balances on the current account.

Figure 4.11. Net Private Capital Flows to Emerging Markets and Foreign Purchases of G3 Bonds and Stocks
(In billions of U.S. dollars)

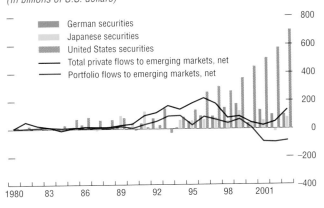

Sources: Bloomberg; and IMF, *World Economic Outlook.*

bailout of partially hedged corporates (region II). Finally, in highly developed financial markets, welfare is maximized by no government intervention (i.e., a laissez-faire regime in region I, where there is no need to accumulate NIR).

Reserve accumulation may be a desirable self-insurance policy and it may also have a positive impact on the development of local bond markets, suggesting that both policies complement and reinforce each other. Sterilization is required to contain the inflationary pressures associated with the rapid accumulation of reserves, and sterilization operations in several emerging markets are conducted by issuing central bank debt—rather than government bonds. Substituting government debt for central bank debt can help accelerate the development of local government bond markets by increasing market size and liquidity (McCauley, 2003a). In turn, a well-developed government bond market can facilitate the development of corporate fixed-income markets, and hence reduce a country's dependence on external capital (IMF, 2002). Special care should be taken, though, to avoid government bond issuance from crowding out corporate bond issuance.

In sum, self-insurance provides a number of arguments to rationalize a higher-than pre-crisis level of reserves—and, hence, a transitional period of emerging markets as net capital exporters. However, it is unclear to what extent self-insurance has been an important motivation behind the large NIR accumulation. Indeed, monetary authorities seem to have been driven by a desire to prevent nominal exchange rate appreciation in the pursuit of export-led growth policies—especially in Asia and after the increase in inflows in 2003–04. While both motivations are likely to be valid and co-existing, several analysts have argued that economic development considerations involve keeping the real exchange rate undervalued in order to bias domestic investment toward export industries. Others have argued that these policies may cause inflationary pressures and that they may also delay the implementation of structural changes needed to reduce future crises (Bird and Rajan, 2003).

Global Factors

In an increasingly globalized capital market, global factors—such as the bursting of the global equity market bubble, the increasing role of China in global trade and production, and global imbalances among the mature markets—are having a progressively more important impact on capital flows to emerging markets. As the emerging market asset class becomes more mainstream, determinants of the global asset allocation process—in particular, risk-adjusted returns across asset classes and countries—become more relevant for emerging markets. Combined with increased geopolitical risks and an increased perception of emerging markets as a risky asset class, these factors have increased investor risk aversion and contributed to a reduction in the supply of funds available for emerging markets in international capital markets—which, in turn, contributes to the emerging markets as capital exporters phenomenon, especially in 2000–02.

In particular, increasing current account deficits in the U.S. have absorbed an increasing share of capital flows.[35] In contrast to the first half of the 1980s, when U.S. deficits were financed mostly by outflows from the euro area, Japan, and other advanced economies, the current episode shows emerging markets also contributing to finance such deficits (see Figure 4.10). Moreover, large increases in international gross asset and liability positions over the past decade are likely to change the international financial adjustment process (see Lane and Milesi-Ferretti, 2003 and 2004; and Gourinchas and Rey, 2004).

[35]The United States' current account deficit represents 71.6 percent of global capital imports (see the Statistical Appendix, Figure 1).

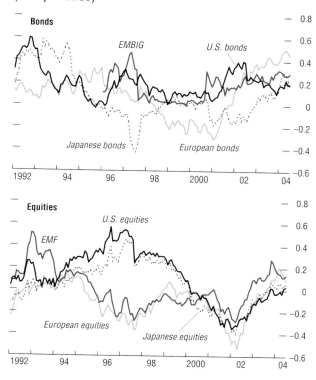

Figure 4.12. Risk-Adjusted Rates of Return (Sharpe ratios)[1]

Source: IMF staff estimates based on Bloomberg.
[1]Sharpe ratios are monthly excess returns divided by rolling volatilities.

These underlying macroeconomic imbalances have affected global fixed-income and equity markets, which, in turn, have repercussions on capital flows to emerging markets. The sharp increase in foreign purchases of U.S. securities since 1999 is negatively correlated with private (and especially) portfolio flows to emerging markets—and also with foreign purchases of German and Japanese securities (see Figure 4.11). This is, however, justified by risk-adjusted returns: Sharpe ratios for U.S. bonds dominate ratios for emerging market, European, and Japanese bonds from 1996 to 2003 (see Figure 4.12). The same can be said about Sharpe ratios for equities, where the dominance of risk-adjusted returns runs from 1994 until 2001.[36] Capital has been flowing to where returns are higher or, perhaps more relevant in these uncertain times, where risks are relatively lower. Over the past 18 months, better risk-adjusted returns have supported a resumption of flows to emerging market assets. However, the beginning of the tightening cycle in the major financial centers could have an impact on flows to emerging market countries (see discussion in Chapter II).

The post-crisis balance sheet adjustments have been accompanied by an important pattern of international risk transfer, which links these adjustments to global imbalances. As noted in previous sections, the strengthening of balance sheets in emerging markets has involved a substantial reduction in external debt and an increase in liquid reserves. Toward the end of this process, emerging markets—particularly in Asia (see McCauley, 2003b)—have been receiving risky equity capital while investing in safe interbank deposits and U.S. treasury and agency securities.[37]

Although there is a cost involved in the process, the risk transfer from emerging to mature markets is likely to contribute to improve the resilience of emerging markets' balance sheets and to a better allocation of risk worldwide. McCauley (2003b) notes that in this process the U.S. economy is playing the role of a global financial intermediary, providing international risk absorption and maturity transformation, and, as such, the U.S. net international investment position can be interpreted as the intermediary's capital base. McCauley also notes that, while there is a latent conflict between the deteriorating net international investment position of the United States and its role in international financial risk intermediation, this conflict appeared to be far from pressing.

Heightened uncertainty and global risk aversion have had a major impact not just on the level of flows to emerging markets but also on the geographical distribution of portfolio investments. Results from the IMF's *Coordinated Portfolio Investment Survey* (CPIS) suggest that there has been a retrenchment of U.S. investors from both crisis and non-crisis countries between 1997 and 2002 (see Table 4.7). This is likely to have been determined by a decline in risk-adjusted returns in emerging markets, compared to returns that could be earned in mature markets, especially in the United States (see Figure 4.12), as well as by the reduction in risk capital allocated to emerging markets by opportunistic investors (hedge funds and the proprietary trading desks of major banks) in the aftermath of regional and global crises. During the same period, the total value of emerging market assets held by European and Asian mature market investors appears to

[36]Although Sharpe ratios are a widely used measure of risk-adjusted returns, some asset managers also consider correlations with market portfolios and benchmarks as guides for their asset allocation decisions. See IMF (2004b) for an analysis of institutional investors' allocation decisions vis-à-vis emerging market assets.

[37]There was a similar exchange of risk between the United States and the euro area in the late 1990s, with the latter absorbing risk while issuing short and low-risk liabilities in order to buy risky equity shares (see McCauley, 2003b).

Table 4.7. Derived Portfolio Investment Liabilities by Nonresident Holder: Equity and Debt Securities
(In millions of U.S. dollars)

| Investment to | Investment from | | | | | | |
| | Industrial Countries | | | Emerging Markets | | | |
	North America	Europe	Asia	Latin America	EM Europe	EM Asia	Total
1997							
Crisis Countries	**153,486**	**72,963**	**32,794**	**7,885**	**0**	**4,826**	**271,955**
Brazil	52,968	22,198	2,572	2,592	0	67	80,397
Argentina	38,648	16,668	3,097	1,439	0	245	60,097
Russia	12,223	12,717	346	3,130	0	984	29,399
Turkey	7,046	861	4,100	18	0	132	12,157
Indonesia	4,532	2,555	1,249	164	0	1,170	9,669
Korea	15,596	8,059	8,665	134	0	18	32,472
Malaysia	9,288	4,919	9,510	157	0	1,011	24,885
Thailand	5,784	2,699	2,239	98	0	647	11,467
Philippines	7,402	2,287	1,018	154	0	552	11,413
Non-Crisis Countries	**105,369**	**39,543**	**15,213**	**2,510**	**0**	**1,085**	**163,719**
Mexico	65,004	19,709	3,773	1,559	0	328	90,374
Chile	8,231	1,359	42	79	0	0	9,712
Colombia	4,147	988	382	22	0	93	5,632
Peru	3,687	763	101	37	0	0	4,588
Czech Republic	869	2,035	448	9	0	1	3,360
Hungary	5,021	4,167	3,425	29	0	53	12,695
Poland	4,531	3,152	145	157	0	21	8,006
China	5,523	3,555	5,038	370	0	306	14,792
India	8,356	3,815	1,857	249	0	283	14,560
Total	**258,855**	**112,506**	**48,007**	**10,395**	**0**	**5,910**	**435,673**
2002							
Crisis Countries	**87,906**	**110,938**	**46,539**	**9,638**	**1,386**	**4,024**	**260,433**
Argentina	234	8,454	1,855	675	1	5	11,224
Brazil	21,181	23,144	4,331	8,159	42	34	56,890
Russia	11,579	18,217	285	142	1,302	6	31,530
Turkey	1,905	14,932	1,460	34	31	12	18,374
Indonesia	2,777	2,387	2,469	34	0	2,962	10,629
Korea	39,532	30,444	17,805	343	4	154	88,282
Malaysia	4,028	5,746	11,027	73	0	509	21,384
Thailand	2,697	4,385	4,646	58	2	225	12,014
Philippines	3,974	3,230	2,659	120	5	117	10,106
Non-Crisis Countries	**67,569**	**68,062**	**15,045**	**5,658**	**691**	**7,947**	**164,971**
Mexico	43,268	20,472	2,180	4,309	15	79	70,323
Chile	4,371	2,924	70	100	0	2	7,467
Colombia	1,165	2,242	375	735	0	2	4,520
Peru	2,019	835	25	138	(5)	0	3,014
Czech Republic	885	2,382	17	0	33	0	3,318
Hungary	2,002	17,061	780	83	320	4	20,250
Poland	3,013	11,399	108	36	327	1	14,884
China	2,986	5,811	10,684	164	1	485	20,130
India	7,860	4,935	807	91	0	7,372	21,065
Total	**155,475**	**179,000**	**61,584**	**15,296**	**2,078**	**11,970**	**425,404**

Source: IMF staff estimates based on Coordinated Portfolio Investment Survey (CPIS) data.
Note: Shaded areas highlight the largest holdings of securities of a particular emerging market.

have increased substantially, contributing to a more balanced investor base for emerging market assets.[38]

Moreover, investments in non-crisis countries, and to a lesser extent those in crisis countries, show a clear trend toward increas-

[38]This last statement should be interpreted with some caution, as it could also be due to improved coverage of these regions in the 2002 survey.

Table 4.8. Derived Portfolio Investment Liabilities by Nonresident Holder: Short- and Long-Term Debt Securities

(In millions of U.S. dollars)

| | Investment from | | | | | | |
| | Industrial Countries | | | Emerging Markets | | | |
Investment to	North America	Europe	Asia	Latin America	EM Europe	EM Asia	Total
1997							
Crisis Countries	75,360	49,404	24,644	5,699	0	4,605	159,711
Brazil	20,280	12,543	2,271	1,822	0	67	36,983
Argentina	25,338	13,465	2,993	1,264	0	245	43,305
Russia	3,680	11,195	331	2,246	0	959	18,411
Turkey	995	100	4,018	0	0	132	5,245
Indonesia	1,881	1,489	786	107	0	1,150	5,413
Korea	10,961	6,769	8,512	111	0	18	26,370
Malaysia	4,320	1,289	3,683	77	0	884	10,252
Thailand	3,464	1,277	1,489	68	0	636	6,934
Philippines	4,440	1,277	561	5	0	515	6,798
Non-Crisis Countries	46,391	23,697	12,911	1,514	0	1,056	85,569
Mexico	29,003	12,207	3,554	1,293	0	325	46,383
Colombia	3,423	596	382	13	0	93	4,506
Chile	3,530	238	5	30	0	0	3,802
Peru	1,263	375	53	5	0	0	1,696
Czech Republic	46	1,476	410	0	0	0	1,932
Hungary	1,364	2,637	3,353	8	0	53	7,415
Poland	2,868	2,380	108	144	0	21	5,521
China	3,160	2,524	4,195	20	0	293	10,192
India	1,734	1,264	851	2	0	271	4,122
Total	121,751	73,100	37,555	7,213	0	5,661	245,280
2002							
Crisis Countries	23,571	56,629	33,252	8,681	842	1,643	124,618
Argentina	216	7,509	1,844	609	1	5	10,185
Brazil	5,083	17,069	4,094	7,703	42	34	34,024
Russia	6,518	10,248	212	76	760	6	17,820
Turkey	1,286	9,045	1,452	34	31	12	11,860
Indonesia	221	687	1,008	24	0	933	2,872
Korea	5,793	7,507	14,614	17	3	85	28,019
Malaysia	1,301	1,470	5,907	62	0	439	9,180
Thailand	46	347	2,032	43	0	40	2,507
Philippines	3,107	2,746	2,088	114	5	90	8,151
Non-Crisis Countries	29,031	42,575	7,589	5,275	635	265	85,370
Mexico	20,315	13,084	1,998	4,089	15	71	39,573
Colombia	988	2,229	375	689	0	2	4,283
Chile	3,625	946	64	70	0	2	4,707
Peru	1,632	594	15	104	(5)	2	2,342
Czech Republic	114	1,186	12	0	20	0	1,332
Hungary	37	14,167	763	33	307	4	15,311
Poland	1,943	8,925	101	35	298	1	11,303
China	377	1,195	3,848	163	1	61	5,644
India	1	247	414	91	0	121	875
Total	52,603	99,203	40,841	13,956	1,476	1,908	209,988

Source: IMF staff estimates based on Coordinated Portfolio Investment Survey (CPIS) data.
Note: Shaded areas highlight the largest holdings of securities of a particular emerging market.

ing regionalization of asset holdings. This is quite noticeable for the pattern of debt holdings (Table 4.8; note the shaded areas that form a diagonal in the lower panel of the table), but holds to a large extent also for holdings of debt and equity securities (Table 4.7). Furthermore, emerging markets in Asia and Latin America have increased substantially their holdings of regional assets, in part owing to the development of local institutional investor bases.[39] This stronger "regional bias" is likely to be due to the fact that higher uncertainty has led investors to purchase more securities in countries where geographic proximity ensures better knowledge of institutional and other fundamental determinants of risk and return profiles.

In retrospect, emerging market securities have remained relatively well-supported by international investors. To the extent that U.S. investors can be considered representative of the mature market investor base in general, this can be seen by examining the main trends in the retail and institutional investor flows into the U.S.-based emerging market, international equity, and international bond mutual funds. As the upper panel of Figure 4.13 shows, during 1998–2002 cumulative net inflows into the U.S.-based emerging market equity funds, which manage both retail and institutional money, remained relatively stable, before picking up sharply in 2003. The dynamics of total net assets of the U.S.-based emerging market equity funds essentially mirrored the performance of the MSCI EMF index. Similarly, total net assets of the U.S.-based emerging market hedge funds, which invest in emerging market equity and debt securities, remained resilient during 1997–2000, and moved more in line with the EMBI Global index (see lower panel of Figure 4.13).[40] Thus, while it may be regrettable that there was no notable pickup in inflows into dedicated emerging market funds during the time of retrenchment in international bank lending, it is encouraging that these funds did not experience major outflows despite a string

Figure 4.13. Emerging Market Mutual and Hedge Fund Assets

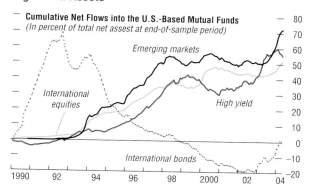

Cumulative Net Flows into the U.S.-Based Mutual Funds
(In percent of total net assest at end-of-sample period)

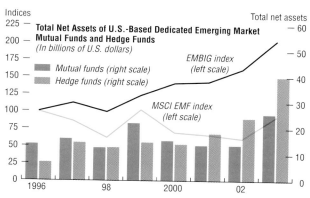

Total Net Assets of U.S.-Based Dedicated Emerging Market Mutual Funds and Hedge Funds
(In billions of U.S. dollars)

Source: Investment Company Institute (U.S.).

[39]See IMF (2004b).

[40]In contrast, the capital under management of global macro hedge funds and proprietary trading desks of international banks—and, therefore, their allocations to emerging markets— were significantly reduced during the same period, but recovered in 2003.

of emerging market crises and increased global risk aversion. Although this asset allocation trend may not be identical to that of other institutional investors, the fact that pension funds and insurance companies are investing in emerging market and alternative securities at the margin, suggests that they may be rather close.[41]

In sum, emerging markets appear to have faced a reasonable supply of foreign funds, despite the turbulence in international markets and the string of crises and costly adjustment processes faced over the last decade or so.

Conclusions and Policy Issues

The perceived anomaly of emerging markets as net capital exporters appears to be less of an anomaly when the bust phase of the 1990s cycle in capital flows is studied in detail. The confluence of ongoing, deep, and long balance sheet adjustments in some emerging markets, with concomitant crises in other emerging markets at the turn of the century, goes a long way in explaining the collective position of emerging markets as net capital exporters in 2000–01. Reserves accumulation was the largest capital outflow associated with emerging markets as net capital exporters in 2002–04, despite increased private capital flows. Global uncertainties and imbalances are likely to have reduced the amount of capital available for emerging markets, but these countries were simultaneously reducing their external financing needs: in all, the reduction of flows to emerging markets is understandable in the context of developments in international capital markets.

Despite the depth and length of the last capital flows cycle, the phenomenon of emerging markets as net capital exporters may be mostly a cyclical, thus temporary, phenomenon. There are a number of institutional factors and capital market frictions that restrict the level of capital flows to emerging markets, and some of them have become more apparent during the crisis episodes.[42] However, the recent pickup in private capital inflows to emerging markets over the past 18 months is likely to be the beginning of a moderate resumption of flows to emerging markets. The strength and persistence of the recovery in flows to emerging markets will depend, among other factors, on how exchange rate policies and global imbalances evolve in the medium term. In particular, emerging markets have already accumulated enough reserves, and some market participants argue that the costs of accumulating more international reserves—including macroeconomic instability—are going to come to the fore and could reduce such accumulation in the near future.[43] However, analysts also argue that some emerging markets (especially, but not exclusively, in Asia) are likely to continue to be net capital exporters for some time, as the massive reallocation of production toward China has left corporates in these nations extremely uncertain about which sectors would be profitable in this new environment. This would reduce investment levels below trend and contribute to net capital exports.

The analysis of the phenomenon of emerging markets as net capital exporters raises several policy issues. The three key reasons behind emerging markets' position as net capital exporters suggest, in turn, three sets of policy issues. In particular, some policy measures and institutional arrangements could facilitate faster and more efficient balance sheet adjustments in both the private and public sectors in emerging markets; also, an

---

[41]See IMF (2004b).

[42]Alfaro, Kalemi-Ozcan, and Volosovych (2003) study the main structural impediments to larger flows to emerging markets and conclude that institutional quality is the most important determinant of the so-called Lucas paradox, which describes why capital does not flow to emerging markets in larger volumes.

[43]See, for instance, Fernandez and Malcolm (2004).

orderly resolution of global imbalances in the mature markets appears to be critical to a sustained resumption of flows to emerging markets.

The first set of policy measures would involve policies aimed at making shorter and more efficient the post-crisis balance sheet adjustments, such that emerging markets can resume growth soon after a major financial shock. The recovery, and the associated resumption of flows, would also be faster if structural reforms improve the environment for investment in general and, in particular, FDI—the largest component of capital flows to emerging markets, and one that tends to behave in a countercyclical fashion. As noted in CMCG (2003), sound macroeconomic policies, improvements in the investment climate, and the development of local financial markets are critical elements for the attraction of FDI. In particular, the removal of regulatory, legal, and tax impediments for FDI would pave the way for a faster recovery after crises. Also, a consistent track record of respect of property rights, a stable and transparent regulatory framework, local sources of finance, and continuous dialogue with the private sector would facilitate the resumption of FDI flows.

In this vein, the chapter has also highlighted the need to improve markets for distressed debt to make less costly and disruptive the period of post-crisis deleveraging. This involves improving not only bankruptcy laws and the enforcement property rights, but also the market infrastructure that allows for a more rapid disposition of and trading of dis-

tressed assets. This would have the double benefit of making the adjustment less severe for local corporates and attracting foreign risk capital to contribute to the restructuring process.[44] The lengthy period of time needed to complete a corporate turnaround and realize the associated capital gains also requires assurances that taxation and repatriation policies are consistent over relatively long periods of time.[45] Moreover, deep and liquid equity and property markets would reduce the overshooting of asset prices and cushion the value of collateral after a sudden stop, stabilizing credit flows to some extent.[46] Also, they would facilitate the transfer of ownership and control, and result in a better allocation of resources.

The second set of policies has to do with what countries can do to self-insure against sudden stops in capital inflows. The pursuit of strong policies that promote macroeconomic stability is a necessary condition for financial stability in the face of sudden stops, but it may not be sufficient. Several emerging markets have been accumulating large amounts of international reserves in part to self-insure, but this may be rather costly and conspire against macroeconomic stability. Hence, the development of local securities markets, as well as other market mechanisms to self-insure, would allow emerging markets to protect themselves against financial crises with a lower reliance on NIR. The optimal policy mix to self-insure depends on the level of development of local securities and derivatives markets, and the development of local markets not only improves the efficiency of the

[44]The amounts involved may be substantial, as a recent survey by Ernst and Young (2004) indicated that while Asia (including Japan) has disposed of $1 trillion in bad loans, the region also has another $1 trillion to manage.

[45]Market participants have noted that, as foreign funds cashed out of investments made in distressed assets in some Asian countries, tax authorities then audited and penalized investors with retroactive taxes on funds that were seen to have made "exorbitant" returns. Since the investor base for these distressed assets is small and very specialized, these policies can have negative "spillovers" across countries and inhibit the supply of risk capital when it is most needed.

[46]Analysts have also noted that some banks that had sold loans to AMCs in the Asian crisis countries, were reluctant to lend again to such corporates despite improvements in their balance sheets. This was in part due to lack of changes in ownership and control of the companies.

allocation of financial capital but also has the added benefit of reducing the cost of self-insurance and leaving it more in the hands of the private sector (see IMF, 2003a).

In the same vein, countries could do much more in terms of improving the management of international reserves. The authorities in emerging markets need to incorporate risk management practices into both sides of their balance sheets, and refine the estimation of the costs and benefits of their holdings of NIR. Several emerging markets have conducted effective liability management operations to improve their debt profiles, and many of them are also becoming more sophisticated managers of their NIR. However, only a few incorporate the trade-offs implicit across both sides of the national balance sheets. Moreover, estimation of the opportunity costs of holding reserves would have to incorporate potential market risks (in particular, relative to exchange rate fluctuations) and macroeconomic risks (such as the inflationary consequences of nonsterilized intervention). The benefits of NIR accumulation are more difficult to estimate as they are related to more elusive precautionary needs—even though this might be reflected in lower borrowing costs.

In particular, some analysts have argued that countries may want to hold a larger but better diversified—perhaps held in an equity fund—level of reserves, rather than a smaller level of liquid reserves (Feldstein, 2003). In other words, that countries may be better off substituting some investment risk for less risk of a speculative attack. As several emerging markets have already accumulated large stocks of NIR, they may want to consider more sophisticated approaches to investing their reserves. For instance, some central banks are managing reserves according to three tranches: one for standard intervention/liquidity needs; another for self-insurance vis-

à-vis major shocks; and a third one for trading/asset management purposes.[47] In Singapore, for example, the Government of Singapore Investment Corporation operates as a professional asset manager and invests in a wide set of mature and emerging market securities. Other countries in the region are also considering the adoption of such a model. However, some analysts have questioned the wisdom of having the official sector manage "excessive" reserves and suggested outsourcing that activity to the private sector.

The final set of policy issues relates to the entrance of emerging market assets into the mainstream in global portfolios. This development puts emerging markets into competition with other asset classes for risk capital. The recent experience has shown that emerging markets have to establish a track record of consistently strong macroeconomic policies and structural reforms, to ensure they can deliver attractive risk-adjusted returns to global investors, thus ensuring a steady flow of capital. Individual countries are competing for global capital not just vis-à-vis their "peer group," but also the universe of assets that participate in the global asset allocation process. And this demands a constant updating and upgrading of structural and macro policies.

Finally, a key issue for a more solid resumption of inflows to emerging markets has to do with the resolution of global macroeconomic imbalances, but is very difficult to predict the outcome and implications for emerging markets. Most analysts argue that a large and disruptive correction in the value of the U.S. dollar vis-à-vis other currencies would disrupt flows to emerging markets. However, some analysts (Gourinchas and Rey, 2004) argue that the large cross-holdings of foreign assets and liabilities means that the asset valuation channel of exchange rate adjustments has grown in importance. This would mean that

---

[47]Recent trends in reserves management show increasing exposure to market and credit risks, as well as currency diversification (McCauley and Fung, 2003).

the imbalances would be resolved by a relatively large U.S. dollar depreciation that would effect large transfers of wealth, without large changes in net exports of goods and services (see, however, Lane and Milesi-Ferretti, 2004, for a somewhat more skeptical view on the role of the valuation channel in the international adjustment process). An orderly resolution of these imbalances is probably the best outcome for a steady flow of capital to emerging markets.

References

Alfaro, Laura, Sebnem Kalemli-Ozcan, and Vadym Volosovych, 2003, "Why Doesn't Capital Flow from Rich to Poor Countries? An Empirical Investigation," (unpublished; Boston: Harvard Business School).

Aizenman, Joshua, and Nancy Marion, 2003, "The High Demand for International Reserves in the Far East: What is Going On?" *Journal of the Japanese and International Economies 17*, pp. 370–400.

Bank for International Settlements, 2004, *74th Annual Report* (Basel: Bank for International Settlements).

Bird, Graham, and Ramkishen Rajan, 2003, "Too Much of a Good Thing? The Adequacy of International Reserves in the Aftermath of Crises," *The World Economy*, Vol. 26, pp. 873–91.

Blejer, Mario I., and Liliana Schumacher, 1998, "VAR for Central Banks," *Risk*, October, pp. 65–69.

Brown, B., 1992, "Capital Flight," *The New Palgrave Dictionary of Money and Finance*, ed. by Peter Newman, Murray Milgate, and John Eatwell, Vol. 1 (New York: Stockton Press), pp. 294–96.

Buiter, William, and Anne Sibert, 1999, "UDROP: A Small Contribution to the New International Financial Architecture," CEPR Discussion Paper No. 2138 (London: Centre for Economic Policy Research).

Caballero, Ricardo J., 2003, "On the International Financial Architecture: Insuring Emerging Markets," NBER Working Paper No. 9570 (Cambridge, Mass.: National Bureau of Economic Research).

———, and Arvind Krishnamurthy, 2003, "Excessive Dollar Debt: Financial Development and Underinsurance," *Journal of Finance*, Vol. 58, pp. 867–94.

Calvo, Guillermo A., 1998, "Capital Flows and Capital-Market Crises: The Simple Economics of Sudden Stops" (unpublished; University of Maryland).

Capital Markets Consultative Group (CMCG), 2003, "Foreign Direct Investment in Emerging Markets" (Washington, September).

Chan-Lau, Jorge A., 2004, "Reserve Holdings and Sovereign Default Risk," (unpublished; Washington: International Monetary Fund).

———, Arnaud Jobert, and Janet Kong, 2004, "An Option-Based Approach to Bank Vulnerabilities in Emerging Markets," IMF Working Paper No. 04/33 (Washington: International Monetary Fund).

Christiano, Lawrence, Christopher Gust, and Jorge Roldos, 2002, "Monetary Policy in a Financial Crisis," NBER Working Paper No. 9005 (Cambridge, Mass.: National Bureau of Economic Research).

Collyns, Charles, and Mohamed A. El-Erian, 1993, "Restructuring of Commercial Bank Debt by Developing Countries: Lessons from Recent Experience," IMF Paper on Policy Analysis and Assessment No. 93/7 (Washington: International Monetary Fund).

Crosbie, Peter J. and Jeffrey R. Bohn. 2003, "Modeling Default Risk." Moody's KMV [online]. Available via the Internet at *http://www.moodyskmv.com.*

Dobson, Wendy, and Gary Clyde Hufbauer, 2001, "World Capital Markets: Challenge to the G-10," (Washington, DC: Institute for International Economics).

Dornbusch, Rudiger, 1990, "Capital Flight: Theory, Measurement and Policy Issues," Occasional Paper No. 2 (Washington: Inter-American Development Bank).

Edison, Hali, 2003, "Are Foreign Exchange Reserves in Asia Too High," in the *World Economic Outlook* (Washington: International Monetary Fund, September), pp. 78–92.

Eichengreen, Barry, and Ashoka Mody, 1998, "What Explains Changing Spreads on Emerging Market Debt?" NBER Working Paper No. 6408 (Cambridge, Mass.: National Bureau of Economic Research).

Ernst and Young, 2004, "Global Nonperforming Loan Report."

Espinosa-Vega, Marco A., and Mercedes Vera-
  Martín, 2004, "On Chile's Holding of Foreign
  Reserves" (unpublished; Washington:
  International Monetary Fund).

Feldstein, Martin, 2003, "An Overview of
  Prevention and Management," in *Economic and
  Financial Crises in Emerging Market Economies*, ed.
  by Martin Feldstein (Chicago and London: The
  University of Chicago Press), pp. 1–29.

Fernandez, David G., and James Malcolm, 2004,
  "An Asian Intervention Reader," *Economic and
  Foreign Exchange Research* (New York: J.P. Morgan,
  March).

Fernandez, Raquel, and Sule Ozler, 1991, "Debt
  Concentration and Secondary Market Prices,"
  World Bank Working Paper No. 570 (Washing-
  ton: World Bank).

Ferrucci, Gianluigi, 2003, "Empirical Determinants
  of Emerging Market Economies' Sovereign Bond
  Spreads," Working Paper No. 205 (London:
  Bank of England).

———, Valerie Herzberg, Farouk Soussa, and
  Ashley Taylor, 2004, "Understanding Capital
  Flows to Emerging Market Economies," *Financial
  Stability Review*, Vol. 16 (London: Bank of
  England, June), pp. 89–97.

Froot, Kenneth A., and Jeremy C. Stein, 1991,
  "Exchange Rates and Foreign Direct Investment:
  An Imperfect Capital Markets Approach," *The
  Quarterly Journal of Economics*, Vol. 106
  (November), pp. 1191–217.

Fung, Ben, George Jason, Stefan Hohl, and
  Guonan Ma, 2004, "Public Asset Management
  Companies in East Asia," BIS Occasional Paper
  No 3 (Basel: Bank for International Settlements,
  February).

Gapen, Michael T., Dale F. Gray, Cheng Hoon
  Lim, and Yingbin Xiao, 2004, "The Contingent
  Claims Approach to Corporate Vulnerability
  Analysis: Estimating Default Risk and Economy-
  wide Risk Transfer," in *Corporate Restructuring:
  International Best Practices*, ed. by Michael
  Pomerleano and William Shaw (Washington:
  World Bank).

Ghosh, Atish, Timothy Lane, Marianne Schulze-
  Ghattas, Ales Bulir, Javier Hamann, and Alex
  Mourmouras, 2002, *IMF-Supported Programs in
  Capital Account Crises*, Occasional Paper No. 210
  (Washington: International Monetary Fund).

Gonzalez-Eiras, Martin, 2002, "The Effect of
  Contingent Credit Lines on Banks' Liquidity

Demand" (unpublished, Buenos Aires:
  Universidad de San Andres).

Gourinchas, Pierre-Olivier, and Hélène Rey, 2004,
  "International Financial Adjustment" (unpub-
  lished; Princeton University Department of
  Economics).

Gray, Dale F., Robert C. Merton, and Zvi Bodie,
  2003, "A New Framework for Analyzing and
  Managing Macrofinancial Risks of an Economy,"
  MfRisk Working Paper No. 1–03. Available via
  the Internet at *http://www.moodys-mfrisk.com*.

Gunter, Frank R., 2004, "Capital Flight from China:
  1984–2001," *China Economic Review*, Vol. 15,
  pp. 63–85.

Hoelscher, David S., and Marc Quintyn, 2003,
  Managing Systemic Bank Crises, IMF Occasional
  Paper No. 224 (Washington: International
  Monetary Fund).

Hviding, Ketil, Michael Nowak, and Luca Antonio
  Ricci, 2004, "Can Higher Reserves Help Reduce
  Exchange Rate Volatility?" (unpublished,
  Washington: International Monetary Fund).

International Monetary Fund, 2000, *World Economic
  Outlook: Supporting Studies* (Washington).

———, 2001, "Emerging Market Financing,"
  Quarterly Report on Developments and Prospects
  (November 14).

———, 2002, *Global Financial Stability Report*, World
  Economic and Financial Surveys (Washington,
  March).

———, 2003a, *Global Financial Stability Report*,
  World Economic and Financial Surveys
  (Washington, March).

———, 2003b, *World Economic Outlook* (Washington,
  September).

———, 2003c, *Global Financial Stability Report*,
  World Economic and Financial Surveys
  (Washington, September).

———, 2004a, "The IMF's Contingent Credit Lines
  (CCL): A Factsheet," (Washington, March).
  Available via the Internet at *http://www.imf.org/
  external/np/exr/facts/ccl.htm*.

———, 2004b, *Global Financial Stability Report*,
  World Economic and Financial Surveys
  (Washington, April).

Kamin, Steven, and Karsten von Kleist, 1999, "The
  Evolution and Determinants of Emerging Market
  Credit Spreads in the 1990s," BIS Working Paper
  No. 68 (Basel: Bank for International Settlements).

Kaminsky, Graciela, and Carmen Reinhart, 1999,
  "The Twin Crisis: The Causes of Banking and

Balance-of-Payments Problems," *American Economic Review*, Vol. 89 (June), pp. 473–500.

Kiyotaki, Nobuhito, and John Moore, 1997, "Credit Cycles," *Journal of Political Economy*, Vol. 105 (April), pp. 211–48.

Kletzer, Kenneth, and Ashoka Mody, 2000, "Will Self-Protection Policies Safeguard Emerging Markets from Crises" (unpublished; Washington: World Bank).

Lane, Philip R., and Gian Maria Milesi-Ferretti, 2003, "International Financial Integration," *IMF Staff Papers*, International Monetary Fund, Vol. 50 (Special Issue), pp. 82–113.

———, 2004, "Financial Globalization and Exchange Rates," paper presented at the international conference organized by the Banco de España and the International Monetary Fund, "Dollars, Debt, and Deficits—60 Years After Bretton Woods," Madrid, June.

Lee, Jaewoo, 2004, "The Insurance Value of Reserves: An Option Pricing Approach," (unpublished; Washington: International Monetary Fund).

LoPucki, Lynn M., and Sara D. Kalin, 2000, "The Failure of Public Company Bankruptcies in Delaware and New York: Empirical Evidence of a "Race to the Bottom," *Vanderbilt Law Review* (July 22). Available via the Internet at *http://ssrn.com/abstract=237029*.

McCauley, Robert, 2003a, "Unifying Government Bond Markets in Asia," *BIS Quarterly Review* (Basel: Bank for International Settlements, December), pp. 89–98.

———, 2003b, "Capital Flows in East Asia Since the 1997 Crisis," *BIS Quarterly Review*, (Basel: Bank for International Settlements, June), pp. 41–55.

———, and Ben S.C. Fung, 2003, "Choosing Instruments in Managing Dollar Foreign Exchange Reserves," *BIS Quarterly Review* (Basel: Bank for International Settlements, March), pp. 39–46.

Mendoza, Ronald U., 2004, "International Reserve-Holding in the Developing World: Self Insurance in a Crisis-Prone Era?," *Emerging Markets Review*, Vol. 5, pp. 61–82.

Ohashi, Kazunari, and Manmohan Singh, 2004, "Japan's Distressed Debt Market," IMF Working Paper No. 04/86 (Washington: International Monetary Fund).

Rogoff, Kenneth, 1999, "International Institutions for Reducing Global Financial Instability," *Journal of Economic Perspectives*, Vol. 13, pp. 21–42.

Shiller, Robert J., 2003, *The New Financial Order: Risk in the 21st Century* (Princeton and Oxford: Princeton University Press).

Solé, Juan, 2004, "Should Central Banks Hedge Foreign Exchange Risk?" (unpublished; Washington: International Monetary Fund, International Capital Markets Department).

Soros, George, 1998, *The Crisis of Global Capitalism* (New York: Public Affairs).

Tweedie, Andrew, 2000, "The Demand for International Reserves—A Review of the Literature" (unpublished; Washington: International Monetary Fund).

GLOSSARY

401(k)	U.S. tax-deferred retirement plan that allows workers to contribute a percentage of their pre-tax salary for investment in stocks, bonds or other securities. The employer may match all or part of employees' contributions.
Accrued benefit	Amount of accumulated pension benefits of a pension plan member.
Accumulated benefit obligation (ABO)	Present value of pension benefits promised by a company to its employees, at a particular date and based on current salaries.
Actuarial gain/loss	An actuarial gain (loss) appears when actual experience is more (less) favorable than the actuary's estimate.
Annuity	A contract that provides an income for a specified period of time, such as a number of years or for life.
Asset/liability management (ALM)	The management of assets to ensure that liabilities are sufficiently covered by suitable assets at all times.
Balance sheet mismatch	A balance sheet is a financial statement showing a company's assets, liabilities and equity on a given date. Typically, a mismatch in a balance sheet implies that the maturities of the liabilities differ (are typically shorter) from those of the assets and/or that some liabilities are denominated in a foreign currency while the assets are not.
Banking soundness	The financial health of a single bank or of a country's banking system.
Beneficiary	Individual who is entitled to a pension benefit (including the pension plan member and dependants).
Book reserve scheme (also known as *Direktzusage*)	In Germany, accounting system whereby the actuarial value of future pension benefits appears as a liability, but is not offset by any specific provision, on the sponsor company's balance sheet.
Brady bonds	Bonds issued by emerging market countries as part of a restructuring of defaulted commercial bank loans. These bonds are named after former U.S. Treasury Secretary Nicholas Brady and the first bonds were issued in March of 1990.
Carry trade	A leveraged transaction in which borrowed funds are used to buy a security whose yield is expected to exceed the cost of the borrowed funds.
Cash securitization	The creation of securities from a pool of pre-existing assets and receivables that are placed under the legal control of investors through a special intermediary created for this purpose. This compares with a "synthetic" securitization where the generic securities are created out of derivative instruments.

Collective action clause	A clause in bond contracts that includes provisions allowing a qualified majority of lenders to amend key financial terms of the debt contract and bind a minority to accept these new terms.
Corporate governance	The governing relationships between all the stakeholders in a company—including the shareholders, directors, and management—as defined by the corporate charter, bylaws, formal policy, and rule of law.
Credit default swap	A financial contract under which an agent buys protection against credit risk for a periodic fee in return for a payment by the protection seller contingent on the occurrence of a credit/default event.
Credit risk	The risk that a counterparty to the insurer is unable or unwilling to meet its obligations causing a financial loss to the insurer.
Credit spreads	The spread between sovereign benchmark securities and other debt securities that are comparable in all respects except for credit quality (e.g., the difference between yields on U.S. Treasuries and those on single A-rated corporate bonds of a certain term to maturity).
Defined benefit plan	Pension plan in which benefits are determined by such factors as salary history and duration of employment. The sponsor company is responsible for the investment risk and portfolio management.
Defined contribution plan	Pension plan in which benefits are determined by returns on the plan's investments. Beneficiaries bear the investment risk.
Dependency ratio	Ratio of pensioners to those of working age in a given population.
Derivatives	Financial contracts whose value derives from underlying securities prices, interest rates, foreign exchange rates, market indexes, or commodity prices.
Dollarization	The widespread domestic use of another country's currency (typically the U.S. dollar) to perform the standard functions of money—that of a unit of account, medium of exchange, and store of value.
EMBI	The acronym for the J.P. Morgan *Emerging Market Bond Index* that tracks the total returns for traded external debt instruments in the emerging markets.
Emerging markets	Developing countries' financial markets that are less than fully developed, but are nonetheless broadly accessible to foreign investors.
Foreign direct investment	The acquisition abroad (i.e., outside the home country) of physical assets, such as plant and equipment, or of a controlling stake (usually greater than 10 percent of shareholdings).
Forward price-earnings ratio	The multiple of future expected earnings at which a stock sells. It is calculated by dividing the current stock price (adjusted for stock splits) by the estimated earnings per share for a future period (typically the next 12 months).

Funded pension plan	Pension plan that has accumulated dedicated assets to pay for the pension benefits.
Funding gap	The difference between the discounted value of accumulating future pension obligations and the present value of investment assets.
Funding ratio	Ratio of the amount of assets accumulated by a defined benefit pension plan to the sum of promised benefits.
Hedge funds	Investment pools, typically organized as private partnerships and often resident offshore for tax and regulatory purposes. These funds face few restrictions on their portfolios and transactions. Consequently, they are free to use a variety of investment techniques—including short positions, transactions in derivatives, and leverage—to raise returns and cushion risk.
Hedging	Offsetting an existing risk exposure by taking an opposite position in the same or a similar risk, for example, by buying derivatives contracts.
Hybrid pension plan	Retirement plan that has characteristics typical of both defined benefit and defined contribution plans.
Individual retirement account (IRA)	In the U.S., tax-deferred retirement plan permitting all individuals to set aside a fraction of their wages (additional contributions are possible on a non-deductible basis).
Interest rate swaps	An agreement between counterparties to exchange periodic interest payments on some predetermined dollar principal, which is called the notional principal amount. For example, one party will make fixed-rate and receive variable-rate interest payments.
Intermediation	The process of transferring funds from the ultimate source to the ultimate user. A financial institution, such as a bank, intermediates credit when it obtains money from depositors and relends it to borrowers.
Investment-grade issues (Sub-investment-grade issues)	A bond that is assigned a rating in the top four categories by commercial credit rating agencies. S&P classifies investment-grade bonds as BBB or higher, and Moody's classifies investment grade bonds as Baa or higher. (Sub-investment-grade bond issues are rated bonds that are below investment-grade.)
Leverage	The proportion of debt to equity. Leverage can be built up by borrowing (on-balance-sheet leverage, commonly measured by debt-to-equity ratios) or by using off-balance-sheet transactions.
Lump sum payment	Withdrawal of accumulated benefits all at once, as opposed to in regular installments.
Mark-to-market	The valuation of a position or portfolio by reference to the most recent price at which a financial instrument can be bought or sold in normal volumes. The mark-to-market value might equal the current market value—as opposed to historic accounting or book value—or the present value of expected future cash flows.

Nonperforming loans	Loans that are in default or close to being in default (i.e., typically past due for 90 days or more).
Occupational pension scheme	Pension plan set up and managed by a sponsor company for the benefit of its employees.
Offshore instruments	Securities issued outside of national boundaries.
Overfunded plan	Defined benefit pension plan in which assets accumulated are greater than the sum of promised benefits.
Pair-wise correlations	A statistical measure of the degree to which the movements of two variables (for example asset returns) are related.
Pay-as-you-go basis (PAYG)	Arrangement under which benefits are paid out of revenue over each period, instead no funding is made for future liabilities.
Pension benefit	Benefit paid to a participant (beneficiary) in a pension plan.
Pension contribution	Payment made to a pension plan by the sponsor company or by plan participants.
Primary market	The market where a newly issued security is first offered/sold to the public.
Private pension plan	Pension plan where a private entity receives pension contributions and administers the payment of pension benefits.
Projected benefit obligation (PBO)	Present value of pension benefits promised by a company to its employees at a particular date, and including assumption about future salary increases (i.e. assuming that the plan will not terminate in the foreseeable future).
Public pension plan	Pension plan where the general government administers the payment of pension benefits (e.g., Social security and similar schemes).
Put (call) option	A financial contract that gives the buyer the right, but not the obligation, to sell (buy) a financial instrument at a set price on or before a given date.
Reinsurance	Insurance placed by an underwriter in another company to cut down the amount of the risk assumed under the original insurance.
Risk aversion	The degree to which an investor who, when faced with two investments with the same expected return but different risk, prefers the one with the lower risk. That is, it measures an investor's aversion to uncertain outcomes or payoffs.
Secondary markets	Markets in which securities are traded after they are initially offered/sold in the primary market.
Solvency	Narrowly defined as the ability of an insurer to meet its obligations (liabilities) at any time. In order to set a practicable definition, it is necessary to clarify the type of claims covered by the assets, e.g., already written business (run-off basis, break-up basis), or would future

new business (going-concern basis) also to be considered. In addition, questions regarding the volume and the nature of an insurance company's business, the appropriate time horizon to be adopted, and setting an acceptable probability of becoming insolvent are taken into consideration in assessing a company's solvency.

Sponsor company

Company that designs, negotiates, and normally helps to administer an occupational plan for its employees and members.

Spread

See "credit spreads" above (the word credit is sometimes omitted). Other definitions include: (1) the gap between bid and ask prices of a financial instrument; (2) the difference between the price at which an underwriter buys an issue from the issuer and the price at which the underwriter sells it to the public.

Syndicated loans

Large loans made jointly by a group of banks to one borrower. Usually, one lead bank takes a small percentage of the loan and partitions (syndicates) the rest to other banks.

Tail events

The occurrence of large or extreme security price movements, that, in terms of their probability of occurring, lie within the tail region of the distribution of possible price movements.

Trustee

Private entity (person or organization) with a duty to receive, manage and disburse the assets of a plan.

Underfunded plan

Defined benefit pension plan in which assets accumulated are smaller than the sum of promised benefits.

Unfunded benefit liability

Amount of promised pension benefits that exceeds a plan's assets.

Vesting

Right of an employee, on termination of employment, to obtain part or all of his accrued benefits.

With-profits policies

The insurance company guarantees to pay an agreed amount at a specific time in the future, and may increase this guaranteed amount through bonus payments. In effect, the policy holders are participating in the profits of the life insurance company.

Yield curve

A chart that plots the yield to maturity at a specific point in time for debt securities having equal credit risk but different maturity dates.

SUMMING UP BY THE CHAIRMAN

The following remarks by the Chairman were made at the conclusion of the Executive Board's discussion of the Global Financial Stability Report *on August 30, 2004.*

Executive Directors had a wide-ranging discussion of financial market developments, prospects, and risks as part of the IMF's surveillance over global financial stability. They welcomed the further strengthening of global financial stability and of key financial intermediaries in the past six months. Directors considered that the combination of broadening global economic growth and low inflationary expectations has created a favorable environment for financial markets. Strong economic growth has boosted corporate and banking sector earnings, facilitated further balance sheet strengthening, and improved credit quality. At the same time, subdued inflationary pressure has contributed to stability and relatively low yields in the major bond markets. This environment has also benefited emerging markets, boosting their growth prospects and credit quality, and facilitating the availability of external financing at relatively low cost. Notwithstanding these favorable developments, Directors noted a number of important risks that remain, suggesting that there is no room for complacency.

Global Financial Market Surveillance

Directors noted that financial markets are adjusting well to the interest rate tightening cycle in mature markets. Markets had been fully prepared for, and responded calmly to, the gradual increases in the U.S. Federal funds rate in June and August 2004. The clear communication by the U.S. Federal Reserve Board of its intention to raise rates con-

tributed to an orderly and timely reduction of speculative leveraged positions that had been built up during a period of exceptionally low interest rates and a relatively steep yield curve. The widespread expectation that continued low inflationary pressure would permit a gradual pace of tightening has also promoted market calm, and volatility across a wide range of assets has remained quite low.

Directors welcomed the further strengthening of corporate, financial, and household sector balance sheets. Increased corporate earnings have contributed to reduced leverage and the accumulation of cash balances in the corporate sector, especially in the United States. Financial intermediaries in the major financial centers have increased their ability to absorb shocks, thus contributing to the improved outlook for financial stability. Although balance sheets of households have strengthened, their debt burden remains high, and Directors pointed to the possibility that this indebtedness could increase the sensitivity of households to economic shocks and amplify any future economic downturn.

Directors noted that the combination of broadening global economic growth, gently rising interest rates, and continued investor appetite for risk have sustained a favorable external financing environment for emerging market countries. Despite some limited turbulence in April and May as markets adjusted to the prospect of higher U.S. interest rates, emerging markets also appear to be taking the transition to tightening in stride. Spreads on emerging market bonds remain at low levels and the appetite for new emerging market issuance is strong, while markets are differentiating more based on fundamentals. Many emerging market borrowers have appropriately taken advantage of the receptive external environment to meet the bulk of their financing needs for 2004 and to begin prefinancing for 2005. Directors welcomed steps taken by several emerging markets to strengthen their public finances and improve the structure of public debt. Directors also noted that banking systems in the major emerging markets have continued to recover, with generally improving capital positions, asset quality, and earnings.

Directors identified several remaining risks to the outlook for financial stability. An unanticipated increase in inflation could transform the market's assumptions about the likely pace of tightening, and result in market turbulence. In that event, bond yields and credit spreads in the United States and elsewhere could overshoot, and hedges against interest rate increases adopted by investors and banks would be tested. Rising interest rates in the major financial centers could also result, as they have in the past, in a less hospitable financing environment for emerging markets. Directors noted, however, that the effective communication strategy pursued so far by the U.S. Federal Reserve Board has helped manage market expectations and limit market volatility. Moreover, the monetary authorities in several mature markets have appropriately indicated that they will respond in a timely way to conditions that potentially threaten price stability. Directors called for close monitoring of the potential impact of continued high oil prices on bond and equity markets.

Directors also discussed the potential for market instability arising from the continued large global external imbalances. Most Directors considered that the persistence of these imbalances and the magnitude of the flows involved remain a potential source of vulnerability in currency markets that could spill over to other asset classes. Directors reiterated that a key policy priority for the inter-national community will remain the pursuit of a cooperative international effort to reduce these imbalances over the medium term.

Directors stressed that emerging market countries should use the current favorable financing environment to increase their resilience to future external shocks and press ahead with growth-enhancing structural reforms. Measures to reduce public debt to manageable levels and to improve the structure of public debt remain key priorities for many emerging markets.

Directors welcomed the opportunity to review several structural issues affecting financial stability. They welcomed staff's work to develop market and credit risk indicators for the mature banking system, assess the linkages of energy trading markets with other financial markets and with underlying supply and demand conditions for energy products, and review the various channels through which financial risk is being transferred from the banking sector to nonbanking institutions.

Directors noted that large capital inflows into hedge funds in recent years, particularly by institutional investors, indicated that hedge funds are an important investor group in global financial markets. Hedge funds are a heterogeneous group engaged in a wide range of dynamic investment strategies. Counterparty risk management by large banks and prime brokers with regard to hedge funds has strengthened in recent years, and hedge fund leverage is currently at relatively moderate levels. Nonetheless, most Directors agreed that more information about hedge funds and their market activities would be helpful in addressing questions about how this important investor group can affect market stability. Several Directors considered that improved transparency and disclosure by hedge funds to investors and counterparties would serve to further strengthen market surveillance and stability. A number of Directors also saw room for closer monitoring of hedge funds by the official sector to achieve a better understanding of hedge funds, their market activities, and potential impact on financial stability, with a few considering that some form of regulation of the industry is unavoidable.

Risk Management in the Pension Fund Industry

Directors continued their review of issues raised by the transfer of risk in mature markets from banking to nonbanking institutions, and welcomed the staff's analysis of the pension fund industry. The size and projected growth of pension funds highlight their growing importance for international capital markets and financial stability and their role as a long-term institutional investor. Directors acknowledged that the roles of state pensions, pension plans in the workplace, and individual savings plans in contributing to retirement pensions vary from country to country. Among workplace pension plans, well-designed defined benefit, defined contribution, and hybrid plans can all continue to play a role in encouraging efficient savings for retirement.

Directors agreed that, while the 2000–02 market downturn had exposed longer-term vulnerabilities at many pension funds, the recent partial recovery in funding ratios provides a window of opportunity for policymakers to introduce measures to encourage better risk management practices and more stable funding strategies. Among such measures, Directors emphasized the development of deeper markets for long-term fixed-income and index-linked instruments to allow pension funds to better match assets and liabilities; regulatory policies that are more closely aligned with the purpose and liability structure of pension funds; the removal or reduction of tax or regulatory obstacles to prudent, continuous funding policies; the development of risk-based approaches to supervision and to guarantee fund premiums; and the promotion of international diversification of pension assets. Directors welcomed the current debate on international accounting standards for

pension assets and liabilities, and agreed that accounting standards should provide an accurate reflection of the financial condition of companies, including their pension plans. Disclosure should be comprehensive, and should include information on sensitivities and risks.

Directors noted that employers and governments have become more aware of the funding challenges pensions face from aging populations and the investment risks involved in funded pension plans. They underscored the importance of effective communication of pension challenges and policy priorities to ensure broad-based public understanding and support of pension reform efforts. In many countries, reductions in state pensions and movements from defined benefit to defined contribution or hybrid pension plans by employers are increasingly transferring risks— including market and longevity risks—to the household sector. This raises the question of how well equipped households are to bear such risks. Directors looked forward to discussing the fund management industry and risk transfer to the household sector in the next issue of the GFSR.

Emerging Markets as Net Capital Exporters

Directors welcomed the discussion of emerging market countries as net capital exporters, in light of the conventional wisdom suggesting that capital normally flows from capital-rich mature markets to capital-scarce emerging markets. They found useful the emphasis placed on financial and balance sheet issues in the staff's analysis of the current episode of net capital outflows, which follows a series of financial crises in emerging markets, as well as changes in global asset allocations and macroeconomic imbalances.

Directors noted that the post-crisis adjustment process in many emerging markets involved substantial restructuring and strengthening of balance sheets in the private and official sectors. In particular, the period 2000–01 was characterized by an important reduction of external liabilities. The reversal in capital inflows and the ensuing external deleveraging process were particularly costly, and Directors stressed the need to improve mechanisms for post crisis balance sheet adjustments—including those that facilitate the transfer of corporate ownership and control, and improve the environment for domestic and foreign investment as well as the functioning of markets for distressed debt.

Directors noted that the shift of emerging markets as net capital exporters during 2002–04 was associated with an unprecedented increase in their net international reserves. This in turn was related to their pursuit of export-led growth policies, supported by competitive exchange rates. Directors acknowledged the challenges involved in establishing a general benchmark for what constitutes a desirable level of international reserves, as circumstances and vulnerabilities differ from country to country. In some cases, the official sector built up reserves beyond pre-crisis levels for precautionary or self-insur-

ance reasons. More generally, Directors considered that policymakers should continue to explore alternative methods to self-insure against sudden reversals in capital flows, including through financial sector reforms and the development of local securities markets, as well as ways to improve the management of international reserves. Several Directors reiterated their call for the IMF to continue to explore the development of effective lending instruments for crisis prevention.

Directors also noted that as emerging market securities become mainstream assets in global portfolios, global factors such as risk-adjusted returns in competing assets, and macroeconomic imbalances in mature markets, are likely to be key determinants of flows. Directors called on emerging market countries to establish a track record of consistently strong policies and reforms to enhance their risk-adjusted returns in order to attract stable inflows. Directors also noted that an orderly resolution of global current account imbalances will contribute to an environment that is conducive to sustained private capital flows to emerging markets.

STATISTICAL APPENDIX

This statistical appendix presents data on financial developments in key financial centers and emerging markets. It is designed to complement the analysis in the text by providing additional data that describe key aspects of financial market developments. These data are derived from a number of sources external to the IMF, including banks, commercial data providers, and official sources, and are presented for information purposes only; the IMF does not, however, guarantee the accuracy of the data from external sources.

Presenting financial market data in one location and in a fixed set of tables and charts, in this and future issues of the GFSR, is intended to give the reader an overview of developments in global financial markets. Unless otherwise noted, the statistical appendix reflects information available up to July 30, 2004.

Mirroring the structure of the chapters of the report, the appendix presents data sepa- rately for key financial centers and emerging market countries. Specifically, it is organized into three sections:

- Figures 1–14 and Tables 1–9 contain infor- mation on market developments in key financial centers. This includes data on global capital flows, and on markets for foreign exchange, bonds, equities, and derivatives, as well as sectoral balance sheet data for the United States, Japan, and Europe.
- Figures 15 and 16, and Tables 10–21 pres- ent information on financial developments in emerging markets, including data on equity, foreign exchange, and bond mar- kets, as well as data on emerging market financing flows.
- Tables 22–28 report key financial soundness indicators for selected countries, including bank profitability, asset quality, and capital adequacy.

List of Tables and Figures

Figure 1. Global Capital Flows: Sources and Uses of Global Capital in 2003

Countries That Export Capital[1]

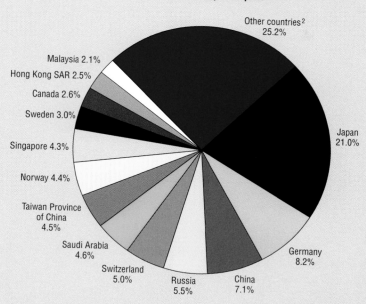

Countries That Import Capital[3]

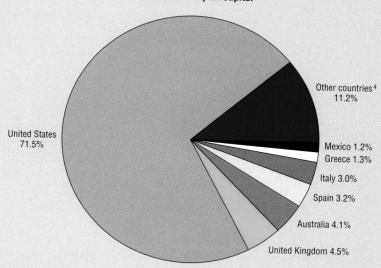

Source: International Monetary Fund, World Economic Outlook database as of August 30, 2004.
[1]As measured by countries' current account surplus (assuming errors and omissions are part of the capital and financial accounts).
[2]Other countries include all countries with shares of total surplus less than 2.1 percent.
[3]As measured by countries' current account deficit (assuming errors and omissions are part of the capital and financial accounts).
[4]Other countries include all countries with shares of total deficit less than 1.2 percent.

Figure 2. Exchange Rates: Selected Major Industrial Countries

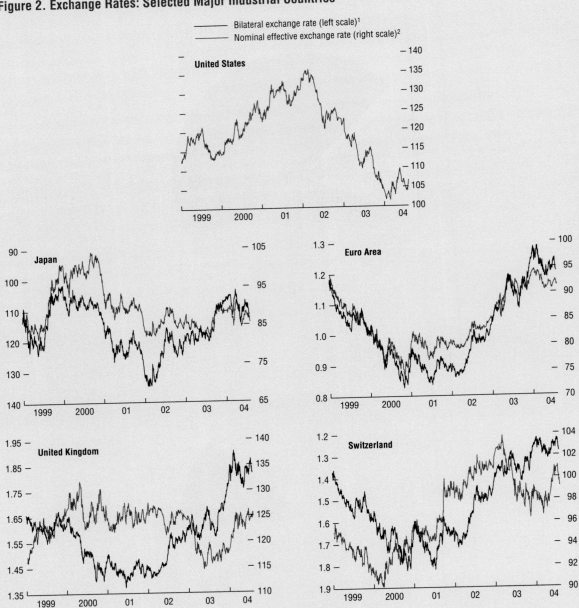

———— Bilateral exchange rate (left scale)[1]
———— Nominal effective exchange rate (right scale)[2]

Sources: Bloomberg L.P.; and the IMF Competitive Indicators System.
Note: In each panel, the effective and bilateral exchange rates are scaled so that an upward movement implies an appreciation of the respective local currency.
[1]Local currency units per U.S. dollar except for the euro area and the United Kingdom, for which data are shown as U.S. dollars per local currency.
[2]1995 = 100; constructed using 1989–91 trade weights.

Figure 3. United States: Yields on Corporate and Treasury Bonds
(Weekly data)

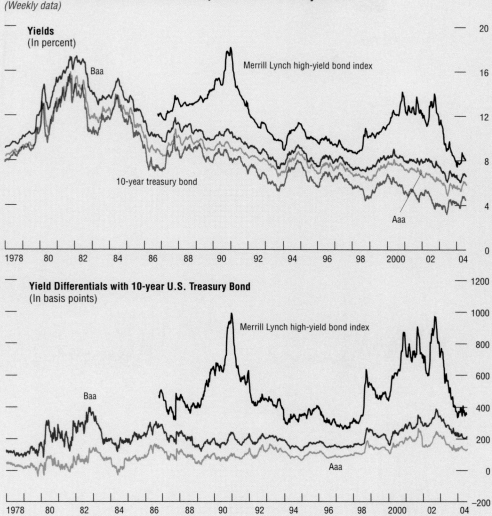

Sources: Bloomberg L.P.; and Merrill Lynch.

173

Figure 4. Selected Spreads
(In basis points)

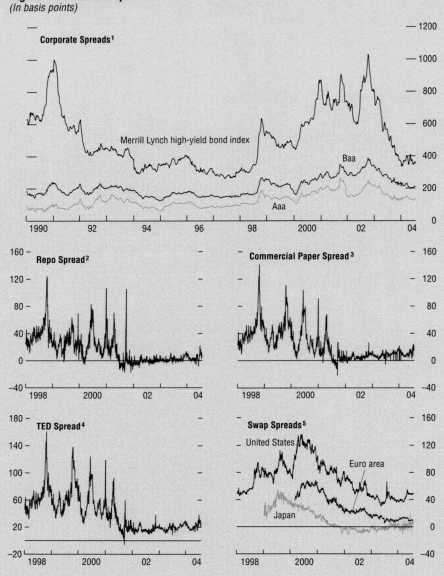

Sources: Bloomberg L.P.; and Merrill Lynch.
[1]Spreads over 10-year U.S. treasury bond; weekly data.
[2]Spread between yields on three-month U.S. treasury repo and on three-month U.S. treasury bill.
[3]Spread between yields on 90-day investment-grade commercial paper and on three-month U.S. treasury bill.
[4]Spread between three-month U.S. dollar LIBOR and yield on three-month U.S. treasury bill.
[5]Spread over 10-year government bond.

Figure 5. Nonfinancial Corporate Credit Spreads
(In basis points)

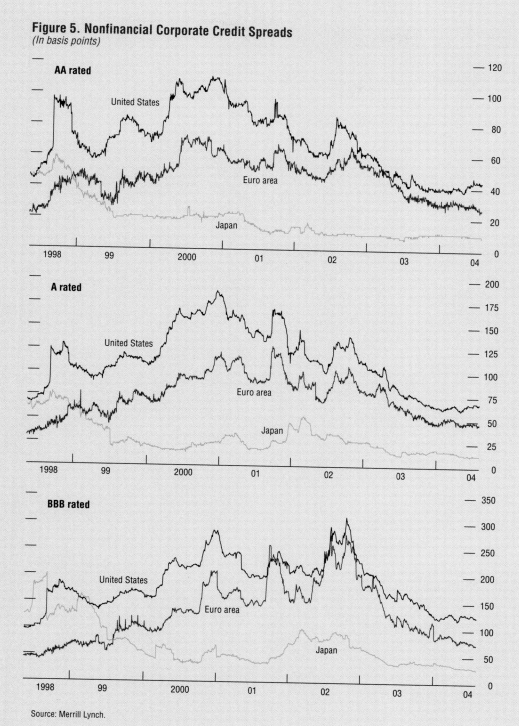

Source: Merrill Lynch.

Figure 6. Equity Markets: Price Indexes
(January 1, 1990 = 100; weekly data)

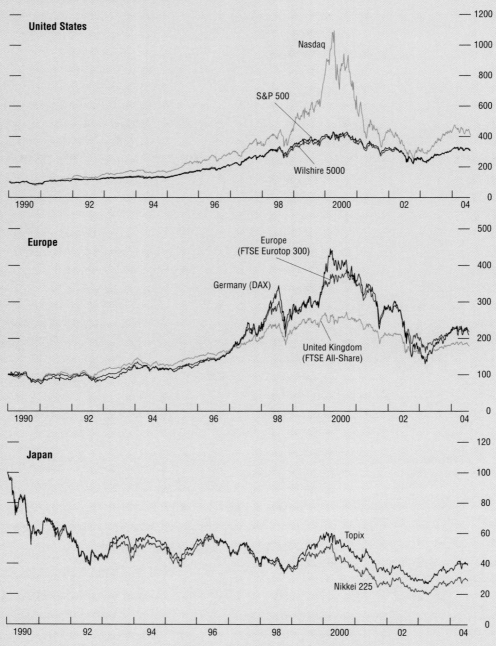

Source: Datastream.

Figure 7. Implied and Historical Volatility in Equity Markets

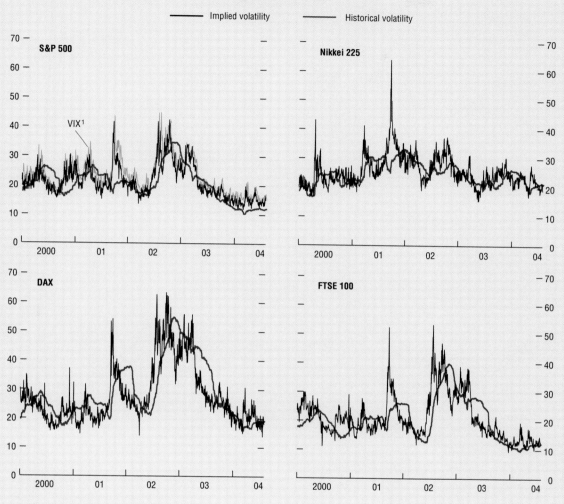

Sources: Bloomberg L.P.; and IMF staff estimates.

Note: Implied volatility is a measure of the equity price variability implied by the market prices of call options on equity futures. Historical volatility is calculated as a rolling 100-day annualized standard deviation of equity price changes. Volatilities are expressed in percent rate of change.

[1]VIX is the Chicago Board Options Exchange volatility index. This index is calculated by taking a weighted average of implied volatility for the eight S&P 500 calls and puts.

Figure 8. Historical Volatility of Government Bond Yields and Bond Returns for Selected Countries[1]

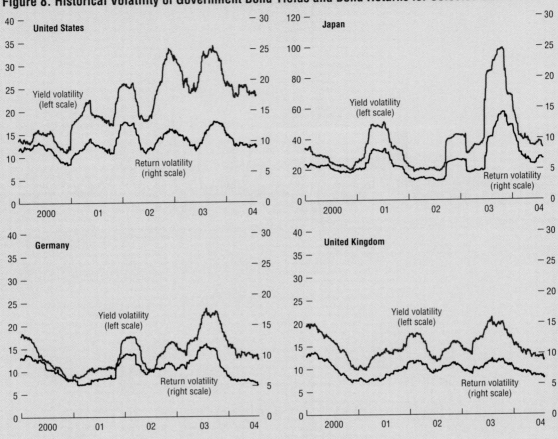

Sources: Bloomberg L.P.; and Datastream.
[1]Volatility calculated as a rolling 100-day annualized standard deviation of changes in yield and returns on 10-year government bonds. Returns are based on 10-plus year government bond indexes.

Figure 9. Twelve-Month Forward Price/Earnings Ratios

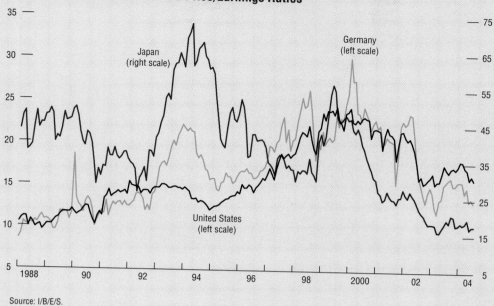

Source: I/B/E/S.

Figure 10. Flows into U.S.-Based Equity Funds

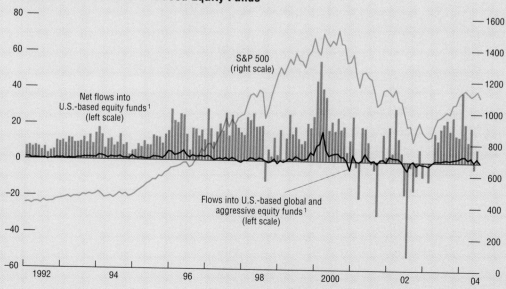

Sources: AMG Data Services; Investment Company Institute; and Datastream.
[1]In billions of U.S. dollars.

Figure 11. United States: Corporate Bond Market

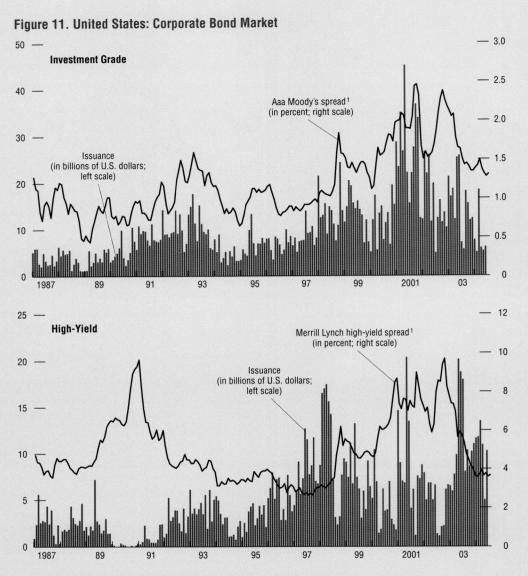

Sources: Board of Governors of the Federal Reserve System; and Bloomberg L.P.
[1]Spread against yield on 10-year U.S. government bonds.

Figure 12. Europe: Corporate Bond Market[1]

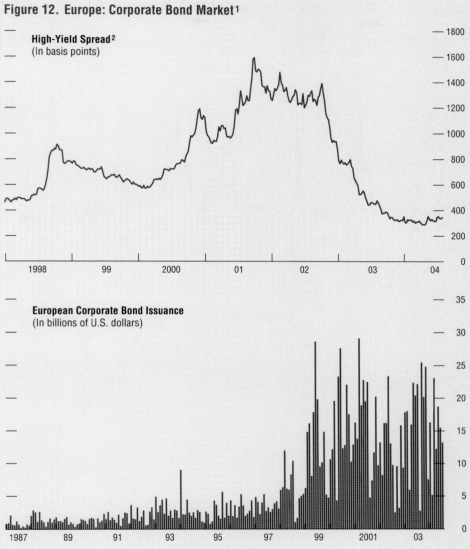

High-Yield Spread[2]
(In basis points)

European Corporate Bond Issuance
(In billions of U.S. dollars)

Sources: Bondware; and Datastream.
[1]Nonfinancial corporate bonds.
[2]Spread between yields on a Merrill Lynch High-Yield European Issuers Index bond and a 10-year German government benchmark bond.

Figure 13. United States: Commercial Paper Market[1]

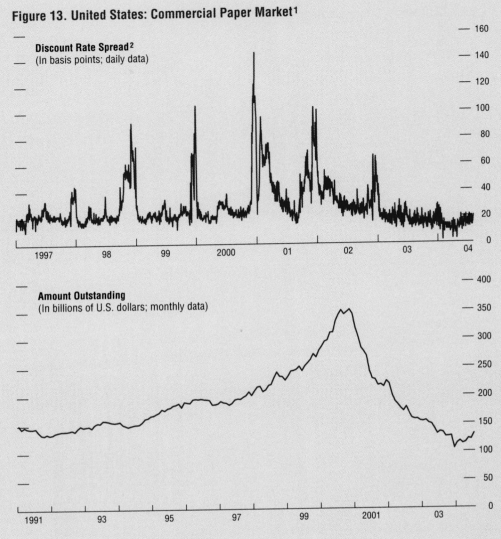

Source: Board of Governors of the Federal Reserve System.
[1]Nonfinancial commercial paper.
[2]Difference between 30-day A2/P2 and AA commercial paper.

Figure 14. United States: Asset-Backed Securities

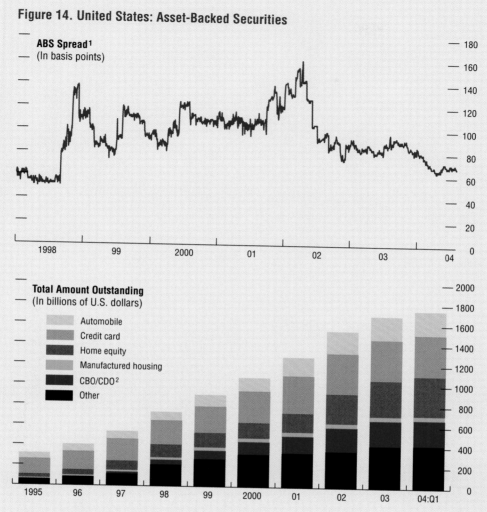

Sources: Merrill Lynch; Datastream; and the Bond Market Association.
[1]Merrill Lynch AAA Asset-Backed Master Index (fixed rate) option-adjusted spread.
[2]Collateralized bond/debt obligations.

Table 1. Global Capital Flows: Inflows and Outflows[1]
(In billions of U.S. dollars)

	Inflows										
	1993	1994	1995	1996	1997	1998	1999	2000	2001	2002	2003
United States											
Direct investment	51.4	46.1	57.8	86.5	105.6	179.0	289.4	321.3	167.0	72.4	39.9
Portfolio investment	111.0	139.4	210.4	332.8	333.1	187.6	285.6	436.6	428.3	427.9	544.5
Other investment	119.7	120.5	170.4	131.8	268.1	57.0	165.2	289.0	187.5	268.0	244.8
Reserve assets	n.a.	n.a.	n.a.	n.a.	n.a.	n.a.	n.a.	n.a.	n.a.	n.a.	n.a.
Total capital flows	282.1	306.0	438.6	551.1	706.8	423.6	740.2	1,046.9	782.9	768.2	829.2
Canada											
Direct investment	4.7	8.2	9.3	9.6	11.5	22.7	24.8	66.1	27.5	20.9	6.3
Portfolio investment	41.4	17.2	18.4	13.7	11.7	16.6	2.7	10.3	24.6	13.4	13.2
Other investment	−6.7	16.0	−3.9	15.7	28.0	5.4	−10.8	0.8	7.5	5.0	10.9
Reserve assets	n.a.	n.a.	n.a.	n.a.	n.a.	n.a.	n.a.	n.a.	n.a.	n.a.	n.a.
Total capital flows	39.4	41.4	23.9	39.1	51.2	44.8	16.6	77.2	59.7	39.3	30.3
Japan											
Direct investment	0.1	0.9	—	0.2	3.2	3.3	12.3	8.2	6.2	9.1	6.2
Portfolio investment	−6.1	64.5	59.8	66.8	79.2	56.1	126.9	47.4	60.5	−20.0	81.2
Other investment	−32.7	−5.6	97.3	31.1	68.0	−93.3	−265.1	−10.2	−17.6	26.6	34.1
Reserve assets	n.a.	n.a.	n.a.	n.a.	n.a.	n.a.	n.a.	n.a.	n.a.	n.a.	n.a.
Total capital flows	−38.7	59.8	157.1	98.1	150.4	−34.0	−125.9	45.4	49.1	15.7	121.5
United Kingdom											
Direct investment	16.5	10.7	21.7	27.4	37.4	74.7	89.5	122.2	53.8	29.2	15.5
Portfolio investment	43.6	47.0	58.8	68.0	43.5	35.2	183.9	255.6	69.6	76.6	149.3
Other investment	191.4	−10.8	106.2	254.4	328.5	103.9	83.6	423.2	333.2	91.1	410.4
Reserve assets	n.a.	n.a.	n.a.	n.a.	n.a.	n.a.	n.a.	n.a.	n.a.	n.a.	n.a.
Total capital flows	251.6	46.9	186.7	349.7	409.4	213.7	357.1	801.0	456.6	196.9	575.3
Euro area[2]											
Direct investment	...	...	...	...	...	...	209.7	404.8	182.5	138.2	117.9
Portfolio investment	...	...	...	...	...	...	282.9	270.7	311.3	273.7	342.7
Other investment	...	...	...	...	...	...	208.3	337.2	241.1	62.6	185.3
Reserve assets	n.a.	n.a.	n.a.	n.a.	n.a.	n.a.	n.a.	n.a.	n.a.	n.a.	n.a.
Total capital flows	...	...	...	...	...	...	700.8	1,012.7	734.8	474.6	645.9
Emerging Markets and Developing Countries[3]											
Direct investment	70.0	95.7	124.0	145.0	182.3	179.4	207.5	213.5	224.0	166.5	175.7
Portfolio investment	94.7	93.5	37.5	113.4	86.2	35.0	113.3	74.7	−8.1	−22.0	62.0
Other investment	40.2	18.8	137.7	86.7	168.4	−108.5	−64.4	−11.6	−43.6	25.5	95.0
Reserve assets	n.a.	n.a.	n.a.	n.a.	n.a.	n.a.	n.a.	n.a.	n.a.	n.a.	n.a.
Total capital flows	204.9	208.0	299.1	345.1	437.0	105.9	256.3	276.6	172.3	170.0	332.8

Sources: International Monetary Fund, *World Economic Outlook* database as of August 30, 2004; and *International Financial Statistics*.
[1]The total net capital flows are the sum of direct investment, portfolio investment, other investment flows, and reserve assets. "Other investment" includes bank loans and deposits.
[2]This aggregate comprises the group of Other Emerging Market and Developing Countries defined in the *World Economic Outlook,* together with Hong Kong SAR, Israel, Korea, Singapore, and Taiwan Province of China.

	Outflows									
1993	1994	1995	1996	1997	1998	1999	2000	2001	2002	2003
−84.0	−80.2	−98.8	−91.9	−104.8	−142.6	−224.9	−159.2	−142.4	−134.8	−173.8
−146.2	−63.2	−122.4	−149.3	−116.9	−124.2	−116.2	−121.9	−84.6	15.9	−72.3
31.0	−40.9	−121.4	−178.9	−262.8	−74.2	−171.2	−288.4	−134.9	−75.4	−38.8
−1.4	5.3	−9.7	6.7	−1.0	−6.7	8.7	−0.3	−4.9	−3.7	1.5
−200.5	−178.9	−352.3	−413.4	−485.5	−347.8	−503.7	−569.8	−366.8	−198.0	−283.4
−5.7	−9.3	−11.5	−13.1	−23.1	−34.1	−17.3	−44.5	−36.2	−26.5	−22.2
−13.8	−6.6	−5.3	−14.2	−8.6	−15.1	−15.6	−43.0	−24.4	−15.9	−9.1
−0.4	−20.4	−8.3	−21.1	−16.2	9.4	10.2	−4.2	−10.5	−8.5	−20.6
−0.9	0.4	−2.7	−5.5	2.4	−5.0	−5.9	−3.7	−2.2	0.2	3.3
−20.8	−35.9	−27.9	−53.9	−45.4	−44.8	−28.5	−95.4	−73.3	−50.7	−48.7
−13.8	−18.1	−22.5	−23.4	−26.1	−24.6	−22.3	−31.5	−38.5	−32.0	−28.8
−63.7	−92.0	−86.0	−100.6	−47.1	−95.2	−154.4	−83.4	−106.8	−85.9	−176.3
15.1	−35.1	−102.2	5.2	−192.0	37.9	266.3	−4.1	46.6	36.4	149.9
−27.5	−25.3	−58.6	−35.1	−6.6	6.2	−76.3	−49.0	−40.5	−46.1	−187.2
−90.0	−170.4	−269.4	−154.0	−271.6	−75.8	13.4	−168.0	−139.2	−127.7	−242.3
−27.3	−34.9	−45.3	−34.8	−62.4	−122.1	−201.6	−245.4	−59.7	−34.2	−51.2
−133.6	31.5	−61.7	−93.1	−85.1	−53.2	−34.2	−97.1	−124.7	1.2	−56.3
−68.5	−42.4	−74.9	−217.8	−276.0	−29.8	−92.8	−417.5	−254.7	−150.5	−432.3
−1.3	−1.5	0.9	0.7	3.9	0.3	1.0	−5.3	4.5	0.6	2.6
−230.5	−47.4	−181.0	−345.1	−419.6	−204.9	−327.5	−765.3	−434.6	−182.9	−537.1
...	...	...	...	...	...	−338.2	−404.9	−283.1	−141.9	−133.9
...	...	...	...	...	...	−330.5	−385.2	−252.8	−162.6	−321.8
...	...	...	...	...	...	−31.0	−166.2	−244.0	−224.2	−265.7
...	...	...	...	...	...	11.6	16.2	16.5	−2.6	35.1
...	...	...	...	...	...	−688.1	−940.1	−763.3	−531.3	−686.4
−16.1	−14.8	−23.5	−28.6	−37.3	−24.2	−33.6	−36.5	−32.8	−23.5	−28.7
1.1	−1.4	−14.1	−31.5	−33.1	0.5	−53.2	−81.6	−95.7	−86.1	−105.2
−25.0	−65.9	−53.3	−95.5	−140.6	37.5	−76.5	−145.9	11.9	−6.1	−114.7
−64.2	−68.2	−130.7	−90.6	−103.6	−34.0	−92.3	−115.1	−113.3	−196.7	−366.6
−104.2	−150.3	−221.6	−246.3	−314.6	−20.2	−255.7	−379.1	−229.9	−312.4	−615.2

Table 2. Global Capital Flows: Amounts Outstanding and Net Issues of International Debt Securities by Currency of Issue and Announced International Syndicated Credit Facilities by Nationality of Borrower
(In billions of U.S. dollars)

	1996	1997	1998	1999	2000	2001	2002	2003	2004:Q1
Amounts outstanding of international debt securities by currency of issue									
U.S. dollar	1,112.6	1,432.9	1,832.6	2,356.5	2,907.1	3,609.6	4,045.9	4,492.5	4,649.5
Japanese yen	462.9	444.4	462.6	497.5	452.5	411.5	433.3	488.6	510.4
Pound sterling	225.7	266.7	322.4	391.1	452.6	506.0	618.6	778.7	832.3
Canadian dollar	76.5	67.2	55.5	56.4	51.5	47.5	51.5	79.3	84.7
Swedish krona	5.1	4.1	7.5	7.2	7.7	8.2	11.1	15.6	15.4
Swiss franc	151.2	138.5	153.5	135.5	132.0	123.6	159.1	195.6	194.1
Euro[1]	832.7	848.9	1,133.9	1,451.6	1,769.2	2,288.7	3,283.1	4,834.5	4,932.5
Other	68.4	78.8	84.3	98.5	97.3	110.2	152.3	217.7	236.9
Total	2,935.1	3,281.5	4,052.3	4,994.3	5,869.9	7,105.3	8,754.9	11,102.5	11,455.8
Net issues of international debt securities by currency of issue									
U.S. dollar	238.7	320.3	399.7	399.7	524.4	550.5	436.3	446.6	80.9
Japanese yen	81.7	34.0	−33.0	−33.0	−23.5	10.9	−17.5	4.0	−3.4
Pound sterling	30.8	46.4	53.9	53.9	77.8	92.1	52.3	86.1	16.4
Canadian dollar	−6.5	−6.2	−7.5	−7.5	−2.3	−2.8	3.6	15.6	0.1
Swedish krona	0.2	−0.4	3.6	3.6	0.1	1.2	1.1	2.0	0.9
Swiss franc	−1.3	−1.6	6.3	6.3	4.0	−0.2	8.0	15.8	1.5
Euro[1]	140.0	130.2	214.6	214.6	507.1	423.7	494.8	786.2	195.3
Other	13.3	23.2	8.9	8.9	14.7	9.1	31.1	38.8	192.8
Total	496.9	545.9	646.5	646.5	1,102.3	1,084.5	1,009.7	1,395.1	484.5
Announced international syndicated credit facilities by nationality of borrower									
All countries	839.3	1,080.6	905.3	1,025.8	1,464.9	1,388.8	1,299.7	1,241.4	244.1
Industrial countries	732.0	903.6	819.4	960.0	1,328.6	1,276.6	1,200.6	1,129.8	218.3
Of which:									
United States	482.2	606.7	575.1	623.0	805.6	850.2	736.9	609.4	132.0
Japan	6.8	6.1	11.4	15.4	17.5	23.8	19.5	18.2	10.4
Germany	17.6	23.6	15.5	34.0	42.4	35.8	85.2	97.1	11.5
France	23.3	38.7	19.8	33.7	72.9	50.1	63.9	65.8	15.2
Italy	5.9	10.1	6.0	16.1	34.9	36.0	22.9	45.3	0.0
United Kingdom	68.4	101.3	79.8	109.0	131.2	105.7	110.0	104.0	22.6
Canada	25.7	37.6	41.4	22.8	37.8	40.6	35.1	28.4	2.5

Source: Bank for International Settlements.
[1]For 1996–98, the euro includes euro area currencies.

Table 3. Selected Indicators on the Size of the Capital Markets, 2003
(In billions of U.S. dollars unless noted otherwise)

	GDP	Total Reserves Minus Gold[1]	Stock Market Capitalization	Debt Securities Public	Debt Securities Private	Debt Securities Total	Bank Assets[2]	Bonds, Equities, and Bank Assets[3]	Bonds, Equities, and Bank Assets[3] (In percent of GDP)
World	36,163.4	3,142.3	31,202.3	20,242.4	31,722.7	51,965.1	40,627.8	123,795.2	342.3
European Union	10,513.1	285.3	7,754.0	6,276.7	10,436.8	16,713.5	18,148.7	42,616.2	405.4
Euro area	8,202.0	186.6	4,882.8	5,480.0	7,966.2	13,446.2	13,136.1	31,762.5	387.3
North America	11,852.4	111.1	15,154.7	5,626.8	16,358.3	21,985.1	6,800.3	43,940.1	370.7
Canada	866.9	36.2	888.7	601.8	370.6	972.4	1,100.3	2,961.4	341.6
United States	10,985.5	74.9	14,266.0	5,025.0	15,987.7	21,012.7	5,700.0	40,978.7	373.0
Japan	4,301.8	663.3	4,904.6	6,154.0	2,260.8	8,414.8	6,218.7	19,538.1	454.2
Memorandum items:									
EU countries									
Austria	253.6	8.5	56.5	203.1	199.7	402.8	282.6	741.9	292.6
Belgium	303.1	11.0	170.7	382.4	314.2	696.6	953.5	1,820.8	600.8
Denmark	210.8	37.1	118.2	115.5	314.7	430.2	426.1	974.5	462.2
Finland	162.2	10.5	170.3	110.7	70.8	181.5	297.4	649.2	400.3
France	1,754.3	30.2	1,237.6	1,045.8	1,538.9	2,584.7	3,495.9	7,318.2	417.2
Germany	2,408.6	50.7	1,079.0	1,165.0	2,881.4	4,046.4	2,890.1	8,015.5	332.8
Greece	174.1	4.4	103.8	225.3	21.2	246.5	176.7	527.0	302.8
Ireland	149.2	4.1	85.1	39.2	137.1	176.3	500.3	761.7	510.6
Italy	1,470.9	30.4	614.8	1,498.7	1,115.4	2,614.1	1,791.8	5,020.8	341.3
Luxembourg	25.9	0.3	37.3	0.0	38.5	38.5	544.4	620.2	2,393.8
Netherlands	512.7	11.0	539.0	257.8	910.3	1,168.1	1,411.1	3,118.1	608.2
Portugal	147.5	5.9	62.4	106.8	120.1	226.9	174.5	463.8	314.4
Spain	840.1	19.8	726.2	445.2	618.6	1,063.8	915.3	2,705.3	322.0
Sweden	301.8	19.7	293.0	167.5	265.5	433.0	288.6	1,014.6	336.2
United Kingdom	1,798.6	41.9	2,460.1	513.7	1,890.4	2,404.1	4,000.5	8,864.7	492.9
Emerging market countries	8,356.5	1,937.7	3,947.3	1,889.3	1,223.7	3,113.0	6,532.4	13,592.8	162.7
Of which:									
Asia	3,871.2	1,248.2	2,942.8	795.4	930.1	1,725.5	4,347.0	9,015.3	232.9
Latin America	1,728.4	195.7	608.1	634.6	212.3	846.9	776.4	2,231.3	129.1
Middle East	812.3	149.5	96.4	10.1	12.7	22.8	693.2	812.4	100.0
Africa	553.8	91.9	168.3	71.6	26.3	97.9	334.3	600.4	108.4
Europe	1,390.9	252.5	131.8	377.6	42.3	419.9	381.6	933.3	67.1

Sources: World Federation of Exchanges; Bank for International Settlements; International Monetary Fund, *International Financial Statistics* (IFS) and *World Economic Outlook;* and ©2003 Bureau van Dijk Electronic Publishing-Bankscope.
[1]Data are from IFS. For the United Kingdom, excludes the assets of the Bank of England.
[2]Assets of commercial banks; data refer to 2002.
[3]Sum of the stock market capitalization, debt securities, and bank assets.

Table 4. Global Over-the-Counter Derivatives Markets: Notional Amounts and Gross Market Values of Outstanding Contracts[1]
(In billions of U.S. dollars)

	Notional Amounts					Gross Market Values				
	End-Dec. 2001	End-June 2002	End-Dec. 2002	End-June 2003	End-Dec. 2003	End-Dec. 2001	End-June 2002	End-Dec. 2002	End-June 2003	End-Dec. 2003
Total	**111,178**	**127,509**	**141,679**	**169,678**	**197,177**	**3,788**	**4,450**	**6,360**	**7,908**	**6,987**
Foreign exchange	**16,748**	**18,068**	**18,460**	**22,088**	**24,484**	**779**	**1,052**	**881**	**996**	**1,301**
Outright forwards and forex swaps	10,336	10,426	10,719	12,332	12,387	374	615	468	476	607
Currency swaps	3,942	4,215	4,503	5,159	6,371	335	340	337	419	557
Options	2,470	3,427	3,238	4,597	5,726	70	97	76	101	136
Interest rate[2]	**77,568**	**89,955**	**101,658**	**121,799**	**141,991**	**2,210**	**2,467**	**4,266**	**5,459**	**4,328**
Forward rate agreements	7,737	9,146	8,792	10,271	10,769	19	19	22	20	19
Swaps	58,897	68,234	79,120	94,583	111,209	1,969	2,213	3,864	5,004	3,918
Options	10,933	12,575	13,746	16,946	20,012	222	235	381	434	391
Equity-linked	**1,881**	**2,214**	**2,309**	**2,799**	**3,787**	**205**	**243**	**255**	**260**	**274**
Forwards and swaps	320	386	364	488	601	58	62	61	67	57
Options	1,561	1,828	1,944	2,311	3,186	147	181	194	193	217
Commodity[3]	**598**	**777**	**923**	**1,040**	**1,406**	**75**	**79**	**86**	**110**	**128**
Gold	231	279	315	304	344	20	28	28	22	39
Other	367	498	608	736	1,062	56	51	58	88	88
Forwards and swaps	217	290	402	458	420	...	...	...	...	...
Options	150	208	206	279	642	...	...	...	...	...
Other	**14,384**	**16,496**	**18,330**	**21,952**	**25,510**	**519**	**609**	**871**	**1,083**	**957**
Memorandum items:										
Gross credit exposure[4]	n.a.	n.a.	n.a.	n.a.	n.a.	1,171	1,317	1,511	1,750	1,986
Exchange-traded derivatives	16,748	18,068	18,460	22,088	24,484	...	...	...	...	...

Source: Bank for International Settlements.

[1]All figures are adjusted for double-counting. Notional amounts outstanding have been adjusted by halving positions vis-à-vis other reporting dealers. Gross market values have been calculated as the sum of the total gross positive market value of contracts and the absolute value of the gross negative market value of contracts with non-reporting counterparties.

[2]Single-currency contracts only.

[3]Adjustments for double-counting are estimated.

[4]Gross market values after taking into account legally enforceable bilateral netting agreements.

Table 5. Global Over-the-Counter Derivatives Markets: Notional Amounts and Gross Market Values of Outstanding Contracts by Counterparty, Remaining Maturity, and Currency[1]
(In billions of U.S. dollars)

	Notional Amounts					Gross Market Values				
	End-Dec. 2001	End-June 2002	End-Dec. 2002	End-June 2003	End-Dec. 2003	End-Dec. 2001	End-June 2002	End-Dec. 2002	End-June 2003	End-Dec. 2003
Total	**111,178**	**127,509**	**141,679**	**169,678**	**197,177**	**3,788**	**4,450**	**6,360**	**7,908**	**6,987**
Foreign exchange	**16,748**	**18,068**	**18,460**	**22,088**	**24,484**	**779**	**1,052**	**881**	**996**	**1,301**
By counterparty										
With other reporting dealers	5,912	6,602	6,845	7,960	8,663	237	372	285	284	395
With other financial institutions	6,755	7,210	7,602	8,955	9,455	319	421	377	427	535
With nonfinancial customers	4,081	4,256	4,012	5,172	6,366	224	259	220	286	370
By remaining maturity										
Up to one year[2]	13,427	14,401	14,533	17,561	18,847	...	...	...	...	...
One to five years[2]	2,340	2,537	2,719	3,128	3,903	...	...	...	...	...
Over five years[2]	981	1,130	1,208	1,399	1,735	...	...	...	...	...
By major currency										
U.S. dollar[3]	15,410	15,973	16,500	19,401	21,429	704	948	813	891	1,212
Euro[3]	6,368	7,297	7,818	9,914	10,145	266	445	429	526	665
Japanese yen[3]	4,178	4,454	4,791	4,907	5,500	313	254	189	165	217
Pound sterling[3]	2,315	2,522	2,462	3,093	4,286	69	112	98	114	179
Other[3]	5,225	5,890	5,349	6,861	7,608	206	345	233	296	329
Interest rate[4]	**77,568**	**89,955**	**101,658**	**121,799**	**141,991**	**2,210**	**2,467**	**4,266**	**5,459**	**4,328**
By counterparty										
With other reporting dealers	35,472	43,340	46,722	53,622	63,579	912	1,081	1,848	2,266	1,872
With other financial institutions	32,510	36,310	43,607	53,133	57,564	945	1,025	1,845	2,482	1,768
With nonfinancial customers	9,586	10,304	11,328	15,044	20,847	353	361	573	710	687
By remaining maturity										
Up to one year[2]	27,886	33,674	36,938	44,927	46,474	...	...	...	...	...
One to five years[2]	30,566	34,437	40,137	46,646	58,914	...	...	...	...	...
Over five years[2]	19,115	21,844	24,583	30,226	36,603	...	...	...	...	...
By major currency										
U.S. dollar	27,427	32,178	34,399	40,110	46,178	952	1,127	1,917	2,286	1,734
Euro	26,230	30,671	38,429	50,000	55,793	677	710	1,499	2,178	1,730
Japanese yen	11,799	13,433	14,650	15,270	19,526	304	326	378	405	358
Pound sterling	6,216	6,978	7,442	8,322	9,884	148	151	252	315	228
Other	5,896	6,695	6,738	8,097	10,610	129	153	220	275	278
Equity-linked	**1,881**	**2,214**	**2,309**	**2,799**	**3,787**	**205**	**243**	**255**	**260**	**274**
Commodity[5]	**598**	**777**	**923**	**1,040**	**1,406**	**75**	**79**	**86**	**110**	**128**
Other	**14,384**	**16,496**	**18,330**	**21,952**	**25,510**	**519**	**609**	**871**	**1,083**	**957**

Source: Bank for International Settlements.

[1]All figures are adjusted for double-counting. Notional amounts outstanding have been adjusted by halving positions vis-à-vis other reporting dealers. Gross market values have been calculated as the sum of the total gross positive market value of contracts and the absolute value of the gross negative market value of contracts with non-reporting counterparties.

[2]Residual maturity.

[3]Counting both currency sides of each foreign exchange transaction means that the currency breakdown sums to twice the aggregate.

[4]Single-currency contracts only.

[5]Adjustments for double-counting are estimated.

Table 6. Exchange-Traded Derivative Financial Instruments: Notional Principal Amounts Outstanding and Annual Turnover

	1987	1988	1989	1990	1991	1992	1993	1994
	(In billions of U.S. dollars)							
Notional principal amounts outstanding								
Interest rate futures	487.7	895.4	1,201.0	1,454.8	2,157.4	2,913.1	4,960.4	5,807.6
Interest rate options	122.6	279.0	386.0	595.4	1,069.6	1,383.8	2,361.4	2,623.2
Currency futures	14.6	12.1	16.0	17.0	18.3	26.5	34.7	40.4
Currency options	59.5	48.0	50.2	56.5	62.9	71.6	75.9	55.7
Stock market index futures	17.6	27.0	41.1	69.1	76.0	79.8	110.0	127.7
Stock market index options	27.7	42.7	70.2	93.6	136.9	163.7	232.4	242.8
Total	729.7	1,304.1	1,764.5	2,286.4	3,521.2	4,638.5	7,774.9	8,897.3
North America	577.8	951.3	1,153.5	1,264.4	2,153.0	2,698.7	4,360.7	4,823.6
Europe	13.3	177.4	250.9	461.4	710.7	1,114.4	1,777.9	1,831.8
Asia-Pacific	138.5	175.5	360.1	560.5	657.0	823.5	1,606.0	2,171.8
Other	0.1	0.0	0.0	0.1	0.5	1.9	30.3	70.1
	(In millions of contracts traded)							
Annual turnover								
Interest rate futures	145.7	156.4	201.0	219.1	230.9	330.1	427.0	628.5
Interest rate options	29.3	30.5	39.5	52.0	50.8	64.8	82.9	116.6
Currency futures	21.2	22.5	28.2	29.7	30.0	31.3	39.0	69.8
Currency options	18.3	18.2	20.7	18.9	22.9	23.4	23.7	21.3
Stock market index futures	36.1	29.6	30.1	39.4	54.6	52.0	71.2	109.0
Stock market index options	139.1	79.1	101.7	119.1	121.4	133.9	144.1	197.6
Total	389.6	336.3	421.2	478.2	510.4	635.6	787.9	1,142.9
North America	318.3	252.3	288.0	312.3	302.6	341.4	382.4	513.5
Europe	35.9	40.8	64.3	83.0	110.5	185.1	263.4	398.1
Asia-Pacific	30.0	34.3	63.6	79.1	85.8	82.9	98.5	131.7
Other	5.4	8.9	5.3	3.8	11.5	26.2	43.6	99.6

Source: Bank for International Settlements.

1995	1996	1997	1998	1999	2000	2001	2002	2003	2004:Q1
(In billions of U.S. dollars)									
5,876.2	5,979.0	7,586.7	8,031.4	7,924.8	7,907.8	9,269.5	9,955.6	13,123.1	16,234.4
2,741.8	3,277.8	3,639.9	4,623.5	3,755.5	4,734.2	12,492.8	11,759.5	20,793.8	26,285.1
33.8	37.7	42.3	31.7	36.7	74.4	65.6	47.0	80.1	75.2
120.4	133.4	118.6	49.2	22.4	21.4	27.4	27.4	37.9	44.6
172.2	195.7	211.3	291.5	340.3	371.5	333.9	325.5	501.8	549.5
337.7	394.5	808.7	907.4	1,510.2	1,148.3	1,574.8	1,700.2	2,196.9	2,681.2
9,282.0	10,017.9	12,407.5	13,934.7	13,589.9	14,257.7	23,764.1	23,815.2	36,733.5	45,869.9
4,852.4	4,841.0	6,348.3	7,355.1	6,930.6	8,167.9	16,203.2	13,693.8	19,503.9	23,737.1
2,241.3	2,828.1	3,587.4	4,397.1	4,008.5	4,197.4	6,141.3	8,800.4	15,405.3	19,864.5
1,990.2	2,154.0	2,235.7	1,882.5	2,401.3	1,606.2	1,308.4	1,191.7	1,607.6	2,073.7
198.1	194.8	236.1	300.0	249.5	286.2	111.2	129.3	216.7	194.6
(In millions of contracts traded)									
561.0	612.2	701.6	760.0	672.7	781.2	1,057.5	1,152.0	1,576.8	454.6
225.5	151.1	116.7	129.6	117.9	107.6	199.6	240.3	302.2	92.4
99.6	73.6	73.5	54.6	37.2	43.6	49.1	42.7	58.7	18.7
23.3	26.3	21.1	12.1	6.8	7.1	10.5	16.1	14.3	2.9
114.8	93.9	115.9	178.0	204.8	225.2	337.1	530.2	725.7	207.7
187.3	172.3	178.2	195.1	322.5	481.4	1,148.2	2,235.4	3,233.9	728.6
1,211.6	1,129.3	1,207.2	1,329.4	1,361.9	1,646.1	2,802.0	4,216.8	5,911.7	1,505.0
455.0	428.4	463.6	530.2	463.0	461.3	675.7	912.2	1,279.7	366.3
354.7	391.8	482.8	525.9	604.5	718.5	957.8	1,074.8	1,346.4	389.0
126.4	115.9	126.8	170.9	207.8	331.3	985.1	2,073.1	3,099.6	685.1
275.5	193.2	134.0	102.4	86.6	135.0	183.4	156.7	186.0	64.6

Table 7. United States: Sectoral Balance Sheets
(In percent)

	1997	1998	1999	2000	2001	2002	2003
Corporate sector							
Debt/net worth	51.3	51.3	51.5	49.0	52.2	51.6	49.5
Short-term debt/total debt	40.5	40.4	38.9	39.5	33.7	30.4	27.7
Interest burden[1]	11.0	12.6	13.4	15.8	18.0	17.3	15.3
Household sector							
Net worth/assets	85.4	85.7	86.1	85.0	83.8	82.0	82.2
Equity/total assets	29.7	31.5	35.0	30.9	26.5	20.7	24.0
Equity/financial assets	42.9	45.0	49.3	45.0	40.1	33.1	37.9
Home mortgage debt/total assets	9.5	9.4	9.1	9.8	10.8	12.3	12.4
Consumer credit/total assets	3.4	3.3	3.1	3.5	3.8	4.0	3.8
Total debt/financial assets	21.0	20.5	19.5	21.8	24.6	28.8	28.1
Debt service burden[2]	12.2	12.1	12.4	12.6	13.1	13.3	13.2
Banking sector[3]							
Credit quality							
Nonperforming loans[4]/total loans	1.0	1.0	1.0	1.1	1.4	1.5	1.2
Net loan losses/average total loans	0.7	0.7	0.6	0.7	1.0	1.1	0.9
Loan-loss reserve/total loans	1.8	1.8	1.7	1.7	1.9	1.9	1.8
Net charge-offs/total loans	0.6	0.7	0.5	0.6	0.8	1.0	0.8
Capital ratios							
Total risk-based capital	12.2	12.2	12.2	12.1	12.7	12.8	13.0
Tier 1 risk-based capital	9.6	9.5	9.5	9.4	9.9	10.0	10.5
Equity capital/total assets	8.3	8.5	8.4	8.5	9.1	9.2	9.2
Core capital (leverage ratio)	7.6	7.5	7.8	7.7	7.8	7.9	7.9
Profitability measures							
Return on average assets (ROA)	1.3	1.3	1.3	1.2	1.2	1.4	1.4
Return on average equity (ROE)	15.6	14.8	15.7	14.8	14.2	14.9	15.2
Net interest margin	4.3	4.0	4.0	3.9	3.9	4.3	4.0
Efficiency ratio[5]	59.2	61.0	58.7	58.4	57.7	55.8	56.6

Sources: Board of Governors of the Federal Reserve System, *Flow of Funds;* Department of Commerce, Bureau of Economic Analysis; Federal Deposit Insurance Corporation; and Federal Reserve Bank of St. Louis.

[1]Ratio of net interest payments to pre-tax income.
[2]Ratio of debt payments to disposable personal income.
[3]FDIC-insured commercial banks.
[4]Loans past due 90+ days and nonaccrual.
[5]Noninterest expense less amortization of intangible assets as a percent of net interest income plus noninterest income.

Table 8. Japan: Sectoral Balance Sheets[1]
(In percent)

	FY1997	FY1998	FY1999	FY2000	FY2001	FY2002	FY2003
Corporate sector							
Debt/shareholders' equity (book value)	207.9	189.3	182.5	156.8	156.0	146.1	121.3
Short-term debt/total debt	41.8	39.0	39.4	37.7	36.8	39.0	37.8
Interest burden[2]	39.1	46.5	36.3	28.4	32.3	27.8	22.0
Debt/operating profits	1,498.5	1,813.8	1,472.1	1,229.3	1,480.0	1,370.0	1079.2
Memorandum items:							
Total debt/GDP	106.5	106.2	107.5	102.0	100.0	98.7	89.5
Household sector							
Net worth/assets	85.3	85.1	85.5	85.4	85.1	85.1	. . .
Equity	4.3	3.1	5.6	4.9	4.5	5.0	. . .
Real estate	40.0	39.5	37.5	36.6	35.4	34.1	. . .
Interest burden[3]	5.5	5.3	5.0	5.1	5.0	4.9	. . .
Memorandum items:							
Debt/equity	345.2	477.6	259.4	299.5	333.4	298.5	. . .
Debt/real estate	36.7	37.8	38.6	40.0	41.9	43.7	. . .
Debt/net disposable income	126.1	127.0	126.7	128.5	130.4	128.7	. . .
Debt/net worth	17.2	17.5	16.9	17.2	17.4	17.5	. . .
Equity/net worth	5.0	3.7	6.5	5.7	5.2	5.9	. . .
Real estate/net worth	46.9	46.4	43.9	42.9	41.6	40.1	. . .
Total debt/GDP	75.9	77.4	77.7	76.4	77.2	76.4	. . .
Banking sector							
Credit quality							
Nonperforming loans[4]/total loans	5.5	6.2	5.9	6.3	8.4	7.4	5.8
Capital ratio							
Stockholders' equity/assets	2.7	4.2	4.5	4.5	4.0	3.4	3.9
Profitability measures							
Return on equity (ROE)	−27.6	−18.0	−0.6	−1.2	−16.3	−19.3	−2.7

Sources: Ministry of Finance, *Financial Statements of Corporations by Industries;* Cabinet Office, Economic and Social Research Institute, *Annual Report on National Accounts;* Japanese Bankers Association, *Financial Statements of All Banks;* and Financial Services Agency, *The Status of Nonperforming Loans.*

[1]Data are fiscal year beginning April 1.
[2]Interest payments as a percent of operating profits.
[3]Interest payments as a percent of income.
[4]From FY1998 onwards, nonperforming loans are based on figures reported under the Financial Reconstruction Law. Up to FY1997, they are based on loans reported by banks for risk management purposes.

Table 9. Europe: Sectoral Balance Sheets[1]

(In percent)

	1997	1998	1999	2000	2001	2002	2003
Corporate sector							
Debt/equity[2]	84.0	82.3	84.8	84.4	84.9	84.1	. . .
Short-term debt/total debt	38.1	37.3	37.7	40.0	39.0	37.5	. . .
Interest burden[3]	17.2	16.8	17.1	19.0	20.0	19.4	. . .
Debt/operating profits	263.3	258.8	288.2	315.9	326.6	337.6	. . .
Memorandum items:							
Financial assets/equity	1.7	1.8	2.1	2.0	1.9	1.6	. . .
Liquid assets/short-term debt	94.5	92.9	89.6	85.6	89.9	94.5	. . .
Household sector							
Net worth/assets	86.2	86.1	86.4	86.0	85.0	83.4	. . .
Equity/net worth	14.2	15.3	17.9	17.1	16.8	14.6	. . .
Equity/net financial assets	37.8	39.8	44.0	43.3	43.1	37.7	. . .
Interest burden[4]	6.3	6.7	6.4	6.5	6.3	6.1	. . .
Memorandum items:							
Nonfinancial assets/net worth	61.2	60.6	58.5	59.8	60.7	61.7	. . .
Debt/net financial assets	45.4	44.0	41.4	43.0	45.3	51.2	. . .
Debt/income	88.6	90.9	93.8	94.8	95.0	98.8	. . .
Banking sector[5]							
Credit quality							
Nonperforming loans/total loans	5.0	6.1	5.6	3.1	2.6	3.1	. . .
Loan-loss reserve/nonperforming loans	74.7	76.5	72.0	77.0	79.6	74.4	75.8
Loan-loss reserve/total loans	2.1	2.7	2.7	2.7	2.7	2.9	2.9
Loan-loss provisions/total operating income[6]	13.2	11.7	9.1	6.7	9.4	12.3	. . .
Capital ratios							
Total risk-based capital	10.7	10.6	10.5	11.0	11.2	11.4	. . .
Tier 1 risk-based capital	7.2	7.0	7.2	7.7	7.7	8.1	. . .
Equity capital/total assets	3.7	3.9	3.8	4.1	4.0	4.0	4.1
Capital funds/liabilities	6.1	6.3	6.2	6.6	6.6	6.6	6.6
Profitability measures							
Return on assets, or ROA (after tax)	0.4	0.4	0.5	0.9	0.4	0.3	0.4
Return on equity, or ROE (after tax)	9.7	11.2	11.7	17.4	9.9	7.5	8.9
Net interest margin	1.9	1.7	1.4	1.4	1.4	1.6	1.5
Efficiency ratio[7]	69.5	68.4	68.6	69.4	71.0	61.6	67.8

Sources: ©2003 Bureau van Dijk Electronic Publishing-Bankscope; ECB *Monthly Bulletin*; and IMF staff estimates.
[1]GDP-weighted average for France, Germany, and the United Kingdom, unless otherwise noted.
[2]Corporate equity adjusted for changes in asset valuation.
[3]Interest payments as a percent of gross operating profits.
[4]Interest payments as percent of disposable income.
[5]Fifty largest euro area banks. Data availability may restrict coverage to less than 50 banks for specific indicators.
[6]Includes the write-off of goodwill in foreign subsidiaries by banks with exposure to Argentina.
[7]Cost to income ratio.

Figure 15. Emerging Market Volatilities

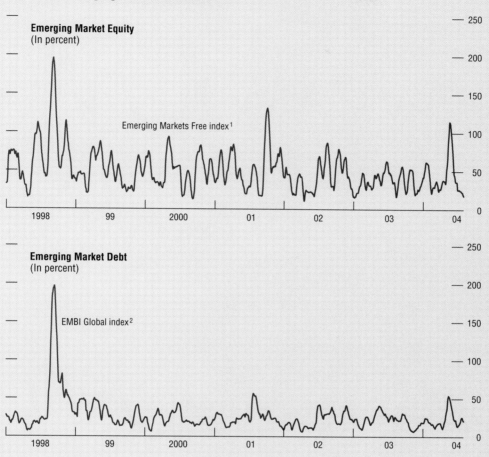

Sources: For "Emerging Market Equity," Morgan Stanley Capital International; and IMF staff estimates. For "Emerging Market Debt," J.P. Morgan Chase & Co.; and IMF staff estimates.
[1]Data utilize the Emerging Markets Free index in U.S. dollars to calculate 30-day rolling volatilities.
[2]Data utilize the EMBI Global total return index in U.S. dollars to calculate 30-day rolling volatilities.

Figure 16. Emerging Market Debt Cross-Correlations

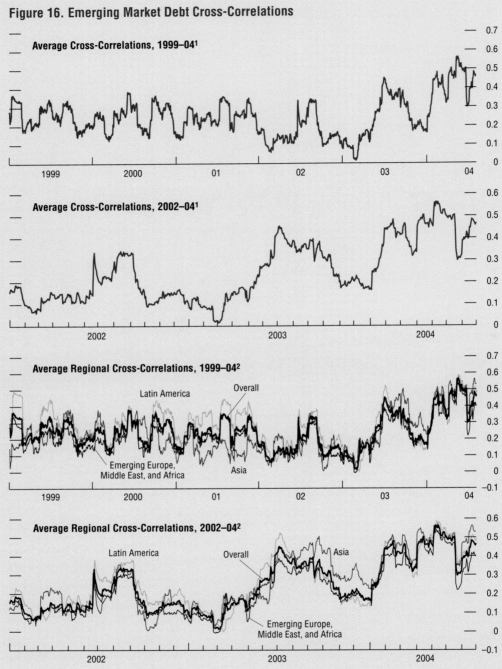

Sources: J.P. Morgan Chase & Co.; and IMF staff estimates.
[1]Thirty-day moving simple average across all pair-wise return correlations of 20 constituents included in the EMBI Global.
[2]Simple average of all pair-wise correlations of all markets in a given region with all other emerging bond markets, regardless of region.

Table 10. Emerging Market Equity Indices

	7/30/2004	2004 End of Period		2003 End of Period				2000	2001	2002	2003	12-Month High	12-Month Low	All-Time High[1]	All-Time Low[1]
		Q1	Q2	Q1	Q2	Q3	Q4								
World	**1,027.0**	**1,059.2**	**1,062.5**	**748.6**	**871.1**	**909.6**	**1,036.3**	**1,221.3**	**1,003.5**	**792.2**	**1,036.3**	**1,085.8**	**870.0**	**1,448.8**	**423.1**
Emerging Markets															
Emerging Markets Free	**423.1**	**482.1**	**432.2**	**272.3**	**332.7**	**377.6**	**442.8**	**333.8**	**317.4**	**292.1**	**442.8**	**497.3**	**347.1**	**587.1**	**175.3**
EMF Latin America	**1,100.3**	**1,169.5**	**1,062.4**	**652.9**	**800.2**	**899.7**	**1,100.9**	**915.6**	**876.2**	**658.9**	**1,100.9**	**1,202.1**	**803.3**	**1,352.5**	**185.6**
Argentina	881.1	1,034.6	847.8	559.9	700.1	733.0	933.6	1,232.7	959.6	470.3	933.6	1,090.5	619.8	2,052.2	152.6
Brazil	742.9	786.9	686.4	410.1	503.1	593.2	802.0	763.2	597.1	395.4	802.0	875.9	491.3	1,306.4	84.1
Chile	783.2	779.6	762.0	446.0	560.4	694.7	800.6	604.7	568.7	445.5	800.6	862.3	592.3	1,119.6	183.0
Colombia	150.1	152.8	145.8	65.9	84.1	85.5	108.6	42.1	57.7	68.3	108.6	171.7	84.1	183.8	41.2
Mexico	2,077.9	2,241.1	2,114.1	1,350.9	1,637.3	1,708.0	1,873.1	1,464.9	1,698.2	1,442.8	1,873.1	2,301.0	1,643.2	2,301.0	308.9
Peru	307.9	364.7	308.8	187.1	207.8	246.1	344.1	125.0	144.1	182.7	344.1	364.7	221.1	364.7	73.5
Venezuela	128.5	123.0	131.7	67.4	125.2	145.3	103.8	106.1	95.4	77.7	103.8	175.7	99.1	278.4	56.1
EMF Asia	**187.3**	**222.1**	**195.0**	**127.2**	**154.4**	**177.5**	**206.4**	**143.6**	**149.7**	**140.4**	**206.4**	**231.7**	**165.4**	**433.0**	**104.1**
China	22.5	24.7	22.5	13.9	16.3	18.9	25.5	22.8	16.8	14.1	25.5	27.1	17.3	136.9	12.9
India	217.0	230.8	201.6	132.4	151.9	188.1	246.2	173.4	141.2	148.8	246.2	258.3	157.2	323.9	77.7
Indonesia	960.2	892.4	927.3	474.9	633.5	728.7	831.1	456.4	437.2	519.6	831.1	1,037.9	578.0	1,077.7	280.0
Korea	220.2	276.1	237.3	158.0	196.7	207.7	246.0	125.6	190.4	184.7	246.0	292.9	206.4	292.9	59.5
Malaysia	310.7	342.6	306.5	240.6	262.8	276.8	300.4	245.2	250.7	244.0	300.4	346.7	272.8	465.7	88.3
Pakistan	193.0	200.7	192.4	140.7	158.9	180.4	188.2	99.1	67.4	146.0	188.2	213.9	162.6	228.9	54.4
Philippines	329.2	296.1	331.8	210.6	257.0	272.6	303.7	352.6	292.2	210.1	303.7	338.9	249.3	917.3	132.6
Taiwan Province of China	228.7	277.0	248.3	184.1	210.9	250.0	259.1	222.2	255.6	189.5	259.1	300.6	224.3	483.5	103.9
Thailand	242.0	240.8	245.3	138.1	170.7	199.6	280.5	102.5	107.5	130.2	280.5	286.5	173.5	669.4	72.0
EMF Europe, Middle East, & Africa	**168.4**	**185.6**	**171.8**	**102.6**	**126.9**	**141.6**	**163.9**	...	**103.5**	**108.4**	**163.9**	**189.2**	**128.0**	**189.2**	**80.8**
Czech Republic	176.4	191.1	178.4	123.1	126.7	142.4	152.9	107.6	97.5	116.2	152.9	199.5	133.2	199.5	62.8
Egypt	313.7	282.6	284.2	114.4	158.5	195.6	234.6	154.9	101.9	97.4	234.6	318.3	149.4	318.3	89.9
Hungary	824.3	782.7	812.9	524.3	538.3	617.4	646.9	582.9	507.9	535.5	646.9	849.4	551.5	941.4	77.1
Israel	148.6	156.5	167.5	97.2	135.8	129.5	141.4	196.0	132.7	90.8	141.4	167.5	123.4	236.2	67.6
Jordan	265.9	250.2	252.5	157.6	182.3	213.8	238.3	116.1	149.5	153.5	238.3	266.6	194.4	266.6	103.1
Morocco	191.6	188.3	189.4	142.5	163.7	166.3	171.4	198.9	180.1	138.5	171.4	197.2	160.8	302.1	99.6
Poland	1,176.1	1,251.6	1,218.3	797.4	914.0	1,049.8	1,118.3	1,307.9	891.9	861.0	1,118.3	1,335.7	986.1	1,792.9	99.6
Russia	432.1	596.7	470.5	264.6	388.6	436.1	461.1	155.2	237.8	270.7	461.1	626.8	354.1	626.8	30.6
South Africa	284.2	302.7	278.9	227.6	244.3	258.5	296.8	244.8	309.3	272.7	296.8	320.0	255.2	350.5	99.7
Turkey	329,483	336,724	303,284	154,022	179,225	225,249	319,808	163,012	234,490	169,900	319,808	350,236	177,412	350,236	426
EMF Sectors															
Energy	283.4	324.4	277.8	161.7	205.8	233.5	287.4	148.5	162.1	163.1	287.4	335.2	201.2	335.2	81.7
Materials	230.8	253.1	222.3	163.5	178.1	206.1	250.1	140.8	173.9	182.8	250.1	268.4	192.6	268.4	98.5
Industrials	98.4	107.2	99.2	60.9	71.3	81.4	98.9	73.4	63.8	61.8	98.9	110.7	74.7	276.8	52.6
Consumer discretionary	215.2	250.9	218.7	130.8	166.8	188.0	233.8	126.0	130.6	138.8	233.8	258.3	175.9	258.3	74.1
Consumer staple	118.0	124.4	117.1	82.8	101.1	105.7	118.6	103.1	94.6	88.2	118.6	129.0	99.4	148.6	80.4
Healthcare	262.8	286.6	291.6	183.8	243.9	252.9	272.5	173.9	146.5	169.8	272.5	300.7	238.0	300.7	83.3
Financials	135.9	151.0	138.8	89.5	106.8	117.9	138.8	112.6	107.7	98.6	138.8	155.4	108.1	185.0	74.6
Information technology	132.9	174.5	149.5	93.5	117.2	140.7	149.6	130.9	134.2	103.9	149.6	187.3	130.8	300.0	74.6
Telecommunications	100.7	108.9	104.1	64.6	80.0	86.2	100.8	113.8	91.9	72.7	100.8	112.7	80.5	211.5	73.1
Utilities	118.9	127.7	114.3	72.7	92.8	107.8	127.2	95.7	91.5	72.4	127.2	134.1	95.0	247.8	63.1

Table 10 (continued)

		2004 End of Period		2003 End of Period								12-Month High	12-Month Low	All-Time High[1]	All-Time Low[1]
	7/30/2004	Q1	Q2	Q1	Q2	Q3	Q4	2000	2001	2002	2003				
World	**−3.3**	**2.2**	**0.3**	**−5.5**	**16.4**	**4.4**	**13.9**	**−14.1**	**−17.8**	**−21.1**	**30.8**	...	...	...	...
Emerging Markets															
Emerging Markets Free	**−2.1**	**8.9**	**−10.3**	**−6.8**	**22.2**	**13.5**	**17.3**	**−31.8**	**−4.9**	**−8.0**	**51.6**	...	...	...	...
EMF Latin America	**3.6**	**6.2**	**−9.2**	**−0.9**	**22.6**	**12.4**	**22.4**	**−18.4**	**−4.3**	**−24.8**	**67.1**	...	...	...	...
Argentina	3.9	10.8	−18.1	19.1	25.0	4.7	27.4	−26.1	−22.2	−51.0	98.5	...	...	...	...
Brazil	8.2	−1.9	−12.8	3.7	22.7	17.9	35.2	−14.2	−21.8	−33.8	102.9	...	...	...	...
Chile	2.8	−2.6	−2.2	0.1	25.7	24.0	15.2	−17.0	−6.0	−21.7	79.7	...	...	...	...
Colombia	2.9	40.7	−4.5	−3.5	27.6	1.7	27.0	−41.2	37.1	18.3	59.0	...	...	...	...
Mexico	−1.7	19.7	−5.7	−6.4	21.2	4.3	9.7	−21.5	15.9	−15.0	29.8	...	...	...	...
Peru	−0.3	6.0	−15.3	2.4	11.1	18.4	39.8	−26.7	15.3	26.8	88.4	...	...	...	...
Venezuela	−2.4	18.5	7.0	−13.3	85.8	16.1	−28.5	0.8	−10.0	−18.6	33.6	...	...	...	...
EMF Asia	**−4.0**	**7.6**	**−12.2**	**−9.3**	**21.4**	**14.9**	**16.3**	**−42.5**	**4.2**	**−6.2**	**47.1**	...	...	...	...
China	0.4	−3.0	−9.1	−1.5	17.1	16.1	34.7	−32.0	−26.0	−16.0	80.3	...	...	...	...
India	7.6	−6.3	−12.6	−11.0	14.7	23.8	30.9	−17.2	−18.6	5.3	65.5	...	...	...	...
Indonesia	3.6	7.4	3.9	−8.6	33.4	15.0	14.1	−49.3	−4.2	18.9	60.0	...	...	...	...
Korea	−7.2	12.2	−14.1	−14.4	24.5	5.6	18.4	−44.6	51.6	−3.0	33.2	...	...	...	...
Malaysia	1.4	14.0	−10.5	−1.4	9.2	5.3	8.6	−17.3	2.3	−2.7	23.1	...	...	...	...
Pakistan	0.3	6.6	−4.1	−3.6	12.9	13.6	4.3	−4.3	−32.0	116.7	28.9	...	...	...	...
Philippines	−0.8	−2.5	12.1	0.2	22.0	6.1	11.4	−32.1	−17.1	−28.1	44.5	...	...	...	...
Taiwan Province of China	−7.9	6.9	−10.4	−2.9	14.6	18.6	3.6	−42.3	15.0	−25.8	36.7	...	...	...	...
Thailand	−1.3	−14.1	1.9	6.0	23.6	17.0	40.5	−50.0	4.9	21.1	115.4	...	...	...	...
EMF Europe, Middle East, & Africa	**−2.0**	**13.2**	**−7.4**	**−5.3**	**23.7**	**11.6**	**15.8**	...	...	**4.7**	**51.2**	...	...	...	...
Czech Republic	−1.1	25.0	−6.6	6.0	2.9	12.4	7.4	5.5	−9.4	19.2	31.6	...	...	...	...
Egypt	10.4	20.5	0.5	17.5	38.6	23.4	19.9	−38.4	−34.2	−4.4	140.8	...	...	...	...
Hungary	1.4	21.0	3.9	−2.1	2.7	14.7	4.8	−19.6	−12.9	5.4	20.8	...	...	...	...
Israel	−11.3	10.7	7.0	7.0	39.7	−4.7	9.2	24.7	−32.3	−31.6	55.7	...	...	...	...
Jordan	5.3	5.0	0.9	2.7	15.6	17.3	11.4	−24.7	28.8	2.6	55.3	...	...	...	...
Morocco	1.1	9.8	0.6	2.9	14.9	1.5	3.1	−20.2	−9.5	−23.1	23.8	...	...	...	...
Poland	−3.5	11.9	−2.7	−7.4	14.6	14.9	6.5	−4.8	−31.8	−3.5	29.9	...	...	...	...
Russia	−8.2	29.4	−21.2	−2.3	46.9	12.2	5.7	−30.4	53.2	13.9	70.3	...	...	...	...
South Africa	1.9	2.0	−7.9	−16.6	7.4	5.8	14.8	−1.2	26.3	−11.8	8.8	...	...	...	...
Turkey	8.6	5.3	−9.9	−9.3	16.4	25.7	42.0	−33.5	43.8	−27.5	88.2	...	...	...	...
EMF Sectors															
Energy	2.0	12.9	−14.4	−0.9	27.2	13.5	23.1	−24.7	9.2	0.6	76.2	...	...	...	...
Materials	3.8	1.2	−12.2	−10.6	8.9	15.8	21.3	−21.0	23.5	5.2	36.8	...	...	...	...
Industrials	−0.9	8.4	−7.4	−1.5	17.2	14.1	21.5	−41.7	−13.1	−3.2	60.1	...	...	...	...
Consumer discretionary	−1.6	7.3	−12.8	−5.8	27.5	12.7	24.3	−41.6	3.6	6.3	68.4	...	...	...	...
Consumer staple	0.8	4.9	−5.8	−6.1	22.1	4.5	12.2	−20.2	−8.2	−6.7	34.4	...	...	...	...
Healthcare	−9.9	5.2	1.7	8.3	32.7	3.7	7.8	0.7	−15.8	15.9	60.5	...	...	...	...
Financials	−2.1	8.8	−8.1	−9.3	19.4	10.4	17.7	−24.3	−4.3	−8.4	40.7	...	...	...	...
Information technology	−11.1	16.7	−14.3	−10.0	25.3	20.1	6.3	−44.9	2.6	−22.6	43.9	...	...	...	...
Telecommunications	−3.2	8.0	−4.4	−11.1	23.8	7.7	17.0	−31.1	−19.2	−20.9	38.7	...	...	...	...
Utilities	4.1	0.4	−10.5	0.5	27.6	16.2	17.9	−25.0	−4.4	−20.9	75.7	...	...	...	...

Period on Period Percent Change

Table 10 (concluded)

	7/30/2004	2004 End of Period Q1	Q2	2003 End of Period Q1	Q2	Q3	Q4	2000	2001	2002	2003	12-Month High	12-Month Low	All-Time High[1]	All-Time Low[1]
Developed Markets															
Australia	697.6	680.5	700.6	580.4	601.6	627.1	655.5	640.1	690.8	604.4	655.5	639.6	539.9	712.9	250.2
Austria	154.8	141.1	150.7	92.8	101.6	104.6	118.0	96.9	94.6	91.8	118.0	105.4	79.7	105.4	96.2
Belgium	66.1	63.6	66.3	44.0	52.3	55.0	60.1	85.8	78.6	55.3	60.1	65.0	38.1	53.9	51.2
Canada	1,049.3	1,062.0	1,058.7	796.3	868.0	922.4	1,019.7	1,156.4	965.8	818.3	1,019.7	886.4	705.8	1,511.4	338.3
Denmark	1,994.9	1,909.4	2,011.5	1,370.1	1,554.7	1,695.1	1,772.7	2,333.3	2,060.1	1,448.8	1,772.7	1,752.8	1,245.8	2,776.6	556.5
Finland	81.1	113.1	91.6	84.0	94.4	92.2	97.4	267.5	171.8	100.3	97.4	126.0	78.8	383.1	78.8
France	96.0	95.3	98.0	69.2	81.2	82.4	93.2	152.0	123.1	81.3	93.2	95.3	63.4	178.6	63.4
Germany	72.5	73.0	75.4	46.9	60.4	61.5	74.6	124.0	100.1	56.0	74.6	78.4	42.9	163.6	41.4
Greece	67.1	67.0	68.5	38.2	50.7	54.9	63.6	106.1	76.8	46.8	63.6	61.9	38.2	197.2	38.2
Hong Kong SAR	6,433.8	6,747.8	6,349.0	4,501.2	4,838.9	6,011.5	6,341.3	7,690.1	6,058.0	4,808.4	6,341.3	5,553.6	4,305.4	10,165.3	1,995.5
Ireland	74.9	71.0	76.4	56.8	60.7	62.0	65.9	92.1	93.1	56.8	65.9	67.1	51.9	107.3	51.9
Italy	81.9	79.8	83.1	62.6	72.2	71.3	78.1	119.9	91.2	69.6	78.1	78.4	58.7	132.1	58.7
Japan	686.7	709.2	714.6	480.4	542.9	613.4	637.3	808.2	650.3	524.3	637.3	628.7	462.1	1,655.3	462.1
Netherlands	66.5	67.4	69.2	53.4	60.3	61.9	68.4	124.5	100.4	66.0	68.4	80.9	47.4	134.9	47.4
New Zealand	120.6	112.8	115.6	88.8	101.4	102.8	107.6	83.9	94.2	90.0	107.6	101.4	86.6	141.0	56.7
Norway	1,461.1	1,407.3	1,475.8	804.4	994.1	1,041.2	1,240.9	1,458.0	1,278.4	898.3	1,240.9	1,116.3	762.2	1,599.1	455.9
Portugal	70.0	74.1	72.7	51.3	55.9	59.6	66.1	97.9	79.5	57.0	66.1	64.6	48.1	123.1	48.1
Singapore	1,068.1	1,048.3	1,041.3	725.6	831.9	932.0	1,005.1	1,173.4	936.8	764.9	1,005.1	922.1	687.3	1,624.2	508.2
Spain	91.0	92.0	92.8	67.8	79.3	77.2	89.6	107.7	99.0	69.9	89.6	81.9	61.1	133.7	27.4
Sweden	5,243.9	5,238.6	5,385.2	3,271.7	3,827.3	4,136.5	4,675.2	7,735.0	6,178.8	3,517.4	4,675.2	4,173.8	2,914.9	12,250.4	787.2
Switzerland	726.0	734.4	735.8	534.3	626.6	656.3	714.3	1,017.0	813.4	603.2	714.3	716.9	481.4	1,032.8	158.1
United Kingdom	1,331.2	1,321.9	1,349.4	1,082.4	1,215.4	1,236.1	1,348.7	1,841.4	1,586.2	1,179.2	1,348.7	1,336.7	986.4	1,974.2	585.4
United States	1,031.2	1,055.9	1,068.9	796.1	916.1	935.6	1,045.4	1,249.9	1,084.5	824.6	1,045.4	950.4	726.5	1,493.0	273.7
Period on Period Percent Change															
Developed Markets															
Australia	−0.4	3.8	3.0	−4.0	3.7	4.2	4.5	3.7	7.9	−12.5	8.5	...	...	...	...
Austria	2.7	19.6	6.8	1.1	9.5	2.9	12.8	−7.6	−2.4	−3.0	28.5	...	...	...	...
Belgium	−0.2	5.8	4.3	−20.4	18.9	5.3	9.2	−13.1	−8.3	−29.7	8.7	...	...	...	...
Canada	−0.9	4.1	−0.3	−2.7	9.0	6.3	10.6	8.1	−16.5	−15.3	24.6	...	...	...	...
Denmark	−0.8	7.7	5.3	−5.4	13.5	9.0	4.6	9.9	−11.7	−29.7	22.4	...	...	...	...
Finland	−11.5	16.2	−19.1	−16.2	12.4	−2.2	5.6	−8.9	−35.8	−41.6	−2.9	...	...	...	...
France	−2.1	2.3	2.9	−14.9	17.3	1.5	13.1	1.4	−19.0	−34.0	14.6	...	...	...	...
Germany	−3.9	−2.2	3.4	−16.2	28.7	2.0	21.2	−10.8	−19.3	−44.0	33.2	...	...	...	...
Greece	−2.0	5.4	2.2	−18.4	32.8	8.3	15.7	−38.6	−27.6	−39.1	35.8	...	...	...	...
Hong Kong SAR	1.3	6.4	−5.9	−6.4	7.5	24.2	5.5	−16.7	−21.2	−20.6	31.9	...	...	...	...
Ireland	−2.0	7.7	7.5	−0.1	7.0	2.1	6.3	−8.5	1.1	−39.0	16.0	...	...	...	...
Italy	−1.4	2.3	4.0	−10.0	15.3	−1.2	9.4	3.9	−24.0	−23.6	12.2	...	...	...	...
Japan	−3.9	11.3	0.8	−8.4	13.0	13.0	3.9	−20.3	−19.5	−19.4	21.6	...	...	...	...
Netherlands	−4.0	−1.5	2.8	−19.1	12.9	2.6	10.6	1.0	−19.4	−34.3	3.6	...	...	...	...
New Zealand	4.4	4.8	2.5	−1.4	14.2	1.4	4.7	−24.9	12.2	−4.4	19.6	...	...	...	...
Norway	−1.0	13.4	4.9	−10.5	23.6	4.7	19.2	7.1	−12.3	−29.7	38.1	...	...	...	...
Portugal	−3.6	12.1	−1.9	−10.1	9.1	6.6	10.8	−6.2	−18.8	−28.3	15.9	...	...	...	...
Singapore	2.6	4.3	−0.7	−5.1	14.6	12.0	7.8	−25.7	−20.2	−18.4	31.4	...	...	...	...
Spain	−1.9	2.6	0.8	−2.9	16.8	−2.5	16.1	−11.2	−8.0	−29.5	28.3	...	...	...	...
Sweden	−2.6	12.1	2.8	−7.0	17.0	8.1	13.0	−13.8	−20.1	−43.1	32.9	...	...	...	...
Switzerland	−1.3	2.8	0.2	−11.4	17.3	4.7	8.8	6.2	−20.0	−25.8	18.4	...	...	...	...
United Kingdom	−1.3	−2.0	2.1	−8.2	12.3	1.7	9.1	−6.7	−13.9	−25.7	14.4	...	...	...	...
United States	−3.5	1.0	1.2	−3.5	15.1	2.1	11.7	−13.6	−13.2	−24.0	26.8	...	...	...	...

Data are provided by Morgan Stanley Capital International. Regional and sectoral compositions conform to Morgan Stanley Capital International definitions.
[1]From 1990 or initiation of the index.

Table 11. Foreign Exchange Rates
(Units per U.S. dollar)

	7/30/2004	2004 End of Period Q1	Q2	2003 End of Period Q1	Q2	Q3	Q4	2000	2001	2002	2003	12-Month High	12-Month Low	All-Time High[1]	All-Time Low[1]
Emerging Markets															
Latin America															
Argentina	2.98	2.86	2.96	2.97	2.81	2.92	2.93	1.00	1.00	3.36	2.93	2.81	3.00	0.98	3.86
Brazil	3.04	2.90	3.09	3.35	2.84	2.90	2.89	1.95	2.31	3.54	2.89	2.78	3.21	0.00	3.95
Chile	641.80	612.40	636.00	733.25	700.90	660.95	592.75	573.85	661.25	720.25	592.75	558.00	714.65	295.18	759.75
Colombia	2,611.90	2,679.55	2,693.20	2,958.00	2,817.00	2,900.80	2,780.00	2,236.00	2,277.50	2,867.00	2,780.00	2,611.90	2,906.90	689.21	2,980.00
Mexico	11.42	11.13	11.49	10.77	10.46	10.99	11.23	9.62	9.16	10.37	11.23	10.58	11.67	2.68	11.67
Peru	3.42	3.46	3.47	3.47	3.47	3.48	3.46	3.53	3.44	3.51	3.46	3.42	3.51	1.28	3.65
Venezuela	1,917.60	1,917.60	1,917.60	1,598.00	1,598.00	1,598.00	1,598.00	699.51	757.50	1,388.80	1,598.00	1,598.00	1,918.00	45.00	1,921.80
Asia															
China	8.28	8.28	8.28	8.28	8.28	8.28	8.28	8.28	8.28	8.28	8.28	8.28	8.28	5.96	8.92
India	46.47	43.60	46.06	47.47	46.49	45.76	45.63	46.68	48.25	47.98	45.63	43.54	46.47	16.92	49.05
Indonesia	9,130	8,564	9,400	8,902	8,275	8,395	8,420	9,675	10,400	8,950	8,420	8,317	9,440	1,977	16,650
Korea	1,170.10	1,147.27	1,155.45	1,254.45	1,193.05	1,150.10	1,192.10	1,265.00	1,313.50	1,185.70	1,192.10	1,140.30	1,203.18	683.50	1,962.50
Malaysia	3.80	3.80	3.80	3.80	3.80	3.80	3.80	3.80	3.80	3.80	3.80	3.80	3.80	2.44	4.71
Pakistan	58.35	57.39	58.08	58.00	57.85	57.90	57.25	57.60	59.90	58.25	57.25	57.00	58.50	21.18	64.35
Philippines	55.95	56.20	56.12	53.53	53.48	54.88	55.54	50.00	51.60	53.60	55.54	54.57	56.46	23.10	56.46
Taiwan Province of China	34.14	33.02	33.78	34.75	34.64	33.74	33.96	33.08	34.95	34.64	33.96	32.80	34.51	24.48	35.19
Thailand	41.32	39.29	40.93	42.84	42.00	40.03	39.62	43.38	44.21	43.11	39.62	38.84	42.07	23.15	55.50
Europe, Middle East, & Africa															
Czech Republic	26.36	26.67	26.17	29.37	27.51	27.36	25.71	37.28	35.60	30.07	25.71	25.05	29.98	25.05	42.17
Egypt	6.21	6.20	6.19	5.76	6.08	6.14	6.17	3.89	4.58	4.62	6.17	6.12	6.24	3.29	6.24
Hungary	206.52	201.68	205.61	227.19	231.27	218.30	208.70	282.34	274.81	224.48	208.70	200.42	238.20	90.20	317.56
Israel	4.52	4.53	4.50	4.70	4.32	4.44	4.39	4.04	4.40	4.74	4.39	4.36	4.63	1.96	5.01
Jordan	0.71	0.71	0.71	0.71	0.71	0.71	0.71	0.71	0.71	0.71	0.71	0.71	0.71	0.64	0.72
Morocco	10.60	9.18	8.85	9.85	9.45	9.33	8.80	10.56	11.59	10.18	8.80	9.62	10.85	7.75	11.28
Poland	3.64	3.86	3.69	4.10	3.90	3.95	3.73	4.13	3.96	3.83	3.73	3.56	4.05	1.72	4.71
Russia	29.11	28.52	29.07	31.39	30.37	30.59	29.24	28.16	30.51	31.96	29.24	28.44	30.73	0.98	31.96
South Africa	6.27	6.29	6.14	7.87	7.47	6.93	6.68	7.58	11.96	8.57	6.68	5.93	7.60	2.50	12.45
Turkey	1,466,000	1,314,500	1,484,000	1,714,000	1,418,500	1,391,500	1,406,500	668,500	1,450,100	1,655,100	1,406,500	1,309,300	1,558,000	5,036	1,769,000
Developed Markets															
Australia[2]	0.70	0.77	0.70	0.60	0.67	0.68	0.75	0.56	0.51	0.56	0.75	0.80	0.64	0.84	0.48
Canada	1.33	1.31	1.33	1.47	1.35	1.35	1.30	1.50	1.59	1.57	1.30	1.27	1.41	1.12	1.61
Denmark	6.19	6.05	6.09	6.80	6.45	6.37	5.91	7.92	8.35	7.08	5.91	5.80	6.87	5.34	9.00
Euro[2]	1.23	1.23	1.22	1.09	1.15	1.17	1.26	0.94	0.89	1.05	1.26	1.28	1.08	1.28	0.83
Hong Kong SAR	7.80	7.79	7.80	7.80	7.80	7.74	7.76	7.80	7.80	7.80	7.76	7.71	7.80	7.70	7.82
Japan	111.35	104.22	108.77	118.09	119.80	111.49	107.22	114.41	131.66	118.79	107.22	103.68	120.32	80.63	159.90
New Zealand[2]	0.64	0.67	0.64	0.56	0.59	0.60	0.66	0.44	0.42	0.52	0.66	0.71	0.57	0.72	0.39
Norway	7.02	6.84	6.93	7.27	7.20	7.04	6.67	8.80	8.96	6.94	6.67	6.63	7.68	5.51	9.58
Singapore	1.72	1.67	1.72	1.76	1.76	1.73	1.70	1.73	1.85	1.73	1.70	1.67	1.76	1.39	1.91
Sweden	7.68	7.54	7.51	8.45	7.99	7.75	7.19	9.42	10.48	8.69	7.19	7.11	8.54	5.09	11.03
Switzerland	1.28	1.27	1.25	1.35	1.35	1.32	1.24	1.61	1.66	1.38	1.24	1.22	1.42	1.12	1.82
United Kingdom[2]	1.82	1.85	1.82	1.58	1.65	1.66	1.79	1.49	1.45	1.61	1.79	1.90	1.57	2.01	1.37

Table 11 (concluded)

		2004 End of Period		2003 End of Period											
	7/30/2004	Q1	Q2	Q1	Q2	Q3	Q4	2000	2001	2002	2003	12-Month High	12-Month Low	All-Time High[1]	All-Time Low[1]
Emerging Markets															
Latin America															
Argentina	−0.7	2.6	−3.4	13.0	5.7	−3.5	−0.5	0.2	−0.2	−70.2	14.7	...	...	...	...
Brazil	1.6	−0.1	−6.1	5.6	17.9	−1.9	0.3	−7.7	−15.6	−34.7	22.4	...	...	...	...
Chile	−0.9	−3.2	−3.7	−1.8	4.6	6.0	11.5	−7.8	−13.2	−8.2	21.5	...	...	...	...
Colombia	3.1	3.7	−0.5	−3.1	5.0	−2.9	4.3	−16.3	−1.8	−20.6	3.1	...	...	...	...
Mexico	0.6	0.9	−3.1	−3.7	3.0	−4.8	−2.2	−1.2	5.1	−11.7	−7.6	...	...	...	...
Peru	1.5	0.1	−0.3	1.2	0.2	−0.4	0.6	−0.5	2.4	−2.0	1.5	...	...	...	...
Venezuela	0.0	−16.7	0.0	−13.1	0.0	0.0	0.0	−7.3	−7.7	−45.5	−13.1	...	...	...	...
Asia															
China	0.0	0.0	0.0	0.0	0.0	0.0	0.0	0.0	0.0	0.0	0.0	...	...	...	...
India	−0.9	4.6	−5.3	1.1	2.1	1.6	0.3	−6.7	−3.3	0.6	5.2	...	...	...	...
Indonesia	3.0	−1.7	−8.9	0.5	7.6	−1.4	−0.3	−26.6	−7.0	16.2	6.3	...	...	...	...
Korea	−1.3	3.9	−0.7	−5.5	5.1	3.7	−3.5	−9.9	−3.7	10.8	−0.5	...	...	...	...
Malaysia	0.0	0.0	0.0	0.0	0.0	0.0	0.0	0.0	0.0	0.0	0.0	...	...	...	...
Pakistan	−0.5	−0.2	−1.2	0.4	0.3	−0.1	1.1	−10.1	−3.8	2.8	1.7	...	...	...	...
Philippines	0.3	−1.2	0.1	0.1	0.1	−2.5	−1.2	−19.5	−3.1	−3.7	−3.5	...	...	...	...
Taiwan Province of China	−1.1	2.8	−2.2	−0.3	0.3	2.7	−0.7	−5.1	−5.3	0.9	2.0	...	...	...	...
Thailand	−0.9	0.8	−4.0	0.6	2.0	4.9	1.0	−13.6	−1.9	2.6	8.8	...	...	...	...
Europe, Middle East, & Africa															
Czech Republic	−0.7	−3.6	1.9	2.4	6.8	0.5	6.4	−3.9	4.7	18.4	16.9	...	...	...	...
Egypt	−0.3	−0.5	0.1	−19.8	−5.1	−1.1	−0.4	−11.5	−15.1	−0.9	−25.1	...	...	...	...
Hungary	−0.4	3.5	−1.9	−1.2	−1.8	5.9	4.6	−10.6	2.7	22.4	7.6	...	...	...	...
Israel	−0.4	−3.0	0.6	1.0	8.7	−2.7	1.1	2.7	−8.1	−7.3	8.0	...	...	...	...
Jordan	0.0	−0.1	0.1	0.0	0.1	0.0	0.0	−0.3	0.2	−0.1	0.1	...	...	...	...
Morocco	−16.5	−4.2	3.8	3.3	4.2	1.3	6.1	−4.6	−8.9	13.9	15.7	...	...	...	...
Poland	1.4	−3.3	4.7	−6.6	5.0	−1.1	5.8	0.4	4.2	3.5	2.6	...	...	...	...
Russia	−0.1	2.5	−1.9	1.8	3.4	−0.7	4.6	−2.2	−7.7	−4.5	9.3	...	...	...	...
South Africa	−2.1	6.2	2.5	9.0	5.3	7.8	3.7	−18.8	−36.6	39.6	28.2	...	...	...	...
Turkey	1.2	7.0	−11.4	−3.4	20.8	1.9	−1.1	−18.6	−53.9	−12.4	17.7	...	...	...	...
Developed Markets															
Australia	0.5	2.0	−8.8	7.6	11.4	1.0	10.6	−14.9	−8.8	10.2	33.9	...	...	...	...
Canada	0.1	−0.9	−1.8	7.1	8.9	−0.4	4.2	−3.5	−5.9	1.3	21.2	...	...	...	...
Denmark	−1.5	−2.2	−0.8	4.1	5.4	1.3	7.7	−6.7	−5.1	17.9	19.8	...	...	...	...
Euro	1.1	−2.2	−0.9	4.0	5.5	1.3	8.1	−6.3	−5.6	18.0	20.0	...	...	...	...
Hong Kong SAR	0.0	−0.4	−0.1	0.0	0.0	0.7	−0.3	−0.3	0.0	0.0	0.4	...	...	...	...
Japan	−2.3	2.9	−4.2	0.6	−1.4	7.5	4.0	−10.4	−13.1	10.8	10.8	...	...	...	...
New Zealand	0.1	2.0	−4.8	5.8	5.9	1.3	10.2	−14.9	−6.1	25.9	25.0	...	...	...	...
Norway	−1.3	−2.6	−1.2	−4.6	1.0	2.3	5.7	−8.9	−1.8	29.2	4.1	...	...	...	...
Singapore	−1.2	1.5	−2.5	−1.7	0.2	1.9	1.7	−4.0	−6.0	6.4	2.1	...	...	...	...
Sweden	−2.1	−4.6	0.3	2.8	5.8	3.0	7.9	−9.5	−10.2	20.6	20.9	...	...	...	...
Switzerland	−2.6	−2.1	1.4	2.4	0.0	2.4	6.5	−1.3	−3.0	20.0	11.7	...	...	...	...
United Kingdom	0.0	3.4	−1.4	−1.7	4.5	0.4	7.5	−7.7	−2.6	10.7	10.9	...	...	...	...

Source: Bloomberg L.P.
[1]High value indicates value of greatest appreciation against the U.S. dollar; low value indicates value of greatest depreciation against the U.S. dollar. "All-Time" refers to the period since 1990 or initiation of the currency.
[2]U.S. dollars per unit.

Table 12. Emerging Market Bond Index: EMBI Global Total Returns Index

| | 7/30/2004 | 2004 End of Period | | 2003 End of Period | | | | 2000 | 2001 | 2002 | 2003 | 12-Month High | 12-Month Low | All-Time High[1] | All-Time Low[1] |
		Q1	Q2	Q1	Q2	Q3	Q4								
Composite	**285**	**292**	**276**	**240**	**264**	**270**	**283**	**196**	**199**	**225**	**283**	**293**	**251**	**293**	**63**
Latin America															
Argentina	72	74	70	60	79	69	67	183	61	57	67	77	65	194	47
Brazil	380	387	364	278	323	344	390	222	238	230	390	407	304	407	68
Chile	166	168	164	153	161	162	162	116	129	150	162	168	153	168	98
Colombia	207	216	199	176	197	195	201	115	149	169	201	216	184	216	70
Dominican Republic	96	97	85	120	110	116	99	. . .	102	117	99	121	83	123	83
Ecuador	473	523	437	302	353	374	464	177	241	230	464	526	325	526	61
El Salvador	113	119	111	105	104	107	110	. . .	. . .	98	110	120	99	120	95
Mexico	289	299	282	264	280	282	284	192	219	254	284	301	261	301	58
Panama	462	475	449	414	438	441	452	300	353	395	452	476	415	476	56
Peru	420	440	408	377	386	420	431	244	307	341	431	449	376	449	52
Uruguay	104	106	94	60	89	91	97	. . .	105	62	97	107	80	107	38
Venezuela	410	398	390	264	319	346	393	224	236	281	393	410	322	410	59
Asia															
China	242	249	240	235	244	243	241	179	203	230	241	250	232	250	98
Malaysia	195	200	191	179	191	192	194	133	150	175	194	201	181	201	64
Philippines	271	265	262	233	258	261	261	157	201	230	261	271	242	271	81
Thailand	185	188	184	176	182	185	184	138	153	174	184	189	177	189	75
Europe, Middle East, & Africa															
Bulgaria	600	594	592	543	559	559	578	372	468	525	578	602	542	602	80
Côte d'Ivoire	57	65	56	58	70	62	58	42	54	43	58	73	54	100	29
Croatia	176	174	176	170	171	173	174	145	162	169	174	176	171	176	71
Egypt	145	145	142	128	136	139	140	. . .	103	122	140	146	135	146	87
Hungary	143	144	142	139	142	142	142	111	122	137	142	144	140	144	97
Lebanon	186	184	185	160	170	171	177	122	130	148	177	186	171	186	99
Morocco	266	264	265	243	252	256	262	199	222	237	262	266	252	266	73
Nigeria	611	618	595	446	511	571	586	267	364	376	586	622	489	622	66
Pakistan	101	160	100	160	160	160	160	. . .	122	160	160	160	96	160	91
Poland	297	306	292	284	302	293	290	221	245	280	290	308	279	308	71
Russia	420	446	417	383	423	419	426	164	256	348	426	447	388	447	26
South Africa	302	312	298	285	294	296	297	190	220	271	297	313	280	313	99
Tunisia	129	134	127	116	126	126	127	. . .	. . .	112	127	135	118	135	98
Turkey	274	290	261	192	223	248	279	144	176	213	279	291	226	291	91
Ukraine	284	295	281	261	268	277	289	127	199	241	289	295	261	295	100
Latin	253	259	244	206	229	236	252	202	177	189	252	261	217	261	62
Non-Latin	344	355	337	302	329	334	342	186	240	291	342	355	314	355	72

Table 12 *(concluded)*

| | Period on Period Percent Change | | | | | | | | | | | | | | |
| | 7/30/2004 | 2004 End of Period | | 2003 End of Period | | | | 2000 | 2001 | 2002 | 2003 | 12-Month High | 12-Month Low | All-Time High[1] | All-Time Low[1] |
		Q1	Q2	Q1	Q2	Q3	Q4								
Composite	**3.0**	**3.4**	**−5.5**	**6.6**	**10.1**	**2.3**	**4.7**	**14.4**	**1.4**	**13.1**	**25.7**	...	...	...	...
Latin America															
Argentina	2.9	9.2	−4.9	5.2	32.1	−11.9	−2.6	7.8	−66.9	−6.4	19.1	...	...	...	...
Brazil	4.4	−0.9	−5.8	20.8	16.4	6.4	13.5	13.0	7.3	−3.6	69.8	...	...	...	...
Chile	1.2	3.5	−2.6	2.2	5.0	0.6	0.3	12.2	11.7	15.8	8.3	...	...	...	...
Colombia	3.7	7.1	−7.6	4.3	11.9	−1.0	3.3	3.0	29.5	13.3	19.4	...	...	...	...
Dominican Republic	12.6	−2.0	−11.9	3.0	−8.3	4.9	−14.5	...	...	13.9	−15.3	...	...	...	...
Ecuador	8.2	12.9	−16.4	31.2	16.9	5.9	24.1	53.9	36.1	−4.7	101.5	...	...	...	...
El Salvador	1.6	7.9	−6.3	6.3	−0.4	3.0	2.7	...	...	...	11.9	...	...	...	...
Mexico	2.4	5.3	−5.6	3.6	6.2	0.6	0.7	17.5	14.3	16.1	11.6	...	...	...	...
Panama	2.7	5.2	−5.5	4.9	5.8	0.5	2.6	8.3	17.6	11.9	14.4	...	...	...	...
Peru	2.7	2.0	−7.1	10.7	2.3	8.8	2.7	0.2	26.2	10.8	26.6	...	...	...	...
Uruguay	10.4	10.2	−11.9	−2.8	48.0	2.2	5.9	...	...	−40.6	55.6	...	...	...	...
Venezuela	5.0	1.4	−2.1	−6.0	20.7	8.6	13.5	16.0	5.6	18.9	39.9	...	...	...	...
Asia															
China	1.0	3.3	−3.6	2.1	3.8	−0.5	−1.0	12.1	13.3	13.6	4.5	...	...	...	...
Malaysia	1.7	3.2	−4.5	1.8	7.2	0.5	0.9	11.6	12.9	16.9	10.7	...	...	...	...
Philippines	3.3	1.4	−0.9	1.1	10.8	1.3	0.1	−2.9	27.6	14.6	13.4	...	...	...	...
Thailand	0.5	2.2	−2.2	1.3	3.6	1.4	−0.4	14.3	11.3	13.5	5.9	...	...	...	...
Europe, Middle East, & Africa															
Bulgaria	1.4	2.6	−0.3	3.4	3.0	0.0	3.4	5.1	25.7	12.2	10.2	...	...	...	...
Côte d'Ivoire	1.7	12.9	−14.3	34.8	21.0	−11.3	−6.8	−20.2	30.5	−20.7	34.8	...	...	...	...
Croatia	0.0	0.3	1.0	1.0	0.6	0.8	0.5	13.7	11.5	4.0	2.9	...	...	...	...
Egypt	1.7	3.8	−2.2	4.3	6.2	2.4	1.0	...	...	18.5	14.4	...	...	...	...
Hungary	0.4	1.4	−1.5	1.7	1.8	0.0	0.2	9.8	10.4	12.3	3.7	...	...	...	...
Lebanon	0.7	3.8	0.8	8.0	6.3	0.7	3.4	8.9	6.2	14.1	19.5	...	...	...	...
Morocco	0.3	0.7	0.4	2.2	4.0	1.4	2.2	5.5	11.1	7.2	10.2	...	...	...	...
Nigeria	2.5	5.4	−3.6	18.4	14.6	11.7	2.7	5.3	36.3	3.3	55.8	...	...	...	...
Pakistan	1.6	0.0	−37.7	−0.2	0.0	0.0	0.0	...	...	31.3	−0.2	...	...	...	...
Poland	1.7	5.4	−4.5	1.7	6.1	−2.9	−0.9	15.9	10.6	14.2	3.7	...	...	...	...
Russia	0.8	4.7	−6.5	10.1	10.4	−1.0	1.7	54.9	55.8	35.9	22.4	...	...	...	...
South Africa	1.3	4.9	−4.4	5.1	3.3	0.7	0.2	8.5	16.2	22.9	9.6	...	...	...	...
Tunisia	1.0	5.1	−4.7	3.5	8.6	−0.3	1.1	...	...	...	13.3	...	...	...	...
Turkey	5.1	4.2	−10.1	−9.9	16.0	11.6	12.2	1.1	22.5	21.1	30.8	...	...	...	...
Ukraine	1.2	2.2	−5.0	8.1	2.9	3.4	4.2	...	57.1	21.0	19.8	...	...	...	...
Latin	3.7	3.1	−5.9	9.0	11.2	2.9	6.5	12.5	−12.4	6.8	33.0	...	...	...	...
Non-Latin	2.0	3.8	−5.0	4.0	8.7	1.5	2.5	18.2	28.8	21.0	17.7	...	...	...	...

Source: J.P. Morgan Chase & Co.

Table 13. Emerging Market Bond Index: EMBI Global Yield Spreads
(In basis points)

	7/30/2004	2003 End of Period				End of Period				12-Month High	12-Month Low	All-Time High[1]	All-Time Low[1]
		Q1	Q2	Q3	Q4	2000	2001	2002	2003				
Composite	**450**	**626**	**515**	**486**	**403**	**735**	**728**	**725**	**403**	**549**	**371**	**1,631**	**215**
Latin America													
Argentina	4,909	6,096	4,485	5,355	5,485	770	5,363	6,342	5,485	6,201	4,401	7,222	381
Brazil	586	1,050	798	692	459	748	864	1,460	459	891	406	2,451	406
Chile	84	156	129	102	90	220	175	176	90	134	79	260	79
Colombia	429	595	447	479	427	755	508	633	427	599	352	1,076	261
Dominican Republic	1,525	527	789	705	1,141	. . .	446	499	1,141	1,750	508	1,750	304
Ecuador	944	1,372	1,178	1,121	799	1,415	1,233	1,801	799	1,280	676	4,764	630
El Salvador	289	348	371	315	284	. . .	. . .	411	284	362	217	434	217
Mexico	198	289	239	216	201	391	306	329	201	267	165	1,149	165
Panama	344	399	361	359	324	501	404	446	324	433	285	769	277
Peru	411	477	491	355	325	687	521	609	325	552	273	1,061	273
Uruguay	595	1,344	720	691	636	. . .	284	1,228	636	811	533	1,982	251
Venezuela	601	1,406	1,001	832	586	958	1,130	1,131	586	886	533	2,658	409
Asia													
China	67	68	52	44	58	160	99	84	58	80	39	364	39
Malaysia	124	200	143	124	100	237	207	212	100	155	94	1,141	94
Philippines	423	536	443	414	415	644	466	522	415	507	377	993	300
Thailand	78	120	94	54	67	173	132	128	67	110	49	951	45
Europe, Middle East, & Africa													
Bulgaria	121	253	229	235	177	772	433	291	177	251	121	1,679	121
Côte d'Ivoire	3,325	2,703	2,474	2,665	3,013	2,443	2,418	3,195	3,013	3,333	2,537	3,333	582
Croatia	117	118	113	115	122	330	187	132	122	151	99	1,014	99
Egypt	99	287	216	158	131	. . .	360	325	131	169	79	646	79
Hungary	25	20	33	37	28	136	93	52	28	57	−29	196	−29
Lebanon	358	592	485	504	421	338	645	776	421	505	297	1,082	111
Morocco	137	372	244	224	160	584	518	390	160	281	128	1,606	128
Nigeria	527	1,292	963	643	499	1,807	1,103	1,946	499	977	409	2,937	409
Pakistan	277	289	289	289	289	. . .	1,115	271	289	348	271	2,225	271
Poland	61	176	68	73	76	241	195	185	76	93	37	410	17
Russia	298	365	284	285	257	1,172	669	478	257	360	211	7,063	211
South Africa	144	187	190	162	152	418	319	250	152	209	127	757	127
Tunisia	130	254	183	171	146	. . .	. . .	273	146	200	91	394	91
Turkey	377	970	751	538	309	803	702	696	309	646	286	1,196	286
Ukraine	335	404	370	363	258	1,953	940	671	258	438	231	2,314	231
Latin	559	810	662	631	518	702	888	981	518	714	472	1,532	401
Non-Latin	294	405	326	295	248	791	523	444	248	357	233	1,812	233

Table 13 *(concluded)*

		Period on Period Spread Change								12-Month High	12-Month Low	All-Time High[1]	All-Time Low[1]
	7/30/2004	2003 End of Period				End of Period							
		Q1	Q2	Q3	Q4	2000	2001	2002	2003				
Composite	**47**	**−99**	**−111**	**−29**	**−83**	**−16**	**−7**	**−3**	**−322**	...	...	...	...
Latin America													
Argentina	−576	−246	−1,611	870	130	237	4,593	979	−857	...	...	...	...
Brazil	127	−410	−252	−106	−233	110	116	596	−1,001	...	...	...	...
Chile	−6	−20	−27	−27	−12	81	−45	1	−86	...	...	...	...
Colombia	2	−38	−148	32	−52	339	−247	125	−206	...	...	...	...
Dominican Republic	384	28	262	−84	436	...	...	53	642	...	...	...	...
Ecuador	145	−429	−194	−57	−322	−1,938	−182	568	−1,002	...	...	...	...
El Salvador	5	−63	23	−56	−31	...	...	...	−127	...	...	...	...
Mexico	−3	−40	−50	−23	−15	30	−85	23	−128	...	...	...	...
Panama	20	−47	−38	−2	−35	91	−97	42	−122	...	...	...	...
Peru	86	−132	14	−136	−30	244	−166	88	−284	...	...	...	...
Uruguay	−41	116	−624	−29	−55	...	...	944	−592	...	...	...	...
Venezuela	15	275	−405	−169	−246	90	172	1	−545	...	...	...	...
Asia													
China	9	−16	−16	−8	14	35	−61	−15	−26	...	...	...	...
Malaysia	24	−12	−57	−19	−24	65	−30	5	−112	...	...	...	...
Philippines	8	14	−93	−29	1	334	−178	56	−107	...	...	...	...
Thailand	11	−8	−26	−40	13	9	−41	−4	−61	...	...	...	...
Europe, Middle East, & Africa													
Bulgaria	−56	−38	−24	6	−58	146	−339	−142	−114	...	...	...	...
Côte d'Ivoire	312	−492	−229	191	348	1,051	−25	777	−182	...	...	...	...
Croatia	−5	−14	−5	2	7	−77	−143	−55	−10	...	...	...	...
Egypt	−32	−38	−71	−58	−27	...	...	−35	−194	...	...	...	...
Hungary	−3	−32	13	4	−9	19	−43	−41	−24	...	...	...	...
Lebanon	−63	−184	−107	19	−83	119	307	131	−355	...	...	...	...
Morocco	−23	−18	−128	−20	−64	204	−66	−128	−230	...	...	...	...
Nigeria	28	−654	−329	−320	−144	770	−704	843	−1,447	...	...	...	...
Pakistan	−12	18	0	0	0	...	...	−844	18	...	...	...	...
Poland	−15	−9	−108	5	3	29	−46	−10	−109	...	...	...	...
Russia	41	−113	−81	1	−28	−1,260	−503	−191	−221	...	...	...	...
South Africa	−8	−63	3	−28	−10	141	−99	−69	−98	...	...	...	...
Tunisia	−16	−19	−71	−12	−25	...	...	...	−127	...	...	...	...
Turkey	68	274	−219	−213	−229	360	−101	−6	−387	...	...	...	...
Ukraine	77	−267	−34	−7	−105	...	−1,013	−269	−413	...	...	...	...
Latin	41	−171	−148	−31	−113	104	186	93	−463	...	...	...	...
Non-Latin	46	−39	−79	−31	−47	−222	−268	−79	−196	...	...	...	...

Source: J.P. Morgan Chase & Co.

Table 14. Total Emerging Market Financing
(In millions of U.S. dollars)

	1999	2000	2001	2002	2003	2003 Q3	2003 Q4	2004 Q1	2004 Q2
Total	**163,569.6**	**216,402.7**	**162,137.7**	**147,395.6**	**206,900.0**	**54,557.3**	**66,585.0**	**69,284.8**	**55,099.3**
Africa	**4,707.2**	**9,382.8**	**6,992.3**	**7,019.0**	**12,073.8**	**4,187.2**	**1,032.7**	**2,606.3**	**2,062.3**
Algeria	...	...	50.0	150.0	40.0	...	...	...	...
Angola	...	...	455.0	350.0	1,522.0	1,205.0	...	550.0	...
Botswana	...	...	22.5	...	...	...	...	...	...
Cameroon	...	...	53.8	...	100.0	...	...	...	...
Chad	...	...	400.0	...	...	...	...	...	...
Côte d'Ivoire	179.0	...	15.0	...	...	...	...	...	...
Ghana	30.0	320.0	300.0	420.0	650.0	650.0	...	...	...
Kenya	...	7.5	80.2	...	134.0	...	...	...	...
Malawi	...	...	...	...	...	...	...	...	...
Mali	...	...	...	150.4	287.6	...	287.6	...	...
Mauritius	160.0	...	...	...	...	...	...	...	...
Morocco	322.2	56.4	136.1	...	474.7	...	...	222.4	...
Mozambique	...	...	200.0	...	35.5	...	...	...	...
Namibia	...	...	...	...	35.0	...	35.0	...	...
Niger	...	...	...	...	27.0	...	...	...	...
Nigeria	90.0	...	100.0	960.0	488.0	...	48.0	30.0	...
Senegal	...	...	...	40.0	...	...	...	80.0	...
Seychelles	...	50.0	...	150.0	...	...	...	...	...
South Africa	3,423.4	8,698.8	4,646.7	4,058.1	7,764.9	2,325.0	523.2	1,179.5	2,027.6
Tanzania	...	135.0	...	...	...	...	...	...	...
Tunisia	352.6	94.3	533.0	740.5	485.2	7.2	108.9	544.5	30.0
Zambia	...	...	...	...	30.0	...	30.0	...	...
Zimbabwe	150.0	...	...	...	...	...	...	...	...
Asia	**55,958.6**	**85,881.0**	**67,483.4**	**67,201.3**	**96,714.5**	**26,850.5**	**35,737.4**	**34,889.0**	**26,857.2**
Brunei	...	...	...	129.0	...	...	...	...	...
China	3,461.8	23,063.4	5,567.3	8,891.6	16,530.9	3,729.5	7,520.1	7,810.5	6,421.9
Hong Kong SAR	11,488.3	21,046.4	18,307.3	12,602.1	11,407.3	2,680.6	5,783.0	2,393.9	2,703.5
India	2,376.2	2,224.2	2,382.2	1,380.8	3,954.5	1,272.1	1,858.1	4,335.5	1,809.4
Indonesia	1,465.3	1,283.1	964.9	974.0	5,486.8	823.7	1,048.9	2,158.0	95.1
Korea	13,542.3	14,230.4	17,021.0	14,693.5	17,921.6	5,019.9	4,174.6	5,822.3	5,179.0
Lao P.D.R.	...	...	...	71.4	...	...	...	...	...
Malaysia	5,177.2	4,506.4	4,432.4	5,597.3	5,497.7	535.5	2,450.5	912.5	2,114.5
Marshall Islands	...	...	...	...	...	...	...	...	...
Pakistan	...	...	182.5	289.1	185.5	7.0	178.5	500.0	...
Papua New Guinea	232.4	...	...	...	153.7	...	153.7	...	...
Philippines	7,181.7	5,021.9	3,658.8	5,458.1	5,122.2	1,285.5	2,063.7	2,520.0	1,232.5
Singapore	4,338.7	6,079.7	10,383.6	3,810.0	7,470.4	925.9	3,275.8	1,315.4	1,438.8
Sri Lanka	...	...	...	...	...	...	...	...	...
Taiwan Province of China	4,019.9	6,703.5	3,794.0	10,959.3	20,122.9	9,507.1	6,269.4	6,138.5	4,752.5
Thailand	2,551.7	1,572.5	684.4	1,927.0	2,623.9	957.7	875.0	982.4	1,075.0
Vietnam	100.0	20.0	...	383.5	51.0	6.0	...	...	...
Europe	**26,191.5**	**37,021.7**	**22,787.7**	**29,566.9**	**47,309.3**	**12,295.9**	**13,447.1**	**14,099.9**	**14,433.2**
Azerbaijan	77.2	...	16.0	...	...	...	...	997.0	...
Belarus	...	...	...	...	24.0	24.0	...	...	...
Bulgaria	53.9	8.9	242.3	1,260.8	702.4	6.2	696.2	...	540.5
Croatia	1,504.9	1,498.7	1,766.0	1,425.4	2,022.4	178.1	528.1	372.7	724.8
Cyprus	288.5	86.3	633.0	547.9	648.2	226.0	422.2	...	...
Czech Republic	540.3	127.1	564.6	453.4	4,438.8	1,605.0	1,331.1	16.6	2,395.6
Estonia	289.2	412.7	202.1	292.6	457.3	...	61.5	...	35.2
Georgia	...	...	...	...	6.0	...	6.0	...	...

Table 14 *(concluded)*

	1999	2000	2001	2002	2003	2003		2004	
						Q3	Q4	Q1	Q2
Europe *(continued)*									
Gibraltar	65.0	80.0	...	...	...	...	...	...	...
Hungary	3,471.2	1,308.8	1,364.7	1,040.2	3,634.3	1,438.2	270.5	1,833.4	1,916.6
Kazakstan	417.0	429.6	573.5	743.5	1,475.0	670.0	725.0	202.0	219.0
Kyrgyz Republic	...	...	...	95.0	...	...	...	...	...
Latvia	288.9	23.0	212.1	74.6	70.7	70.7	...	493.5	84.3
Lithuania	959.7	683.8	247.3	374.3	431.7	...	...	754.2	...
Macedonia	...	...	...	...	...	...	...	...	...
Malta	57.0	...	85.0	...	...	...	...	...	...
Moldova	40.0	...	...	...	114.7	114.7	...	...	...
Poland	3,780.7	5,252.9	4,836.6	5,913.2	7,633.5	1,448.3	2,455.7	3,524.0	529.5
Romania	176.0	594.4	1,347.2	1,442.2	1,738.8	77.2	448.0	244.7	91.0
Russia	166.8	3,950.7	3,200.1	8,496.0	11,788.8	2,947.3	3,857.1	1,756.9	5,032.0
Slovak Republic	994.7	1,466.7	219.9	143.1	940.6	...	286.9	...	1,235.3
Slovenia	687.7	672.7	827.2	309.3	394.8	61.5	11.8	76.2	309.4
Turkey	11,900.0	20,385.4	6,405.1	6,376.0	9,349.5	3,018.7	2,217.0	3,128.6	1,320.0
Ukraine	290.7	...	15.0	514.0	1,400.0	410.0	130.0	700.0	...
Uzbekistan	142.0	40.0	30.0	46.0	37.8	...	...	...	...
Middle East	**15,387.4**	**14,999.7**	**11,020.3**	**10,685.4**	**8,281.7**	**2,207.1**	**2,601.8**	**5,418.2**	**3,611.6**
Bahrain	361.1	1,391.0	207.0	665.0	1,750.0	...	...	...	...
Egypt	1,533.7	919.4	2,545.0	670.0	155.0	...	155.0	200.0	...
Iran, I.R. of	...	...	...	986.3	...	...	...	...	...
Israel	3,719.0	2,908.5	1,602.6	344.4	750.0	...	...	758.1	1,264.7
Jordan	...	60.0	...	80.9	...	...	...	...	...
Kuwait	147.5	250.0	770.0	750.0	365.0	...	365.0	300.0	...
Lebanon	1,421.4	1,752.4	3,300.0	990.0	160.0	160.0	...	...	1,268.0
Libya	...	50.0	...	...	...	...	...	...	...
Oman	356.8	685.0	...	2,332.0	818.3	...	818.3	98.6	360.0
Qatar	2,000.0	1,980.0	913.0	1,536.7	880.8	658.0	97.9	1,125.0	719.0
Saudi Arabia	4,374.8	2,200.9	275.0	280.0	569.5	169.5	...	718.0	...
United Arab Emirates	781.0	2,045.0	520.7	370.0	2,133.2	1,219.6	465.6	2,066.0	...
Latin America	**61,324.9**	**69,117.6**	**53,854.0**	**32,923.0**	**42,520.6**	**9,016.6**	**13,766.0**	**12,271.4**	**8,134.9**
Argentina	17,844.4	16,648.5	3,423.9	824.2	130.0	...	100.0	250.0	100.0
Bolivia	...	...	20.0	90.0	...	...	...	...	...
Brazil	12,951.9	23,238.2	19,532.9	10,925.6	11,899.7	3,744.8	3,633.0	3,834.5	2,169.6
Chile	8,031.7	5,782.5	3,935.3	2,959.6	4,631.0	1,310.0	1,452.0	1,300.0	469.2
Colombia	3,555.8	3,093.2	4,895.0	2,096.0	1,911.3	515.0	646.3	500.0	...
Costa Rica	300.0	250.0	250.0	250.0	490.0	...	40.0	310.0	...
Dominican Republic	...	74.0	531.1	258.0	650.4	...	46.0	31.0	...
Ecuador	73.0	...	910.0	10.0	...	...	...	...	...
El Salvador	316.5	160.0	488.5	1,251.5	381.0	...	32.5	...	...
Grenada	...	...	...	100.0	...	...	...	...	...
Guadeloupe	...	...	...	17.4	...	...	...	...	...
Guatemala	222.0	505.0	325.0	44.0	300.0	300.0	...	59.3	...
Jamaica	...	421.0	726.5	345.0	49.6	1.3	...	247.9	125.0
Mexico	14,099.5	15,313.4	13,823.5	10,040.6	16,964.3	800.5	5,846.2	4,401.7	3,771.1
Nicaragua	...	...	...	...	...	...	...	22.0	...
Paraguay	55.0	...	70.0	...	...	...	...	...	...
Peru	1,618.4	465.4	137.5	1,993.0	1,375.0	125.0	500.0	90.0	500.0
St. Lucia	...	...	...	...	20.0	20.0	...	...	...
Trinidad & Tobago	230.0	301.0	70.0	303.0	46.0	...	...	100.0	...
Uruguay	465.0	602.1	1,147.4	400.0	...	...	...	...	...
Venezuela	1,561.7	2,263.3	3,417.5	1,015.0	3,672.5	2,200.0	1,470.0	1,125.0	1,000.0

Source: Data provided by the Bond, Equity and Loan database of the International Monetary Fund sourced from Capital Data.

Table 15. Emerging Market Bond Issuance
(In millions of U.S. dollars)

	1999	2000	2001	2002	2003	2003 Q3	2003 Q4	2004 Q1	2004 Q2
Developing Countries	**82,359.4**	**80,475.4**	**89,036.9**	**61,647.4**	**97,388.2**	**24,601.4**	**24,732.5**	**38,372.5**	**26,859.7**
Africa	**2,345.5**	**1,485.8**	**2,109.6**	**2,161.1**	**5,511.9**	**2,000.0**	...	**1,180.7**	**1,100.0**
Mauritius	160.0	...	...	...	...	...	...	...	...
Morocco	151.5	...	...	...	464.9	...	...	...	...
South Africa	1,804.7	1,485.8	1,647.7	1,511.1	4,690.0	2,000.0	...	636.2	1,100.0
Tunisia	229.3	...	462.0	650.0	357.0	...	...	544.5	...
Asia	**23,424.7**	**24,501.4**	**35,869.2**	**22,532.7**	**34,389.3**	**9,834.9**	**11,768.5**	**13,729.9**	**9,375.0**
China	1,060.0	1,770.7	2,341.9	602.8	2,034.2	318.8	1,665.4	38.8	...
Hong Kong SAR	7,124.8	7,058.9	10,458.6	1,951.6	1,236.2	583.0	468.7	296.9	140.0
India	100.0	100.0	99.3	153.0	450.0	100.0	350.0	888.1	575.0
Indonesia	...	...	125.0	375.0	609.0	192.4	...	1,300.0	25.3
Korea	4,905.8	7,653.0	7,756.3	6,705.5	11,531.3	3,305.8	2,089.0	5,129.9	3,811.7
Malaysia	2,062.4	1,419.7	2,150.0	1,880.0	962.5	...	962.5	325.0	550.0
Pakistan	...	...	...	...	...	...	...	500.0	...
Philippines	4,751.2	2,467.3	1,842.4	4,773.8	3,799.6	1,055.0	1,520.0	2,150.0	650.0
Singapore	2,147.1	2,333.8	8,664.7	562.1	4,336.8	652.1	2,278.8	302.3	500.0
Taiwan Province of China	475.0	1,698.0	2,152.4	5,480.8	9,129.7	3,627.8	2,434.1	2,799.0	2,123.0
Thailand	798.4	...	278.6	48.0	300.0	...	...	...	1,000.0
Europe	**13,872.8**	**14,202.5**	**11,558.6**	**14,997.0**	**24,411.4**	**5,201.3**	**3,389.1**	**10,358.3**	**7,728.7**
Bulgaria	53.9	...	223.4	1,247.8	...	...	...	...	...
Croatia	601.2	858.0	934.0	847.5	983.6	...	...	372.7	724.8
Cyprus	288.5	...	480.5	479.8	648.2	226.0	422.2	...	...
Czech Republic	421.7	...	50.7	428.4	3,168.4	1,546.2	150.0	...	2,011.4
Estonia	84.9	335.7	65.5	292.6	323.3	...	...	...	35.2
Hungary	2,410.5	540.8	1,247.8	70.5	2,211.4	1,130.1	...	1,239.5	1,350.4
Kazakstan	300.0	350.0	250.0	209.0	100.0	...	100.0	100.0	100.0
Latvia	236.7	...	180.8	...	...	...	...	493.5	36.0
Lithuania	531.5	376.2	222.4	355.6	431.7	...	...	754.2	...
Poland	1,652.6	1,553.5	2,773.7	2,679.9	4,301.2	549.0	1,000.0	3,080.2	422.2
Romania	...	259.5	908.6	1,062.2	813.6	...	...	...	...
Russia	...	75.0	1,352.7	3,391.5	4,005.0	150.0	1,330.0	850.0	1,100.0
Slovak Republic	800.2	978.3	219.9	143.1	861.3	...	286.9	...	1,198.8
Slovenia	439.1	384.7	490.0	30.2	...	...	...	...	...
Turkey	5,761.2	8,490.8	2,158.7	3,259.8	5,253.8	1,250.0	...	2,768.2	750.0
Ukraine	290.7	...	...	499.0	1,310.0	350.0	100.0	700.0	...
Middle East	**4,409.8**	**4,670.6**	**5,920.7**	**3,706.6**	**1,860.0**	**160.0**	**200.0**	**2,710.0**	**2,518.0**
Bahrain	209.1	188.5	...	325.0	750.0	...	...	...	...
Egypt	100.0	...	1,500.0	...	...	...	...	...	...
Iran, I.R. of	...	...	...	986.3	...	...	...	...	...
Israel	1,679.2	1,329.7	1,120.7	344.4	750.0	...	...	645.0	1,000.0
Jordan	...	...	...	80.9	...	...	...	...	...
Kuwait	...	...	...	750.0	200.0	...	200.0	...	...
Lebanon	1,421.4	1,752.4	3,300.0	990.0	160.0	160.0	...	...	1,268.0
Oman	...	...	...	...	...	...	...	...	250.0
Qatar	1,000.0	1,400.0	...	...	...	...	...	665.0	...
United Arab Emirates	...	...	...	230.0	...	...	...	1,400.0	...
Latin America	**38,306.7**	**35,615.2**	**33,578.8**	**18,250.0**	**31,215.5**	**7,405.3**	**9,375.0**	**10,393.6**	**6,138.0**
Argentina	14,182.8	13,024.8	1,500.5	...	100.0	...	100.0	...	100.0
Brazil	8,585.8	11,382.1	12,238.8	6,375.5	10,709.9	3,190.3	3,515.0	2,905.0	1,264.7
Chile	1,763.8	679.7	1,536.0	1,728.9	2,900.0	900.0	850.0	1,150.0	...
Colombia	1,675.6	1,547.2	4,263.3	1,000.0	1,765.0	515.0	500.0	500.0	...
Costa Rica	300.0	250.0	250.0	250.0	490.0	...	40.0	310.0	...
Dominican Republic	...	...	500.0	...	600.0	...	...	...	...
El Salvador	150.0	50.0	353.5	1,251.5	348.5	...	...	...	...
Grenada	...	...	...	100.0	...	...	...	...	...
Guatemala	...	...	325.0	...	300.0	300.0	...	50.0	...
Jamaica	...	421.0	690.7	300.0	...	...	...	247.9	125.0
Mexico	9,854.0	7,078.4	9,231.7	4,914.1	9,082.1	300.0	2,400.0	4,130.7	3,148.3
Peru	...	...	...	1,930.0	1,250.0	...	500.0	...	500.0
Trinidad & Tobago	230.0	250.0	...	...	...	...	...	100.0	...
Uruguay	350.0	442.6	1,106.1	400.0	...	...	...	...	...
Venezuela	1,214.7	489.4	1,583.2	...	3,670.0	2,200.0	1,470.0	1,000.0	1,000.0

Source: Data provided by the Bond, Equity and Loan database of the International Monetary Fund sourced from Capital Data.

Table 16. Emerging Market Equity Issuance
(In millions of U.S. dollars)

	1999	2000	2001	2002	2003	2003 Q3	2003 Q4	2004 Q1	2004 Q2
Developing Countries	**23,187.4**	**41,772.8**	**11,245.9**	**16,359.4**	**28,671.0**	**7,092.7**	**18,373.7**	**13,061.3**	**10,044.2**
Africa	**658.7**	**103.3**	**150.9**	**340.5**	**977.4**	**. . .**	**223.2**	**223.3**	**927.6**
Morocco	. . .	56.4	6.8	. . .	. . .	. . .	. . .	. . .	. . .
South Africa	658.7	46.9	144.1	340.5	977.4	. . .	223.2	223.3	927.6
Asia	**18,271.8**	**31,567.7**	**9,591.5**	**12,411.4**	**24,612.9**	**6,906.0**	**15,478.1**	**12,007.9**	**7,884.3**
China	1,477.4	20,239.7	2,810.4	2,546.0	6,864.4	339.8	5,677.9	6,387.5	5,284.4
Hong Kong SAR	3,370.0	3,088.6	297.1	2,857.7	2,962.2	493.6	2,382.6	857.4	553.9
India	874.4	916.7	467.2	264.8	1,299.7	330.4	969.3	2,509.0	. . .
Indonesia	522.2	28.2	347.2	281.0	1,008.4	131.3	607.1	338.0	19.8
Korea	6,590.6	784.8	3,676.4	1,553.7	1,222.6	465.1	488.5	94.4	937.3
Macao	. . .	29.5		. . .	. . .	. . .	. . .	. . .	. . .
Malaysia	. . .	. . .	15.4	891.2	618.2	155.9	454.6	104.3	11.2
Papua New Guinea	232.4	. . .	. . .	. . .	153.7	. . .	153.7	. . .	. . .
Philippines	221.7	194.6	. . .	11.3	. . .	. . .	. . .	. . .	. . .
Singapore	1,725.6	2,202.2	625.8	891.6	1,168.7	123.3	563.7	493.4	145.2
Taiwan Province of China	2,500.4	3,951.5	1,126.6	3,057.9	8,276.3	4,702.8	3,305.7	1,062.9	932.5
Thailand	757.3	132.0	225.3	56.3	1,038.7	163.7	875.0	161.0	. . .
Europe	**1,411.6**	**3,339.8**	**259.4**	**1,612.4**	**2,253.3**	**33.0**	**2,132.4**	**693.5**	**282.7**
Bulgaria	. . .	. . .	. . .	. . .	442.0	. . .	442.0	. . .	. . .
Croatia	. . .	. . .	22.3	. . .	. . .	. . .	. . .	. . .	. . .
Czech Republic	. . .	. . .	. . .	. . .	824.6	. . .	824.6	. . .	146.9
Estonia	190.3	. . .	. . .	. . .	. . .	. . .	. . .	. . .	. . .
Hungary	529.2	19.1	. . .	. . .	13.2	. . .	13.2	349.7	. . .
Latvia	. . .	. . .	. . .	22.7	. . .	. . .	. . .	. . .	. . .
Lithuania	. . .	150.5	. . .	. . .	. . .	. . .	. . .	. . .	. . .
Poland	636.3	358.9	. . .	217.3	604.9	33.0	552.1	. . .	107.4
Russia	55.8	387.7	237.1	1,301.0	368.7	. . .	300.5	237.4	28.5
Turkey	. . .	2,423.8	. . .	71.4	. . .	. . .	. . .	106.5	. . .
Middle East	**2,084.0**	**1,618.1**	**86.8**	**. . .**	**. . .**	**. . .**	**. . .**	**136.6**	**264.7**
Egypt	89.2	319.4	. . .	. . .	. . .	. . .	. . .	. . .	. . .
Israel	1,994.8	1,298.7	86.8	. . .	. . .	. . .	. . .	113.1	264.7
Oman	. . .	. . .	. . .	. . .	. . .	. . .	. . .	23.6	. . .
Latin America	**761.3**	**5,143.9**	**1,157.2**	**1,995.0**	**827.4**	**153.6**	**540.0**	**. . .**	**684.9**
Argentina	349.6	393.1	34.4	. . .	. . .	. . .	. . .	. . .	. . .
Brazil	161.4	3,102.5	1,122.9	1,148.5	287.4	153.6	. . .	. . .	499.7
Chile	. . .	. . .	. . .	. . .	. . .	. . .	. . .	. . .	105.4
Dominican Republic	. . .	74.0	. . .	. . .	. . .	. . .	. . .	. . .	. . .
Mexico	162.0	1,574.3	. . .	846.6	540.0	. . .	540.0	. . .	79.8
Peru	88.4	. . .	. . .	. . .	. . .	. . .	. . .	. . .	. . .

Source: Data provided by the Bond, Equity and Loan database of the International Monetary Fund sourced from Capital Data.

Table 17. Emerging Market Loan Syndication
(In millions of U.S. dollars)

	1999	2000	2001	2002	2003	2003 Q3	2003 Q4	2004 Q1	2004 Q2
Total	**58,022.8**	**94,154.5**	**61,854.9**	**69,388.9**	**80,840.8**	**22,863.2**	**23,478.7**	**17,850.9**	**18,195.3**
Africa	**1,703.0**	**7,793.7**	**4,731.8**	**4,517.4**	**5,584.6**	**2,187.2**	**809.4**	**1,202.4**	**34.8**
Algeria	...	...	50.0	150.0	40.0	...	...	...	...
Angola	...	...	455.0	350.0	1,522.0	1,205.0	...	550.0	...
Botswana	...	...	22.5	...	...	...	...	...	...
Cameroon	...	...	53.8	...	100.0	...	...	...	...
Chad	...	...	400.0	...	...	...	...	...	...
Côte d'Ivoire	179.0	...	15.0	...	...	...	...	...	...
Ghana	30.0	320.0	300.0	420.0	650.0	650.0	...	...	...
Kenya	...	7.5	80.2	...	134.0	...	...	...	...
Malawi	...	...	...	...	...	...	...	...	4.8
Mali	...	...	...	150.4	287.6	...	287.6	...	...
Morocco	170.6	...	129.3	...	9.8	...	...	...	...
Mozambique	...	...	200.0	...	35.5	...	...	222.4	...
Namibia	...	...	...	...	35.0	...	35.0	...	...
Niger	...	...	...	...	27.0	...	...	...	...
Nigeria	90.0	...	100.0	960.0	488.0	...	48.0	30.0	...
Senegal	...	...	...	40.0	...	...	...	...	...
Seychelles	...	50.0	...	150.0	...	...	...	80.0	...
South Africa	960.0	7,166.1	2,855.0	2,206.5	2,097.5	325.0	300.0	320.0	...
Tanzania	...	135.0	...	...	...	...	...	...	...
Tunisia	123.4	94.3	71.0	90.5	128.2	7.2	108.9	...	30.0
Zambia	...	...	...	...	30.0	...	30.0	...	...
Zimbabwe	150.0	...	...	...	...	...	...	...	...
Asia	**14,262.0**	**29,812.0**	**22,022.7**	**32,257.3**	**37,712.3**	**10,109.7**	**8,490.8**	**9,151.3**	**9,597.9**
Brunei	...	...	...	129.0	...	...	...	...	...
China	924.4	1,053.1	415.0	5,742.8	7,632.4	3,070.9	176.9	1,384.2	1,137.5
Hong Kong SAR	993.5	10,898.9	7,551.6	7,792.9	7,208.9	1,604.0	2,931.7	1,239.6	2,009.6
India	1,401.8	1,207.6	1,815.7	963.1	2,204.8	841.7	538.8	938.5	1,234.4
Indonesia	943.1	1,254.9	492.6	318.0	3,869.4	500.0	441.9	520.0	50.0
Korea	2,046.0	5,792.6	5,588.2	6,434.3	5,167.7	1,249.0	1,597.0	598.0	430.0
Lao P.D.R.	...	...	...	71.4	...	...	...	...	...
Malaysia	3,114.8	3,086.7	2,267.0	2,826.1	3,917.1	379.6	1,033.4	483.2	1,553.3
Marshall Islands	...	...	...	34.7	...	...	...	...	...
Pakistan	...	...	182.5	289.1	185.5	7.0	178.5	...	...
Philippines	2,208.9	2,360.0	1,816.4	673.0	1,322.5	230.5	543.7	370.0	582.5
Singapore	466.0	1,543.7	1,093.2	2,356.3	1,964.8	150.5	433.3	519.7	793.6
Sri Lanka	23.0	100.0	105.0	...	186.0	100.0	86.0	...	35.0
Taiwan Province of China	1,044.5	1,054.0	515.0	2,420.5	2,716.9	1,176.5	529.7	2,276.7	1,697.0
Thailand	996.0	1,440.5	180.5	1,822.7	1,285.2	794.0	...	821.3	75.0
Vietnam	100.0	20.0	...	383.5	51.0	6.0	...	...	...
Europe	**10,907.1**	**19,479.3**	**10,969.7**	**12,957.5**	**20,644.6**	**7,061.6**	**7,925.7**	**3,048.0**	**6,421.8**
Azerbaijan	77.2	...	16.0	...	...	...	...	997.0	...
Belarus	...	...	...	...	24.0	24.0	...	...	...
Bulgaria	...	8.9	18.9	13.0	260.4	6.2	254.2	...	540.5
Croatia	903.6	640.7	809.8	577.8	1,038.9	178.1	528.1	...	...
Cyprus	...	86.3	152.5	68.1	...	...	...	...	...
Czech Republic	118.6	127.1	513.9	25.0	445.9	58.7	356.5	16.6	237.4
Estonia	14.0	77.0	136.6	...	133.9	...	61.5	...	...
Georgia	...	...	...	...	6.0	...	6.0	...	...
Gibraltar	65.0	80.0	...	...	...	...	...	...	...

Table 17 (concluded)

	1999	2000	2001	2002	2003	2003 Q3	2003 Q4	2004 Q1	2004 Q2
Europe (continued)									
Hungary	531.6	748.9	116.9	969.7	1,409.7	308.2	257.3	244.3	566.2
Kazakstan	117.0	79.6	323.5	534.5	1,375.0	670.0	625.0	102.0	119.0
Kyrgyz Republic	...	...	...	95.0	...	...	...	...	...
Latvia	52.2	23.0	31.3	51.9	70.7	70.7	...	...	...
Lithuania	428.2	157.2	24.9	18.8	...	...	...	...	48.3
Macedonia	...	...	...	...	...	...	...	...	...
Malta	57.0	...	85.0	...	...	...	...	...	...
Moldova	40.0	...	...	...	114.7	114.7	...	...	...
Poland	1,491.9	3,340.5	2,062.9	3,016.0	2,727.4	866.3	903.6	...	...
Romania	176.0	334.9	438.6	380.0	925.2	77.2	448.0	443.8	...
Russia	111.0	3,488.1	1,610.3	3,803.5	7,415.1	2,797.3	2,226.6	244.7	91.0
Slovak Republic	194.5	488.3	...	...	79.3	...	...	669.5	3,903.5
Slovenia	248.6	288.0	337.2	279.0	394.8	61.5	11.8	...	36.5
Turkey	6,138.8	9,470.9	4,246.4	3,044.8	4,095.7	1,768.7	2,217.0	76.2	309.4
Ukraine	...	...	15.0	15.0	90.0	60.0	30.0	253.9	570.0
Uzbekistan	142.0	40.0	30.0	46.0	37.8	...	...	...	...
Middle East	**8,893.7**	**8,711.0**	**5,012.7**	**6,978.8**	**6,421.7**	**2,047.1**	**2,401.8**	**2,571.5**	**829.0**
Bahrain	152.0	1,202.5	207.0	340.0	1,000.0	...	...	...	...
Egypt	1,344.5	600.0	1,045.0	670.0	155.0	...	155.0	200.0	...
Iran, I.R. of	692.0	757.7	887.0	1,680.1	700.0	...	700.0	152.5	...
Israel	45.0	280.0	395.0	...	...	...	...	...	...
Jordan	...	60.0	...	...	...	...	...	...	...
Kuwait	147.5	250.0	770.0	...	165.0	...	165.0	300.0	...
Libya	...	50.0	...	...	...	...	...	...	...
Oman	356.8	685.0	...	2,332.0	818.3	...	818.3	75.0	110.0
Qatar	1,000.0	580.0	913.0	1,536.7	880.8	658.0	97.9	460.0	719.0
Saudi Arabia	4,374.8	2,200.9	275.0	280.0	569.5	169.5	...	718.0	...
United Arab Emirates	781.0	2,045.0	520.7	140.0	2,133.2	1,219.6	465.6	666.0	...
Latin America	**22,257.0**	**28,358.5**	**19,118.0**	**12,677.9**	**10,477.7**	**1,457.7**	**3,851.1**	**1,877.8**	**1,312.0**
Argentina	3,312.1	3,230.6	1,889.0	824.2	30.0	...	...	250.0	...
Bolivia	...	...	20.0	90.0	...	...	...	...	...
Brazil	4,204.7	8,753.6	6,171.3	3,401.7	902.4	400.9	118.0	929.5	405.2
Chile	6,267.9	5,102.8	2,399.3	1,230.7	1,731.0	410.0	602.0	150.0	363.8
Colombia	1,880.2	1,546.0	631.7	1,096.0	146.3	...	146.3	...	...
Costa Rica	...	...	150.0	...	...	...	...	...	...
Dominican Republic	...	...	31.1	258.0	50.4	...	46.0	31.0	...
Ecuador	73.0	...	910.0	10.0	...	...	...	...	...
El Salvador	166.5	110.0	135.0	...	32.5	...	32.5	...	...
Guadeloupe	...	...	...	17.4	...	...	...	...	...
Guatemala	222.0	505.0	...	44.0	...	...	...	9.3	...
Jamaica	...	...	35.8	45.0	49.6	1.3	...	...	...
Mexico	4,083.6	6,660.7	4,591.8	4,280.0	7,342.2	500.5	2,906.3	271.0	543.0
Nicaragua	...	...	...	...	...	...	...	22.0	...
Paraguay	55.0	...	70.0	...	...	...	...	...	...
Peru	1,530.0	465.4	137.5	63.0	125.0	125.0	...	90.0	...
St. Lucia	...	...	...	...	20.0	20.0	...	...	...
Trinidad & Tobago	...	51.0	70.0	303.0	46.0	...	...	...	...
Uruguay	115.0	159.5	41.3	...	...	...	...	...	...
Venezuela	347.0	1,773.9	1,834.3	1,015.0	2.5	...	...	125.0	...

Source: Data provided by the Bond, Equity and Loan database of the International Monetary Fund sourced from Capital Data.

Table 18. Equity Valuation Measures: Dividend-Yield Ratios

	2004		2003						
	Q2	Q1	Q3	Q4	1999	2000	2001	2002	2003
Argentina	1.08	0.98	1.23	1.08	3.29	4.62	5.16	3.42	1.08
Brazil	3.46	3.27	4.36	3.46	2.95	3.18	4.93	5.51	3.46
Chile	1.76	1.96	1.74	1.76	1.88	2.33	2.31	2.76	1.76
China	2.19	2.26	2.96	2.19	3.14	0.95	1.95	2.41	2.19
Colombia	3.92	3.06	4.48	3.92	6.78	11.12	5.63	4.78	3.92
Czech Republic	6.85	7.35	7.36	6.85	1.36	0.95	2.28	2.36	6.85
Egypt	4.69	4.23	4.23	4.69	3.92	5.75	6.48	7.53	4.69
Hong Kong SAR	2.82	2.84	3.20	2.82	2.31	2.58	3.25	3.85	2.82
Hungary	0.94	0.78	0.99	0.94	1.14	1.46	1.30	1.40	0.94
India	1.47	1.61	1.88	1.47	1.25	1.59	2.03	1.81	1.47
Indonesia	3.83	3.66	4.00	3.83	0.91	3.05	3.65	4.17	3.83
Israel	1.10	1.01	0.80	1.10	1.87	2.26	2.24	1.47	1.10
Jordan	2.36	2.25	2.65	2.36	4.24	4.54	3.51	3.77	2.36
Korea	1.82	1.88	2.14	1.82	0.81	2.05	1.54	1.38	1.82
Malaysia	2.38	1.92	2.49	2.38	1.15	1.70	1.87	2.04	2.38
Mexico	1.83	1.66	2.02	1.83	1.27	1.63	1.98	2.30	1.83
Morocco	4.18	3.79	4.32	4.18	2.49	3.59	3.97	4.84	4.18
Pakistan	8.63	8.20	8.78	8.63	4.00	5.12	16.01	10.95	8.63
Peru	1.75	1.70	2.31	1.75	2.86	3.38	3.16	2.37	1.75
Philippines	1.43	1.53	1.33	1.43	1.08	1.44	1.43	1.97	1.43
Poland	1.28	1.14	1.39	1.28	0.70	0.68	1.87	1.84	1.28
Russia	2.38	2.00	1.61	2.38	0.14	0.92	1.11	1.87	2.38
Singapore	2.03	1.98	2.34	2.03	0.86	1.40	1.80	2.27	2.03
South Africa	3.22	2.93	3.67	3.22	2.09	2.75	3.47	3.83	3.22
Sri Lanka	2.51	2.27	1.84	2.51	3.22	5.59	4.79	3.35	2.51
Taiwan Province of China	1.86	1.73	1.91	1.86	0.97	1.71	1.42	1.60	1.86
Thailand	1.69	2.43	2.57	1.69	0.70	2.13	2.02	2.48	1.69
Turkey	0.89	1.44	1.26	0.89	0.76	1.91	1.15	1.35	0.89
Venezuela	3.68	3.03	4.48	3.68	5.80	5.05	3.89	2.38	3.68
Emerging Markets	2.25	2.16	2.52	2.25	1.52	2.09	2.30	2.43	2.25
EM Asia	1.96	1.97	2.28	1.96	1.01	1.71	1.73	1.81	1.96
EM Latin America	2.61	2.43	3.03	2.61	2.28	2.69	3.37	3.64	2.61
EM Europe & Middle East	1.81	1.75	1.53	1.81	1.16	1.84	1.69	1.71	1.81
ACWI Free	1.99	2.03	2.16	1.99	1.27	1.46	1.72	2.25	1.99

Data are from Morgan Stanley Capital International. The countries above include the 27 constituents of the Emerging Markets Free index as well as Hong Kong SAR and Singapore. Regional breakdowns conform to Morgan Stanley Capital International conventions. All indices reflect investible opportunities for global investors by taking into account restrictions on foreign ownership. The indices attempt to achieve an 85 percent representation of freely floating stocks.

Table 19. Equity Valuation Measures: Price-to-Book Ratios

| | 2004 | | 2003 | | | | | | | |
	Q2	Q1	Q3	Q4	1998	1999	2000	2001	2002	2003
Argentina	1.79	2.00	1.38	1.79	1.31	1.47	1.04	0.86	1.20	1.79
Brazil	1.81	1.79	1.37	1.81	0.52	1.24	1.18	1.11	1.24	1.81
Chile	1.55	1.33	1.50	1.55	1.16	1.69	1.49	1.39	1.15	1.55
China	2.16	2.13	1.63	2.16	0.63	0.69	2.75	1.88	1.30	2.16
Colombia	1.34	1.81	1.11	1.34	0.71	0.71	0.49	0.53	1.18	1.34
Czech Republic	1.06	1.30	0.95	1.06	0.73	0.80	1.00	0.81	0.84	1.06
Egypt	2.17	2.67	1.81	2.17	2.13	3.57	2.32	1.39	1.05	2.17
Hong Kong SAR	1.47	1.56	1.38	1.47	1.31	2.27	1.67	1.38	1.10	1.47
Hungary	1.97	2.28	1.94	1.97	3.05	3.35	2.33	2.03	1.91	1.97
India	3.79	3.53	2.88	3.79	2.00	3.55	2.71	2.13	2.15	3.79
Indonesia	2.26	2.42	2.11	2.26	1.39	2.41	1.03	2.72	2.23	2.26
Israel	2.46	2.75	2.33	2.46	1.48	2.53	3.04	2.22	1.74	2.46
Jordan	1.98	2.08	1.82	1.98	1.05	1.03	1.02	1.38	1.26	1.98
Korea	1.52	1.71	1.35	1.52	0.99	1.42	0.82	1.33	1.21	1.52
Malaysia	1.85	2.11	1.74	1.85	1.25	1.98	1.59	1.76	1.54	1.85
Mexico	2.20	2.49	2.04	2.20	1.72	2.31	1.91	1.99	1.77	2.20
Morocco	1.50	1.64	1.45	1.50	4.27	3.53	2.56	1.79	1.40	1.50
Pakistan	2.31	2.41	2.23	2.31	1.07	1.48	1.41	0.88	2.04	2.31
Peru	2.77	3.01	2.07	2.77	1.41	1.92	1.13	1.29	1.84	2.77
Philippines	1.40	1.36	1.33	1.40	1.48	1.64	1.27	1.11	0.85	1.40
Poland	1.72	1.92	1.68	1.72	1.47	2.12	2.10	1.33	1.37	1.72
Russia	1.33	1.64	1.34	1.33	0.67	2.41	0.90	1.27	1.22	1.33
Singapore	1.62	1.67	1.52	1.62	1.55	2.56	2.05	1.63	1.26	1.62
South Africa	1.95	1.96	1.70	1.95	1.52	2.75	2.68	1.81	1.72	1.95
Sri Lanka	1.52	1.57	2.02	1.52	1.15	1.00	0.60	0.83	1.22	1.52
Taiwan Province of China	2.10	2.25	2.11	2.10	2.21	3.46	1.87	1.98	1.53	2.10
Thailand	2.94	2.49	2.30	2.94	1.14	2.04	1.51	1.68	1.83	2.94
Turkey	2.02	2.06	1.49	2.02	2.55	9.21	2.72	3.80	1.76	2.02
Venezuela	1.41	1.78	1.14	1.41	0.57	0.63	0.67	0.48	0.87	1.41
Emerging Markets	1.90	2.01	1.67	1.90	1.21	2.12	1.64	1.59	1.45	1.90
EM Asia	1.95	2.06	1.71	1.95	1.40	2.09	1.53	1.68	1.41	1.95
EM Latin America	1.90	1.95	1.59	1.90	0.87	1.57	1.36	1.35	1.44	1.90
EM Europe & Middle East	1.67	1.95	1.59	1.67	1.88	3.41	2.15	1.70	1.42	1.67
ACWI Free	2.46	2.48	2.27	2.46	3.49	4.23	3.46	2.67	2.07	2.46

Data are from Morgan Stanley Capital International. The countries above include the 27 constituents of the Emerging Markets Free index as well as Hong Kong SAR and Singapore. Regional breakdowns conform to Morgan Stanley Capital International conventions. All indices reflect investible opportunities for global investors by taking into account restrictions on foreign ownership. The indices attempt to achieve an 85 percent representation of freely floating stocks.

Table 20. Equity Valuation Measures: Price-Earnings Ratios

	2004		2003						
	Q2	Q1	Q3	Q4	1999	2000	2001	2002	2003
Argentina	18.25	27.81	7.96	13.72	24.82	20.69	19.13	−12.86	13.72
Brazil	9.99	9.05	9.37	10.34	18.64	12.83	8.49	11.23	10.34
Chile	22.26	23.37	34.42	30.81	46.40	31.96	18.02	17.16	30.81
China	17.09	15.16	13.05	17.11	14.97	40.60	14.09	12.14	17.11
Colombia	12.12	11.80	8.57	8.94	20.30	−103.44	64.91	9.55	8.94
Czech Republic	16.91	22.38	11.51	12.49	−42.04	16.49	9.21	10.40	12.49
Egypt	13.23	10.51	9.07	10.90	16.54	9.35	6.28	7.33	10.90
Hong Kong SAR	21.83	21.37	17.08	20.00	30.81	7.64	20.47	14.91	20.00
Hungary	13.23	12.14	11.09	13.11	18.50	14.82	19.34	10.06	13.11
India	17.62	14.52	15.97	18.96	22.84	15.61	13.84	13.56	18.96
Indonesia	11.06	10.75	8.31	10.37	−48.73	18.68	8.37	7.14	10.37
Israel	32.58	41.55	52.96	34.05	25.51	23.88	228.84	−46.62	34.05
Jordan	22.45	28.39	20.18	21.38	13.51	−107.11	15.10	12.39	21.38
Korea	15.26	12.56	11.46	13.93	23.24	8.12	15.23	11.44	13.93
Malaysia	18.98	15.80	15.37	16.33	−8.41	20.63	22.62	13.21	16.33
Mexico	17.32	14.29	14.96	15.70	14.64	13.78	14.23	14.07	15.70
Morocco	24.79	22.85	21.94	22.46	18.65	9.30	10.77	9.87	22.46
Pakistan	9.46	9.18	8.44	8.68	17.60	8.39	4.53	8.07	8.68
Peru	30.59	20.52	14.26	26.45	18.46	15.44	14.08	20.42	26.45
Philippines	19.09	17.79	20.25	20.18	142.83	−35.06	43.72	18.21	20.18
Poland	25.13	15.75	28.67	19.50	22.33	14.30	18.32	−261.14	19.50
Russia	12.47	8.92	13.96	11.13	−126.43	5.69	5.03	7.33	11.13
Singapore	19.93	15.51	21.54	21.38	41.18	18.94	16.53	21.07	21.38
South Africa	13.78	13.22	10.93	12.75	18.73	14.87	11.30	10.50	12.75
Sri Lanka	11.95	12.99	14.83	12.69	7.59	4.24	8.53	14.35	12.69
Taiwan Province of China	27.76	16.76	36.01	25.70	38.26	14.06	21.08	73.13	25.70
Thailand	13.23	12.38	12.49	15.24	−8.94	−14.61	16.67	15.52	15.24
Turkey	9.95	8.32	7.98	11.01	38.60	11.77	25.51	101.33	11.01
Venezuela	26.55	19.33	16.56	24.40	17.68	21.76	18.43	13.43	24.40
Emerging Markets	2.16	2.55	13.84	15.03	27.17	14.85	13.99	13.95	15.03
EM Asia	1.97	2.30	14.97	16.72	40.98	15.47	16.73	14.85	16.72
EM Latin America	2.43	2.95	12.21	13.18	18.28	14.93	11.67	13.84	13.18
EM Europe & Middle East	1.75	2.22	16.28	14.65	37.25	14.05	13.10	16.27	14.65
ACWI Free	2.03	2.05	21.36	21.94	35.70	25.44	26.76	23.18	21.94

Data are from Morgan Stanley Capital International. The countries above include the 27 constituents of the Emerging Markets Free index as well as Hong Kong SAR and Singapore. Regional breakdowns conform to Morgan Stanley Capital International conventions. All indices reflect investible opportunities for global investors by taking into account restrictions on foreign ownership. The indices attempt to achieve an 85 percent representation of freely floating stocks.

Table 21. United States Mutual Fund Flows
(In millions of U.S. dollars)

	2004		2003						
	Q2	Q1	Q3	Q4	1999	2000	2001	2002	2003
Asia Pacific (Ex-Japan)	−423.4	1,068.2	442.5	962.9	151.7	−1,207.9	−496.2	−43.0	1,510.8
Corporate High Yield	−3,807.3	−1,601.7	310.5	3,739.2	−510.1	−6,162.3	5,938.3	8,082.4	20,261.9
Corporate Investment Grade	−1,560.3	3,095.3	−1,721.6	752.8	7,136.3	4,253.7	21,692.0	32,688.3	16,660.2
Emerging Markets Debt	−243.6	325.2	−175.7	437.2	18.4	−499.9	−447.7	449.7	889.0
Emerging Markets Equity	−914.1	3,112.0	1,644.6	2,676.0	23.5	−349.9	−1,662.7	−330.7	4,672.7
European Equity	−96.6	374.2	−1.9	−722.9	−1,664.9	620.9	−1,790.8	−1,044.8	−947.4
Global Equity	1,609.2	2,574.7	−436.9	719.8	4,673.2	12,626.7	−3,005.5	−5,152.1	−1,995.4
Growth-Aggressive	4,081.0	6,022.1	4,654.5	5,286.7	15,247.5	46,610.3	17,882.8	5,611.6	11,464.9
International & Global Debt	221.2	2,159.0	−96.1	1,498.9	−1,581.6	−3,272.2	−1,602.2	−823.0	3,225.0
International Equity	5,268.1	14,256.4	4,873.3	7,688.9	2,998.5	13,322.4	−4,488.2	4,240.0	14,650.8
Japanese Equity	1,314.6	1,541.4	755.7	570.7	731.0	−830.6	−269.8	−82.0	1,863.3
Latin American Equity Funds	−53.0	−39.7	61.7	107.7	−120.9	−94.6	−146.7	32.7	185.7

Data are provided by AMG Data Services and cover net flows of U.S.-based mutual funds. Fund categories are distinguished by a primary investment objective that signifies an investment of 65 percent or more of a fund's assets. Primary sector data are mutually exclusive, but emerging and regional sectors are all subsets of international equity.

Table 22. Bank Regulatory Capital to Risk-Weighted Assets
(In percent)

	1998	1999	2000	2001	2002	2003	2004:Q1
Latin America							
Argentina	20.4	20.8	19.5	17.9	. . .	14.0	14.0
Bolivia	11.6	12.2	13.4	14.6	16.1	15.3	16.1
Brazil	15.6	15.5	14.3	15.3	16.7	18.9	. . .
Chile	12.5	13.5	13.3	12.7	14.0	14.1	15.0
Colombia	10.3	10.8	12.2	12.4	12.1	12.4	13.2
Costa Rica	14.4	17.5	16.7	15.1	15.8	16.5	. . .
Dominican Republic	13.3	12.5	12.1	11.8	12.0	11.4	12.3
Ecuador	11.2	14.7	13.1	13.5	11.8	12.2	12.2
Honduras	7.5	11.4	12.3	12.7	12.9	13.0	13.1
Mexico	14.4	16.2	13.8	14.7	15.5	14.2	14.5
Paraguay[1]	. . .	17.2	17.2	16.2	17.9	20.1	20.8
Peru	11.2	12.0	12.9	13.4	12.5	13.3	14.2
Uruguay[1,2]	11.2	10.2	11.7	11.3	20.9	11.3	10.7
Venezuela	. . .	. . .	. . .	. . .	. . .	. . .	. . .
Emerging Europe							
Armenia	29.8	27.8	25.0	31.7	30.5	33.8	35.6
Bulgaria	36.7	41.8	35.6	31.3	25.2	22.0	21.3
Croatia	12.7	20.6	21.3	18.5	16.6	15.7	. . .
Czech Republic	12.0	13.2	14.8	15.4	14.3	14.5	15.2
Estonia	17.0	16.1	13.2	14.4	15.3	14.5	14.0
Hungary	16.5	14.9	13.7	13.9	13.0	11.6	. . .
Israel	9.2	9.4	9.2	9.4	9.9	10.4	. . .
Latvia	17.0	16.4	14.3	14.2	13.1	12.6	. . .
Lithuania	23.8	17.4	16.3	15.7	14.8	13.2	. . .
Macedonia	25.9	28.7	36.7	34.3	28.1	. . .	. . .
Malta	. . .	14.3	16.0	15.9	16.0	. . .	. . .
Poland	11.7	13.2	12.9	15.1	13.8	13.8	. . .
Russia	11.5	18.1	19.0	20.3	19.1	19.1	18.7
Slovak Republic	6.6	12.6	12.5	19.8	21.3	21.6	21.0
Slovenia	15.3	14.0	13.5	11.9	11.9	11.5	. . .
Turkey	. . .	8.2	9.3	20.8	25.1	30.9	32.1
Ukraine	. . .	19.6	15.5	20.7	18.0	15.1	14.8
Western Europe							
Austria	13.5	13.0	13.3	13.7	13.3	14.4	14.0
Belgium	11.3	11.9	11.9	12.9	13.1	12.8	. . .
Denmark	10.7	11.1	11.3	12.1	12.6	12.8	. . .
Finland	11.5	11.9	11.6	10.5	11.7	18.9	. . .
France	. . .	12.7	11.9	12.1	12.3	12.0	. . .
Germany	11.4	11.5	11.7	12.0	12.7	12.9	. . .
Greece	10.2	16.2	13.6	12.5	10.6	10.7	. . .
Iceland	10.4	10.6	9.7	11.4	12.3	12.4	. . .
Ireland	11.6	10.8	10.7	10.6	12.3	13.9	. . .
Italy	11.3	10.6	10.1	10.4	11.2	11.2	. . .
Luxembourg	12.9	13.1	13.4	13.7	15.0	17.7	. . .
Netherlands	11.1	10.9	10.7	11.0	11.5	11.5	. . .
Norway	12.4	12.0	12.1	12.6	12.2	12.4	12.0
Portugal	11.1	10.8	9.2	9.5	9.8	10.0	. . .
Spain	12.9	12.6	12.4	12.9	12.5	12.6	. . .
Sweden	10.4	11.4	9.9	10.0	10.1	10.1	10.0
Switzerland	11.3	11.3	12.7	11.8	12.1	11.2	. . .
United Kingdom[3]	13.2	14.0	13.0	13.2	12.2	12.5	. . .

Table 22 *(concluded)*

	1998	1999	2000	2001	2002	2003	2004:Q1
Asia							
Bangladesh	7.3	7.4	6.7	6.7	7.5	...	...
China	...	12.8	13.5	12.3	11.2	...	...
Hong Kong SAR	18.5	18.7	17.8	16.5	15.8	15.4	...
India	11.6	11.2	11.1	11.4	11.9	12.6	...
Indonesia	−13.0	−6.7	21.6	18.2	20.1	22.3	...
Korea	8.2	10.8	10.5	10.8	10.5	10.5	...
Malaysia	11.8	12.5	12.5	13.0	13.2	13.7	13.5
Pakistan	12.5	12.2	11.4	11.3	12.6	11.1	11.1
Philippines[4]	17.7	17.5	16.2	14.7	15.5	16.3	...
Singapore	18.1	20.6	19.6	18.1	16.9	17.9	...
Thailand	10.9	12.4	11.9	13.9	13.7	14.0	12.7
Middle East and North Africa							
Egypt	...	...	...	...	...	...	...
Jordan	21.7	21.2	19.4	17.4	16.7	15.9	...
Kuwait	22.5	23.7	22.2	22.0	19.7	18.4	...
Lebanon	18.9	15.0	16.9	18.0	19.4	22.3	...
Morocco	12.6	12.1	12.8	12.6	12.2	10.1	...
Oman	...	16.5	16.5	15.6	16.9	...	...
Saudi Arabia	21.2	21.2	21.0	20.3	18.7	19.0	...
Tunisia	11.7	11.6	13.3	10.6	10.6	...	...
United Arab Emirates	20.0	20.5	20.2	20.0	18.9	18.2	...
Sub-Saharan Africa							
Ghana	11.1	11.5	11.6	14.7	13.4	...	...
Kenya	...	...	17.5	17.1	17.4	17.2	18.1
Mauritius	11.9	13.3	12.3	13.0	13.1	...	...
Nigeria	12.7	19.0	17.5	16.1	...	...	...
South Africa	10.1	11.5	12.5	11.4	12.6	12.2	12.7
Tanzania	6.5	3.8	9.6	9.6	8.6	...	...
Uganda	11.0	13.6	20.5	23.1	23.7	20.5	...
Zimbabwe	...	...	44.0	44.5	30.6	16.2	...
Other							
Australia	10.3	10.1	9.8	10.5	9.9	10.1	10.1
Canada	10.6	11.7	11.8	12.2	12.2	13.3	13.3
Japan[5]	9.6	11.9	12.2	11.7	10.9	10.4	...
United States[6]	12.2	12.2	12.1	12.7	12.8	12.8	12.8

Sources: National authorities; and IMF staff estimates.
[1]Private banks.
[2]Excludes suspended banks and mortgage banks.
[3]Includes mortgage banks.
[4]Data not strictly comparable. The data for 1998–2000 are for the net worth-to-risk assets ratio based on the old General Banking Act.
[5]All internationally active banks.
[6]All commercial banks.

Table 23. Bank Capital to Assets
(In percent)

	1998	1999	2000	2001	2002	2003	2004:Q1
Latin America							
Argentina	11.3	10.6	10.4	13.2	13.9	12.2	11.5
Bolivia	8.5	9.2	9.8	10.5	11.9	12.1	12.4
Brazil	10.5	11.6	12.1	13.6	13.5	16.2	. . .
Chile	7.5	7.8	7.5	7.2	7.2	7.3	7.8
Colombia	9.6	10.9	10.1	9.4	9.3	9.8	10.0
Costa Rica	9.8	10.9	10.8	12.9	12.6	13.6	13.4
Dominican Republic	10.8	10.8	9.4	10.0	10.7	7.8	7.4
Ecuador	14.5	12.9	12.9	8.8	10.3	10.2	10.0
Honduras	9.9	10.0	9.8	10.0	9.1	. . .	. . .
Mexico	8.3	8.0	9.6	9.4	11.1	11.4	11.5
Paraguay	14.9	12.6	12.4	12.1	10.9	10.0	10.0
Peru	8.7	8.9	9.1	9.8	10.1	9.3	10.0
Uruguay	15.3	14.7	11.7	8.1	−1.9	3.0	. . .
Venezuela	14.0	13.5	13.0	14.1	15.9	14.3	13.9
Emerging Europe							
Armenia	11.7	11.8	12.3	13.6	15.0	13.0	. . .
Bulgaria	14.0	15.3	15.2	13.6	13.3	13.2	12.9
Croatia	18.3	15.2	11.9	10.4	9.4	9.5	8.8
Czech Republic	. . .	6.3	5.4	5.2	5.2	5.7	6.1
Estonia	16.2	15.5	12.6	13.3	12.1	11.3	11.2
Hungary	9.7	9.7	9.8	9.5	10.0	9.8	. . .
Israel	6.7	6.8	7.3	7.7	6.5	7.2	7.2
Latvia	3.7	2.0	8.5	9.1	8.8	8.6	8.5
Lithuania	13.9	9.9	9.2	9.4	9.9	9.8	. . .
Macedonia	. . .	. . .	. . .	. . .	. . .	. . .	. . .
Malta	. . .	5.7	6.5	6.7	6.6	. . .	. . .
Poland	7.0	7.1	7.1	8.0	8.7	8.3	. . .
Russia	7.3	10.6	12.1	14.4	14.0	14.6	14.5
Slovak Republic	9.8	8.7	5.9	7.9	9.8	10.0	. . .
Slovenia	. . .	. . .	10.1	8.8	8.4	8.4	8.2
Turkey	8.7	5.2	6.1	9.6	11.6	13.6	14.6
Ukraine	. . .	23.0	17.5	16.6	15.6	12.9	12.4
Western Europe							
Austria	4.9	5.2	5.2	5.1	5.6	5.8	5.6
Belgium	4.0	4.1	4.6	4.4	4.7	4.3	4.2
Denmark	6.3	6.1	6.9	5.9	5.2	5.6	6.0
Finland	5.9	5.6	6.3	10.2	10.1	9.6	8.8
France	6.4	6.8	6.7	6.7	6.8	6.7	6.5
Germany	4.0	4.1	4.2	4.3	4.5	4.5	4.3
Greece	. . .	10.1	8.9	9.2	9.4	7.6	7.9
Iceland	7.0	6.8	6.4	6.6	7.4	7.3	. . .
Ireland	7.2	7.3	6.5	5.9	5.5	5.2	5.0
Italy	6.8	6.8	6.7	6.7	6.5	6.5	. . .
Luxembourg	3.5	3.8	3.9	3.9	3.7	3.8	. . .
Netherlands	5.0	4.8	5.1	4.8	4.7	4.3	. . .
Norway	6.9	7.1	7.0	6.8	6.3	6.0	5.9
Portugal	5.9	6.0	5.8	5.6	5.7	5.9	5.9
Spain	6.6	6.4	7.3	7.2	7.0	7.0	. . .
Sweden	5.0	5.5	5.3	5.6	5.2	5.2	. . .
Switzerland	4.4	4.3	5.8	5.5	5.4	5.3	. . .
United Kingdom[1]	7.0	7.5	6.5	6.6	6.7	6.8	. . .

Table 23 *(concluded)*

	1998	1999	2000	2001	2002	2003	2004:Q1
Asia							
Bangladesh	5.0	4.3	3.5	3.5	4.1	3.2	. . .
China	. . .	5.2	5.3	5.1	4.6	. . .	. . .
Hong Kong SAR	7.7	8.1	9.0	9.8	10.7	11.5	. . .
India	6.7	5.8	5.7	5.3	5.5	5.8	. . .
Indonesia	−12.9	−4.6	6.0	5.3	7.1	8.7	. . .
Korea	2.8	3.9	3.8	4.1	4.0	4.1	. . .
Malaysia	8.2	8.4	8.5	8.5	8.7	8.5	. . .
Pakistan	5.6	5.0	4.9	4.6	6.1	6.2	. . .
Philippines	14.1	14.5	13.6	13.6	13.4	13.1	12.7
Singapore	10.0	11.0	10.0	10.0	11.0	11.0	. . .
Thailand	5.9	6.0	4.3	5.1	5.8	6.4	. . .
Middle East and North Africa							
Egypt	5.1	5.4	5.6	5.2	4.8	5.3	4.8
Jordan	8.5	7.9	7.0	6.6	6.2	6.4	. . .
Kuwait	11.4	11.6	11.5	11.2	10.4	10.8	. . .
Lebanon	6.6	6.6	6.4	6.2	6.4	6.2	. . .
Morocco	9.8	9.9	9.2	9.3	8.9	8.2	. . .
Oman	. . .	13.0	13.0	12.6	12.5	. . .	. . .
Saudi Arabia	10.0	9.6	9.7	9.9	10.2	10.8	. . .
Tunisia	. . .	. . .	. . .	. . .	. . .	. . .	. . .
United Arab Emirates	. . .	. . .	. . .	. . .	. . .	. . .	. . .
Sub-Saharan Africa							
Ghana	12.2	11.9	11.8	12.5	12.0	12.0	. . .
Kenya	10.7	8.9	8.7	8.8	8.0	7.7	7.1
Mauritius	7.1	8.1	7.8	8.4	9.3	. . .	. . .
Nigeria	9.3	8.2	7.4	8.6	9.5	. . .	. . .
South Africa	8.2	8.2	8.7	7.8	8.2	7.0	6.9
Tanzania	6.5	3.8	9.6	9.6	8.6	. . .	. . .
Uganda	. . .	7.0	9.8	10.0	9.5	9.9	. . .
Zimbabwe	8.0	9.4	9.4	9.3	9.5	9.0	. . .
Other							
Australia[2]	7.6	7.3	6.9	7.1	6.3	5.8	5.9
Canada	4.2	4.7	4.7	4.6	4.6	4.7	4.7
Japan	2.4	4.6	4.8	4.2	3.0	. . .	. . .
United States[3]	8.5	8.4	8.5	9.1	9.2	9.1	9.2

Sources: National authorities; and IMF staff estimates.
[1]Data for U.K. large commercial banks (exclusive of mortgage banks and other banks).
[2]Tier 1 capital to total assets.
[3]All commercial banks.

Table 24. Bank Nonperforming Loans to Total Loans
(In percent)

	1998	1999	2000	2001	2002	2003	2004:Q1
Latin America							
Argentina	5.3	8.9	9.8	14.0	37.4	30.5	27.7
Bolivia	4.6	6.6	10.3	14.4	17.7	17.1	18.7
Brazil***	10.2	8.7	8.4	5.7	5.3	4.4	. . .
Chile	1.5	1.7	1.7	1.6	1.8	1.6	1.6
Colombia	10.7	13.6	11.0	9.7	8.7	6.8	6.7
Costa Rica	3.5	2.7	3.5	2.4	3.2	1.7	. . .
Dominican Republic	2.4	2.2	2.6	2.6	4.9	8.9	8.6
Ecuador	8.1	26.0	31.0	27.8	8.4	7.9	8.4
Honduras	11.2	11.2	12.5	13.0	12.4	8.7	9.0
Mexico	11.3	8.9	5.8	5.1	4.6	3.2	3.2
Paraguay [1]	8.1	9.3	12.0	12.3	14.7	15.0	13.1
Peru	7.0	8.7	9.8	9.0	7.6	5.8	5.8
Uruguay[1,2]	. . .	8.7	8.5	9.3	13.9	15.0	7.2
Venezuela	5.5	7.8	6.6	7.0	9.2	7.7	6.8
Emerging Europe							
Armenia	6.0	8.0	6.2	6.0	4.9	5.4	5.8
Bulgaria[3]	. . .	26.7	17.3	13.1	8.6	7.3	7.0
Croatia***	9.3	10.3	9.5	7.2	5.8	5.1	. . .
Czech Republic	20.3	22.0	19.9	13.7	10.6	4.9	4.8
Estonia	1.4	1.7	1.0	1.3	0.8	0.4	0.4
Hungary	4.9	4.2	3.0	2.2	2.0	3.4	. . .
Israel*	9.9	9.0	6.7	8.1	9.9	10.3	. . .
Latvia	6.0	6.0	4.6	2.8	2.0	1.9	1.5
Lithuania**	12.9	12.5	11.3	8.3	6.5	3.0	. . .
Macedonia[4]	32.9	41.3	34.8	33.7	15.9	15.1	. . .
Malta	. . .	13.0	14.0	18.0	16.2	. . .	. . .
Poland**	10.5	13.3	15.0	17.9	21.1	20.9	. . .
Russia	17.3	13.4	7.7	6.2	5.6	5.0	5.0
Slovak Republic	31.6	23.7	15.3	14.0	11.2	9.1	7.8
Slovenia	5.4	5.2	6.5	7.0	7.0	6.5	. . .
Turkey	6.7	10.5	11.1	25.2	17.6	11.5	10.2
Ukraine[5]	. . .	35.8	29.6	25.1	21.9	28.3	28.0
Western Europe							
Austria	2.6	1.7	1.9	1.3	1.3	. . .	. . .
Belgium	2.7	2.7	2.7	2.9	2.9	3.4	. . .
Denmark	0.8	0.6	0.5	0.5	0.6	0.6	. . .
Finland*	1.2	1.0	0.6	0.7	0.6	0.4	0.5
France	6.3	5.7	5.0	5.0	5.0	4.8	. . .
Germany	4.5	4.6	5.1	4.9	5.0	4.8	. . .
Greece	13.6	15.5	12.3	9.2	8.1	8.4	. . .
Iceland	2.4	2.5	2.0	2.8	3.4	3.4	. . .
Ireland	1.2	1.0	1.0	1.0	1.0	0.9	. . .
Italy	11.8	9.8	7.8	6.7	6.5	6.8	. . .
Luxembourg	0.5	0.5	0.5	0.4	0.4	0.3	. . .
Netherlands	2.6	2.7	2.3	2.4	2.5	2.4	. . .
Norway	1.4	1.4	1.3	1.4	2.0	1.8	1.6
Portugal	3.3	2.4	2.0	1.9	2.1	2.4	. . .
Spain	2.0	1.6	1.6	1.4	1.4	1.1	. . .
Sweden	2.6	1.7	1.7	1.6	1.4	1.3	. . .
Switzerland	5.2	4.6	3.8	4.1	3.6	3.6	. . .
United Kingdom[6]	3.2	3.0	2.5	2.6	2.6	2.2	. . .

FINANCIAL SOUNDNESS INDICATORS

Table 24 *(concluded)*

	1998	1999	2000	2001	2002	2003	2004:Q1
Asia							
Bangladesh	40.7	41.1	34.9	31.5	28.0	...	...
China[7]	...	...	...	29.8	25.5	22.0	...
Hong Kong SAR[8]	5.3	7.2	6.1	5.7	4.5	3.9	...
India	14.4	14.7	12.7	11.4	10.4	8.8	...
Indonesia	48.6	32.9	18.8	11.0	6.2	5.8	...
Korea	7.4	8.3	6.6	2.9	1.9	2.6	...
Malaysia	18.6	16.6	15.4	17.8	15.8	13.9	13.8
Pakistan	19.5	22.0	19.5	19.6	17.7	13.7	13.2
Philippines	12.4	14.6	16.6	19.0	16.6	16.1	16.5
Singapore	...	5.3	3.4	3.6	3.4	3.2	...
Thailand	42.9	38.6	17.7	10.5	15.8	12.8	12.1
Middle East and North Africa							
Egypt	...	...	...	...	...	...	
Jordan	11.1	14.4	18.4	19.3	21.0	19.9	...
Kuwait	10.3	12.8	19.2	10.3	7.8	7.0	...
Lebanon[9]	3.6	5.8	7.8	10.0	12.4	12.8	12.2
Morocco	14.6	15.3	17.5	16.8	17.2	18.1	...
Oman	6.4	6.0	7.5	10.6	11.3		...
Saudi Arabia	8.4	11.4	10.4	10.1	9.2	8.2	...
Tunisia	19.5	18.8	21.6	19.2	20.7	...	...
United Arab Emirates	13.5	13.6	12.7	15.7	15.3	14.3	...
Sub-Saharan Africa							
Ghana	17.2	12.8	11.9	19.6	22.7	...	...
Kenya	27.0	33.7	32.7	29.2	28.7	22.5	22.2
Mauritius	9.1	8.3	7.7	8.0	8.6	...	...
Nigeria	19.4	25.6	22.6	16.0	17.3	17.0	...
South Africa*	4.1	4.9	4.3	3.3	3.3	2.5	2.3
Tanzania	22.9	25.2	17.3	12.0	9.2	...	...
Uganda****	20.2	11.9	9.8	6.5	3.6	8.0	...
Zimbabwe	...	...	19.6	11.4	4.2	4.7	...
Other							
Australia	0.7	0.6	0.5	0.7	0.6	0.4	0.4
Canada	1.1	1.2	1.2	1.5	1.6	1.2	1.0
Japan	5.4	5.8	6.1	6.6	8.9	7.2	...
United States[10]	1.0	1.0	1.1	1.4	1.5	1.2	1.1

Sources: National authorities; and IMF staff estimates.
[1]Private banks.
[2]Excluding suspended banks and mortgage banks.
[3]Total loans exclude interbank loans.
[4]Under the new methodology adopted in 2002, interbank loans are also included in total loans which results in a significant decline in the NPL ratio. Under the old methodology, the ratio remains at about one-third of all loans.
[5]The sudden increase in NPLs in 2003 reflects a revision in the official definition.
[6]Includes mortgage banks.
[7]Data for state-owned commercial banks only.
[8]Classified loan ratio as reported in the FSSA.
[9]Net of provisions. The latest observation refers to May 2004.
[10]All commercial banks.
Note: (*) Based on net nonperforming loans (NPLs)
  (**) 30-day NPL classification
  (***) 60-day NPL classification
  (****) 180-day NPL classification

Table 25. Bank Provisions to Nonperforming Loans
(In percent)

	1998	1999	2000	2001	2002	2003	2004:Q1
Latin America							
Argentina	61.2	69.4	67.7	75.7	73.3	81.2	83.8
Bolivia	58.0	55.8	61.2	63.9	63.3	72.4	68.7
Brazil	110.9	125.1	82.1	126.1	143.5	165.6	. . .
Chile	131.4	152.9	145.5	146.5	128.1	130.9	142.0
Colombia	37.9	36.8	54.5	73.9	86.3	98.3	100.9
Costa Rica	130.1	126.8	100.8	113.2	102.6	145.9	. . .
Dominican Republic	117.9	120.5	121.6	112.3	64.9	65.0	74.7
Ecuador	99.6	109.0	104.0	102.2	131.4	127.3	120.5
Honduras	19.3	23.1	26.7	29.5	37.4	36.8	39.3
Mexico	66.1	107.8	115.3	123.8	138.1	167.1	167.4
Paraguay[1]	48.1	45.1	39.2	39.8	50.3	59.2	53.0
Peru	92.1	99.5	104.3	114.2	133.2	141.1	142.5
Uruguay[1,2]	62.8	48.4	47.5	45.4	60.2	37.3	. . .
Venezuela	123.4	101.8	93.6	92.4	97.9	103.7	107.2
Emerging Europe							
Armenia	. . .	. . .	. . .	. . .	. . .	. . .	. . .
Bulgaria	75.0	71.9	79.3	73.5	74.3	52.8	52.9
Croatia	84.4	78.7	79.8	75.7	68.1	60.8	. . .
Czech Republic	54.3	52.1	46.8	60.3	77.5	77.1	76.8
Estonia	. . .	. . .	. . .	. . .	. . .	. . .	. . .
Hungary	45.2	51.4	56.4	57.7	51.3	47.7	. . .
Israel	49.5	45.7	55.8	57.1	54.7	53.8	. . .
Latvia	78.0	79.3	74.1	80.4	95.5	98.5	. . .
Lithuania	47.5	37.5	34.6	34.2	18.6	21.6	. . .
Macedonia	. . .	. . .	. . .	. . .	. . .	. . .	. . .
Malta	. . .	. . .	. . .	. . .	. . .	. . .	. . .
Poland	. . .	. . .	46.0	48.5	46.8	51.7	. . .
Russia	42.8	73.9	102.6	108.1	112.5	118.0	. . .
Slovak Republic	. . .	42.5	78.4	82.5	72.5	81.1	85.7
Slovenia[3]	. . .	114.9	101.0	100.5	102.0	101.5	. . .
Turkey	44.2	61.9	63.1	48.9	64.2	88.5	89.8
Ukraine	. . .	. . .	38.4	39.2	39.6	22.7	21.8
Western Europe							
Austria	. . .	. . .	. . .	. . .	. . .	. . .	. . .
Belgium	61.0	58.0	57.0	57.0	51.8	46.3	. . .
Denmark	. . .	. . .	. . .	. . .	. . .	. . .	. . .
Finland	. . .	. . .	. . .	. . .	. . .	. . .	. . .
France	58.5	60.7	60.8	59.9	58.4	57.7	. . .
Germany	73.3	76.9	81.8	85.7	. . .	. . .	. . .
Greece	24.1	26.1	36.8	43.3	45.3	. . .	. . .
Iceland	51.9	50.5	52.5	46.8	43.7	. . .	. . .
Ireland	60.0	82.0	105.0	118.0	129.0	. . .	. . .
Italy	42.8	48.1	48.6	50.0	53.6	55.1	. . .
Luxembourg	. . .	. . .	. . .	. . .	. . .	. . .	. . .
Netherlands	. . .	93.1	90.8	88.8	67.3	. . .	. . .
Norway[4]	48.3	45.1	37.8	30.6	35.7	34.2	. . .
Portugal	. . .	. . .	66.7	66.8	62.8	72.6	. . .
Spain	53.8	57.4	61.6	64.7	67.7	76.0	72.7
Sweden	42.3	55.5	60.0	64.9	73.8	. . .	. . .
Switzerland	. . .	. . .	. . .	. . .	. . .	. . .	. . .
United Kingdom	56.0	71.2	65.0	69.5	72.3	. . .	. . .

Table 25 *(concluded)*

	1998	1999	2000	2001	2002	2003	2004:Q1
Asia							
Bangladesh	53.5	51.4	59.1	60.5	55.8	. . .	. . .
China	. . .	. . .	. . .	. . .	. . .	. . .	. . .
Hong Kong SAR	. . .	. . .	. . .	. . .	. . .	. . .	. . .
India	. . .	. . .	. . .	. . .	. . .	. . .	. . .
Indonesia	28.6	77.7	88.8	94.0	119.6	143.2	. . .
Korea	46.2	66.6	81.8	85.2	109.4	. . .	. . .
Malaysia	. . .	39.0	41.0	37.7	38.1	38.9	38.0
Pakistan	58.6	46.6	53.9	53.2	58.2	64.7	66.1
Philippines	36.4	45.2	43.7	45.3	50.2	51.5	51.0
Singapore	. . .	86.2	87.2	90.1	96.7	107.8	. . .
Thailand	29.2	37.9	47.2	54.9	61.8	72.8	69.0
Middle East and North Africa							
Egypt	. . .	. . .	. . .	. . .	. . .	. . .	. . .
Jordan	45.8	44.7	34.6	36.4	36.7	38.9	. . .
Kuwait	68.2	53.2	50.1	53.7	64.3	72.4	. . .
Lebanon	57.4	72.5	72.5	69.3	68.2	73.3	. . .
Morocco	52.6	51.8	45.7	53.0	57.1	66.5	. . .
Oman	70.3	75.0	71.9	68.5	79.7	. . .	. . .
Saudi Arabia	83.0	88.0	99.0	107.0	110.4	118.9	. . .
Tunisia	. . .	. . .	. . .	. . .	. . .	. . .	. . .
United Arab Emirates	. . .	. . .	. . .	. . .	. . .	. . .	. . .
Sub-Saharan Africa							
Ghana	89.4	67.2	58.6	46.4	63.6	. . .	. . .
Kenya	. . .	. . .	. . .	. . .	. . .	. . .	. . .
Mauritius	. . .	. . .	. . .	. . .	. . .	. . .	. . .
Nigeria	. . .	46.7	49.7	73.6	60.9	. . .	. . .
South Africa	41.3	41.5	43.8	36.4	42.9	52.0	. . .
Tanzania	. . .	. . .	. . .	. . .	. . .	. . .	. . .
Uganda	54.2	51.9	50.5	. . .	. . .	. . .	. . .
Zimbabwe	. . .	. . .	44.4	28.3	52.8	70.1	. . .
Other							
Australia[5]	37.9	44.2	38.4	37.0	36.5	40.8	39.7
Canada	50.3	45.4	42.8	44.0	41.1	43.5	46.2
Japan	49.9	40.3	35.5	31.8	31.6	34.9	. . .
United States[6]	183.2	178.0	149.4	132.4	127.2	145.8	156.2

Source: National authorities; and IMF staff estimates.

[1]Private banks.
[2]Excluding suspended banks and mortgage banks.
[3]Actual provisioning as a percentage of required provisioning.
[4]Loan-loss provision ratio for enterprise loans.
[5]Specific provisions.
[6]Loss allowance to noncurrent loans and leases, all commercial banks.

Table 26. Bank Return on Assets
(In percent)

	1998	1999	2000	2001	2002	2003	2004:Q1
Latin America							
Argentina	. . .	0.4	0.3	−0.2	−9.7	−2.5	−3.2
Bolivia	0.7	0.8	−0.9	−0.4	0.1	0.3	−0.2
Brazil	0.6	1.6	1.0	0.2	1.9	1.6	. . .
Chile	0.9	0.7	1.0	1.3	1.1	1.3	1.6
Colombia	−2.2	−3.2	−2.0	0.6	1.5	1.9	. . .
Costa Rica	0.9	1.6	1.5	1.7	1.8	2.1	. . .
Dominican Republic	1.7	2.4	1.6	1.9	2.3	—	0.3
Ecuador	0.8	0.2	−2.8	−6.6	1.5	1.5	1.9
Honduras	1.7	1.2	0.8	0.8	0.7	1.6	1.8
Mexico	0.6	0.7	0.9	0.8	−1.1	1.7	1.7
Paraguay	. . .	2.2	1.4	2.2	1.0	0.4	−0.2
Peru	0.7	0.3	0.3	0.4	0.8	1.1	1.2
Uruguay[1]	0.9	1.3	0.9	−0.3	−4.8	−2.1	−0.1
Venezuela	4.9	3.1	2.8	2.8	5.3	6.2	7.1
Emerging Europe							
Armenia	4.2	2.3	−1.9	−9.1	3.9	2.7	. . .
Bulgaria	1.7	2.7	3.1	2.9	2.1	2.4	2.5
Croatia	−2.8	0.8	1.2	1.3	1.3	1.3	. . .
Czech Republic	−0.2	−0.3	0.7	0.7	1.2	1.2	1.2
Estonia[2]	−1.2	1.4	1.1	2.5	2.6	2.2	. . .
Hungary	−2.0	0.6	1.3	1.7	1.7	1.9	. . .
Israel	0.5	0.5	0.5	0.3	0.1	0.4	. . .
Latvia	−1.5	1.0	2.0	1.5	1.5	1.4	. . .
Lithuania	0.9	0.2	0.5	−0.1	1.0	1.4	. . .
Macedonia	2.0	0.8	0.8	−0.7	0.4	. . .	. . .
Malta	. . .	0.9	0.8	0.8	0.8	. . .	. . .
Poland[2]	1.8	1.6	1.5	1.4	0.8	1.0	. . .
Russia	−3.5	−0.3	0.9	2.4	2.6	2.6	3.2
Slovak Republic	−0.5	−2.3	1.5	1.0	1.2	1.2	1.2
Slovenia	1.2	0.8	1.1	0.5	1.1	1.0	0.9
Turkey	1.9	−0.4	−3.0	−6.1	1.4	2.2	0.4
Ukraine	. . .	2.0	−0.1	1.2	1.2	1.0	1.0
Western Europe							
Austria	0.4	0.3	0.4	0.5	0.3	0.4	. . .
Belgium	0.3	0.4	0.6	0.4	0.4	0.4	. . .
Denmark	0.8	0.7	0.8	0.8	0.7	0.8	. . .
Finland	1.2	1.0	1.2	0.7	0.9	0.9	. . .
France	0.3	0.4	0.5	0.5	0.4	0.5	. . .
Germany	0.6	0.2	0.2	0.2	−0.1	−0.1	. . .
Greece	0.8	2.4	1.4	1.0	0.5	0.7	. . .
Iceland	0.9	1.3	0.6	0.8	1.1	1.1	. . .
Ireland[3]	. . .	1.3	1.2	0.9	1.5	. . .	. . .
Italy	0.5	0.6	0.8	0.6	0.5	0.5	. . .
Luxembourg	0.6	0.4	0.5	0.5	0.4	0.5	. . .
Netherlands	0.4	0.6	0.5	0.5	0.3	0.4	. . .
Norway[2]	0.9	1.4	1.4	0.9	0.6	0.7	1.0
Portugal	0.9	0.9	0.9	0.8	0.8	0.8	0.8
Spain	0.9	1.0	1.0	1.0	0.9	1.0	. . .
Sweden	0.7	0.7	0.9	0.8	0.6	0.7	. . .
Switzerland	0.7	0.8	0.9	0.6	0.5	0.7	. . .
United Kingdom[2,4]	0.8	1.0	0.9	0.5	0.9	1.1	. . .

Table 26 *(concluded)*

	1998	1999	2000	2001	2002	2003	2004:Q1
Asia							
Bangladesh	0.3	0.2	—	0.7	0.5	. . .	. . .
China	. . .	0.1	0.1	0.1	0.1	. . .	. . .
Hong Kong SAR	0.4	0.4	0.8	0.8	0.8	0.8	. . .
India	0.8	0.5	0.7	0.5	0.8	1.0	. . .
Indonesia	−19.9	−8.7	0.3	0.6	1.4	1.6	. . .
Korea[2]	−3.2	−1.3	−0.6	0.8	0.6	0.1	. . .
Malaysia	. . .	0.7	1.5	1.0	1.3	1.4	. . .
Pakistan	0.5	−0.3	—	0.0	0.8	1.4	1.1
Philippines	0.8	0.4	0.4	0.4	0.8	1.1	1.1
Singapore	0.4	1.2	1.3	0.8	0.8	0.9	. . .
Thailand[2]	−5.6	−5.7	−1.7	−0.1	0.3	0.8	. . .
Middle East and North Africa							
Egypt	0.9	0.9	0.9	0.8	0.7	0.5	0.5
Kuwait	. . .	1.8	2.0	2.0	1.8	. . .	. . .
Jordan	0.7	0.3	0.3	0.7	0.5	0.7	. . .
Lebanon	1.5	1.0	0.7	0.5	0.6	0.7	. . .
Morocco	0.9	0.7	0.7	0.9	0.3	0.6	. . .
Oman	1.9	1.6	1.3	0.1	1.4	. . .	. . .
Saudi Arabia[2]	. . .	0.9	2.0	2.2	2.3	2.4	. . .
Tunisia	1.2	1.2	1.2	1.1	0.7	. . .	. . .
United Arab Emirates	2.0	1.5	1.8	2.6	2.2	2.3	. . .
Sub-Saharan Africa							
Ghana	8.8	8.5	9.8	8.7	6.7	. . .	. . .
Kenya	0.8	—	0.5	1.6	1.2	2.4	2.0
Mauritius[2]	2.4	2.2	2.3	2.2	2.3	. . .	. . .
Nigeria	4.5	4.1	4.0	5.2	. . .	. . .	. . .
South Africa	1.1	1.0	1.1	0.7	0.4	0.8	1.2
Tanzania	1.9	0.1	1.3	1.2	1.3	. . .	. . .
Uganda	. . .	3.7	4.4	4.4	3.3	3.5	. . .
Zimbabwe	. . .	. . .	6.0	5.1	4.0	6.7	. . .
Other							
Australia	1.0	1.2	1.3	1.0	1.2	1.1	. . .
Canada	0.6	0.7	0.7	0.7	0.4	0.7	. . .
Japan[2]	−0.6	−0.9	0.3	0.1	−0.7	−0.6	. . .
United States[5]	1.2	1.3	1.2	1.2	1.3	1.4	1.4

Sources: National authorities; and IMF staff estimates.
[1]Private banks, excludes suspended banks and mortgage banks.
[2]Before tax.
[3]Data for 2002 corresponds to Allied Irish Bank and Bank of Ireland only.
[4]Includes mortgage banks.
[5]All commercial banks.

Table 27. Bank Return on Equity
(In percent)

	1998	1999	2000	2001	2002	2003	2004:Q1
Latin America							
Argentina	. . .	4.0	3.1	−1.5	−69.9	−20.6	−27.7
Bolivia	8.0	8.7	−9.5	−4.3	0.7	2.8	−1.8
Brazil	7.4	18.9	11.3	2.4	20.8	16.4	. . .
Chile	11.5	9.4	12.7	17.7	14.4	16.7	18.6
Colombia	−19.2	−29.5	−17.3	5.4	13.7	18.0	27.2
Costa Rica	8.4	15.9	16.3	18.7	17.1	19.5	. . .
Dominican Republic	22.9	24.7	26.1	21.7	21.0	−0.5	3.4
Ecuador	5.3	1.3	−21.3	−36.0	15.3	14.0	19.3
Honduras	20.2	14.0	9.0	8.9	8.2	13.3	15.9
Mexico	6.9	5.8	10.4	8.6	−10.4	14.2	14.4
Paraguay	. . .	20.1	12.4	21.2	9.0	4.5	−2.0
Peru	8.4	4.0	3.1	4.5	8.4	10.8	12.3
Uruguay	7.3	7.8	4.6	−18.7	−45.4	−19.4	. . .
Venezuela	41.4	24.0	23.1	20.3	35.6	44.0	53.0
Emerging Europe							
Armenia	35.0	19.6	12.0	−6.3	. . .	. . .	. . .
Bulgaria	21.5	20.9	22.6	19.3	14.9	17.9	20.3
Croatia	−16.1	5.0	10.5	6.7	20.4	18.7	. . .
Czech Republic	−17.8	−4.3	13.1	16.6	27.4	23.8	22.5
Estonia[1]	−6.4	7.8	8.6	18.8	20.5	20.7	. . .
Hungary	−26.7	6.7	15.1	20.2	19.7	25.8	. . .
Israel	9.9	11.3	11.7	5.9	2.8	7.6	. . .
Latvia	−12.9	11.2	18.6	19.0	16.4	. . .	. . .
Lithuania	11.9	1.3	5.0	−1.2	9.8	13.5	. . .
Macedonia	8.2	3.5	3.8	−3.2	2.1	. . .	. . .
Malta	. . .	15.7	13.3	11.9	12.3	. . .	. . .
Poland	9.2	12.9	14.5	12.8	5.2	5.9	. . .
Russia	−28.6	−4.0	8.0	19.4	18.0	17.8	22.4
Slovak Republic	−13.4	−36.5	25.2	22.7	29.4	27.2	26.4
Slovenia	11.3	7.8	11.4	4.8	13.3	12.6	. . .
Turkey	23.1	−7.2	−43.7	−57.5	11.2	15.8	2.4
Ukraine	. . .	8.7	−0.5	7.5	8.0	7.6	7.5
Western Europe							
Austria	7.1	6.9	9.4	9.8	5.4	7.2	. . .
Belgium	11.0	17.1	20.4	13.7	11.8	13.6	. . .
Denmark	12.9	11.8	13.5	12.6	11.7	12.5	. . .
Finland	25.8	19.4	22.4	13.5	11.5	10.3	. . .
France	8.4	9.1	9.7	9.6	9.4	10.2	. . .
Germany	8.5	5.4	5.3	4.2	2.0	. . .	. . .
Greece	12.0	29.0	15.0	12.4	6.8	. . .	. . .
Iceland	13.5	19.3	9.7	13.4	18.1	19.7	. . .
Ireland[2]	. . .	23.0	22.0	16.0	27.0	. . .	. . .
Italy	7.4	9.6	11.5	8.8	6.2	7.9	. . .
Luxembourg	. . .	34.0	36.7	40.7	36.4	34.9	. . .
Netherlands	11.0	14.2	14.7	10.8	9.2	11.0	. . .
Norway[1]	. . .	18.0	19.2	13.0	9.2	12.0	. . .
Portugal	13.6	14.7	15.2	14.9	11.7	13.7	14.3
Spain	. . .	18.3	18.5	16.5	14.6	16.6	. . .
Sweden	14.2	16.0	15.7	13.0	10.1	12.3	13.4
Switzerland	17.1	18.8	18.2	11.2	8.6	. . .	. . .
United Kingdom[3]	26.1	26.0	20.8	18.0	17.3	19.0	. . .

Table 27 (concluded)

	1998	1999	2000	2001	2002	2003	2004:Q1
Asia							
Bangladesh	6.6	5.2	0.3	15.9	11.6	...	...
China	...	...	...		...	...	...
Hong Kong SAR	7.8	11.1	13.5	13.9	13.3	13.5	...
India	...	...	12.8	10.4	11.9	13.1	...
Indonesia			19.6	13.4	22.7	22.1	...
Korea[1]	−52.5	−23.1	−11.9	15.9	11.7	2.7	...
Malaysia	...	11.5	19.6	13.3	16.3	17.1	...
Pakistan	9.1	−6.2	−0.3	−0.3	13.8	22.1	17.4
Philippines	5.9	2.9	2.6	3.2	5.8	8.5	8.6
Singapore	4.2	10.7	12.6	7.7	7.6	8.3	...
Thailand[1]	−38.9	−47.3	−16.2	−1.9	3.9	8.6	...
Middle East and North Africa							
Egypt	...	14.7	16.1	13.7	12.4	8.9	9.5
Jordan	8.6	3.5	4.4	10.9	8.7	10.2	...
Kuwait	13.8	15.3	17.6	18.2	17.4	18.6	...
Lebanon	20.3	15.7	11.1	8.4	9.4	10.4	...
Morocco	9.5	8.2	8.1	10.2	1.9	6.8	...
Oman	16.7	13.2	12.0	1.2	14.3	...	...
Saudi Arabia[1]	...	9.1	21.0	21.9	22.2	22.7	...
Tunisia	13.2	12.7	14.9	14.0	7.4	...	...
United Arab Emirates	17.7	12.8	14.9	16.7	15.6	16.4	...
Sub-Saharan Africa							
Ghana	30.8	62.8	60.8	42.3	33.8	...	...
Kenya	8.9	0.3	5.3	17.3	13.0	24.1	20.9
Mauritius[1]	23.9	20.7	22.1	20.6	22.0	...	...
Nigeria	...	46.7	51.6	54.9	...	...	...
South Africa	12.5	12.2	12.0	9.1	6.0	12.1	17.7
Tanzania	45.6	2.1	20.5	21.4	17.6	...	...
Uganda	...	56.5	53.1	45.8	33.5	...	...
Zimbabwe	...	...	43.2	42.7	57.7	114.8	...
Other							
Australia	15.0	18.0	19.4	15.6	18.2	17.3	...
Canada	13.4	15.8	15.3	13.9	9.4	14.7	10.1
Japan[1]	−20.0	−25.1	6.8	1.2	−19.5	−19.4	...
United States[4]	14.0	15.3	14.0	13.1	14.5	15.3	15.5

Sources: National authorities; and IMF staff estimates.
[1] Before tax.
[2] Data for 2002 corresponds to Allied Irish Bank and Bank of Ireland only.
[3] U.K. large commercial banks.
[4] All commercial banks.

Table 28. Moody's Weighted Average Bank Financial Strength Index[1]

	Financial Strength Index				Percent Change from Dec. 2003
	Dec. 2001	Dec. 2002	Dec. 2003	May 2004	
Latin America					
Argentina	13.3	0.0	0.0	0.0	0.0
Bolivia	25.0	8.3	2.1	2.1	0.0
Brazil	37.9	25.0	24.3	24.3	0.0
Chile	50.6	52.5	56.5	56.5	0.0
Colombia	23.3	24.2	24.2	24.2	0.0
Ecuador	8.3	8.3	8.3	. . .	. . .
Mexico	36.3	39.6	39.6	37.4	−5.5
Paraguay	. . .	. . .	. . .	. . .	. . .
Peru	22.9	23.3	23.3	25.0	7.1
Uruguay	31.3	0.0	0.0	0.0	. . .
Venezuela	28.8	15.4	8.3	8.3	0.0
Emerging Europe					
Bulgaria	. . .	16.7	20.8	20.8	0.0
Croatia	33.3	33.3	33.3	33.3	0.0
Czech Republic	29.2	32.5	33.9	38.0	12.0
Estonia	38.3	46.7	46.7	46.7	0.0
Hungary	41.7	45.0	42.5	42.5	0.0
Israel	48.3	45.8	45.8	45.8	0.0
Latvia	29.2	32.1	32.1	35.4	10.3
Lithuania	. . .	. . .	. . .	. . .	. . .
Poland	29.6	28.3	29.5	29.5	0.0
Russia	12.5	10.8	10.8	10.8	0.0
Slovak Republic	9.6	15.0	17.5	20.8	18.9
Slovenia	40.2	40.8	45.2	45.2	0.0
Turkey	30.0	20.4	20.4	19.0	−6.9
Ukraine	8.3	8.3	8.3	8.3	0.0
Western Europe					
Austria	62.5	61.7	61.7	61.7	0.0
Belgium	75.0	75.0	75.0	75.0	0.0
Denmark	80.0	80.0	80.0	85.0	6.3
Finland	70.0	73.3	73.3	74.8	2.0
France	71.9	74.2	71.2	71.2	0.0
Germany	61.7	54.2	46.7	46.7	0.0
Greece	40.0	40.0	44.8	44.8	0.0
Ireland	69.2	70.0	71.7	71.7	0.0
Italy	64.6	63.3	63.3	63.3	0.0
Luxembourg	68.7	68.3	66.7	66.7	0.0
Netherlands	87.5	84.2	84.2	84.2	0.0
Norway	63.3	65.0	67.5	65.0	−3.7
Portugal	64.6	64.2	64.2	65.7	2.4
Spain	77.1	75.0	76.7	76.7	0.0
Sweden	72.5	73.3	75.0	77.0	2.7
Switzerland	70.8	72.1	72.1	72.1	0.0
United Kingdom	83.8	83.8	83.3	83.3	0.0

Table 28 (concluded)

	Financial Strength Index				Percent Change from Dec. 2003
	Dec. 2001	Dec. 2002	Dec. 2003	May 2004	
Asia					
China	10.0	10.0	10.0	10.0	0.0
Hong Kong SAR	66.6	62.3	62.3	62.3	0.0
India	25.8	27.5	27.5	27.5	0.0
Indonesia	1.7	3.0	3.0	7.3	143.3
Korea	14.2	16.7	18.3	20.0	9.0
Malaysia	30.4	31.7	33.3	36.8	10.5
Pakistan	2.1	5.0	9.6	9.6	0.0
Philippines	17.5	20.4	20.4	19.2	−6.2
Singapore	75.0	74.7	74.7	74.7	0.0
Thailand	15.8	15.8	15.8	16.7	5.3
Middle East					
Egypt	22.9	22.9	22.9	22.9	0.0
Jordan	25.0	19.2	19.2	19.2	0.0
Lebanon	33.3	33.3	33.3	33.3	0.0
Morocco	35.8	35.8	35.8	35.8	0.0
Oman	31.7	29.2	29.2	29.2	0.0
Saudi Arabia	43.3	43.3	43.3	43.3	0.0
Tunisia	16.7	16.7	16.7	16.7	0.0
Africa					
Ghana	...	...	...	...	...
Kenya	...	...	...	...	...
Nigeria	...	...	...	...	...
South Africa	53.5	49.0	50.0	50.0	0.0
Uganda	...	...	...	...	...
Zambia	...	...	...	...	...
Zimbabwe	...	...	...	...	...
Other					
Australia	71.7	72.5	72.5	72.5	0.0
Canada	77.1	75.0	75.0	75.0	0.0
Japan	16.7	12.9	12.0	12.0	0.0
United States	77.1	75.0	75.0	75.0	0.0

Source: Moody's.

[1]Constructed according to a numerical scale assigned to Moody's weighted average bank ratings by country. "0" indicates the lowest possible average rating and "100" indicates the highest possible average rating.

World Economic and Financial Surveys

This series (ISSN 0258-7440) contains biannual, annual, and periodic studies covering monetary and financial issues of importance to the global economy. The core elements of the series are the *World Economic Outlook* report, usually published in April and September, and the semiannual *Global Financial Stability Report*. Other studies assess international trade policy, private market and official financing for developing countries, exchange and payments systems, export credit policies, and issues discussed in the *World Economic Outlook*. Please consult the IMF *Publications Catalog* for a complete listing of currently available World Economic and Financial Surveys.

World Economic Outlook: A Survey by the Staff of the International Monetary Fund

The *World Economic Outlook,* published twice a year in English, French, Spanish, and Arabic, presents IMF staff economists' analyses of global economic developments during the near and medium term. Chapters give an overview of the world economy; consider issues affecting industrial countries, developing countries, and economies in transition to the market; and address topics of pressing current interest.

ISSN 0256-6877.

$49.00 (academic rate: $46.00); paper.
2004. (April). ISBN 1-58906-337-6. **Stock #WEOEA200401.**
2003. (April). ISBN 1-58906-212-4. **Stock #WEOEA0012003.**
2002. (Sep.). ISBN 1-58906-179-9. **Stock #WEOEA0022002.**
2002. (April). ISBN 1-58906-107-1. **Stock #WEOEA0012002.**

Global Financial Stability Report: Market Developments and Issues

The *Global Financial Stability Report,* published twice a year, examines trends and issues that influence world financial markets. It replaces two IMF publications—the annual *International Capital Markets* report and the electronic quarterly *Emerging Market Financing* report. The report is designed to deepen understanding of international capital flows and explores developments that could pose a risk to international financial market stability.

$49.00 (academic rate: $46.00); paper.
April 2004 ISBN 1-58906-328-7. **Stock #GFSREA0012004.**
September 2003 ISBN 1-58906-236-1. **Stock #GFSREA0022003.**
March 2003 ISBN 1-58906-210-8. **Stock #GFSREA0012003.**
December 2002 ISBN-1-58906-192-6. **Stock #GFSREA0042002.**
September 2002 ISBN 1-58906-157-8. **Stock #GFSREA0032002.**

Emerging Local Securities and Derivatives Markets

by Donald Mathieson, Jorge E. Roldos, Ramana Ramaswamy, and Anna Ilyina

The volatility of capital flows since the mid-1990s has sparked an interest in the development of local securities and derivatives markets. This report examines the growth of these markets in emerging market countries and the key policy issues that have arisen as a result.

$42.00 (academic rate: $35.00); paper.
2004. ISBN 1-58906-291-4. **Stock #WEOEA0202004.**

Official Financing: Recent Developments and Selected Issues

by a staff team in the Policy Development and Review Department led by Martin G. Gilman and Jian-Ye Wang

This study provides information on official financing for developing countries, with the focus on low-income countries. It updates the 2001 edition and reviews developments in direct financing by official and multilateral sources.

$42.00 (academic rate: $35.00); paper.
2003. ISBN 1-58906-228-0. **Stock #WEOEA0132003.**
2001. ISBN 1-58906-038-5. **Stock #WEOEA0132001.**

Exchange Arrangements and Foreign Exchange Markets: Developments and Issues

by a staff team led by Shogo Ishii

This study updates developments in exchange arrangements during 1998–2001. It also discusses the evolution of exchange rate regimes based on de facto policies since 1990, reviews foreign exchange market organization and regulations in a number of countries, and examines factors affecting exchange rate volatility.

ISSN 0258-7440
$42.00 (academic rate $35.00)
2003 (March) ISBN 1-58906-177-2. **Stock #WEOEA0192003.**

World Economic Outlook Supporting Studies

by the IMF's Research Department

These studies, supporting analyses and scenarios of the *World Economic Outlook,* provide a detailed examination of theory and evidence on major issues currently affecting the global economy.

$25.00 (academic rate: $20.00); paper.
2000. ISBN 1-55775-893-X. **Stock #WEOEA0032000.** E

Exchange Rate Arrangements and Currency Convertibility: Developments and Issues

by a staff team led by R. Barry Johnston

A principal force driving the growth in international trade and investment has been the liberalization of financial transactions, including the liberalization of trade and exchange controls. This study reviews the developments and issues in the exchange arrangements and currency convertibility of IMF members.

$20.00 (academic rate: $12.00); paper.
1999. ISBN 1-55775-795-X. **Stock #WEOEA0191999.**

Available by series subscription or single title (including back issues); academic rate available only to full-time university faculty and students. For earlier editions please inquire about prices.

The IMF *Catalog of Publications* is available on-line at the Internet address listed below.

Please send orders and inquiries to:
International Monetary Fund, Publication Services, 700 19th Street, N.W.
Washington, D.C. 20431, U.S.A.
Tel.: (202) 623-7430   Telefax: (202) 623-7201
E-mail: publications@imf.org
Internet: http://www.imf.org